"This ingenious archive of working class history, organized as an extended calendar, overflows with both little and better-known events. Reading through the text, the power, fury, and persistence of the working class struggles shine. 'Working class' is broader than unions and job struggles; rather, it includes all emancipatory acts of working class people, be they Indigenous peoples fighting for land rights, African Americans massively protesting against police killings, anticolonial liberation movements, women rising up angry, or mass mobilizations worldwide against imperialist wars. It is international in scope, as is the working class. This is a book the reader will open every day to recall and be inspired by what occurred on that date. I love the book and will look forward to the daily readings."
—Roxanne Dunbar-Ortiz, author of *An Indigenous Peoples' History of the United States* (Beacon Press 2015)

"One thing most people in the world have in common—whatever our gender, race, age, culture, or condition—is that we have to work for a living, and most of us have to work for someone else. That means either we have to obey their will or find ways to resist it. This book provides a panoramic compendium of that resistance. I've been studying and writing about labor history for more than half a century, but I've never even heard about most of these thousand or more strikes, uprisings, and protests from around the world—or about the violence that was so often used against them. I've found this book an easy and fun way to fill that gap."
—Jeremy Brecher, author of *Strike! 50th Anniversary Edition* (PM Press 2020)

"The Working Class History project has hit upon a novel way to communicate our shared history to a new generation of budding radicals and working class revolutionaries and, with this book, presents centuries of solidarity and rebellion in an easily digestible (and endlessly engrossing) catalogue of dissent. They make it clear that today's victories build upon yesterday's struggles, and that to push forward into the liberated, equitable future we want, we must remember how far we've come—and reckon with how much further there is to go."
—Kim Kelly, journalist and labor columnist at *Teen Vogue*

T0043547

"A perfect present for busy activists. Just a few minutes a day is all it takes to learn fascinating and often poignant facts about working class history. As I've come to expect from our friends at Working Class History, the content is global, diverse, and clear, bringing to our attention *our* history, which has so often been ignored, neglected, or misrepresented. Buy a copy for yourself too!"
—Mike Jackson, cofounder of Lesbians and Gays Support the Miners

"I've learned so much from reading *Working Class History*. It's a fountainhead of vital and inspiring information about the international class struggle and a crucial antidote to the twenty-first-century post-truth right-wing media blitz 24/7 assault on our senses. It's important to have revolutionary heroes and knowledge of past struggles to inspire the rebel souls of the future. Long may *Working Class History* inspire!"
—Bobby Gillespie, lead singer of Primal Scream

"*Working Class History* is essential reading for those seeking awareness of people who made history in efforts and events meant to create a better world."
—John O'Brien, Stonewall rebellion participant,
Gay Liberation Front cofounder

"How do I love *Working Class History*? Let me count some of the ways! This collection lets us honor our dead and fight for the living. It allows us to go on romantic revolutionary dates. It is a daily inspirational affirmation, yet with substance. It reminds us to be brave and bold, and that much is always possible even in the bleakest of times. The book is love embodied, making you want to embrace each and every rebel ancestor."
—Cindy Milstein, author of *Paths Toward Utopia* (PM Press 2012)

"This is an unusual and fascinating book. *Working Class History* tells the collective tales of the imagination and energy of working class rebels, as well as showing the price paid by working class people who resisted and subverted the demands of labor and capital."
—Andrej Grubačić, professor of anthropology at CIIS-San Francisco, coauthor of *Wobblies and Zapatistas* (PM Press 2008) and *Living at the Edges of Capitalism: Adventures in Exile and Mutual Aid* (University of California Press 2016)

"Capitalist society does not encourage information or ideas that contradict its purpose. Working class history is not taught in our schools for this reason. Often it is lost and forgotten. *Working Class History* have listened for these stories, researched and documented them, and now presents them for us to witness and cherish in the light of our reality. This book provides fuel for our souls, and for this I thank the editors."
—Al Glatkowski, Vietnam Veterans Against the War, *Columbia Eagle* mutineer

"By recounting day-to-day struggles, the editors of this important book concretely reveal that social progress is the legacy of centuries of people's blood, sweat, and tears. While billionaires may today claim ownership of humanity's vast social wealth, the events detailed here reveal the outlines of a better future."
—George Katsiaficas, author of *The Global Imagination of 1968: Revolution and Counterrevolution* (PM Press 2018)

"*Working Class History* is a wonderful global collection of stories of fierce workers' resistance and rebellion that comes at a critical time, as power's policies worldwide continue to consolidate obscene wealth for the few on the backs of workers and the environment. This collection challenges the dominant histories and the splashy headlines of the self-made industry titans to reveal the narrative of international exploited workers who refused to obey, fighting instead against great odds for their basic rights and dignity and ultimately for workers' collective liberation."
—scott crow, author of *Black Flags and Windmills: Hope, Anarchy, and the Common Ground Collective* (PM Press 2014)

WORKING CLASS HISTORY
EVERYDAY ACTS OF RESISTANCE & REBELLION

Working Class History: Everyday Acts of Resistance & Rebellion
© 2020 Working Class History
This edition © 2020 PM Press

ISBN: 978–1–62963–823–2 (print)
ISBN: 978–1–62963–839–3 (ebook)
Library of Congress Control Number: 2020934730

Cover by Michael Oswell
Interior design by briandesign

10 9 8 7 6 5 4 3 2

PM Press
PO Box 23912
Oakland, CA 94623
www.pmpress.org

Printed in the USA.

Contents

Foreword

Noam Chomsky

My personal engagements with social movements have been mostly with anti-war mobilization and resistance and with solidarity movements globally, in Latin America, Asia, and the Middle East. But apart from these, from childhood the movements that I've found truly inspiring have been workers' struggles. I grew up during the Great Depression, and vivid childhood memories range from security forces violently attacking women picketing a textile plant to the crucial role of union membership in the lives of my (mostly unemployed) extended family. And, at barely a step removed, as a child I followed closely the leading role of militant union activists in establishing the New Deal programs that have greatly improved the lives of most Americans, and which have been under severe attack in recent years. And it continues through the years, with many dramatic and inspiring struggles—Lordstown,[1] the Decatur strikes and lockouts of the 1990s,[2] today's spontaneous teachers' strikes calling for reconstructing the woefully underfunded public education system,[3] and many others.

Though the situation has somewhat improved in recent years, our education system does not even come close to adequately reflecting the impact of these movements of ordinary people on our history. One major contribution was Howard Zinn's *People's History of the United States* and the companion *Voices* volume,[4] which lifted the veil from central parts of history that had been concealed or sidelined in the standard patriotic versions. But

---

1   See, for example, our entry for March 4, 1972. In subsequent footnotes we will just give the dates of relevant examples. [editor's note]
2   See June 26, 1993.
3   See February 22, 2018.
4   Howard Zinn, *A People's History of the United States: 1492—Present* (New York: Harper & Row, 2009 [1980]); Howard Zinn and Anthony Arnove, eds., *Voices of a People's History of the United States* (New York: Seven Stories Press, 2004).

there is a long way to go. In particular, labor history is virtually effaced in the educational system, as well as in the media. Not long ago the press had fine journalists covering the labor movement. Today, almost none. Every newspaper has a business section; none could even imagine a labor section, addressing the interests and concerns of a large majority of the population. Social movements receive cursory attention, usually highly misleading. The one that receives by far the most attention is the civil rights movement. There is even a national holiday in memory of Martin Luther King Jr. But it is instructive to see how it is handled.

The uplifting rhetoric on Martin Luther King Jr. Day typically reaches as far as his "I have a dream" speech at the huge demonstration in Washington in August 1963. But King did not terminate his activities then. He went on to become a prominent critic of the Vietnam War and to organize and support struggles for housing, workers' rights, and other popular needs in the North. He was assassinated in 1968 while supporting a garbage workers' strike,[5] the day after he had delivered another memorable speech that is barely known. He was organizing a poor people's movement and another march on Washington to demand human and civil rights for all Americans, including Aboriginal and white Americans. None of this was tolerable to establishment liberalism. He was bitterly condemned for supposedly losing his way. It's fine to condemn racist Alabama sheriffs—but "not in my backyard." His major commitments are omitted from the schools and the media. Other movements fare similarly.

Today, social movements face more challenges than ever before. Each January since 1947, the *Bulletin of Atomic Scientists* sets the minute hand of its Doomsday Clock at a certain distance from midnight—which means terminal disaster. Once, in 1953, it was set at two minutes to midnight, after the US and then the USSR exploded thermonuclear weapons, demonstrating that human intelligence had developed the means to destroy everything. It did not reach that grim setting again until Donald Trump had been in office for a year. By then the analysts added the immense threat of global warming to the extreme danger of nuclear war, both existential threats to survival. In January 2019 the clock was again set to two minutes to midnight, now described as "the new abnormal." And analysts added a third existential threat, the erosion of democracy, the sole hope for addressing serious

---

5   See April 4, 1968.

challenges. These judgments seem valid to me, and each threat has been significantly intensified since the clock was last set.[6]

Furthermore, the neoliberal assault on the population since Ronald Reagan and Margaret Thatcher has radically concentrated wealth, while real wages for the majority stagnate or decline and benefits are eroded, along with functioning democracy, as governments fall into the hands of private wealth and corporate power even more than before.[7]

Another major thrust of policy has been to undermine popular organization, particularly the labor movement, traditionally its leading force. Organized, militant popular action has been the critical factor in driving such progress as has been made in confronting the primary challenges to decent survival—and innumerable others. It remains the hope for today.

Fortunately, it is reviving, particularly among younger people. Neoliberalism has elicited widespread anger and resentment, which can be exploited by demagogues in ugly ways, facts all too obvious on the present scene. But there are also counterforces. In light of the severity of the crises that are looming and imminent, which of these prevails will—quite literally—determine the fate of the species.

Nuclear war and environmental catastrophe will spare no one, not even those deluded ultra-rich who believe they can escape to gated communities on mountain tops—or colonize Mars. The impressive achievements of young activists around the world are having a major impact—Extinction Rebellion and many others. In the US, young activists of the Sunrise Movement, supported by a few members of Congress (notably Alexandria Ocasio-Cortez), succeeded, with direct action, in placing a Green New Deal on the legislative agenda, something essential for survival in some form, an achievement almost unimaginable a few years ago.

A core concern is revival of the labor movement, battered by the neoliberal offensive. Many commentators associate the labor movement with mostly male, white, native-born blue-collar workers, often excluding "unpaid labor," mostly "women's work"; but, in truth, workers around the world are predominantly people of color, diverse in terms of gender,

6 With the addition of "cyber-enabled disinformation campaigns" to the already existing threats of nuclear weapons and climate change, the Doomsday Clock now stands at 100 seconds to midnight; see Science and Security Board, "Closer Than Ever: It Is Now 100 Seconds to Midnight," *Bulletin of Atomic Scientists*, January 23, 2020, accessed May 21, 2020, https://thebulletin.org/doomsday-clock/current-time.
7 "Neoliberalism" refers to free market economic policies, including privatization and reduction of publicly funded social security and services.

immigration status, sexuality, and sector. Resurrecting this movement is not an idle dream.

In the 1920s, the vigorous and militant US labor movement was virtually destroyed by often violent state and corporate repression. A few years later, it rose in new forms and spearheaded the New Deal reforms. To take a more recent precedent, in the early 1970s, there was a significant rise in labor militancy, mostly but not entirely repressed. Tony Mazzocchi and his Oil, Chemical and Atomic Workers International Union (OCAW)[8]—who are right on the front line, facing destruction of the environment every day at work—were the driving force behind the establishment of the Occupational Safety and Health Act (OSHA), protecting workers on the job. And they went on from there. Mazzocchi was a harsh critic of capitalism, as well as a committed environmentalist. He held that workers should "control the plant environment," while also taking the lead in combatting industrial pollution. As the Democrats abandoned working people, Mazzocchi began to advocate for a union-based Labor Party, an initiative that made considerable progress in the 1990s but couldn't survive the decline of the labor movement under a severe business-government attack reminiscent of the 1920s.

In these tumultuous times, *Working Class History: Everyday Acts of Resistance & Rebellion* is important, because a functioning democracy requires active citizen participation in setting social policy. I can return to the latest setting of the Doomsday Clock, highlighting the existential crises of global warming and nuclear war and adding, for the first time, the erosion of democracy. We can look forward to a day when citizen participation becomes direct decision-making in the workplace and the community and on a larger scale up to the international dimension.

For now, the critical task is to organize activist popular movements to change popular consciousness and understanding, to shape legislation, and to create facts on the ground: worker-owned industries, cooperatives, and other structures of democratic participation. We can learn a great deal from the long and hard struggles for social justice in past years, and we can and must move forward to build on their achievements and to surpass them. Given the urgency of the crises we face, there is no time to lose.

---

8   See November 13, 1974.

Introduction

Why Working Class?

Some clever people once said, "The history of all hitherto existing society is the history of class struggles."[1] Like them, we also believe that historical change has primarily been the result of struggle between classes. Any improvement in the lives of ordinary people—the creation of the weekend,[2] the abolition of slavery,[3] and the collapse of empires—has been the result of the struggles of the oppressed and exploited against the systems that oppress and exploit us.

Today, in our current capitalist society, the working class is numerically the largest class. When we say "working class," we are talking about it in an economic rather than cultural sense, as it is often perceived. Broadly speaking, it refers to those of us who do not own factories, farms, offices, or stocks therein (also known as "means of production") and so need to sell our ability to work to people who do.

Capitalism is based on this arrangement, which famous physicist Albert Einstein explained quite simply:

> The owner of the means of production is in a position to purchase the labor power of the worker. By using the means of production, the worker produces new goods which become the property of the capitalist. The essential point about this process is the relation between what the worker produces and what he [sic] is paid, both measured in terms of real value.... What the worker receives is determined not by the real value of the goods he produces, but by his minimum needs

---

1   Karl Marx and Friedrich Engels, "Manifesto of the Communist Party," in Karl Marx and Frederick Engels, *Selected Works*, vol. 1 (Moscow: Progress Publishers, 1969), 99–137.
2   See December 26, 1904.
3   See December 25, 1831.

and by the capitalists' requirements for labor power in relation to the number of workers competing for jobs. It is important to understand that even in theory the payment of the worker is not determined by the value of his product.[4]

So, depending on market conditions, we are paid the minimum amount necessary to ensure we keep turning up for work each day.

The difference between the value we produce and the lower value of our wages (known as "surplus value") is how businesses make profit and expand. This exploitative relationship is at the heart of capitalist society and is the cause of the central conflict within it, namely, that employers want workers to work the longest hours for the least pay, whereas we would rather work shorter hours for more pay.[5] This gives all workers a shared economic interest in fighting capitalism.

Because capitalism is entirely dependent on our labor, we are also potentially the most powerful class in society. The primary reason we fail to exert our potential power is that we are divided in a myriad of ways:

- We are divided into employed and unemployed, so those of us in work have to fear losing our jobs, and those not in work have to compete among ourselves to work for the lowest rates.
- We are divided into different enterprises that compete against one another, so companies that make the most profit—often by paying the lowest wages and ignoring environmental standards—succeed, while others either fail or get taken over.
- We are divided by gender roles, whereby much of the world's work is seen as "women's work" and is entirely unpaid, particularly care and domestic work.
- We are divided into different nation-states, so if workers in one country win better pay and working conditions, production can be relocated to lower-wage parts of the world.
- We are divided by racism, whereby certain racial and ethnic groups, e.g., Black people in the US, are systemically disadvantaged and oppressed. This gives workers of dominant groups at least the illusion of a stake

---

4   Albert Einstein, "Why Socialism?" *Monthly Review* 1 (May 1949), accessed April 20, 2020, https://monthlyreview.org/2009/05/01/why-socialism.

5   See May 1, 1886.

in maintaining the status quo and enables employers and authorities to play different groups off against one another.[6]

- We are divided by citizenship status, so within many countries there is a much more exploitable migrant labor force that can be denied basic legal rights, and workers who try to fight back can be deported if they try to fight back.[7]

These are just a few of the ways we are split up and set against one another, to prevent us from uniting and fighting for our collective self-interest and reclaiming more of our "surplus value" from those who exploit us. Fighting against these divisions and showing solidarity with different groups of workers has to be an essential part of any movement to improve the lot of the working class or any section thereof.

All other types of discrimination and privilege in our society intersect with class. Take, for example, abortion rights and gender; whatever laws are in place, the wealthy are almost always able to access abortions, whereas for poor and working class people it may be impossible.

For every system of oppression, from racism to homophobia to transphobia to sexism to ableism—to name just some—worse outcomes are experienced by poor people compared to the wealthy. Therefore, struggles of oppressed groups like women,[8] people of color in the US,[9] or LGBT+ people,[10] for example, should not be dismissed, as some do, as being merely related to "identity"; these are also inherently class struggles.

Any victory for one group of workers is a victory for all of us. For example, a group of underpaid migrant workers successfully improving their pay and conditions also means that employers are unable to employ super-exploited workers to undercut native-born workers.[11]

Similarly, environmental destruction and the resultant climate chaos disproportionately affect poor and working class people, especially in the colonized world. This will only get worse in the coming years, so fighting to protect our planet is also an existential issue for our class.[12]

---

6   See November 23, 1887.
7   See June 29, 1936.
8   See June 14, 1991.
9   See May 2, 1968.
10 See June 28, 1969.
11 See June 8, 2017.
12 See June 17, 1971.

Struggles of Indigenous peoples,[13] of peasants,[14] and struggles against colonialism[15] have also been, in large part, struggles against dispossession, struggles against being turned into a working class—disconnected from the land and means of production—in the first place.

All this considered, we take an expansive, intersectional, and internationalist view of class, and we present snapshots of all kinds of battles against exploitation and oppression.

Why History?

The Working Class History project came out of conversations a number of us were having back in 2014. We had all been involved in a number of activities, including workplace organizing and campaigning against austerity and, before that, the Iraq War. However, our activity was cut off from the mass, radical working class movements of the past; like many people our age (and even a little older), we grew up and entered the workforce following the defeats of the 1980s and subsequent dismantling of workers' organizations. By the time we were politicized, the shared knowledge of struggle and culture of solidarity that had previously defined working-class life, had, in many places, disappeared.

To access this knowledge, we read a lot of history, and we were struck by how many vital lessons there were that could inform our struggles today. Yet while a lot has been written about working class struggle around the world, much of that writing is inaccessible to most people, hidden in dusty archives or behind online pay walls, or it is online but written in convoluted academic or political jargon.

So we decided to set up a database of historical events, in which we would include short, clearly written summaries, primarily about struggles that have taken place for a better world and the people who took part in them. We also included information about atrocities carried out by the rich and powerful to counter those struggles,[16] as well as those sometimes carried out in the name of making a better world.[17] We believe it is important not only to counter dominant narratives that sanitize the history of capitalism and colonialism but also to learn from the mistakes (as well as successes) of those who have fought against them.

---

13   See June 25, 1878.
14   See April 10, 1919.
15   See March 26, 1953.
16   See October 17, 1961.
17   See December 17, 1933.

For people without money, social media can be a useful tool for getting information out to a wide audience, so that was the forum we initially decided to prioritize. We speculated that posting on anniversaries of events would be the most likely way to make content about things that had happened, in some cases hundreds of years ago, go viral; information about a random strike in the 1800s may not seem immediately relevant, but reading about something that happened on this date in the past does seem to give a more tangible connection to the event, making it easier to relate to.

Our hope was that these short viral posts would allow readers to glimpse a snapshot of these historical movements and the people who helped make our world what it is today. This could then both educate people about how we can organize ourselves to defend or improve our conditions and inspire people in that fight.

The project has far surpassed our initial hopes. We now have over seven hundred thousand followers across our various online platforms, reaching an audience of over eleven million per month. People from all over the world have volunteered to help out and contribute, and much of our content has been translated into Arabic, French, Persian, Spanish, Norwegian, and Turkish.

More recently, we launched a podcast to look at some of these issues in more detail and to speak to participants and historians of these movements, to dig deeper into events, what people did, and how we can apply the lessons of those struggles today.

How to Read This Book

This book is a curated selection of some of the texts from our archive: two for each day of the year, many of which have never appeared online.

For this work we have decided to focus on historical events rather than individuals. As such, we have omitted the birth and death dates of the people who have been involved in various movements, unless their death was of particular historical note in itself—for example, if they were assassinated.

This book does not pretend to be comprehensive. We do not claim to recount every movement or incident of importance to our collective history of struggle. We do not have the space in this volume to even approach such a task.

We have attempted to present a diverse range of historical events, but due to our locations, primarily the UK and the US, the languages we speak, and the nature and biases of sources available to us, there is, unfortunately but unavoidably, a bias in the events toward the European languages of English, Spanish, French, and Italian and toward countries with colonial relationships with those languages.

We have written it so that it can be read in any order. You don't have to read from January 1, you can start out with any date—today's date, your birthday, an anniversary—and just dip in and out as you see fit. The only slight issue here could be that we only explain particular organizations and concepts the first time they are mentioned, so reading nonsequentially would require a basic knowledge of political terminology.

We use dates in the standard current calendar, so, for example, dates in the Russian Old Style calendar have been converted. Dates are given in the country where the events occurred (which sometimes might have been reported as a different date in countries in different time zones).

Our articles are intended to give a brief snapshot of the people and movements that have helped improve our world. We don't claim to tell the full story of any of the historical events addressed herein, and we do encourage people to learn more about the stories that interest them. We provide sources and further reading for each date in the references section at the back of the book.

In cases when there are *Working Class History* podcast episodes available where readers can learn more, we highlight this with 🎙 where the number indicates the number of the relevant episode(s).

To listen to podcast episodes, find them at workingclasshistory.com/podcast. Alternatively, you can listen to them on all major podcast apps (like Apple Podcasts, Google Play, or Spotify) by searching for *Working Class History*.

We have made every effort to be as accurate as possible. However, given the scope of this text it seems likely that at least one error might have slipped through the cracks of our fact-checking and proofreading processes. If this is the case, we apologize. We also recognize that the understanding of historical events changes over time as more evidence comes to light. So if you do spot any errors or notice anything that has been superseded by new evidence, please do get in touch to let us know about it, so we can make any corrections in our archive and in future editions of this book.

Finally, the history of those without money and power, i.e., the vast majority of us, often goes unwritten. So if you have a story for us, or if you would like to help us record and publicize our collective history of resistance, please get in touch.

Email: info@workingclasshistory.com
Instagram: @workingclasshistory
Twitter: @wrkclasshistory
Facebook: facebook.com/workingclasshistory

Content note: due to the disturbing nature of much people's history, many of our entries include descriptions of violence, racism, genocide, homophobia, torture, and death, and some of them include mentions of sexual violence. Pages containing mentions of sexual violence will be indicated with ⚠ at the top of the page. Some of the images may be disturbing for some people.

Acknowledgments

First, we would like to extend huge thanks to our Patreon supporters. Our work is entirely funded by our readers and listeners, at patreon.com/workingclasshistory. Without their help, neither writing this book nor running the Working Class History project more generally would have been possible.

Thanks also to everyone who has helped out with our project, to everyone who has read and given feedback on early versions of this manuscript, and to everyone who has spoken with us on our podcast and inspired us with their stories.

Special thanks in no particular order to Matti Ron, Rakan Budeiri, Linda Towlson, Hayley Friel, Robyn Karina, Steven Johns, Sebastian Porreca, Jingying Wang, Nathan Gilchrist, Har Ham, Jeff Gandy, Christine, Biswadip Dasgupta, Mike Harman, Eliza Wormell, John Shepherd, DD Johnston, Bettina Escauriza, LD, Arno, Bryan Zubalsky, Christine Homitsu White, Daan, Emilia Lena Fernández, Lewis Gavin, Lizzie Derrington, Martina Domladovac, Emily Webb, Matthew Wilson, Rodrigo Costa, Ritwik Khanna, Michael Ryan, John Yates, Brian Layng, Chris Dodge, and Michael Oswell. Thanks also to PM Press for suggesting this book and making it happen.

Finally, thank you for buying this book and helping support our work.

This book is dedicated to all those who have fought to defend their fellow workers and for a better world and whose names have never been written down. We may never know who you were, but whatever we have today, we owe it in part to you.

JANUARY

1 **January 1, 1804** Haiti became an independent republic, following a revolution that had begun thirteen years earlier as a rebellion against slavery and French colonialism.

Previously known as Saint-Domingue, it was the most profitable colony in the world, generating greater revenue than all of the continental North American colonies combined. This immense wealth was generated by the sweat and blood of enslaved Africans who were being worked to death in their tens of thousands on coffee and sugar plantations.

On August 22, 1791, shortly after the French Revolution, which espoused the ideals of "liberty, equality, and fraternity," a slave rebellion erupted, demanding that those ideals be realized and slavery and colonialism be abolished. Over the coming years, the rebels successfully defeated the combined armies of the world's biggest colonial powers: France, Spain, and Britain.

The 1804 declaration of independence abolished the colony of Saint-Domingue and reinstated the Indigenous Taíno name of Hayti. Europe and the US promptly embargoed the fledgling republic, causing it severe economic hardship.

In 1825, France finally agreed to recognize Haiti's independence, provided it compensate former slaveowners to the tune of 150 million gold francs ($21 billion today)—a ransom that deeply impoverished the state and was not fully repaid until 1947. The United States only recognized Haiti's independence in 1862. This, however, did not prevent the United States from invading and occupying Haiti in 1915.

January 1, 1994 The Zapatista uprising began, with Indigenous people in Chiapas, Mexico, rising up and taking control of their communities,

Zapatista women, 2018 *(Courtesy Global Justice Now Flickr, CC by SA 2.0 https://www.flickr.com/photos/wdm/41047778152)*

redistributing power and organizing new, directly democratic ways of running society. Despite state repression, violence, and massacres, their movement of around three hundred thousand people remains self-managed to this day.

2 **January 2, 1858 and 1904** US troops in two warships landed in Uruguay to protect US-owned property during a revolution in Montevideo. They departed on January 27, 1858.

On the same date, just under half a century later, in 1904, US and British naval forces intervened in the Dominican Republic, again to protect US interests during a revolution, remaining until February 11.

January 2, 1920 The second Palmer raids began. The raids were an attempt by the US Department of Justice to arrest and deport foreign-born radical workers and leftists, especially anarchists. Between three and ten thousand people were arrested and held without trial, most of them US citizens. The majority of those arrested were released without charge, but more than five hundred foreign citizens were eventually deported.

Radicals awaiting deportation on Ellis Island, January 3, 1920 *(Courtesy Corbis Images for Education/Wikimedia Commons)*

3 **January 3, 1913** The Little Falls textile strike in New York ended when the workforce of predominantly migrant women organized in the revolutionary Industrial Workers of the World union (IWW; aka Wobblies) won their demands. They had walked out on October 9, and in the face of violent police repression, the workers held firm and achieved a reduction in weekly working hours from sixty to fifty-four, with no loss of pay. 🔊 **6, 16**

January 3, 1966 Military veteran and civil rights activist Sammy Younge Jr. was murdered in Alabama. He was the first Black college student to be killed for involvement in the civil rights movement. Younge was shot by

Sammy Younge Jr. enlistment photograph, 1964 *(Courtesy United States Navy/Wikimedia Commons)*

a gas station attendant in Macon County for trying to use the "whites-only" restroom. Following mass protests, the killer was indicted in November of that year but was later acquitted by an all-white jury.

January 4, 1917 A ten-day strike of wharf workers started in Guyana. As a consequence of World War I, the prices of foodstuffs and other commodities rose, while wages remained the same. Against a background of labor unrest due to deteriorating living conditions, the wharf workers won an increase in wages and a shorter workweek and sparked a national wave of strikes.

January 4, 1938 Four to five hundred workers at the Serge Island Estate in Saint Thomas, Jamaica, forced a general work stoppage on the farm. They were demanding pay increases before they would start reaping crops. Police sent in by British colonial authorities took steps to break the strike, arresting sixty-three workers and trying them over three days beginning on January 13. Three "ringleaders" were given one-month prison sentences, with hard labor, eighteen were fined, and the others were discharged.

January 5, 1939 Lithuanian-Jewish anti-fascist and Spanish Civil War fighter Samuel Kaplan was transferred by Communist Party authorities to the Montjuich prison in Barcelona. He had been held without charge since February of the previous year. Kaplan had travelled to Spain to help Republican forces resist the coup attempt by General Francisco Franco's nationalist and fascist forces.

Having previously been imprisoned for his political activities both by the Soviet Union and by Nazi Germany in the Dachau concentration camp, which he escaped, he described his treatment by his Republican "allies" as the worst he had ever suffered. He had even taken part in a hunger strike with several other anti-fascist prisoners.

We thought that nothing more had been heard from him after nationalist forces took over the city on January 21, until his son, a reader of the Working Class History Facebook page, got in touch and informed us that Samuel Kaplan had escaped once again, eventually fleeing to Mexico, where he lived out the rest of his days. 🎙 **39–40**

January 5, 1960 Anti-fascist guerrilla Francesc Sabaté Llopart—"El Quico"— was assassinated by police in Catalonia. He fought against the nationalists in the Spanish Civil War, then fought with the French resistance during World

War II, after which he joined the underground resistance in Spain, becoming its most celebrated and longest-serving fighter, before he was killed.

6 **January 6, 1945** Four women were hanged in the Auschwitz concentration camp for their role in a prisoner rebellion the previous October. Ala Gertner had stolen gunpowder from the munitions factory where she was an enslaved laborer, which she provided to underground resistance member Roza Robota, who delivered it to Soviet Jewish detainees, who built bombs for the rebellion. Estusia Wajcblum and Regina Safirsztajn had also been involved and were also executed. Hanged publicly in front of the other women prisoners, Robota appealed to them from the gallows: "Be strong and be brave."

Ala Gertner, 1943 *(Courtesy Wikimedia Commons)*

January 6, 2005 Local residents of Bayview, in Durban, South Africa, successfully fought off a local government water disconnection team. This was especially brave given that a council security team had previously murdered a teenage boy, Marcel King, elsewhere in the city, when he attempted to help his mother during a disconnection of her electricity. The council, run by the African National Congress (ANC), said that they would be back with greater force.

Since being elected in 1994, the ANC had pursued a neoliberal agenda and disconnected the water supply to over one million homes, while thousands of people continued to die each year from diarrhea, mostly caused by unsafe water.

7 **January 7, 1913** A strike for a maximum eight-hour workday began in Peru after workers rejected proposals from employers. In El Callao, there was a total stoppage of industry, as gasworkers, mill workers, typographers, bakers, and other unionized workers went out on strike.

January 7, 1919 The series of events known in Argentina as the Tragic Week began. Maritime workers at the port of Buenos Aires voted to strike for better pay and shorter hours, while police at the nearby British-owned Vasena plant attacked striking metalworkers, killing five and wounding twenty. Over the next few days, strikes spread through the city, with riots breaking out and workers seizing arms.

Meanwhile, police and soldiers fought workers, and right-wing mobs launched pogroms, attacking Jewish areas and beating and murdering Jews, whom the anti-Semites associated with anarchists and communists. In crushing the rebellion, troops killed between one hundred and seven hundred people, injured four hundred to two thousand, and imprisoned over fifty thousand.

8 **January 8, 1811** Possibly the biggest slave uprising in United States history took place on the Louisiana coast. Hundreds of enslaved people attacked their masters, then marched toward New Orleans, carrying banners, drums, and farm tools as weapons. They burned plantations and recruited more rebels on their way, and, despite their lack of firearms, they fought the local militia. Their advance was eventually stopped when a second brigade arrived from Baton Rouge.

January 8, 1896 The world's first explicitly anarchist-feminist newspaper, *La Voz de la Mujer* (Woman's Voice), was published in Buenos Aires, Argentina. It advocated class struggle, women's liberation, and sexual freedom.

9 **January 9, 1907** In Rio Blanco, Mexico, the army finally crushed a labor rebellion by striking textile workers demanding better pay, shorter working hours, and improved working conditions. Two hundred workers were killed, 400 were arrested, and 1,500 were fired.

January 9, 1973 In Durban, South Africa, workers at the Coronation Brick and Tile factory went out on strike. By the end of March, close to one hundred thousand mainly Black African workers, approximately half the entire Black African workforce in Durban, were on strike. The Coronation workers and many others ended up winning pay increases.

10 **January 10, 1918** Two hundred housewives marched through working class districts of Barcelona calling textile workers, most of whom were women, out on strike against the high cost of living. Strikes, demonstrations, and attacks on shops and coal yards continued even after a new military governor declared a state of siege and suspended civil rights.

January 10, 1966 The home of biracial voting rights activist Vernon Dahmer was firebombed by the Ku Klux Klan in Mississippi. While he managed to save his wife and child, he died from severe burns and smoke inhalation the following day. He had offered to pay the poll tax for anyone who could not afford to register to vote, which would have helped more Black people vote.

11 **January 11, 1912** The Lawrence strike, also known as the Bread and Roses strike, broke out. Polish women working in cotton mills in New England noticed their pay had been reduced and stopped their looms, leaving the mill shouting "Short pay!" Other workers, mostly women and girls, also walked out, and within a week twenty thousand were out. Despite savage repression, they held out until mid-March and won all of their demands, which were also then granted by other employers who wanted to avoid similar strikes.

The popular name for the strike came from a line in a speech by socialist Rose Schneiderman: "The worker must have bread, but she must have roses too." Young girls began inscribing the demand on their banners in Lawrence.

Lawrence strikers marching in the city, 1912 *(Courtesy Lawrence History Center Photograph Collection/Wikimedia Commons)*

January 11, 1998 Twenty-four thousand villagers in India occupied the proposed site for the construction of a Narmada River dam. They successfully blocked the project, which would have displaced 320,000 people.

12 **January 12, 1922** After shipping companies refused to increase salaries by 40 percent, seamen from Hong Kong and Canton (now Guangzhou) went on strike for higher wages. Led by the Seamen's Union, the strike quickly garnered over thirty thousand participants, greatly disrupting everyday life and food shipments to Hong Kong. Though the strike was declared illegal by the British colonial government, negotiations took place after fifty-two days, with employers capitulating on March 5, 1922, and agreeing to wage increases of 15 to 30 percent.

January 12, 1964 The Zanzibar Revolution occurred when the Black African majority overthrew the ruling sultan. The rebellion ended two hundred years of often racist Arab minority rule—which had been preserved and strengthened during the island's occupation by Britain—which had ended the previous year. Ethnic reprisals began against Arab and South Asian civilians, with hundreds, possibly thousands, killed, despite the presence of British troops nearby. British military forces were, however, only to be used if a left-wing party took power, which did not happen.

13 **January 13, 1943** Nineteen-year-old Ukrainian anti-Nazi resistance fighter Ulyana Matveevna Gromova was executed by German forces. Arrested three days earlier, she endured brutal torture as the Nazis tried to force her to disclose the names of her comrades. They beat her, whipped her with metal, burned her with hot irons, flayed and mutilated her, tore out her hair, and rubbed salt in her wounds, but she refused to betray her comrades. She also raised the spirits of her fellow detainees by reciting poetry.

January 13, 1947 Fifteen thousand workers declared a general strike in Mombasa, Kenya, then part of the British Empire, with numerous grievances, in particular at wage differentials between Black and non-Black workers. Railway workers, dockers, domestic servants, hotel workers, and many others walked out. The government declared the strike illegal, but three-quarters of the workforce participated in it anyway, bringing Mombasa to a standstill. The strike lasted twelve days, until a tribunal was formed that awarded pay increases of as much as 20 to 40 percent, as well as numerous other improvements, including paid overtime, paid vacation, and housing allowances.

14 **January 14, 1929** At Port Adelaide, Australia, six hundred striking union dockworkers rushed the Mareeba steamship, which was filled with scab workers (i.e., strikebreaking, nonunion replacement workers). Strikebreakers and police fought the workers, who retaliated with stones, injuring some thirty scabs. One of the scabs pulled out a revolver and began shooting into the crowd. He was not arrested by police. The events were part of a protracted dispute over working conditions and unionization at the port.

January 14, 1930 Albrecht "Ali" Höhler, a gangster and militant in the German Communist Party's paramilitary organization the Roter Frontkämpferbund (League of Red Front Fighters) shot Horst Wessel, leader of Berlin's Nazi SA (Sturmabteilung; storm troopers). Wessel was made into a martyr by the Nazis, while Höhler was sentenced to six years in prison, only to be dragged out and killed when the Nazis came to power.

15 **January 15, 1919** Revolutionary socialists Rosa Luxemburg and Karl Liebknecht were murdered in Berlin by the right-wing para-military Freikorps, who were acting on the orders of the Sozialdemokratische Partei Deutschlands (Social Democratic Party of Germany; SPD). Luxemburg and Liebknecht had played an important part in the German Revolution of 1918–1919.

Rosa Luxemburg, c.1900
(Courtesy Wikimedia Commons)

January 15, 1934 The popular UK tabloid the *Daily Mail* published an article titled "Hurrah for the Blackshirts!" in support of Oswald Mosley's fascist movement. The article was written by Viscount Rothermere, whose family still owns the *Mail*. The newspaper continues to be one of the most right-wing British tabloids, publishing false and misleading articles about anti-fascists and others.

16 **January 16, 1973** Students at the University of Sussex initiated a rent strike against the government's plans to cut student grants. They would be joined by students from around the UK, with forty-four universities taking part in rent strikes by the end of February.

January 16, 1997 Indian trade union leader Dutta Samant was assassinated. Famously, he was a key organizer during the massive textile workers' strike in Mumbai in 1982. He was shot seventeen times by four gunmen believed to be contract killers connected to the criminal underworld.

Patrice Lumumba in Brussels, 1960 *(Photo by Behrens, Herbert/Anefo, courtesy Nationaal Archief)*

17 **January 17, 1961** Patrice Lumumba, the first democratically elected prime minister of Congo, which had gained its independence from Belgium the previous year, was murdered following a coup backed by the US and Belgium. Initially the CIA had intended to assassinate the socialist independence leader, but instead he and two colleagues were arrested, brutally beaten, tortured, and then shot. Belgian troops then dug up the bodies, dismembered them, and dissolved them in sulfuric acid, grinding what was left into powder and scattering it.

January 17, 1969 Bunchy Carter and John Huggins, two members of the revolutionary Black Panther Party, were murdered by a member of the US Organization, a Black nationalist group that was being manipulated by the FBI as part of its COINTELPRO program, with the intention of causing deadly division.

18 **January 18, 1958** The Battle of Hayes Pond took place near Maxton, North Carolina, with Native Americans routing a Ku Klux Klan rally. The Klan, which considered the local Lumbee tribe as a "mongrel" race of "half n——s," were unhappy with interracial relationships involving white men and thought that due to their small numbers and marginalized status the Lumbee would be an easy target.

Klan members began by burning a cross on the lawn of a Lumbee woman who was dating a white man. Their activities escalated and culminated in a rally on January 18 that was intended to end "race mixing" once and for all. The Klan declared that five thousand people would attend.

On the day, they only mustered around fifty Klan members and one hundred other white supremacists, while five hundred Lumbee, led by World War II veterans and armed with shotguns, clubs, and rocks turned out to oppose them. The Native Americans opened fire and attacked, slightly wounding four Klansmen, who returned fire but failed to hit anyone. The KKK were

Lumbee residents confront white supremacists at Hayes Pond *(Photo by Bill Shaw, courtesy State Archives of North Carolina/Wikimedia Commons)*

totally defeated and forced to flee. The Lumbee seized their audio equipment and burned their Klan outfits and banners on a makeshift bonfire until police arrived and teargassed the revelers.

In the wake of the incident, public sentiment swung against the KKK, and the local leader was later convicted for incitement to riot and jailed for two years. The humiliation ended Klan activity in the local area, and the incident is celebrated each year as a Lumbee holiday.

January 18, 1977 Workers and poor people across Egypt rose up against the ending of state subsidies for basic goods. Despite the government killing hundreds of people, strikes, demonstrations, and riots forced authorities to back down in just two days.

19 **January 19, 1915** The Roosevelt massacre took place in New Jersey when sheriff's deputies in the pay of fertilizer bosses opened fire on a crowd of unarmed striking workers, killing two and injuring eighteen. The workers were fighting to reverse a 20 percent pay cut. It is likely that those killed were Alessandro Tessitore, twenty-eight, and Kalman Batyi, thirty-eight. The deputies were gunmen for a private detective agency hired to help break the strike. Despite the murders, the workers held firm and successfully overturned the pay cut. Although unusual in the case of US labor massacres, a number of the deputies were arrested, and nine were later convicted of manslaughter and jailed for two to ten years.

January 19, 1984 Protests began in the Rif area of northern Morocco against the introduction of baccalaureate subscription fees in public schools mandated by a structural adjustment program imposed by the International Monetary Fund. Students were joined by workers and the unemployed in days of protests that were met by savage repression from the regime of Hassan II, who described the poor people of the Rif as *awbash*—savages or scum. Troops killed and jailed hundreds to suppress the movement.

20 **January 20, 1900** Health officials in Honolulu, Hawaii, battling a plague epidemic attempted to conduct controlled burnings of homes and businesses in Chinatown, which quickly got out of control. The fire accidentally set light to the wooden roof of the old Kaumakapili Church, then continued to spread for seventeen days, devastating a thirty-eight-acre area that included four thousand homes of mostly Chinese and Japanese residents.

Authorities disregarded evidence that rats spread the disease and instead scapegoated Asian residents for an outbreak of bubonic plague that had killed a Chinese bookkeeper. They based their tactics not on science but on racist stereotypes about Chinese homes being dirty and set up a cordon sanitaire, effectively quarantining people of Asian descent in the city for weeks.

Their possessions were thrown into the street, their homes sprayed with carbolic acid, and they were forced to shower in public in mass, makeshift cleaning stations. Officials then began burning the homes of Chinese and Japanese people.

When the January fire first started spreading out of control, residents fleeing for their lives were turned back by the National Guard, backed up by white vigilantes. Eventually a single exit in the cordon was opened to allow people to escape the fire.

The *Honolulu Advertiser* declared that "intelligent Anglo-Saxon methods" had been employed to combat a "disease wafted to these shores from Asiatic countries." Another local paper celebrated the fire for supposedly eradicating the plague, while also clearing valuable real estate. After the fire, many of the residents made homeless were never able to return to the area, and its demographics were permanently altered.

January 20, 1964 A battalion of around 1,350 troops in Tanzania (then Tanganyika) mutinied to protest against low pay and the fact that they were still commanded by British officers, despite having gained independence two years previously. The rebellion spread to a further battalion the next day, as rebels took European officers hostage and gained control of key locations in Dar es Salaam, including the radio station, airport, and telegraph office. Looting also broke out.

Trade unions planned to launch a general strike on January 26, but, on January 25, the government of the socialist independence leader Julius Nyerere requested British troops to help suppress the revolt. The next day, British commandos arrived and attacked the mutineers, killing three soldiers and arresting hundreds more, while police arrested two hundred people, including several union leaders and the general secretary of the Tanganyika Federation of Labour (TFL). Nyerere's government subsequently broke up the TFL, replacing it with a state-run "union," whose role was to support government policies.

Mutinies with similar demands also broke out in Uganda and Kenya, with the new anti-colonial leaders in these countries also requesting assistance from British forces to suppress them.

21 **January 21, 1921** Striking workers in Santa Cruz, Argentina, seized the La Anita and La Primavera ranches, taking their owners and the deputy police commissioner hostage. The strikers, mostly wool workers and rural laborers, were demanding better pay and conditions, including Saturdays off, better food, and a pack of candles per month each.

The workers had organized themselves into columns and were marching from workplace to workplace, seizing food and weapons. Subsequently, some clashes took place with police, but after the arrival of the army, the workers agreed to give up their weapons and release their hostages in return for most of their demands being met.

However, later that year, authorities raided union offices, and when workers launched a general strike in response, a colonel named Héctor

Benigno Varela arrived with two hundred troops and set about trying to crush the strike with brute force. By January 1922, as many as 1,500 workers had been killed.

January 21, 1946 The largest strike in United States history, in terms of number of participants, took place, with 750,000 steelworkers going on strike, as part of a massive strike wave in the wake of World War II.

22 **January 22, 1826** Members of the Acjachemen Nation, who were field hands at Mission San Juan Capistrano, in California, refused to work, engaging in what may have been the first farmworker strike in the state, then part of Mexico. Over one hundred workers gathered, rose in rebellion, and demanded that the local padre (priest) be placed in the stocks. They reportedly insulted the local captain of the guard and threatened to put him in the stocks if he failed to do so.

There had been a long history of Native American resistance to the missions and other colonizers before this point, so this may just be the first reported work stoppage.

January 22, 1969 Black workers at the Eldon Chrysler plant in Detroit marched on the United Auto Workers union (UAW) with a list of grievances. The workers had formed the Eldon Revolutionary Union Movement (ELRUM) and called a strike the next day, keeping out two-thirds of the workforce. The company retaliated by firing and disciplining dozens of militants. ELRUM was able to rebuild its presence at the plant over the following year, nonetheless. 🎙 **12**

23 **January 23, 1913** Ten thousand clothing workers went on strike in Rochester, New York, for the eight-hour day, a 10 percent wage increase, union recognition, and extra pay for overtime and holidays. Six people were injured over the course of the strike, and one worker, eighteen-year-old Ida Braiman, was shot to death by a sweatshop contractor. The

Garment workers on strike, Rochester, 1913 *(Courtesy Albert R Stone Collection/ Wikimedia Commons)*

strike was called off in April when manufacturers agreed not to discriminate against workers for joining a union.

January 23, 1982 All Formula One Grand Prix drivers except two went on strike, barricading themselves in a room to protest against new "superlicense" conditions. The new licenses would tie drivers to three-year contracts and, worse, would forbid any criticism of their governing body, the Fédération Internationale de l'Automobile (FIA), with a penalty of a lifetime ban if a driver did so. The drivers were fined, but the new licenses were withdrawn.

24 **January 24, 1964** Kenyan independence leader and prime minister Jomo Kenyatta invited British colonial troops to put down a mutiny of soldiers who were conducting a sit-down protest against low pay and the continued presence of British officers in the Kenyan military. A US destroyer also rushed to the area to back up UK forces. In the repression, one African soldier was killed, and one soldier and one passerby were injured. It was the third such rebellion that week in East Africa.

January 24, 1977 Nine left-wing lawyers were shot in an attack by fascists in Madrid, in what is known as the Atocha massacre. The fascists entered the offices of the Comisiones Obreras union (Workers' Commissions; CCOO) with machine guns looking for a communist transport strike organizer. When they didn't find him, they shot a lawyer, and then lined eight others up against a wall and shot them as well, killing five and seriously wounding the others, including a pregnant woman.

Elsewhere in the city, on that same day, twenty-one-year-old student María Luz Nájera Julián was killed by police during a demonstration against the fascist murder of left-wing bricklayer Arturo Ruiz the previous day, at a demonstration calling for the release of political prisoners. Police let his attackers escape and instead charged Ruiz's fellow demonstrators.

25 **January 25, 1911** Kanno Sugako, a Japanese anarchist feminist, was executed for her part in a plot to assassinate the emperor. She remains the only woman to be executed in Japan for treason. Radicalized at the age of fourteen, after being raped, in addition to being a pioneering feminist, she was one of Japan's first female journalists and a prolific writer of fiction and nonfiction. She was inspired by Sophia Perovskaya, who helped assassinate the Russian czar.

Kanno Sugako, pre-1910 *(Courtesy Wikimedia Commons)*

Sugako admitted her guilt in the plot, as did her half a dozen or so coconspirators. Nonetheless, twenty-four anarchists, most of whom were innocent, were sentenced to death, which enraged Sugako. In her prison diary she wrote: "Needless to say, I was prepared for the death sentence. My only concern day and night was to see as many of my . . . fellow defendants saved as possible. . . . I am convinced our sacrifice is not in vain. It will bear fruit in the future. I am confident that because I firmly believe my death will serve a valuable purpose I will be able to maintain my self-respect until the last moment on the scaffold. I will be enveloped in the marvelously comforting thought that I am sacrificing myself for the cause. I believe I will be able to die a noble death without fear or anguish." In her final entry she wrote of her happiness upon learning that twelve of her fellow defendants were reprieved, their lives thereby spared.

January 25, 2011 The Egyptian Revolution began. Groups of young people chose the date of the annual Egyptian "police day" to protest against police brutality. Millions of protesters took to the streets in an ongoing rebellion that would eventually bring down the government of Hosni Mubarak.

Demonstrators praying in Tahrir Square (Photo by Lilian Wagdy from Flickr, CC by SA 2.0 https://www.flickr.com/photos/lilianwagdy)

26 **January 26, 1932** Four thousand mainly Jewish tenants in New York attacked police reserve forces that were trying to evict seventeen tenants. The mob was led by women poised on rooftops directing the action with megaphones and hurling missiles at police.

January 26, 1952 The Cairo fire, or Black Saturday riots, began when protesters burned and looted hundreds of European-owned buildings in protest at British occupation troops killing fifty Egyptian policeman the previous day. The events began when airport workers refused to service four British planes.

27 **January 27, 1918** Revolution broke out in Finland as workers took over Helsinki, with many of the country's other large towns following in the next few days. The "People's Republic of Finland" instituted numerous far-reaching reforms, including women's suffrage, workers' control of production, a maximum eight-hour workday, the abolition of the old mode of land distribution, and the emancipation of domestic servants and farmhands.

However, to end conflict with the Central Powers in World War I, Finland, along with other territories, was surrendered to Germany by the Russian Bolshevik government in the March 1918 Treaty of Brest-Litovsk. The following month counterrevolutionary White forces drowned the revolution in blood, killing thousands of workers and socialists and throwing tens of thousands more into internment camps.

January 27, 1923 Anarchist miner Kurt Wilckens assassinated Argentinian army officer Colonel Héctor Benigno Varela, who was responsible for the killing of 1,500 workers in Patagonia in 1921–1922. Wilckens was arrested and soon murdered in prison by a former police officer smuggled in by prison guards. After his death an indefinite general strike broke out across the country.

28 **January 28, 1917** Carmelita Torres, a seventeen-year-old Mexican maid who worked in the US, refused to take the mandatory gasoline bath given to day laborers at the border and convinced thirty other trolley passengers to join her. Her protest spread in what became known as the Bath Riots.

Torres was one of many workers who crossed the border between Juárez and El Paso each day. In the name of public health, Mexican workers were frequently subjected to degrading and humiliating treatment. The workers had to strip naked, undergo a toxic gasoline bath, and have their clothes steamed. The stated aim of the program was to kill lice, which can spread typhus. However, it was not applied to everyone crossing the border: just working class Mexicans.

In addition to gasoline being poisonous, it was also a deadly fire risk. A group of prisoners in El Paso being treated with gasoline were burned to death in an accidental fire. Furthermore, US health workers were secretly photographing naked Mexican women.

Anger at the practice finally exploded, and within a few hours Torres had amassed a crowd of several thousand mostly women protesters. They blocked all traffic and trolleys into El Paso. They pelted immigration officers with rocks and bottles when they tried to disperse them, and when US and then Mexican troops arrived they received the same treatment. The riots were eventually suppressed by the soldiers, and Torres was arrested, which appears to have had the effect of discouraging future protests.

The enforced bathing and fumigation of Mexican workers with toxic chemicals like gasoline, and later DDT and Zyklon B, continued until the 1950s. The use of Zyklon B at the border appealed to scientists in Nazi Germany, who in the late 1930s began using the agent at borders and in concentration camps for delousing. Notoriously, they later also used it to exterminate millions of people in the Holocaust.

January 28, 1946 A massacre took place in Bulnes Square, in Santiago, Chile, when police fired on thousands of workers who were demonstrating against rising prices, killing six and injuring several others. A strike of saltpeter workers, protesting against an increase in prices at company grocery stores, had been suppressed and thousands of other workers were marching to support them.

29 **January 29, 1911** In northern Mexico, the first battle of the so-called Tijuana revolt occurred. A pre-dawn raid by a mix of international supporters of the anarchist Partido Liberal de México (Liberal Party of Mexico; PLM) and Industrial Workers of the World union (IWW) members seized the town of Mexicali, killing the jailer. The revolt, despite serious flaws, would spread in the border areas, peaking in May with the capture of the town of Tijuana.

January 29, 1935 Workers at a sugar factory in Saint Kitts joined a strike of cane cutters for a pay increase that had begun the previous day. The workers assembled in the yard at Buckley's plantation. When they failed to disperse, the manager fired his gun into the crowd, injuring several workers. British armed police then arrived, but workers still refused to disperse, demanding that the manager be arrested. Instead the police opened fire on the workers, killing three and injuring eight. The following day, a British warship arrived, and marines disembarked to suppress the strike. Thirty-nine strikers were arrested and six jailed for two to five years.

30 **January 30, 1965** Former British prime minister Winston Churchill's funeral took place. One of its most memorable moments was when cranes on the London docks dipped as his funeral barge went past. It later emerged that the dockworkers had originally refused to dip the cranes, as they "didn't like" Churchill, and had to be paid extra to do it.

While presented as a national hero today, Churchill was, in fact, hated by many, especially working class people, which is why he lost the 1945 election. A virulent racist, he supported using poison gas on civilians, sent troops against striking workers, and helped kill up to four million Bengalis in an enforced famine.

National Liberation Front guerrillas, 1966 *(Courtesy Wikimedia Commons)*

January 30, 1968 The North Vietnamese military and the National Liberation Front (NLF) in the South launched the Tet offensive—a major operation against US and South Vietnamese Army of the Republic of Vietnam (ARVN) forces—to coincide with Vietnamese New Year. The offensive was a tactical failure, with North Vietnamese forces and the NLF suffering massive casualties. However, it showed the US public that the propaganda that the war was nearly over and that victory for the US was close was a lie. Thus, it ended up being a political success for the anti-colonial forces and helped swing public sentiment against US involvement in the region, including among US troops. 🎧 **10–11, 14**

31 **January 31, 1938** Pecan shellers at the Southern Pecan Shelling Company in Texas went on strike against low wages. Led by firebrand Emma Tenayuca, the mostly Latina women workers held out for a month and won.

January 31, 1957 Three hundred fifty Jewish bagel bakers in New York City went on strike. At first, bagel truck drivers did not strike with them; however, bakers slashed tires, hijacked trucks, stole keys, and appealed to drivers to join them until they agreed. They were also joined by 385 workers at the Pechter Baking Company. The bakers remained out for thirty-three days until the city's thirty-four bakeries agreed to improved pay and benefits for the strikers.

FEBRUARY

The Greensboro Woolworth, which is now a civil rights museum, 2018 *(Photo by bobistraveling from Flickr CC by SA 2.0 https://www.flickr.com/photos/bobistraveling/42234330014)*

1 **February 1, 1960** Four Black college students refused to move from a Woolworth lunch counter when they were denied service in Greensboro, North Carolina. By the following September over seventy thousand people had participated in sit-ins against Jim Crow segregation laws.

February 1, 2012 The Port Said stadium massacre occurred in Egypt, with dozens of people killed and hundreds injured, after fans of the Al-Masry football team, many of them armed with rocks and knives, attacked Al-Ahly fans. Eyewitnesses reported that police did nothing when the attack began and refused to open gates to allow people to escape. Many people believe that the attack was retaliation against the Ultras Ahlawy, a group of Ahly fans who were active in the 2011 revolution and in opposing the ruling Supreme Council of the Armed Forces. Numerous people were subsequently charged in connection with the deaths, including nine police officers.

2 **February 2, 1902** The first workers' union federation in the Philippines, the Unión Obrera Democrática Filipina (Democratic Workers Union of the Philippines; UOD) was set up by Isabelo de los Reyes. By the following year, it had 150 member unions,
Isabelo de los Reyes, date unknown *(Courtesy Wikimedia Commons)*

totaling twenty thousand members. The union's principles were based on the ideas of German communist Karl Marx and Italian anarchist Errico Malatesta. Reyes had spent time in Spain, where he was jailed for inciting strikes. He came across anarchist and Marxist ideas in prison and brought numerous books by the likes of Marx and Russian anarchist Mikhail Bakunin back to the Philippines with him.

February 2, 1988 Four lesbians abseiled into the UK House of Lords to protest an ongoing debate about introducing the homophobic section 28 law, which would come into force that May. Section 28 of the Local Government Act 1988 prohibited local authorities, including schools, from teaching "the acceptability of homosexuality as a pretended family relationship."

In 2017, four other lesbians climbed onto the Houses of Parliament to put up a blue plaque commemorating the 1988 action.

3 **February 3, 1988** With inflation at nearly 5 percent, 2,500 nurses across the UK went on strike against a pay increase offer of only 3 percent. Workers at car manufacturer Vauxhall and some miners joined them on sympathy strikes. Despite press attacks, most people supported them, and they won some concessions.

February 3, 1994 Workers in Ecuador held a national general strike to protest against the economic policies of President Sixto Durán-Ballén's conservative government, particularly a 71 percent increase in the price of gasoline. The walkout followed a general strike of students the previous day.

4 **February 4, 1899** Fighting broke out between the United States and the Philippine Republic when the US decided to take over the newly independent country. It waged a vicious counterinsurgency campaign and officially declared victory in 1902, although many citizens continued to battle the occupiers for several years thereafter.

Philippines casualties on the first day of the war
(Courtesy US Army/Wikimedia Commons)

February 4, 1924 Around 175 Industrial Workers of the World union (IWW) members took on the Ku Klux Klan, patrolling the streets of Greenville, Maine, after the KKK tried to intimidate IWW organizers. "We are going to stick, and if the Klan wants to start something, the IWW are going to finish it," declared Bob Pease, a local Wobbly, who also alleged that the Klan were in the pay of the lumber industry in which the IWW was active. 🎙 **6, 9**

5 **February 5, 1885** King Leopold of Belgium declared his new colony the Congo Free State. What followed was one of the most horrific examples of European colonialism. The regime began the ruthless exploitation of the local population, forcing them to extract natural resources, particularly rubber, which

Nsala, a Congolese man, looks at the severed hand and foot of his five-year-old daughter, who was mutilated and eaten by militia, 1904 *(Courtesy Wikimedia Commons)*

were shipped back to Belgium. Eight to ten million Africans were killed, with many more mutilated, for acts as minor as failing to hit production targets.

February 5, 1981 The 240 mostly women workers at the Lee Jeans factory in Greenock, Scotland, occupied their workplace when they learned that it was due to be closed and production moved elsewhere. They barricaded the doors with chairs, and two of them climbed onto the roof and down a drainpipe to buy 240 portions of fish and chips and Irn Bru (a popular Scottish carbonated soft drink). They kept up the occupation for seven months, until management caved in and agreed to a buyout, securing jobs for the 140 workers still occupying the plant.

6 **February 6, 1916** The Cabaret Voltaire nightclub opened in Zürich, Switzerland. Often described as "history's wildest nightclub," it was the spiritual home of the anarchic Dada art movement, formed by radical artists revolted by the capitalist carnage of World War I.

February 6, 1919 The Seattle general strike, perhaps the most spectacular strike in US history, began. Nearly one hundred thousand downed tools in support of striking shipyard workers, but, more importantly, they then elected a general strike committee and began running the city and essential services themselves. While the shipyard workers did not get their pay increase, the five-day general strike was a historic and successful experiment that demonstrated that workers could run society themselves.

On the same day, workers in Butte, Montana, responded to a dollar per day wage cut by launching their own general strike. To prevent disunity, workers formed a Workers' and Soldiers' Council to conduct the strike.

7 **February 7, 1919** Construction union activists representing 75,000 members in Essex, New Jersey, voted to strike in the event of alcohol prohibition coming into force on July 1. Two days later, it was reported that 200,000 workers in New York City also voted to strike, with a further 150,000 due to vote over the following two weeks. New York unions received letters from union branches in LA, Cincinnati, Seattle, San Francisco, Chicago, Saint Louis, Kansas City, Milwaukee, and elsewhere. Workers who supported the movement wore pins that declared: "No beer, no work." However, union leaders called off the action the following month, stating it would have made them "look ridiculous."

February 7, 1974 Grenada achieved independence from Britain, following a turbulent period of civil unrest, including a nationwide general strike protesting against police and paramilitary brutality, among other things, which had been ongoing since January 1.

8 **February 8, 1517** Hernández de Córdoba set sail with three ships from Cuba heading west to explore the shores of southern Mexico in search of Indigenous people to enslave and use as forced labor in mines. He was defeated by the Maya and forced to retreat, dying from his wounds shortly after returning to Cuba.

February 8, 1968 The Orangeburg massacre took place when police opened fire on Black South Carolina State students protesting at a segregated bowling alley, killing three and wounding twenty-seven. The incident is much less well-known than the May 5, 1970, killing of white students at Kent State.

9 **February 9, 1912** A group of women workers in Gundry's net and rope factory in Bridgeport, Dorset, staged a wildcat strike over pay and conditions. They walked around the town singing suffragette songs and collecting money for a strike fund. They refused arbitration from the local

MP, returning to work the following week when a London trade union official signed them up and settled the dispute.

February 9, 1995 The Mexican government called off the peace process with Zapatista rebels and invaded their Chiapas strongholds after an adviser to the US Chase Manhattan Bank demanded that the government take action.

A secret Chase memo, which was leaked, stated: "While Chiapas, in our opinion, does not pose a fundamental threat to Mexican political stability, it is perceived to be so by many in the investment community. The government will need to eliminate the Zapatistas to demonstrate their effective control of the national territory and of security policy." The memo went on to say that the governing party should "consider carefully whether or not to allow opposition victories if fairly won at the ballot box." However, the autonomous Zapatista communities held out.

10 **February 10, 1960** The sit-ins that had been sweeping North Carolina arrived in Raleigh. Black students demonstrated against whites-only lunch counters at drugstores across the city. The drugstores responded by closing the counters.

February 10, 1979 Striking lettuce grower Rufino Contreras was killed by a foreman in California. Four thousand three hundred workers, mostly organized in the United Farm Workers (UFW) union, were on strike in Imperial Valley in a violent dispute. Authorities declined to prosecute the murderer, citing insufficient evidence.

11 **February 11, 1967** A protest against police repression was held outside the LGBT+ Black Cat Tavern in Los Angeles. It was part of a series of demonstrations against police raids and harassment of countercultural young people held that night around the city.

The Black Cat was chosen as the location of one of the protests because it had been the site of a violent police raid on January 1, with police attacking customers, arresting fourteen for same-sex kissing. The protest was endorsed by gay rights group PRIDE (Personal Rights in Defense and Education), which was formed the previous year. This may have been the first use of the term *pride* in the LGBT+ rights movement.

February 11, 2004 Eighty unemployed workers looted a supermarket in the town of Levoča, Slovakia, kickstarting a militant wave of protest against sweeping benefit cuts, primarily by Roma people, that ended up winning better conditions for all unemployed people.

12 **February 12, 1920** The first strike organized by women in Colombia took place at the textile factory in Bello, Antioquia. Some four hundred women walked out demanding equal pay with men, an end to sexual harassment by managers, the abolition of fines for sick leave, reduced surveillance and searches of workers, and that salaries be paid directly to women workers rather than to their fathers or husbands.

Key organizers included Teresa Tamayo, Adelina González, Carmen Agudelo, Teresa Piedrahita, Matilde Montoya, and Betsabé Espinoza. Most male workers at the factory crossed the picket lines, and police tried to break the strike. But the women, who had widespread public support and received donations from other workers, especially in Medellín, held firm.

On March 4, the women won most of their demands, including a 40 percent pay increase, reduced working hours, better health and safety, and the abolition of fines, as well as the dismissal of a number of abusive managers.

February 12, 1978 In Aotearoa/New Zealand 250 members of the Māori Tainui Awhiro tribe and its allies occupied the Raglan Golf Course, preventing games from being played. The course had been built on the site of an Indigenous burial ground that was seized by the government during World War I. Eventually, the tribal occupants were evicted, their homes and graves destroyed, and the land sold to private developers.

Eva Rickard, a member of both the golf club and the tribe, was a key organizer of protests, which began in 1972, when the club planned to expand and destroy more burial grounds. At the occupation, Tainui Awhiro religious leaders held a ceremony and danced a traditional haka welcome.

Eva Rickard, 1979 *(Photo courtesy Nambassa Trust and Peter Terry, www. nambassa.com Wikimedia Commons)*

By the afternoon, the police began making arrests. They violently arrested Rickard, permanently injuring her wrist, and seventeen others. In response, a prominent member of the Te Matakite tribe, Ben Matthews, played a round of golf on parliament's front lawn in front of television cameras. Eventually, the prime minister phoned Rickard and offered to sell the land back to the tribe, but Rickard rejected the offer, arguing that the government never paid for the land in the first place.

Direct action by Māori people continued until 1983, when the government gave in and returned the land, which is now home to a community center open to all.

13 **February 13, 1913** Eighty-two-year-old labor activist Mother Jones was arrested in Charleston, West Virginia, after martial law was declared to suppress a coal miners' strike. She was charged with inciting a riot— reportedly for attempting to read the Declaration of Independence—and conspiracy to commit murder. Tried and convicted in a military court, she was sentenced to

Mother Jones, 1924 *(Courtesy of the Library of Congress)*

twenty years in prison. Jones declared: "Whatever I have done in West Virginia . . . I have done it all over the United States. And when I get out, I will do it again." She was released and pardoned after serving eighty-five days. She had, however, contracted pneumonia in prison.

February 13, 1951 Aotearoa/New Zealand's biggest ever industrial dispute began when dockworkers started an overtime ban, demanding the same 15 percent pay increase that all industrial workers had just been awarded. Waterside workers had only been offered a 9 percent pay increase by the mostly British-owned shipping companies.

The employers responded by locking out the workers, and the government backed them up by introducing emergency laws, deploying the army and navy to work as scabs, and deregistering the Waterside Workers' Federation (WWF). The national umbrella union group, the Federation of Labour, supported the government, and the opposition Labour Party also failed to support the Waterside workers.

Despite all the forces ranged against them, up to twenty thousand other workers took solidarity strike action in support of the dockers, and thousands more refused to handle scab goods. Nonetheless, after 151 days, the workers were forced to concede defeat. In the wake of the dispute, many militants were blacklisted and prevented from working on the docks for years afterward.

14 **February 14, 1874** The drawing below was published in *Penny Illustrated* magazine in London depicting the Bihar famine of 1873–1874. A drought in the region endangered food supplies, so the newly appointed British governor of Bengal, Richard Temple, organized a massive relief effort, importing hundreds of thousands of tons of rice from Burma (now Myanmar) and organizing relief packages to provide three hundred million units of relief (each unit catering for one person for one day). The swift action meant that there were few or no deaths from the famine.

Famine street scene, 1874 *(Penny Illustrated)*

However, Temple was strongly rebuked by the British government for spending too much. So when the next famine hit South and South West India in 1876, Temple massively reduced aid, while hundreds of thousands of tons of food were exported to England, and around five and a half million Indians died.

February 14, 1939 After ten firemen returned to work following a short stoppage, worker unrest at the Leonora sugar plantation in Guyana escalated when eighty to ninety members of a shovel gang refused an offer of nine cents per bed for fieldwork. The workers demanded twelve cents. Two days later, British police massacred the protesting workers.

15 **February 15, 1851** A crowd of African Americans and abolitionists raided the Boston courthouse and rescued Shadrach Minkins, aka Frederick Jenkins, an imprisoned runaway enslaved person, then smuggled him to freedom in Canada.

February 15, 1913 A strike of rubber workers in Akron, Ohio, organized by the Industrial Workers of the World union (IWW) had grown to 3,500 strikers. Earlier that month three hundred mostly nonunion workers at Firestone walked out. They turned to the IWW, which helped spread the strike to up to twenty thousand workers at multiple firms. Facing repression and violence from the police, the strike ended a few weeks later with no real concessions. But within two decades, Akron rubber workers were solidly organized and began to win massive gains with sit-down strikes. 👤 **6**

16 **February 16, 1924** Nearly two hundred thousand dockworkers in Britain walked out on strike. The Labour Party was in power for the first time at this point, and Prime Minister Ramsay MacDonald responded by bringing the full force of the law down on the workers, invoking the Emergency Powers Act 1920. Still, the workers held out, and a week later they voted to accept a pay increase of two shillings per day.

February 16, 1937 A group of predominantly Polish women cigar makers in Detroit sat down demanding a 10 percent raise, kickstarting a militant wave of sit-down strikes across the industry in the city.

17 **February 17, 1964** A nationwide strike of sugar workers broke out in Guyana demanding that the Sugar Producers' Association recognize for the Guyana Agricultural and General Workers Union (GAWU). The British-owned companies used African scab workers to try to break the strike of the predominantly East Indian workers, which worsened racial tensions in the country and culminated in killings of Asians later in the year.

February 17, 1977 During an occupation of Sapienza University in Rome, Luciano Lama, general secretary of the Confederazione Generale Italiana del Lavoro union (Italian General Confederation of Labor; CGIL) and a member of the Communist Party, went to the occupation to "talk sense" to the occupying students. He brought with him a couple of hundred heavies in his security team. The factory workers he brought had been told they were there to fight "fascists," but, seeing that this was a lie, many of them left. In the area where he was due to speak, Lama found another platform already rigged up by the Metropolitan Indians, with a dummy of himself on it that included a big red cutout of a Valentine's heart and a slogan punning his name: *Nessuno L'Ama* (Lama Nobody, or Nobody Loves Him).

A violent clash ensued between the students and the goons, resulting in Lama and his team having their speakers smashed and being chased off campus, in an event that would become famous and further strengthen the extraparliamentary left in Italy.

The Metropolitan Indians were a group of Italian radicals who used humor and ridicule as weapons in the class war.

18 **February 18, 1946** The Royal Indian Navy mutiny began when sailors at Bombay (now Mumbai) harbor went on strike for better food and improved living conditions. The rebellion, which rapidly spread across the country, involving ten thousand sailors on sixty-six ships and at shore establishments, was accompanied by widespread rioting, a one-day general strike in Bombay, and smaller mutinies in the Royal Indian Air Force and local police forces. It was heavily repressed by British troops and Royal Navy warships. Rebellious ships raised three flags: the red flag and the flags of the Indian National Congress (INC) and the Muslim League. However, both organizations officially condemned the revolt and eventually pressured the strikers to give up. Authorities then began arresting and court-martialing mutineers, eventually dismissing 476 sailors, none of whom were reinstated into the Indian or Pakistani Navies following independence.

February 18, 2010 The *Accra Times* newspaper in Ghana reported that sex workers in the city organized in the Industrial and Commercial Workers' Union (ICU) were fighting to collectively raise their prices in response to high inflation.

19 **February 19, 1927** A general strike was called in Shanghai, China. It shut post offices, all cotton mills, and most essential services but was defeated after fierce street fighting and bloody repression. However, this didn't break the working class, which rose up again the following month.

February 19, 1951 A general strike of agricultural workers and laborers broke out on the island of Grenada, then part of the British Empire, demanding pay increases and recognition for the Grenada Manual & Mental Workers Union (GMMWU). British troops were called in, as were colonial police from elsewhere in the Caribbean, and several men and women who were supporting the strike were shot and killed. Despite the violent repression, the workers fought on and, on May 19, won a 50 percent pay increase and, for the first time, paid leave—seven days per year for those working at least two hundred days. It was part of a wave of strikes in the Caribbean in the wake of World War II.

20 **February 20, 1834** The first Lowell "mill girls" strike occurred in New England, with eight hundred women textile workers walking out in opposition to a 15 percent pay cut. They also immediately withdrew all of their savings, causing a run on two local banks. While the stoppage failed to prevent the pay cut, it was a powerful message that women workers in the area would no longer be meek and pliable.

February 20, 1990 Mineworkers won a ten-month strike and occupation of Pittston Coal plant in Virginia. Sit-ins, sabotage, and the actions of thousands of strike supporters and women played a key role in this success. While a month-long Soviet coal strike dominated US news broadcasts, the much longer Pittston strike garnered almost no mainstream press coverage.

21 **February 21, 1936** Korean anarchist Shin Chaeho died in prison. He and his partner had been arrested by Japanese police, and he was sentenced to ten years of hard labor for belonging to a secret organization. He had been Korea's most prominent journalist, and he was well-known for his idiosyncrasies. For example, he only washed his face standing upright, meaning he would always be splashed with water, as he refused to ever bow.

February 21, 1965 El-Hajj Malik El-Shabazz, better known as Malcolm X, instrumental speaker and activist of the US civil rights and Black power movements, was assassinated while preparing to address a crowd of supporters in New York. An ardent opponent of white supremacy, Malcolm X was a critic of the principle of absolute nonviolence, if nonviolence would delay the emancipation of Black people. He also became critical of all forms of exploitation. A month before his murder, he told an interviewer: "All my life, I believed that the fundamental struggle was Black versus white. Now I realize that it is the haves against the have-nots."

Malcolm X, 1964 *(Courtesy of the Library of Congress, New York World-Telegram & Sun Collection)*

22 **February 22, 1927** The first union for Korean casual laborers in Japan, the Jiyü Rōdōsha Kumiai (Casual Workers' Union) was formed. It was organized by Korean anarchists Mun Seong-hun, Lee Si-woo, O Seong-mun, and others.

February 22, 2018 Some twenty thousand teachers across the state of West Virginia walked out on a wildcat strike, protesting against low pay and a new inferior health insurance scheme. Rank-and-file teachers, who had organized themselves in individual schools and across counties and the state in Facebook groups, initiated the walkout in defiance of the law and their own unions. They shut schools in all fifty-five counties, affecting a quarter of a million students.

Four days later, union leaders attempted to call off the action following a verbal agreement with the governor, but teachers again organized themselves and remained determined to stay out until a genuine deal passed the legislature, which occurred on March 6, when a bill was passed giving teachers and other state employees a 5 percent pay increase.

Their example inspired teachers to take similar action in Kentucky, Oklahoma, and Arizona that year, and Denver, Oakland, and Los Angeles the next.

23 **February 23, 1910** Textile workers in New York decided to end their five-month strike, also known as the Uprising of the Twenty Thousand, after winning higher wages. Workers at the soon-to-be-infamous Triangle Shirtwaist factory were at the center of the strike, organized primarily by migrant Jewish and Italian workers, most of whom were women. Workers decided to return to work, despite not having won union recognition.

February 23, 2004 In Trebišov, Slovakia, a major clash occurred between security forces and unemployed workers, most of them Roma, protesting against welfare cuts. Police attacked four hundred demonstrators using tear gas and water cannons. The next day they attacked the settlement where the protesters lived, conducting illegal searches and torturing residents, including pregnant women and disabled people, with batons and electric cattle prods. Nonetheless, the protests continued, successfully winning improvements to benefits for all unemployed people in the country.

24 **February 24, 1912** During the Bread and Roses Strike of around twenty thousand mostly women textile workers in the Industrial Workers of the World union (IWW), police clubbed strikers and their children who were being transported to stay with other families. One pregnant woman miscarried after a beating.

Many of the children were being looked after by strike supporters in New York City, to help parents bear the hardship of being on strike. The tactic was proving very successful, so, on this day, city authorities tried to prevent one hundred children from going to Philadelphia. When the women

Police repression against strikers and their children *(By Ernest Collier, Collier's Weekly)*

and children were arrested, they refused to pay fines, instead choosing to go to jail. The police violence backfired and galvanized support across the US. 🎙 **6, 16**

February 24, 1932 The chief of police of Montevideo, Uruguay, Luis Pardeiro, and his chauffeur were assassinated. Pardeiro was notorious for torturing anarchists in custody, including Miguel Arcángel Roscigno, who had robbed banks alongside legendary Spanish revolutionary Buenaventura Durruti. The attack was attributed to five Uruguayan anarchists. At Pardeiro's wake that night, someone wrote in his book of condolences: "Eye for eye, tooth for tooth."

25 **February 25, 1941** A general strike was called in Netherlands against the anti-Jewish measures of the occupying Nazis. Organized by communists, it was largely suppressed the next day, with key activists sent to the concentration camps.

February 25, 1986 US-backed, anti-communist dictator of the Philippines Ferdinand Marcos was toppled by mass protests and forced to flee the country, in what became known as the People Power Revolution.

26 **February 26, 1860** In what is known as the Wiyot massacre, white settlers attacked and murdered up to 250 Indigenous Wiyot people at Tuluwat, on modern-day Indian Island, in Eureka, California. The Wiyot people had never had conflict with white settlers and so did not expect an attack. On the day of the attack, most of the young men of the tribe were away gathering supplies.

The settlers armed themselves with clubs, axes, knives, and a few guns and attempted to systematically murder everyone on the island: mostly women, children, and elders. Over the coming days more Wiyot people in the area were murdered.

While many white people criticized the murders, no one was prosecuted for them, and one journalist who wrote an editorial condemning the murderers was forced to leave the area due to death threats.

After the killings, the surviving Wiyot were prohibited from returning to their land. Many of the survivors tried to resist, launching attacks on nearby white settlements, but they were eventually removed to reservations.

They and their descendants never gave up the fight for their home. The Wiyot tribe purchased a parcel of their old land in 2000, and, in 2019, the city gave back the bulk of the remaining land.

February 26, 1931 The La Placita raid took place in Los Angeles, with armed immigration officers, some in military uniforms, sealing off the popular La Placita Park in a mostly Mexican neighborhood. They demanded that everyone in the park present their papers, and then arrested dozens of people, later deporting many of them. The raids were part of what became known as the Mexican Repatriation, an illegal series of raids and the deportation of up to 1.8 million people, most of whom were actually US citizens who had been born and raised in the US. In 1929, President Herbert Hoover had decided to try to "create jobs" for white workers during the Depression by removing those deemed to be "Other": namely Mexicans and US citizens of Mexican descent. Under President Franklin D. Roosevelt, the practice continued until 1936, with the support of labor unions.

27 **February 27, 1943** The Rosenstrasse protests— the only mass public demonstration by Germans against the deportation of Jews—began. The protests outside a detention center on Rosenstrasse lasted

Sculpture commemorating the Rosenstrasse protests *(By Ingeborg Hunzinger, photo by Manfred Brückels/ Wikimedia Commons CC by SA 3.0)*

until March. They were organized by non-Jewish wives and relatives of Jewish men who had been picked up in a brutal wave of arrests across Berlin. The tenacity of the women, who had refused to divorce their husbands and had shown that they were willing to die to protect their Jewish families, may have forced Nazi authorities to temporarily back down. Unlike most European Jews, those who were detained in Rosenstrasse survived the Holocaust.

February 27, 1973 Armed Native American activists occupied Wounded Knee, South Dakota, to protest tribal corruption and the continuing failure of the US government to fulfil treaties they had signed with Indigenous people. Choosing the site of the 1890 massacre of Native Americans by US troops, they held out for seventy-one days, frequently exchanging fire with government forces and suffering casualties, some fatal.

Though eventually broken, the occupation galvanized huge support for the American Indian Movement, famously including Marlon Brando, who boycotted that year's Oscars, sending the Apache actor Sacheen Littlefeather in his place to collect his best actor award. Littlefeather delivered a speech about Wounded Knee to reporters backstage after she was threatened with arrest for speaking on the podium.

28 **February 28, 1948** British colonial police in Ghana killed three Ghanaian people and injured many others when they opened fire on a procession of unarmed ex-servicemen. The men, who had fought for the British Army, were attempting to present a petition to the governor requesting action against the rising cost of living. Six Africans were subsequently arrested and deported without trial. Riots that broke out across the country in response were suppressed.

February 28, 1969 Black Panthers held an armed demonstration at the capitol in Olympia, Washington, to protest against state attempts to disarm them. Following numerous police murders of unarmed Black people, the revolutionary socialist Black Panther Party started armed self-defense patrols.

The Republican mayor of Seattle had already passed a similar law, so state legislators proposed a law that would make exhibiting "firearms or other weapons in a manner manifesting intent to intimidate others" a gross misdemeanor. Lawmakers rushed through the legislation, and upon hearing of Panther plans to demonstrate, police panicked, drafting in dozens of armed state troopers and mounting a machine gun on the roof of the capitol.

The Panthers arrived in four cars and unloaded their weapons at the request of the police. While one of them, Aaron Dixon, entered the building and made a five-minute statement to the legislature, others held the doors shut, forcing the officials to listen. Despite the protest, Governor Dan Evans signed the bill into law.

The National Rifle Association, supposedly a gun rights advocacy group, did not support the Panthers and elsewhere supported Republican legal moves to take away the Panthers' guns.

29 **February 29, 1864** The three hundred women members of the Collar Laundry Union in Troy, New York, won their six-day strike for a 25 percent pay increase. Most employers caved in to the women's demands on this day, after a smaller number had given in the day before.

February 29, 2004 Haitian president Jean-Bertrand Aristide was ousted in a right-wing military coup, which he claims was backed by the United States, a claim supported by substantial evidence, including testimony from US members of Congress. He had been president on two previous occasions and had made himself unpopular with the army by trying to bring them under civilian control, with the rich by bringing in measures to prevent the country's wealth being plundered, and with the former French colonial power by demanding restitution for the ransom extorted from Haiti in the nineteenth and twentieth centuries. His government also introduced various progressive reforms, including doubling the minimum wage, subsidizing food for the poor, and building a huge number of schools and hospitals.

MARCH

1 **March 1, 1919** The Sam-il Movement, also known as the March 1st Movement—a series of protests for independence from Japanese colonialism—began in Korea. Over the next six weeks, around two million Koreans, 10 percent of the population, took part in 1,500 demonstrations. Japanese police and armed forces violently suppressed the movement, killing around 7,500 people, some in public executions, wounding nearly 16,000, and arresting over 46,000. In contrast, Japanese authorities claimed that eight security forces personnel were killed. Despite the repression, the protests catalyzed the Korean independence movement, and, since 1949, March 1 has been a national holiday in South Korea.

March 1, 1968 Chicane students at the Woodrow Wilson High School in East Los Angeles walked out on strike in protest at the cancellation of a student play. A few days later, on March 6, coordinated student strikes began, involving approximately fifteen thousand students from seven or more different high schools. Their goals were to get more Latine teachers in their schools and to change textbooks so they included Mexican American history.[1]

Chicane students were not allowed to speak Spanish in class and were often discouraged from applying to college by guidance counsellors and teachers. The dropout rate for Mexican American students in 1967 was as high as 57.5 percent in one high school. Police and school administrators tried to stop the walkout by blocking school doors and arresting many students who tried to peacefully protest, but the students were undeterred.

Following the walkouts, on March 11, students had a special meeting with the Los Angeles Board of Education, where they listed dozens of demands. Unfortunately, the board said that though it agreed with the vast majority of the demands, lack of funds meant it couldn't follow through on them.

Even if not entirely successful, the walkouts contributed to bringing together and radicalizing working class Chicane youth.

2 **March 2, 1921** A workers' uprising of a multinational group of around two thousand miners began in Labin, Croatia. The miners were rebelling against an Italian fascist attack on a union militant the previous day. A few days later, they declared a republic, which lasted until April, when a thousand soldiers arrived and put down the revolt.

---

1   "Latine," "Chicane," and "Filipine" are used in this book as gender-neutral versions of Latino, Chicano, and Filipino.

March 2, 1955 In Montgomery, Alabama, Claudette Colvin, a fifteen-year-old African American, refused to give up her seat on a bus that she had been ordered to vacate for a white passenger. She was arrested and charged with multiple offences for violating the city's segregation laws. Leaders of the Black community considered attempting to make her case a cause célèbre and a test case for the civil rights movement, but, according to some local activists, Claudette's dark skin and working class background caused concern. One, Gwen Patton, told *Guardian* journalist Gary Younge, "It was partly because of her color and because she was from the working poor. . . . It was a case of 'bourgey' Blacks looking down on the working class Blacks." After Colvin became pregnant as a result of a statutory rape, the leadership decided against pursuing her case.

Claudette Colvin, 1953 *(Courtesy of the Visibility Project/Wikimedia Commons)*

When Rosa Parks—educated, married, and lighter-skinned—was arrested later that year, civil rights leaders had their standard-bearer.

3 **March 3, 1816** Juana Azurduy, a mestiza woman of Quechua descent born in what is now Bolivia, led one of her anti-colonial military detachments, including a women's unit known as the Amazonas, to victory in battle against Spanish troops near Villa.

March 3, 1959 The Hola massacre took place in Kenya when the commander of a British concentration camp for Kenyan civilians had its eighty-eight detainees severely beaten with clubs. Eleven died and the other seventy-seven sustained serious permanent injuries. In an effort to stamp out the Mau Mau anti-colonial

Wambugu Wa Nyingi, one of the survivors of the massacre, 2018 *(Photo by Hellen Masido, Museum of British Colonialism)*

uprising, the British government had thrown around four hundred thousand civilians into concentration camps and forced over a million others into villages supervised by the army that were essentially prison camps.

4 **March 4, 1919** Canadian troops in the British Army awaiting demobilization (return home) in Kinmel Park, Wales, mutinied. Fifteen thousand men were stranded at the camp, in overcrowded and squalid conditions, on half rations and having received no pay in over a month. When the camp commander went to Rhyl for an evening out, tempers exploded. The soldiers looted camp supplies and sergeants' messes and started fires. They managed to grab a few rifles and improvised other makeshift weapons by attaching razors to handles.

Officers and loyal soldiers were armed to suppress the riot, arresting twenty mutineers. Other soldiers then broke them free. Eventually, officers opened fire and by 4:30 a.m. had regained control of the camp. The events left three rioters and two guards dead, seventy-eight rioters arrested, and twenty-five convicted of mutiny and sentenced to up to ten years in prison. However, military authorities massively accelerated demobilization of the men.

March 4, 1972 Thousands of autoworkers in the Lordstown General Motors plant walked out on strike over numerous grievances. The walkout occurred amid a widespread unofficial campaign of sabotage and absenteeism. For example, to slow down the inhumanly fast production line, workers would often just fail to perform their designated task. The plant manager told the Cleveland *Plain Dealer*: "We've had cases of engine blocks

Lordstown plant workers, 1970 *(Courtesy of the Walter P. Reuther Library, Archives of Labor and Urban Affairs, Wayne State University)*

passing 40 men without them doing their work." Other workers slashed upholstery, scratched paint, and bent metal parts. Management responded by disciplining and suspending 1,200 workers and laying off nearly 700.

Workers held the line for twenty-two days, winning concessions, including cancellation of most of the layoffs and disciplinary measures.

The United Auto Workers union (UAW) declared a complete victory despite management not conceding on speed-up and workloads, which were the main problem for workers.

One worker's subsequent complaint outlined the feelings of the rank and file: "Before the strike the union local was in favor of not working faster than you could. Now people are afraid not to work. The union and the company say everything's settled."

The dispute was a lesson to some radical workers, showing the importance of strikers themselves running disputes rather than leaving it to the union leadership.

5 **March 5, 1943** A strike broke out at the Fiat Mirafiori plant in Turin, in fascist Italy when a handful of workers walked out at 10:00 a.m. on Friday. Over the weekend, the strike call spread through working class districts of the city, and by Monday rail workers and other factory workers joined the action, some by working to rule—following the workplace rules so strictly as to slow down production. Within a week, one hundred thousand workers were out, with various different demands in addition to a general demand for a war bonus payment. Authorities arrested 850 workers but were unable to break the strike and were forced to concede to most of the workers' demands. In the wake of the dispute, resistance to fascism escalated, and the protest contributed to the popularity of armed resistance later that year.

March 5, 1984 The great UK miners' strike began when miners at Cortonwood colliery walked out in response to the Conservative government's announcement of a pit closure plan. Some other pits were already on strike in other disputes, but the strikes against closures spread across Yorkshire, and four days later the National Union of Mineworkers (NUM) called a national strike, which was joined by a majority of miners around the country.

Women, many of them miners' wives, played a crucial role in supporting the strike, helping the workers to remain out for nearly a year.

Prime Minister Margaret Thatcher and her government were determined to break the power of workers' organizations and push through mass privatization and free market reforms. They had learned from their previous defeats in miners' strikes in 1972 and 1974. They built up coal stocks, so they could withstand a long strike, and then deliberately provoked the strike by announcing the closure plan in spring when coal was in less demand than during the cold winter months. The defeat of the miners, who had been the most well-organized and most militant group of workers in Britain, marked a decisive turning point in the balance of power between workers and employers in the country. 🔊 **13, 27–29**

6 **March 6, 1922** A wave of rent strikes in Veracruz, Mexico, was triggered when sex workers barricaded a street with their rented mattresses, chairs, and other furniture, planning to start a giant bonfire. Police quelled the action at the last minute, but news of the protest spread and sparked tenant protests across the city.

March 6, 1974 UK coal miners called off their four-week strike after accepting a 35 percent pay offer, in a massive victory that had already brought down the Conservative government.

7 **March 7, 1860** Up to a thousand striking women shoe workers took part in a Great Ladies Procession in Lynn, Massachusetts, amid a blizzard and thick snow drifts. They were accompanied by five thousand striking men, who had walked out two weeks earlier, demanding pay increases, with the women joining a few days later. Despite women's involvement in the dispute garnering it national publicity and the support of Abraham Lincoln, the men failed to support the women's pay demands. They feared that the employers might not listen to them if they added the women's demands. The women ended up returning to work, and, while some men did end up winning a 10 percent pay increase, for most workers the strike petered out and ended in defeat.

March 7, 1932 The Ford Hunger March massacre took place in Detroit, with police and Ford security guards killing four unemployed workers and injuring sixty others when they opened fire on a demonstration organized by the Communist Party USA's Unemployed Council.

8 **March 8, 1917 and 1918** Thousands of housewives and women workers in Saint Petersburg, Russia, defied union leaders' appeals for calm and took to the streets against high prices and hunger, thus igniting the February Revolution, so called because the date was February 23, 1917, on the Old Style calendar in use in Russia at the time. The following day, two hundred thousand workers joined them, striking and shouting slogans against the czar and the war. Some military units began to join the workers, and, on March 15, Czar Nicholas II was forced to abdicate.

Russian women demonstrate in Saint Petersburg, March 8, 1917 *(Courtesy of State Museum of Political History of Russia/Wikimedia Commons)*

On March 8, 1918, women in Austria celebrated International Women's Day on this date for the first time, as thousands took to the streets protesting against World War I.

There is a popular myth that March 8 was chosen on the anniversary of an 1857 strike of women workers in New York, and a further stoppage on the same date in 1908, but that is incorrect.

March 8, 1926 Around six hundred mostly women strikers in the International Fur & Leather Workers Union (IFLWU) in New York City marched through Manhattan and were beaten by police, who claimed that the strikers had been "insulting" them and had "booed and hissed." The *New York Times* reported that "police clubs were used freely" to disperse the workers. The workers were undeterred and remained out for eighteen weeks, until the employers' association agreed to a 10 percent pay increase and a forty-hour, five-day workweek.

9 **March 9, 1883** A large demonstration of the unemployed in Paris was broken up by police. The crowd, led by former Paris communard Louise Michel and brandishing black flags, looted bakeries and clashed with police. Michel and co-organizer, the syndicalist Émile Pouget, were later sentenced to six and eight years in prison, respectively.

Syndicalism, an influential current in the French workers' movement at the time, is the theory and practice of revolutionary unionism, in which workers organize and fight for improvements now, eventually calling a general strike to reorganize society in the interests of workers rather than capitalists.

Louise Michel, 1871 (*Courtesy Wikimedia Commons*)

March 9, 1910 The Westmoreland County coal strike began in Pennsylvania when fifteen thousand coal miners, mostly Slovak migrants, walked out. They shut down sixty-five mines for over a year, until police violence, which killed sixteen, and hardship finally forced them to give in.

10 **March 10, 1906** The Catastrophe de Courrières occurred in France: the worst mining disaster of the twentieth century, with 1,060 workers killed in a coal dust explosion. Forty-five thousand miners subsequently went on strike for fifty-five days against horrific working conditions. The government brought in the army to crush the strike.

March 10, 1952 Fulgencio Batista led a coup in Cuba and appointed himself president. Backed by the US, business, and the wealthy elite, his government killed thousands in anti-communist purges. He was overthrown by the 1959 revolution.

Senator John F. Kennedy later described his rule in a speech:

Fulgencio Batista murdered 20,000 Cubans in seven years—a greater proportion of the Cuban population than the proportion of Americans who died in both World Wars, and he turned democratic Cuba into a complete police state—destroying every individual liberty.

Yet, our aid to his regime, and the ineptness of our policies, enabled Batista to invoke the name of the United States in support of his reign of terror.

Administration spokesmen publicly praised Batista—hailed him as a staunch ally and a good friend—at a time when Batista was murdering thousands, destroying the last vestiges of freedom, and stealing hundreds of millions of dollars from the Cuban people, and we failed to press for free elections.

11 **March 11, 1845** The Battle of Kororāreka took place in Aotearoa/New Zealand, with Māori rebels defeating British forces and seizing the town (now called Russell) during the Flagstaff War. The conflict ended in a stalemate early the following year.

March 11, 1977 Police shot and killed twenty-four-year-old Francesco Lorusso, activist in the far-left extraparliamentary group Lotta Continua (Continuous Struggle), in Bologna, Italy. His murder resulted in two days of heavy rioting, leading the interior minister to send armored vehicles into the university area and other centers of militancy around the city.

Painting of Hone Heke cutting down the British flag from Flagstaff Hill, Kororāreka *(By Arthur David McCormack, courtesy of Wikimedia Commons)*

12 **March 12, 1912** Employers caved in to all of the demands of the Bread and Roses strike of twenty thousand mostly women garment workers in Lawrence, Massachusetts. The stoppage, started by Polish women, was organized by the Industrial Workers of the World union (IWW). The workers faced down savage police and military repression, with at least two workers killed and many others beaten and jailed, eventually winning big concessions across the garment industry. 🎙 **6, 16**

March 12, 1951 Following a successful campaign against transport price rises, three hundred thousand workers took part in a general strike in Barcelona and nearby cities to protest against the Franco dictatorship. Despite the mobilization of thousands of police and civil guards, the strikers held out for two weeks, with the government, terrified of the prospect of further unrest, releasing the vast majority of those arrested and paying full wages to the workers who had been on strike.

13 **March 13, 1940** Indian revolutionary Udham Singh assassinated former lieutenant governor of the Punjab Michael O'Dwyer at a meeting in London. The assassination was revenge for the 1919 Jallianwala

Bagh massacre (also known as the Amritsar massacre), the result of O'Dwyer dispatching troops to attack a peaceful protest, resulting in around 1,800 people being killed and over 1,200 injured. O'Dwyer referred to the events as a "correct action."

While in custody, Singh called himself Ram Mohammad Singh Azad: the first three words of the name reflect the three major religions of Punjab (Hindu, Muslim, and Sikh), while the last, *azad*, means *free*. Convicted of murder, Singh was sentenced to death. Speaking at his trial, Singh explained, "He deserved it. He was the real culprit. He wanted to crush the spirit of my people, so I have crushed him. For full twenty-one years, I have been trying to seek vengeance. I am happy that I have done the job."

March 13, 1945 Two working class sisters, Vera and Libera Arduino, were executed in Italy by fascists, alongside their father, a houseguest, and some neighbors. Factory workers around the region sent delegations to the funeral and stopped work while it was ongoing. One girl raised a red flag on the roof of her factory, while an electrician disconnected wiring to prevent the fascists calling for backup. The sisters had been active in the anti-fascist women's resistance group, the Gddd.

14 **March 14, 1970** Two sailors, Alvin Glatkowski and Clyde McKay, mutinied to protest the war and took control of the SS *Columbia Eagle*, which was carrying ten thousand tons of napalm for the US military in Vietnam. They then sailed the ship to Cambodia, which was neutral at the time, to prevent the cargo being used. Initially, they appeared to have succeeded, as the Cambodian government agreed to their demands and gave them asylum. But, unfortunately for the mutineers, just days later, there was a military coup, and a new pro-US regime took power.

Alvin Glatkowski, c.1975 *(Courtesy of Alvin Glatkowski)*

Glatkowski and McKay were locked up and the ship handed back to US forces. McKay managed to escape from prison and joined Khmer Rouge guerrillas in the countryside. The guerrillas later killed him. Glatkowski eventually returned to the US and was jailed for ten years. 🎧 **21–24**

March 14, 2018 Marielle Franco, a bisexual Afro-Brazilian socialist and feminist was assassinated in Rio de Janeiro. Raised in a favela (shanty town) in
the city, she began work at the age of eleven, and later raised a daughter
as a single mother working for the minimum wage, before being elected
to the city council in 2016. The day before her murder, she had spoken out
against extrajudicial killings by police and paramilitaries. The bullets that
killed her had been purchased by the federal police. The minister of public
security claimed that the bullets were stolen from a post office, but this lie
was retracted when the post office publicly stated it was untrue.

At the time of writing, four suspects have been arrested for the murder,
all with ties to state security forces, and two of them with links to the family
of right-wing president Jair Bolsonaro. Another suspect, a former police
officer, was shot and killed by police in February 2020, as they were attempting to arrest him.

15 **March 15, 1908** The Rochester *Democrat and Chronicle* newspaper in
New York State denounced anarchist women with this headline:
"Women Anarchists Have Become the Terror of World's Police." The article
went on to state: "the guardians of the world nearly always find a woman
implicated when a ruler is stricken down—emotional women lose sense of
fear."

March 15, 1917 Czar Nicholas II abdicated as the February Revolution swept
Russia. Nicholas, already unpopular for his oppressive and brutal reign,
became widely hated when Russia became embroiled in World War I. The
war caused the deaths of over three million people in the Russian Empire,
and labor shortages in the countryside drastically affected the country's
food supply, causing widespread hunger and starvation.

16 **March 16, 1965** Mounted police in Montgomery, Alabama, violently
attacked a peaceful civil rights demonstration. Police officers armed
with clubs and canes rode into a crowd of six hundred people and began
beating them, hospitalizing eight and injuring others. The next day, double
the number of protesters took to the streets.

March 16, 1979 Workers at Ireland's first two McDonald's restaurants in
Dublin walked out on strike for better pay and union recognition. Despite
court injunctions on picketing and McDonald's bribing scabs with free fries,
the strikers stayed out for six months and won concessions, including a

24 percent pay increase. McDonald's, however, continued to mistreat the workers, for example, cutting hours to negate pay increases, with no retaliation from the Irish Transport and General Workers' Union (ITGWU), of which the workers were members.

17 **March 17, 1876** US troops attacked sleeping Cheyenne and Oglala Sioux people in Montana in the Battle of Powder River, marking the beginning of the Great Sioux War. They destroyed and looted the village. But, despite firing nearly two thousand bullets, US forces only managed to inflict a single casualty, whereas the Cheyenne and Sioux warriors, with only around two hundred bullets, killed four soldiers and seriously wounded six others. They also recaptured five hundred of their horses the next morning.

The US commanding officer, Colonel Joseph Reynolds, was court-martialed and suspended from duty following the failed assault.

The incident likely galvanized resistance to the enforced relocation of Native Americans from the Black Hills to a reservation.

March 17, 1920 The right-wing Kapp Putsch, which aimed to roll back the changes since the 1918 German Revolution, collapsed. A general strike of twelve million workers, the biggest in German history, shut down the country. Adolf Hitler flew to Berlin to aid the putsch but was met by strikers at the airfield and had to disguise himself.

Naval brigade in Berlin during the putsch, March 1920
(Courtesy of Bundesarchiv, Bild 119-1983-0012/CC-BY-SA 3.0)

18 **March 18, 1871 and 1911** The Paris Commune, the first ever attempt at a working class uprising to create socialism, was established. The workers of Paris, joined by mutinous national guardsmen, seized the city, and set about reorganizing society based on workers' councils. The communards were able to hold out until late May 1871, when, upon retaking the city, troops massacred thirty thousand workers in bloody revenge.

Paris Commune barricade *(Courtesy of Wikimedia Commons)*

On this same date in 1911, the fortieth anniversary of the Paris Commune, the first International Women's Day was held in Europe to publicize the need for women's rights and suffrage. The date was later moved to March 8.

March 18, 1970 Activists from several feminist groups staged a sit-in at the *Ladies' Home Journal* headquarters in New York City. They were not happy with the journal's lack of women's representation at the corporate level (the entire senior staff were male) or the depiction of women in its advertisements and columns. The sit-in ended the same day when the editor agreed to some of their demands and gave the activists their own column in the magazine.

19 **March 19, 1969** British troops and police invaded the Caribbean island of Anguilla, after a British diplomat was forced to flee the island at gunpoint. The British colonial government had placed Anguilla and the island of Nevis under the authority of the government in Saint Kitts and its premier Robert Bradshaw. Bradshaw was open about his hatred of Anguilla and had said he would "reduce . . . that place to a desert."

Bradshaw did his best to run the island down, sending telephone repairmen to the island in 1960 to deactivate the telephone system and preventing the installation of electricity. So, in 1967, Anguilla seceded from the Saint

Kitts and Nevis and Anguilla body, disarmed the Saint Kitts police, and sent them home.

The British government sent a hapless diplomat, William Whitlock, to try to resolve the situation, but he was dismissive of the Anguillans, so they chased him off the island. He then told reporters that the island was controlled by "gangster" and "Mafia" types, and that local people were wearing "a Black power–type uniform"—which turned out to be morning coats with white gloves.

Local people deployed a number of "antiaircraft goats" on the airfield to prevent British planes from landing. The Labour government responded by sending two hundred paratroopers by sea, along with forty Metropolitan Police officers, expecting to confront an army of criminals and Black radicals but only finding the goats. The incident was so farcical that Britain had to eventually agree to Anguilla's independence from Saint Kitts. It became, and remains, a British overseas territory.

March 19, 2019 Up to 1.4 million young people around the world took part in school strikes demanding government action to halt climate change. Children walked out of class and took to the streets in over two thousand towns and cities in 128 countries, after being inspired by Greta Thunberg, the Swedish fifteen-year-old with autism, who went on strike from school by herself the previous August.

For two weeks, instead of attending lessons, Thunberg stood outside the Swedish parliament building protesting and handing out leaflets that declared: "I

Greta Thunberg outside the Swedish parliament. Her sign reads "school strike for climate." *(Courtesy of Anders Hellberg, CC BY-SA 4.0, https://creativecommons. org/licenses/by-sa/4.0)*

am doing this because you adults are shitting on my future." Further international student walkouts subsequently took place.

20 **March 20, 1927** During a conference of the Kolaba District Depressed Classes in Mahad, India, the Mahad Satyagraha took place. A procession of 2,500 Dalits (sometimes known as "untouchables"), led by Dalit social reformer B.R. Ambedkar, marched through the main streets of Mahad toward a public water tank to assert their right to access it like other members of the community.

While legally people of all castes had the right to use public amenities, in reality this was not the case. So Ambedkar, and then others, drank from the water tank before leaving. In response to this peaceful protest, a mob of caste Hindus attacked the Dalits at the end of their conference. Dalits were beaten up, their homes ransacked, and their grain supplies destroyed. Many sought refuge in the homes of Muslims. Brahmins (the highest caste Hindus) subsequently felt the need to "purify" the now "contaminated" lake, which they did by pouring in dozens of containers of a mixture of cow dung and urine, milk, curds, and ghee.

The direct action was a culmination of four years of organizing. This had included strikes and Dalit military veterans establishing schools for Dalit children. In December that year, ten thousand Dalits took part in a second Mahad Satyagraha. Untouchability was outlawed by the 1955 Indian constitution, but ingrained discrimination against Dalits continues.

March 20, 1975 Operation Red Snake of the Paraná began in Argentina when the government of Isabel Perón sent hundreds of police and troops into the town of Villa Constitución to break the organization of militant industrial workers. They arrested 307 workers, but the working class fought back, going on strike and occupying their plants, demanding that the detainees be released. The occupations lasted until March 26, when they were forcibly broken up by police.

Over the next two months the government continued to arrest, blacklist, and kill workers in the name of fighting "subversion." This sort of repression under the military dictatorship is well-known but repression under Perón, who had the support of most unions, much less so.

21 **March 21, 1937** Police massacred nineteen people and injured hundreds of others at a peaceful demonstration in Ponce, Puerto Rico. Protesters were marching for the release of imprisoned separatist leader Pedro Albizu Campos. Police acted on the orders of the US-appointed governor and after the murders staged photos with a press photographer to try to claim self-defense.

March 21, 1973 The Mental Patients Union was founded in London by a small group of mental health patients and their supporters. They argued that psychiatry was a form of control of the working class under capitalism and that mental health patients needed to organize in the same way that workers organized to advance their interests.

22 **March 22, 1986** Thousands of striking workers from US military bases in the Philippines blockaded the gates of United States Navy and Air Force bases near Manila. Violence also broke out in many locations, as over twenty thousand striking workers pursuing better severance benefits built barricades and clashed with US service personnel attempting to cross the picket lines.

March 22, 2009 Prison riots began in Greece following the death of activist prisoner Katerina Goulioni on March 18. Inmates in the women's prison in Thebes refused to return to their cells, set fires, and destroyed property, while protesters outside the prison clashed with riot police. Two hundred inmates in Athens also held a protest in solidarity.

Goulioni was a prominent incarcerated activist, who had campaigned against lack of facilities for physically disabled prisoners, prison transfers in which many prisoners suspiciously died, and vaginal inspections, which she termed "informal rape." In the wake of the rebellion, the government promised a review of vaginal inspection methods and other prison conditions.

Goulioni's fellow inmates sent the press the following goodbye statement: "All your life was full of thirst. Thirst for struggle and justice. You fought for all and for everything without concern for the consequences. And, at the end, the consequences of your struggles rewarded you in the worst of manners, with a violent, unexpected, sudden death. But we are still here, Katerina, and we shall remember you and continue the struggle you began. You are everywhere. We sense you, and we thank you for taking care of us. For us, you will live forever. Have a great journey!"

23 **March 23, 1931** Indian revolutionary socialists Bhagat Singh, Sukhdev Thapar, and Shivaram Rajguru were executed by British colonial authorities in what is now Punjab, Pakistan. They had been sentenced to death for assassinating a senior British police officer in 1928, to avenge the police killing of Lala Lajpat Rai during an anti-colonial demonstration. While they opposed British colonialism, rather than narrow nationalism, they advocated working class revolution against both British and Indian capitalists. They were all just twenty-two or twenty-three years old.

Following their sentencing, Mohandas Gandhi appealed to the Viceroy of India to commute their sentences, but he also appealed to huge crowds not to take action to secure their release, as he had signed a truce agreement with authorities. After they were executed, Gandhi was greeted by a crowd he described as "incensed," flying black flags and shouting, "Gandhi go back," "Down with Gandhism," "Gandhi's truce has sent

Bhagat Singh, 1929 (*Courtesy of Wikimedia Commons*)

Bhagat Singh to gallows," and "Long live Bhagat Singh." After the executions, Bhagat Singh in particular became a national hero.

March 23, 1944 The most significant attack on Nazi occupation forces by the Italian partisan resistance took place on Via Rasella, in Rome. Around a dozen of the communist-led partisan Gruppi di Azione Patriottica (Patriotic Action Groups; GAP) attacked an SS company of over 150

SS casualties after the attack (*Courtesy of Wikimedia Commons*)

ethnic Germans that was tasked with fighting the resistance.

The partisans detonated a homemade bomb, then opened fire with mortars, hand grenades, and guns before vanishing. The resistance unit suffered no casualties, while over thirty SS members were killed and more than one hundred wounded.

Unable to capture those responsible, the following day the enraged Nazis massacred 335 people, some of whom had been arrested for resistance activities but most of whom were unrelated civilians.

24 **March 24, 1976** A right-wing coup backed by the US took place in Argentina, overthrowing populist Isabel Perón. The new military government stepped up Perón's war against radical workers and communists, murdering and "disappearing" tens of thousands. US secretary of state Henry Kissinger advised the junta to wipe out its opponents quickly before an outcry over human rights abuses could grow.

March 24, 1987 Two hundred fifty members of new AIDS rights direct-action group ACT UP demonstrated on Wall Street, in New York City, to demand greater access to treatment and national action to fight the disease. Seventeen participants were arrested.

25 **March 25, 1911** The Triangle Shirtwaist Factory fire in New York killed 147 workers. The victims were mostly women and young girls aged thirteen to twenty-three working in sweatshop conditions. Some were burned and others were trampled to death desperately trying to escape via stairway exits that were illegally locked to prevent "the interruption of work." Fifty died leaping from the high-rise building to escape the flames. The company owners were charged with seven counts of manslaughter but were found not guilty.

March 25, 1969 Pakistan's dictator General Mohammad Ayub Khan resigned, following mass protests against his regime that had begun in October. Initially the government violently repressed student protests, but that triggered increased opposition. In the countryside, peasants killed landowners and police, while, in the cities, industrial workers held *gheraos*— mass pickets encircling factories. The following year the first elections in Pakistan's history took place.

26 **March 26, 1953** Mau Mau guerrillas fighting British colonialism in Kenya attacked the Naivasha police station. They inflicted a humiliating defeat on the police and released 173 prisoners from an adjoining detention camp, many of them Mau Mau. While the uprising was eventually crushed by British forces, independence was achieved a few years later.

March 26, 1978 Four days before the opening of Japan's Narita International Airport, protesters angry about the construction of the airport destroyed the control tower with molotov cocktails, delaying the opening by nearly two months.

27 **March 27, 1942** France's collaborationist Vichy government issued the barbershop decree, demanding that barbers collect cut hair and donate it to the war effort to make slippers and sweaters. The rebellious Zazous refused and grew their hair long. Zazous were anti-fascist youths who wore dapper suits, listened to jazz and swing music by largely Black musicians, and fought the fascists in the street. Police rounded them up, and Vichy fascist youth groups hunted them down and cut their hair. 🎙 4

March 27, 1943 Gay anti-fascist resistance fighter Willem Arondeus led a group in bombing the Amsterdam public records office. His unit made fake identity papers for Dutch Jews and intended to destroy records that could be used to verify identity documents. Thousands of files were, in fact, destroyed in the attack, but, within a week, Arondeus and the other members of the group were arrested.

One of the group, Frieda Belinfante, a musician and lesbian, managed to evade capture. But twelve, including Arondeus, were executed that July by firing squad. In his last message before his execution, Arondeus said, "Let it be known that homosexuals are not cowards."

Willem Arondeus, 1943 (*Courtesy of Marco Entrop/Het Verzetsmuseum Amsterdam/Wikimedia Commons*)

28 **March 28, 1919** Arkansas joined the majority of other US states in introducing a law prohibiting anarchism and communism. The law, to "define and punish anarchy and . . . Bolshevism," banned any "attempt to overthrow [the] present form of government of the State of Arkansas or the United States" and "exhibit[ing] any flag, etc, which is calculated to overthrow present form of government." Violations could incur fines of up to $1,000 and imprisonment of up to six months.

March 28, 1977 More than 1,300 mostly Black sanitation workers in Atlanta walked off the job for a fifty cent an hour pay increase. The city's first Black mayor, who had come to power on the back of the civil rights and Black power movements and to whom the workers looked for support, fired them all, with the support of civil rights leaders, including Martin Luther King

Sr. (not to be confused with Martin Luther King Jr.). It was an early lesson that having representatives of color doesn't necessarily benefit working class people of color.

29 **March 29, 1986** Anti-fascists got wind of a secret meeting that was due to take place in the small Dutch town of Kedichem to unify two fascist political parties: the Centrum Partij (Center Party) and Centrum Democraten (Center Democrats). Protesters threw a smoke bomb into the hotel where the meeting was taking place, accidentally setting the curtains on fire. Within minutes the building went up in flames, forcing the fascists to flee into a riot that had begun outside. The proposed merger didn't take place.

March 29, 1988 Half a million workers in the Philippines went on a general strike in pursuit of an across-the-board flat rate pay increase.

30 **March 30, 1919** The Transvaal Native Congress launched a campaign against the racist pass laws in South Africa. Pass laws were an internal passport system designed to segregate the population. The campaign lasted three months, and some seven hundred Africans were arrested and charged. At that point, conservatives within the movement regrouped and shut down the campaign, adopting a more moderate approach. The laws were not overturned for decades.

March 30, 1976 A general strike and mass protests were launched in Palestine/Israel in opposition to the Israeli government's extensive seizure of land owned by Arabs in Galilee to construct Jewish settlements and military facilities. A solidarity strike took place in most Palestinian refugee camps in Lebanon. There were widespread clashes with security forces, and six unarmed demonstrators were shot by police and the military, with around one hundred people injured and hundreds of others arrested.

The protests and anger at the repression galvanized a sense of Palestinian Arab solidarity in the area, sparking greater agitation for Palestinian rights.

While the expropriation plan was successful in proportionately reducing the Arab population of Galilee from 92 percent to 72 percent, significant expropriations of land in the area largely ceased in the 1980s. March 30 is now commemorated annually in Palestine/Israel as Land Day, with demonstrations and general strikes.

31 **March 31, 1979** A group of around fifteen men, including off-duty San Francisco vice squad officers, attacked patrons and workers at a lesbian bar in the city. The men, who were having a bachelor party, were denied admission to Peg's Place by the door person, as they were drunk and carrying beer. Some of the men were reported to have shouted, "Let's get the d–kes," forcing their way in, attacking the woman working the door, and beating the woman who owned the bar with a pool cue. When the men were told the women were calling the police, they responded, "We are the cops, and we'll do as we damn well please."

Patrons claim that when on-duty officers eventually arrived, they did not provide any medical assistance to the injured and refused to take witness statements. One woman who was attacked was hospitalized for ten days with head injuries. In the end, one police officer was convicted for his part in the attack but served no jail time, and he and the other officers involved kept their jobs.

The outrageous incident was a contributing factor to growing anger in the LGBT+ community that would explode some weeks later following the failure to convict on murder charges the killer of gay member of the city's Board of Supervisors Harvey Milk.

March 31, 2009 Around forty workers in the Caterpillar factory in Grenoble, France, stormed their bosses' offices and took four of them hostage, demanding better severance packages for workers being laid off. More than seven hundred French Caterpillar workers were being made redundant. The action was successful, and the company increased its pot of redundancy money by €1.5 million (approximately $US2.1 million), leading to an average payout of €80,000 (approximately US$111,000) per worker.

APRIL

1 **April 1, 1649** A farmer and writer named Gerrard Winstanley and a small group of thirty to forty men and women occupied St. George's Hill, in Surrey, England, and began collectively tilling the land. Over the following months, numerous local people joined them to form the movement that became known as the Diggers.

Winstanley was a Protestant who began to write pamphlets criticizing the Church—which traditionally held that "God is in the heavens above the skies." Instead he argued that God was "the spirit within you." In a pamphlet published in January 1649, he wrote: "In the beginning of time God made the earth. Not one word was spoken at the beginning that one branch of mankind should rule over another, but selfish imaginations did set up one man to teach and rule over another."

The politics of the Diggers were a form of protocommunist anarchism, advocating direct action, common ownership, and the dissolution of hierarchy.

April 1, 1982 Oil company Exxon produced a classified internal report on carbon dioxide (CO_2) and the greenhouse effect. A summary of the report circulated to senior management said that CO_2 in the atmosphere was concentrated at 340 parts per million, and that burning fossil fuels and clearing forests was causing this figure to increase, stating that there was "currently no unambiguous scientific evidence that the Earth is warming," while going on to say that global warming could be detectable by 1995. It further warned that this warming might be irreversible and that mitigating against negative effects of global warming would require a reduction in fossil fuel combustion. Exxon scientists projected that surface temperatures would warm 3 to 6°C above preindustrial levels by the year 2100.

The report proves that as early as the 1970s Exxon, like many fossil fuel companies, knew that their products were going to cause devastating climate change to the planet, even though it was not yet directly observable. However, Exxon took no corrective action but instead funneled $31 million to fund misinformation campaigns to try to manufacture doubt about climate change.

2 **April 2, 1920** Military forces began their assault against the workers' March uprising in the Ruhr region of Germany. The Social Democratic government sent the troops to suppress the unruly workers, despite the fact that these military units contained the protofascist forces that had supported and taken part in the Kapp Putsch against the government mere days earlier. At least a thousand participants in the uprising were massacred before fighting ended.

April 2, 1980 Hundreds of Black residents of Bristol, England, fought back against police harassment after a police raid on the only part Black-owned cafe still open in the town. When rioting began, they were joined by hundreds of white Bristolians.

3 **April 3, 1948** A left-wing uprising began on the Korean island of Jeju. Jeju had been largely self-governing following the end of World War II, when Korea was divided by the USSR and the US into North and South after the defeat of Japan. Jeju islanders were angry with violent US-backed police and feared that planned elections organized by the UN in South Korea would reinforce the division between North and South. They attacked police stations and right-wing paramilitaries, in particular targeting those who collaborated with the Japanese imperialists.

The US military government sent troops to the island, and the US-backed South Korean authorities brutally suppressed the rebellion, massacring many thousands, including women and children. When the uprising was finally crushed the following year, 10 percent of the island's population were dead and 70 percent of villages had been destroyed. Subsequent US-backed dictatorships in South Korea banned any mention of the Jeju uprising, and speaking of it was punished with beatings, torture, and lengthy prison sentences.

April 3, 1974 A thousand pupils from schools in Brixton, London, most of them Black, went out on strike in support of three Black youths who had been jailed after police attacked a crowd of people in Brockwell Park. They held a rally and march, parading past the local courthouse, the police station, Tulse Hill School—where another one hundred pupils joined them—and Brockwell Park.

4 **April 4, 1935** The bodies of German anti-Nazi activists Dora Fabian and Mathilde Wurm were found in their flat in London. They had been poisoned. The flat had previously been burgled twice, and they had received threatening letters. While many historians believe they were likely murdered, the inquest declared a double suicide the most likely cause of death. The British government and media, at that point mostly appeasers or supporters of Hitler, were eager to defuse the case and move on.

April 4, 1968 Civil rights activist, socialist, and advocate of nonviolence Martin Luther King Jr. was assassinated while in Memphis supporting a strike of Black sanitation workers, part of a wave of stoppages across the US during the Vietnam War. His ideas had become increasing radical in previous years, and, in addition to opposing racism, he had begun opposing US imperialism in Vietnam and elsewhere and capitalism itself. He had begun organizing a Poor People's Campaign, meant to unite working class and poor people of all races.

Martin Luther King Jr. in Washington, DC, 1963 *(Courtesy National Archives, CC by SA 2.0 https://www.flickr.com/photos/usnationalarchives/5102447354)*

Though King is widely lauded by establishment figures now, at the time he was hated by the rich and powerful, as well as by most white Americans. Fueled by negative media coverage, only 22 percent of Americans approved of Freedom Rides for the desegregation of public transport, and 63 percent disapproved of King.

The FBI's domestic intelligence chief William Sullivan called him "the most dangerous Negro of the future in this Nation from the standpoint of communism, the Negro and national security" and later sent King an anonymous letter attempting to blackmail him into suicide.

His murder left many disillusioned with pacifism, and riots broke out across the US, in the biggest explosion of social unrest since the Civil War. 👥 8

5 **April 5, 1932** In Newfoundland, a crowd of ten thousand people demonstrated outside the central government building in protest at price increases and pension cuts. Police attacked the demonstrators, clubbing a child in the head, and got more than they bargained for. One officer was pulled from his horse and beaten, while the mob smashed up the building, set it on fire, and stormed it in search of the prime minister. A group of police and priests attempted to get the PM to safety, but he was cornered a couple of times and punched in the face once before he managed to escape. Then the demonstrators set about looting all of the downtown liquor stores. The government subsequently collapsed.

April 5, 1971 A communist uprising began in Sri Lanka (then called Ceylon) when militants attacked police stations across the country. The insurgents were mostly young people organized by the Janatha Vimukthi Peramuna (People's Liberation Front; JVP). They had previously supported the United Front (UF) government, which included the Communist Party (CP) and the Lanka Sama Samaja Party (LSSP), which supported the ideology of Russian Bolshevik Leon Trotsky. The election of the UF had been greeted with much joy across the international left, which considered it a victory for "anti-imperialism."

JVP forces initially took control of several towns and rural areas. But then an unlikely coalition emerged to suppress it. Ceylon government forces were given support, troops and weaponry by the UK, the former colonial power, the US, Australia, Egypt, India, and Pakistan, as well as China, the Soviet Union, and Yugoslavia. By June the rebellion had been suppressed, leaving an estimated one to five thousand dead.

While calling themselves communist, the JVP, the CP, and the LSSP were all majority Sinhala organizations that espoused forms of nationalism and engaged in racism and ethnic cleansing against the minority Tamil population. Especially in more recent years, the JVP has become much more openly and virulently racist against Tamils, and in the early 2000s became the primary force opposing the peace process between the government and Tamil rebels, which prolonged the deadly civil war.

6 **April 6, 1871** Rebel national guard troops of the 137th Battalion in the Paris Commune seized the local guillotine, smashed it to pieces, and burned it outside the town hall of the 11th arrondissement to the applause of a huge crowd of onlookers.

The government had recently created a new type of guillotine that was quicker and easier to transport. The

Engraving depicting destruction of the guillotine
(Courtesy of Wikimedia Commons)

arrondissement commune committee had voted to seize these "servile instruments of monarchist domination" and destroy them "once and forever ... for the purification of the district and the consecration of our new freedom."

While some on the left glorify the guillotine, it has, in fact, mostly been used as a weapon against radicals and the powerless. For example, while the guillotine is most famously remembered in connection with the execution of aristocrats during the French Revolution, the new "revolutionary" government soon began using it against those on its left.

The German Nazi government was also a big proponent of the guillotine, executing over sixteen thousand people with the device, including many resistance activists, Sophie and Hans Scholl among them.

More recently it was used in a number of places, including the French colonies in the Caribbean, state socialist East Germany, and France itself, where its last use was against a Tunisian agricultural worker, who was convicted of murder and beheaded in 1977.

April 6, 1968 Just two days after the assassination of Martin Luther King Jr., seventeen-year-old Black Panther "Little" Bobby Hutton was murdered by police in Oakland, California. Hutton had been the very first recruit to the Black Panther Party (BPP). He surrendered following a shootout with the police. He laid down his weapon, took off his shirt, and emerged from the basement where he was holed up, barechested with his hands up. He had been advised by a comrade to surrender naked, but he was embarrassed and left his pants on. Police shot him at least ten times, killing him. Six days later, over a thousand people came to his funeral, at which actor Marlon Brando delivered the eulogy. His killing spurred the rapid growth of the BPP.

7 **April 7, 1926** Violet Gibson, a forty-nine-year-old Irish aristocrat and peace activist, attempted to assassinate Italy's fascist dictator Benito Mussolini in Rome. She was armed with a pistol wrapped in a shawl and a rock to break his car window, if needed. As she fired at his head, Mussolini moved and the bullet hit his nose, travelling through both nostrils. She tried to shoot again but the gun misfired. She was violently beaten and almost killed by an angry mob before being arrested by police.

Gibson endeavored to obtain release by convincing doctors she was

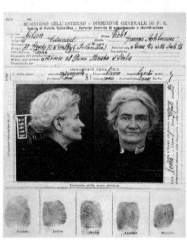

Violet Gibson's police record (Courtesy of the Italian Ministry of the Interior/ Wikipedia)

mad. While her conversations and correspondence were lucid and rational, her lack of children was interpreted as psychologically abnormal. That, a previous suicide attempt, and a violent reaction she had to a fascist inmate got her deemed "insane." She was deported to Britain, where she spent the rest of her life in a mental hospital. When she died, no one attended her funeral.

April 7, 2010 Eight hundred Carlsberg factory workers in Copenhagen, Denmark, walked out on strike to protest against a new management policy restricting beer drinking at work. The company's truck drivers joined the strike in sympathy. The previous week, Carlsberg had removed beer coolers that contained free beer for workers to drink throughout the day from the factory floor, declaring that workers would only be allowed to drink beer in the canteen at lunch hour. The strike lasted for five days but ended in defeat. The following month workers walked out again, this time for a pay increase.

8 **April 8, 1929** Socialist anti-colonial revolutionary Bhagat Singh and his comrade Batukeshwar Dutt threw two bombs into the Delhi Central Legislative Assembly, shouting, "*Inquilab zindabad*" (long live the revolution), and distributed leaflets protesting against the passage of two repressive bills. Their leaflets, scattered on the floor of the assembly, began with the line, "It takes a loud voice to make the deaf hear." Although the bombs were thrown toward an area where there were no people, to avoid causing injury, the two were punished severely with life sentences.

April 8, 1958 Sugarcane workers on two adjoining plantations in Barbados refused to cut cane unless they were given a wage increase of fifteen cents per ton. After being told they were only entitled to a raise of six cents per ton, the cane cutters walked off the job, kickstarting the 1958 sugar workers' wildcat strike, which spread to dozens of plantations around the country.

9 **April 9, 1945** Georg Elser, a factory worker and folk musician who tried singlehandedly to kill Hitler, was murdered in the Dachau concentration camp.
Some years earlier, while working in a weapons factory and then a quarry, he had gradually accumulated an arsenal of stolen explosives, which in 1939 he planted in a pub in Munich that he knew Hitler visited every year on November 8 and 9 to celebrate the Nazi putsch of 1923. Unfortunately, Hitler left early, and the bomb missed him by minutes, killing six senior

Nazis and, tragically, a waitress. Elser was later arrested and tortured but he insisted he acted alone and refused to give up any names, other than one of a communist who had already died. He was sent to a concentration camp, where he was murdered on the orders of SS leader Heinrich Himmler just a few days before the camp's liberation.

April 9, 1948 The Deir Yassin massacre took place, with around 120 fighters from the Zionist paramilitary groups Irgun and Lehi attacking the Palestinian village of Deir Yassin, near Jerusalem. One hundred to 150 or more Palestinians, including many women and children, were killed, some of them decapitated, disemboweled, mutilated, and raped. Many Palestinians fled in terror, and the incident played a key early role in the Israel-Palestine conflict. 🎙 **17–18**

10 **April 10, 1919** Emiliano Zapata, a Nahua mestizo peasant leader during the Mexican Revolution, was assassinated in Chinameca, Ayala municipality, by General Pablo González of the "revolutionary" Venustiano Carranza government.

Early in life, he began to advocate for the rights of Indigenous people in Morelos. When he saw wealthy landowners continually stealing their land, with no response from the government, he began taking part in armed land occupations.

With the outbreak of revolution in 1910, Zapata became the leader of the Liberation Army of the South. The force was a peasant

Emiliano Zapata, 1914 *(Photo by Gustavo Casasola, courtesy of Wikimedia Commons)*

militia fighting for "*tierra y libertad*" (land and freedom), a slogan adopted from Mexican anarchist Ricardo Flores Magón.

When Francisco Madero took power in 1911, Zapata denounced him for betraying the revolution and drafted the Plan of Ayala: a radical program of land reform. Madero himself was then overthrown by counterrevolutionary Victoriano Huerta.

Zapata's southern army allied with the revolutionary armies in the north, led by Pancho Villa and Venustiano Carranza. They soon overthrew Huerta and called a convention to form the new government, which Zapata declined to participate in, as none of the organizers had been elected.

Once in power, Carranza only implemented moderate reforms, which fell well short of the Ayala plan, so the Zapatistas fought on. Carranza put a bounty on Zapata's head, hoping that one of his own fighters would betray him, but none of them did. In the end, he was lured to a meeting with one of Carranza's men who pretended to be interested in defecting. When Zapata arrived at the meeting he was riddled with bullets and his body photographed for propaganda purposes.

To this day, he remains a national hero, and Indigenous rebels in Chiapas, who rose up in 1994 and created an autonomous territory, named themselves after him.

April 10, 1932 Thousands of mostly women mill workers joined a strike against the reduction in rations in Teykovo, in the Soviet Union. The workers complained that the 30 to 50 percent reduction in rations would leave them starving, while managers and Communist Party and secret police officials received plenty of food. Women called on their colleagues to join them, sabotaged machines, and denounced those who refused to walk out as "traitors." They gathered around the town and converged on the town square, making speeches, and dragging a CP member off the rostrum after he condemned the strike. The following morning, only 130 workers went in to work. The secret police made numerous arrests, and, by April 17, the strike had been broken. While no women were prosecuted, several men who had been active in the strike were exiled or sentenced to three years in a labor camp.

11 **April 11, 1945** As US forces approached, the inmate resistance seized control of Buchenwald concentration camp in Germany. However, according to the United States Holocaust Memorial Museum, when the Allies took control of the concentration camps, some of those interned for homosexuality were not freed but were required to serve out the full term of the sentences they had received under the homophobic Nazi penal code.

Thousands of LGBT+ people were interned in concentration camps, most made to wear a pink triangle. Many of them were subjected to medical experiments, castrated, or murdered.

After "liberation," the US army handbook for the occupation of Germany established that, while most Holocaust survivors should be released from concentration camps, "criminals with a prison sentence still to serve will be transferred to civil prisons." Gay and bisexual men and trans women had been convicted under paragraph 175 of the German criminal code, which had been strengthened by the Nazis, and were therefore considered common criminals. Homosexuality was also against the law at that time in Allied countries, including the US, the UK, and the USSR.

One prisoner, Hermann R, who was detained at Landsberg Fortress, southwest of Dachau, joined liberation celebrations. But two weeks later, an American military commissioner visited his cell holding Hermann's file, and told him: "Homosexual—that's a crime. You're staying here!"

US occupation authorities kept the Nazified paragraph 175 on the books, and in the first four years after the end of the war, around 1,500 men per year were arrested under it. After the occupation, West Germany kept it as well and convicted over fifty thousand men before it was finally revoked in 1969. East Germany, on the other hand, reverted to the pre-Nazi paragraph 175, and convicted some four thousand men before revoking it in 1968.

LGBT+ people were not recognized as victims of the Holocaust and had their pensions deducted for the time they spent interned in concentration camps, with most never receiving any compensation.

April 11, 1972 Over two hundred thousand public sector employees in Québec took part in a general strike, bringing the province to a standstill. Though the government tried to crack down on the revolt, this only brought out more workers, with over three hundred thousand taking part in a spontaneous and self-organized strike wave, in which factories were occupied, and even a radio station taken over and broadcast from by the strikers.

12 **April 12, 1920** Workers in Ireland launched a general strike in support of pro-independence prisoners who were on hunger strike in Mountjoy Prison, Dublin. The postal service, public transport, shops, pubs, and public toilets were all shut. After two days, the British government caved in and released all the prisoners.

April 12, 1927 The Shanghai massacre began, with thousands of communists, workers, and students murdered or "disappeared" by Chiang Kai-shek's Kuomintang nationalist movement. The Chinese Communist Party and the Soviet Union, as well as some anarchists, had earlier joined forces with the Kuomintang against domestic warlords and foreign imperial powers to try to unite and modernize China. Over the following twelve months, more than three hundred thousand people would be killed in the Kuomintang's anti-communist purges.

Despite the killings, a minority of Chinese anarchists maintained their involvement with the Kuomintang and attempted to recruit others to join them. This was rejected by most of the movement, including Hua Lin, who argued that militants who entered into a relationship with the Kuomintang effectively stopped being anarchists.

13 **April 13, 1916** The Glasgow Corporation, as the Glasgow city council was then known, introduced a bylaw restricting the right of free assembly. The law came into force in 1922 to prevent working class and radical meetings on Glasgow Green, setting in motion a free speech struggle. Over the next decade, protests were organized, meetings were held in defiance of the law, and speakers arrested and jailed, while crowds of up to one hundred thousand fought the police, rioted, and looted shops, until the law was overturned.

April 13, 1919 The Jallianwala Bagh massacre took place in Amritsar, India, when British troops opened fire on a crowd of predominantly Sikh pilgrims, murdering a thousand or more people and injuring many more. As well as pilgrims, there were large numbers of Muslims and Hindus, many of whom were farmers, traders, and merchants attending a horse and cattle fair. The youngest victim was just six weeks old. The killings were not reported in Britain until December, and no one was charged with any offence. The incident sparked widespread outrage and led to the noncooperation movement that began the following year.

14 **April 14, 1816** A slave uprising, known as Bussa's rebellion, named after its leader, broke out on Easter Sunday night in Barbados. It was to be the island's largest rebellion of enslaved Africans.

Enslaved people took advantage of the temporary freedom from work and the cover of permitted gathering for Easter festivities to organize themselves. They chose a leader on each sugarcane plantation and were assisted by three free Black men who travelled around meeting with rebels.

The revolt began with the burning of cane fields in Saint Philip, and soon around four hundred men and women working on over seventy other estates had joined

Emancipation statue, commonly referred to as the Bussa statue, Barbados *(Photo by Dogfacebob, courtesy of Wikimedia Commons)*

in. British colonial authorities declared martial law the following day and quickly suppressed the uprising. While only two whites were reported killed, 120 enslaved people were killed during the repression, with 144 executed and 132 deported in the aftermath.

April 14, 1919 In Limerick, Ireland, a general strike was called to protest against the British establishment of a "special militarized zone" in the area. The general strike saw the creation of the short-lived Limerick soviet, with the city taken over by the workers.

15 **April 15, 1916** In its newspaper, the Industrial Workers of the World (IWW) announced the formation of its Domestic Workers Union in Denver, Colorado. One of its activists, Jane Street, wrote a letter to another domestic worker organizer in Tulsa, Oklahoma, in 1917, in which she described how they organized and took action to improve pay and conditions:

> [I]f you want to raise a job from $20 to $30 ... you can have a dozen girls answer an ad and demand $30—even if they do not want work at all. Or call up the woman and tell her you will accept the position at $20. Then she will not run her ad the next day. Don't go. Call up the next day and ask for $25 and promise to go (and don't go). On the third day she will say, "Come on out and we will talk the matter over." You can get not only the wages, but shortened hours and lightened labor as well.

 16

April 15, 1989 Reformist Chinese Communist Party leader Hu Yaobang died, prompting a gathering of workers in Tiananmen Square within an hour, eventually sparking a wave of protests by students and workers across the country that would only be crushed by the military several weeks later. While the rebellion is generally described in the West as a student movement calling for liberal capitalist democracy, the reality is more complex, and the working class was deeply involved.

When students faced police repression, many workers took action to support them. In Beijing, after the declaration of martial law, workers took to the streets, built barricades, and fraternized with advancing soldiers, effectively stopping them from reaching the city center.

While students and intellectuals who spoke English did talk in abstract terms about "democracy," workers were primarily concerned with economic problems that were being exacerbated by market reforms introduced by the government, which they saw as the result of an undemocratic bureaucracy. As one worker put it:

> [I]n the workshop, does what the workers say count, or what the leader says? We later talked about it. In the factory, the director is a dictator; what one man says goes. If you view the state through the factory, it's about the same: one-man rule.... Our objective was not very high; we just wanted workers to have their own independent organization.

When the military crackdown finally occurred around the country on June 4, workers were the most numerous victims, with extensive fighting in working class districts around Beijing. The exact number of victims of the repression is unknown, but estimates range from the official Chinese government figure of three hundred up to several thousand. Families of the victims have identified around two hundred people who were killed.

16 **April 16, 1970** A white foreman at a Chrysler plant in Detroit threatened to murder a Black worker. When the worker complained, Chrysler took steps to fire the worker, claiming he had a knife. Around one thousand workers, white and Black, walked out on strike in protest, shutting the plant for an entire weekend, until management backed down. 🔊 **12**

April 16, 1979 Nicaraguan revolutionary Idania Fernandez was murdered in custody by troops of the US-backed dictatorship of Anastasio Somoza Debayle. She had been betrayed by an informant. However, her death inspired more to take up resistance, and within a month the regime was overthrown.

17 **April 17, 1920** Dockers in Dublin refused to load foodstuffs destined for England. The action helped relieve severe food shortages in Dublin, which had been dire since 1917, with many staple goods like butter, eggs, and sugar almost unavailable, while huge quantities of food were being shipped to Britain.

April 17, 1976 The far-right National Front organized a march through the main Asian area in Bradford, northern England. Local politicians organized a counter-rally in the center of town, but hundreds of young Asians broke away, fought through police lines, and attacked the racists. Many of the young people were members of the Bradford Asian Youth Movement, an organization of people of South Asian descent who campaigned against racism, fought fascists in the streets, supported workers' and anti-colonial struggles, and campaigned in support of migrant families. 🎙 **33–34**

18 **April 18, 1888** The Imperial British East Africa Company was founded in London to run what is now Uganda and Kenya as British colonies. As in all of Britain's colonies, the British outlawed homosexuality and propagated homophobic values. In 2017, half of all the world's countries that criminalize being gay, including Uganda and Kenya, had been part of the British Empire.

April 18, 2001 Police in Kabylie, Algeria, murdered a young man named Massinissa, sparking a nationwide uprising that came to be known as the "Black Spring." Following the killing, protests and riots broke out across the country, demanding democratic rights and cultural rights for Amazigh people (also known as Berbers). Police killed upwards of 120 people, quelling the rebellion.

19 **April 19, 1943** The Warsaw Ghetto Uprising began, with Jews fighting back against Nazi attempts to deport them to the Treblinka extermination camp. Although defeated, it was the biggest armed Jewish rebellion against the fascists during the Holocaust.

April 19, 1960 The South Korean April Revolution began in earnest, with thousands of students from Korea University in Seoul marching against the US-backed dictatorship the day after other protesting students were attacked by government supporters. Police opened fire on the crowd, massacring 180, and the government declared martial law. However, the movement grew, and the following week the army refused to fire on protesters. One day later, President Syngman Rhee stepped down.

20 **April 20, 1853** The formerly enslaved woman turned abolitionist Harriet Tubman began working on the Underground Railroad, which smuggled enslaved people to freedom. She personally rescued some seventy people and assisted many more.

Harriet Tubman, c.1885 *(Photo by Horatio Seymour Squyer, courtesy of Wikimedia Commons)*

April 20, 1914 US troops opened fire with machine guns on a camp of striking miners and their families in Ludlow, Colorado.

Twelve thousand miners had gone out on strike the previous September against the Rockefeller family–owned Colorado Fuel and Iron Corporation (CF&I), following the killing of a United Mine Workers of America (UMWA) activist. They demanded better safety at work and to be paid in money instead of company scrip (tokens that could only be redeemed in the company store).

The Rockefellers evicted the striking miners and their families from their homes, so they set up collective "tent cities," which miners' wives helped run. Company thugs harassed strikers and occasionally drove by camps riddling them with machine-gun fire, killing and injuring workers and their children.

Eventually the National Guard was ordered to evict all the strike encampments, and, on the morning of April 20, they attacked the largest camp in Ludlow. They opened fire with machine guns on the tents of the workers and their families, who returned fire. The main organizer of the camp, Louis Tikas, went to visit the officer in charge of the National Guard to arrange a truce, but he was beaten to the ground and shot repeatedly in the back, killing him. That night, troops entered the camp and set fire to it, killing eleven children and two women, in addition to thirteen other people who were killed in the fighting. The youngest victim was Elvira Valdez, aged just three months.

Protests against the massacre broke out across the country, but the workers at CF&I were defeated, and many of them were subsequently sacked and replaced with nonunion miners. Over the course of the strike, sixty-six people were killed, but no guardsmen or company thugs were prosecuted.

21 **April 21, 1856** Stonemasons in Melbourne, Australia, went on strike demanding a maximum eight-hour workday—down from ten hours per day Monday to Friday and eight hours on Saturday. They marched from their construction site, the Old Quadrangle building at Melbourne University, brandishing a banner demanding "8 hours work, 8 hours recreation, 8 hours rest." The workers were extremely well organized and soon achieved their goal, with no loss of pay for workers engaged in public works in the city. They celebrated on Monday, May 12, the Whit Monday holiday, with a parade of nearly seven hundred people from nineteen trades.

April 21, 2007 One hundred fifty garment workers, mostly women, occupied the Mansoura-España textile factory in Egypt, protesting against job losses

and unpaid wages. Management tried various tricks to break the occupation, even threatening to fabricate prostitution charges against the women
workers for sleeping away from home under the same roof as men who
were not their husbands. But the workers held out against both the bosses
and their union, occupying their factory for two months before winning
concessions on both job losses and unpaid wages.

Pauli Murray in later life (*Courtesy University of North Carolina at Chapel Hill/Wikimedia
Commons*)

22 **April 22, 1944** Two hundred Black people, mostly students at Howard
University, held a sit-in demonstration at Thompson's, a segregated
restaurant in Washington, DC—where Jim Crow laws were not in effect but
segregation by custom existed. After the number of paying customers was
slashed, the restaurant was ordered by its headquarters to begin serving
African Americans. The university, in fear of losing federal grants, subsequently directed its students to cease direct action, and Thompson's
promptly restored segregation.

One of the key organizers of the action was Pauli Murray, a young
Black activist and feminist who identified as part female and part male, and
whose only significant romantic relationships were with women.

Washington, DC, banned segregation in restaurants in 1953.

April 22, 1993 Stephen Lawrence, a Black British teenager, was murdered in a racist attack while he waited for a bus in Eltham. Rather than devote adequate resources to finding the killers, the London Metropolitan Police infiltrated the Lawrence family's campaign for justice to find ways to smear and discredit the family. Years of campaigning forced the government to acknowledge the institutional racism of the police force, and two of the killers were convicted in 2012.

23 **April 23, 1951** Sixteen-year-old Black schoolgirl Barbara Johns led her fellow pupils in a walkout against racist and substandard conditions in her school in Prince Edward County, Virginia. The school was one of the case studies examined by the Supreme Court, which eventually declared segregation unconstitutional. Rather than desegregate, the local school board closed all of its schools, and the private schools that local white children went to did not desegregate until 1986.

April 23, 1971 Nearly a thousand Vietnam War veterans returned their combat medals to the government. The Vietnam vets had planned to return the medals in body bags, but authorities erected a fence around the capitol, so the veterans threw their medals over it. Some of the vets, before tossing their medals, dedicated them to comrades—both American and Vietnamese—who had died in battle. One of the protesters, Peter Brannigan, gestured toward the capitol as he threw back his medal, saying, "I got a purple heart here, and I hope I get another one fighting these motherfuckers." 🎙 **10–11**

24 **April 24, 1912** Two hundred eighty-four firemen aboard RMS *Olympic*— the sister ship to the *Titanic*, due to depart the following day—went on strike in protest at the unseaworthy collapsible lifeboats that had just been installed, many of which were rotten. Bosses then brought in replacement scab workers from Southampton and Liverpool. The following day a deputation of strikers witnessed a test of the collapsible boats, and upon seeing that only one was faulty, they agreed to set sail if it was replaced.

Management tried to keep the nonunion scabs at work, but the crew objected, and fifty-four sailors left the ship in protest, forcing the cancellation of its departure. All of them were arrested and tried for mutiny, but, while convicted, none were punished, and the bosses let them return to work, fearing public support for the strikers. The ship and its mutinous crew set sail on May 15.

April 24, 1954 British colonial authorities in Nairobi, Kenya, began Operation Anvil, to ethnically cleanse Kikuyu people from the city. Against the background of the Mau Mau insurgency, which was largely made up of members of the Kikuyu community, the British believed they could destroy the movement for "land and freedom," which they thought was led from Nairobi.

Over a two-week period, troops shut down the city block by block and abducted every member of the Kikuyu and related Embu and Maru tribes. They were interrogated, then divided into groups depending on their alleged support for the Mau Mau movement. Those believed to be more militant were sent for interrogation, torture, and detention, while those without Mau Mau affiliation were deported to overcrowded "reserves."

By the time it was over, apart from a small number of workers with long-term contracts with European employers, nearly the entire Kikuyu population of the city was gone, with twenty thousand sent for "screening" and thirty thousand to reserves. Those abducted could only take one bag of possessions, if that, with the rest looted by British troops. Rather than quell the insurgency, the brutal repression caused opposition to colonial rule to increase.

25 **April 25, 1974** Portugal's fascist dictatorship was overthrown by a military coup, which was then followed by a working class uprising. Urban workers took over their factories, and farmworkers took over their farms, in what would become known as the Carnation Revolution, as few shots were fired, and people adorned troops with carnations.

The key factor in the unpopularity of the regime was the long-running colonial war against independence movements in Angola, Mozambique, and Guinea-Bissau. After the revolution, these colonies, as well as Cape Verde and São Tomé and Principe, soon achieved independence. 🎙 **41–42**

April 25, 2013 Hundreds of thousands of Bangladeshi garment workers walked out in protest the day after the Rana Plaza building collapsed, killing over a thousand of their colleagues. They barricaded highways, fought police, and attacked factories, shops, and the headquarters of the garment employers' federation.

While many media outlets essentially blamed working class consumers buying cheap clothes for the poor conditions of garment workers in Bangladesh, in fact, labor and factory safety costs would be largely insignificant to consumers. Labor costs in the underdeveloped world typically only constitute 1 to 3 percent of the cost of a garment, and it has been estimated that bringing every factory in Bangladesh up to Western standards would add less than ten cents to the cost of each garment. However, these changes would negatively impact employers' profit margins.

26 **April 26, 1797** Sailors on fifteen Royal Navy ships in Plymouth, England, joined a mutiny that had begun two weeks earlier in Spithead, near Portsmouth, demanding better pay and working conditions. They elected delegates and sent them to join negotiations with the other mutineers. Together the men won most of their demands.

April 26, 1982 The trial of the Bradford 12 began at Leeds Crown Court. The twelve were activists of the United Black Youth League, arrested on conspiracy charges for preparing to defend their community from fascists. The trial lasted nine weeks, with the defense arguing that the failure of police to defend Asian and Afro-Caribbean people in Britain from racist attacks meant that those communities had the right to self-defense. In a landmark decision, all twelve defendants were acquitted. 🎙 **33–34**

27 **April 27, 1934** The Federación Obrera de Chile (Federation of Chilean Workers; FOCH) union headquarters in Santiago, Chile, was attacked by police and bosses' militias. Seven workers and one child were murdered and two hundred workers badly injured.

April 27, 1981 Nine white supremacists from the US and Canada were arrested as they prepared a boat full of weapons, bedecked with a Nazi flag, for an attempted invasion of Dominica. The racists, including Ku Klux Klan members and the later founder of neo-Nazi website Stormfront, planned to establish a white dictatorship in the 99 percent non-white nation and trade with apartheid South Africa. They were all sentenced to a paltry three years in prison.

28 **April 28, 1945** Italy's fascist dictator Benito Mussolini was executed by anti-fascist partisans in the village of Giulino de Mezzegra, northern Italy.

After his reign of terror was deposed in 1943, Mussolini was broken from captivity by Nazi troops and put in charge of a puppet government in German-occupied northern Italy.

As more of Italy was liberated by partisan and Allied forces, he tried to escape to Switzerland disguised in a German uniform. But he was spotted by a resistance member who called out, "We've got Big-Head!"

Mussolini was executed near Lake Como, alongside a number of other senior fascists and his mistress. Their bodies were then taken to Milan and dumped in Piazzale Loreto in the early hours of the following morning, where they were soon hung up from the frame of a petrol station. The previous year, the Milan Gestapo had publicly executed fifteen Italian partisans in that square. Mussolini was reported to have said, "For the blood of Piazzale Loreto, we shall pay dearly."

April 28, 1965 Twenty thousand US marines invaded the Dominican Republic on the orders of President Johnson to prevent the creation of "a second Cuba."

29 **April 29, 1992** Following the acquittal of the police officers caught on film beating Rodney King, riots erupted across Los Angeles, in the biggest urban revolt since the 1960s, with widespread arson, looting, and property damage estimated at over $1 billion.

April 29, 2020 Workers at the Arby's fast food outlet in Morris, Illinois, walked out on strike in protest against understaffing, lack of personal protective equipment, and not receiving hazard pay amid the global Covid-19 pandemic. It was just one of a significant number of strikes around the world related to health and safety amid the outbreak.

30 **April 30, 1963** A bus boycott was launched in Bristol, England, by a group of Caribbean migrant workers to protest the bar on Black and Asian workers in bus crews in the city. The "color bar" was enforced by the Transport and General Workers' Union (TGWU) and the state-owned Bristol Omnibus Company, after white union members had threatened to walk out if workers of color were employed. After months of the boycott and mass protests, bus workers voted at a mass meeting in August to end the ban. In September, the first bus conductor of color was recruited. Two years later, the Race Relations Act was introduced, forbidding race discrimination in public places.

April 30, 1977 Coordinated women-only "Take Back the Night" marches against sexual harassment were held in towns and cities across West Germany.

MAY

1 **May 1, 1886** Between three hundred thousand and half a million workers went on strike and rallies were held throughout the United States, under the rubric of the "eight-hour day with no cut in pay." Chicago was the center of the movement, which employers and the government were determined to crush. On May 3, police killed one worker and injured several protecting scab workers crossing picket lines. The following day, anarchist workers called for a mass protest meeting in Haymarket Square. There, a bomb was thrown by an unidentified individual, and police opened fire. Seven officers and several civilians were killed.

Illustration of the Haymarket martyrs by Walter Crane, 1894 *(Courtesy Wikimedia Commons)*

Eight anarchists who were involved in the eight-hour workday movement were subsequently charged, although some of them had no connection to the Haymarket protest and had not even been present, and none of them were accused of throwing the bomb. Seven were sentenced to death and the eighth to fifteen years in prison. Four of them were later executed, with a fifth cheating the hangman by suicide. The remaining three prisoners were released when all eight defendants were later pardoned.

May 1 was later designated International Workers' Day by socialist and communist organizations to commemorate the Haymarket martyrs and the eight-hour workday movement. It is now a public holiday in numerous countries around the world, although many people are unaware of its radical origins.

May 1, 1974 Hundreds of mostly East African Asian women workers at the Imperial Typewriter Company plant in Leicester, England, began a three-month strike. Although unsuccessful, it was a key moment in galvanizing Asian working class resistance in the UK.

2 **May 2, 1967** A group of Black Panthers armed with rifles and shotguns marched into the California State Capitol protesting against a gun control bill that targeted them. To fight police violence and harassment of African Americans, the Panthers used radios to listen to police calls, then members would attend scenes of arrest with law books, openly carrying shotguns—which was legal—and advise arrestees of their constitutional rights. To stop this self-defense against the police, authorities brought in the Mulford Bill—dubbed the "Panther Bill" by the media—to ban the open carrying of loaded firearms in public. The National Rifle Association supported Republican governor Ronald Reagan's signing of the legislation into law.

May 2, 1968 Four thousand workers in the Hamtramck auto plant in Detroit walked out against speedup—an increase in the speed of the production line. Several Black strikers met in a bar across the road and founded the Dodge Revolutionary Union Movement (DRUM) to organize Black workers. Two months later they organized their first wildcat strike. DRUM inspired similar groups at other plants, and these groups later came together to form the League of Revolutionary Black Workers (LRBW). 🎙 **12**

3 **May 3, 1926** At 11:59 p.m., a general strike began in the UK, with nearly two million workers downing tools in support of locked out miners facing pay cuts. Despite solid action lasting over a week, the Trades Union Congress (TUC) caved in without achieving any concessions.

May 3, 1953 Women nightshift workers at the Ivan Karadjov tobacco warehouse in Plovdiv, Bulgaria, drove out guards and barricaded themselves in to protest against casualization. Following nationalization, conditions in the tobacco industry had deteriorated, with the mostly women workers losing permanent jobs and receiving seasonal short-term contracts, with no benefits or accommodation during the off-season. After the death of Joseph Stalin, leader of the Soviet Union, workers took the opportunity to protest.

On the morning of May 4, militia arrived, and women working at two other nearby warehouses walked out on strike and confronted the militia, with other tobacco workers joining them. Communist Party authorities ordered the troops to open fire on the workers, and several were killed, dozens injured, hundreds arrested, many of whom were subsequently sent to the gulags, effectively breaking the strike.

4 **May 4, 1919** Fifty thousand factory workers in Rio de Janeiro walked out, demanding a maximum eight-hour workday and a 20 percent pay increase. In June, workers in São Paulo joined them, and, in July, having failed to break the strike, the government forced the employers to give in to both demands.

May 4, 1961 Freedom Riders began using direct action to fight the segregation of interstate bus travel in the Southern United States. Despite segregation being illegal, the law was not enforced, and police collaborated with the Ku Klux Klan and violent racist white mobs that attacked the Black and white riders. But the riders kept fighting, with some taking up arms to protect themselves, and, by November, segregation on the bus system had ended.

Racists attack Freedom Riders in Alabama, 1961 *(Photo courtesy of the Federal Bureau of Investigation/Wikimedia Commons)*

5 **May 5, 1906** During Cinco de Mayo celebrations, workers at the Cananea Consolidated Copper Company in Sonora, Mexico, who earned 40 percent less than American employees doing the same work, protested against pay discrimination. Authorities responded by declaring martial law. The following month, the Mexican miners went on strike, and many of them were killed by company thugs.

May 5, 1970 Hundreds of thousands of university students in the US walked out of class and took to the streets in a nationwide student strike against the Vietnam War and to protest against the killing of four students at Kent State University by National Guard troops the previous day.

6 **May 6, 1933** Nazis raided the Institut für Sexualwissenschaft (Sexology Institute) in Berlin. Run by Magnus Hirschfeld, the institute was a pioneering organization that supported gay and transgender rights and equality for women. Hirschfeld coined the term "transsexualism." The

Nazis plunder the Institut für Sexualwissenschaft's library, May 6, 1933 *(United States Holocaust Memorial Museum, courtesy of National Archives and Records Administration, College Park)*

institute employed at least one transgender worker and had begun offering the first modern gender affirmation surgery.

A few days after the raid, the institute's huge library was burned in the streets while propaganda minister Joseph Goebbels delivered a speech. The Nazis then stepped up persecution of all LGBT+ people.

May 6, 1937 Four hundred Black women tobacco stemmers went on strike at the I.N. Vaughan Company in Richmond, Virginia, amid a wave of unrest in the industry. With assistance from the Southern Negro Youth Congress (SNYC), the women walked out for better pay and conditions and were joined on picket lines by white women textile workers. After forty-eight hours, they won better pay, a maximum eight-hour day, a five-day week, and union recognition.

7 **May 7, 1912** The first general strike of waiters and hotel workers in New York City began when 150 workers at the Belmont Hotel walked out. Organized by the Industrial Workers of the World union (IWW), at the strike's peak over six thousand workers were out, demanding one day off per week, higher wages, and no discrimination against union members. The employers tried to stoke racial hatred by hiring African American strikebreakers, so the workers allied with the Colored Waiters' Association and called on Black workers to join the strike.

Various individual hotels agreed to some of the strikers' demands, and a combination of police violence, media harassment, and an increasing number of scabs, including local college students, brought the strike to an end by late June, with some key organizers blacklisted. Nonetheless, hotel workers continued to strike in the coming years, and today hotel workers in New York City remain among the best paid in the world. 🎙 6

May 7, 1980 The US-backed military dictatorship in Sabuk-eup, South Korea, reneged on its promise to coal miners and their wives of an amnesty for protests the previous month. They arrested over seventy people and took them to the joint investigation headquarters, where they were brutally tortured. Thirty of them were later sentenced to one to five years in prison. Three of those tortured died prematurely from their injuries.

On April 21, the working class mining community had seized police weapons and dynamite from the mines and taken control of the town, setting up a "liberated zone" during a strike for a 40 percent pay increase. The following day, three hundred armed police arrived, but five thousand protesters succeeded in driving them from the area. Local women, housewives, and other residents took an active part in the struggle, with the community setting up its own security detachments.

By April 24, employers and authorities agreed to all of the workers' demands, including a pay increase and an amnesty for the protesters, in return for workers laying down their weapons.

8 **May 8, 1928** Luisa Lallana, an eighteen-year-old Argentinian anarchist factory worker, was murdered by a strikebreaker during a dockers' strike. The previous month, stevedores in Rosario walked out, demanding their first pay increase in five years. Lallana and some of her colleagues from the Mancini burlap bag factory were distributing leaflets from the Women's Port Committee in support of the dockworkers, when Juan Romero, a scab and member of the extreme right paramilitary Liga Patriótica Argentina (Argentine Patriotic League), shot her in the head. She died that afternoon.

The following day, local unions, the anarchist union the Federación Obrera Regional Argentina (Argentine Regional Workers' Federation; FORA), and the Communist Party called a general strike in protest. Thousands of people downed tools and marched, and Lallana's funeral procession was led by a column of a thousand women. Police violently attacked the mourners, and two warships arrived in the port to reinforce the police and para-militaries. In all, eleven workers were killed during the strike that month. Nonetheless, strikes and demonstrations in the city continued to escalate and grow for over a year.

May 8, 1942 A group of Black and white young people staged a sit-in at the segregated Jack Spratt Coffee House in Chicago—the first sit-in of the civil rights movement. The restaurant called police, but they refused to remove the occupiers, as they had not broken any laws. As a result, the restaurant dropped its discriminatory policy. The occupation was organized by the Congress of Racial Equality (CORE), which had been set up the previous year.

9 **May 9, 1914** Suffragettes battled police who attempted to raid a meeting on women's rights in Glasgow, Scotland. Police storming the hall faced a barrage of flying flowerpots, tables, and chairs, while audience members and bodyguards trained in jiujitsu armed themselves with clubs, batons, poles, planks of wood, and even a revolver loaded with blanks and fought off the police. When police attempted to arrest the speakers, they were slowed by barbed wire that had been hidden in the garlands bedecking the stage.

Cartoon titled "The Suffragette That Knew Jiu-Jitsu" *(Punch 1910, courtesy of Wikimedia Commons)*

May 9, 1936 In Thessaloniki, Greece, police and soldiers attacked a workers' demonstration during a general strike against police repression, killing twelve. The funerals of the workers became mass demonstrations of over two hundred thousand people, and a further nationwide protest strike took place a few days later.

Just three months later, General Ioannis Metaxas declared a dictatorship to end the disorder, but he was forced to introduce a maximum eight-hour workday and social protections like pensions and welfare payments.

10 May 10, 1920 Workers on the East India Docks in London, England, stopped work upon discovering that the *SS Jolly George* ship had been loaded with munitions to be used to fight against the Russian Revolution. They refused to continue loading the ship, with coalheavers refusing to bring aboard coal for the ship's engines, until the weaponry had been unloaded.

The workers were successful, and, on May 15, the munitions were unloaded back onto the docks. Former suffragette and left communist Sylvia Pankhurst played a key role in organizing the

Sylvia Pankhurst in Trafalgar Square, 1932 *(Courtesy of Spaarnestad Photo, via Nationaal Archief)*

boycott, as did another woman known only as "Mrs. Walker from Poplar."

May 10, 1941 The Strike of the One Hundred Thousand took place in Nazi-occupied Belgium on the first anniversary of the German invasion. Beginning in a steelworks in East Belgium, tens of thousands walked out, forcing authorities to grant an 8 percent pay increase, before arresting hundreds of strikers and sending many to the concentration camps.

11 **May 11, 1923** After months of agitation, 150 mostly women rent strikers who had been jailed in the Mexican town of Veracruz the previous year were freed by the governor. The women had organized strikes in detention, and fought with prison guards, while workers outside threatened a general strike for their freedom. The tenants left the jail in groups of ten, the women wearing cream dresses and straw hats with red ribbons, while their supporters sang songs, shouted slogans, and set off firecrackers. The group then paraded through the main streets of the city to the office of the renters' union, where they declared their commitment to continue their direct action against landlords.

May 11, 1972 A group called OPR-33 (Organización Popular Revolucionaria-33; Popular Revolutionary Organization-33), the armed wing of the Federación Anarquista Uruguaya (Uruguayan Anarchist Federation; FAU), kidnapped a shoe manufacturer named Sergio Molaguero, whose workers were on strike. They received a ransom of $10 million, which they used to publicize the crimes of the Uruguayan dictatorship internationally.

12 **May 12, 1916** Irish socialist, trade unionist, and independence activist James Connolly was executed by firing squad at Kilmainham Gaol, in Dublin. Along with fourteen others, he had been sentenced to death for his leading role in the Easter Rising against British colonial authorities. He had been wounded in the fighting and was unable to stand in front of the firing squad, so he was tied to a chair and shot.

James Connolly, pre-1916 *(Courtesy of Wikimedia Commons)*

May 12, 1978 In spite of living under a military regime, dayshift toolroom workers at the Saab-Scania auto plant in São Bernardo, Brazil, decided to stop work. The strike spread, and within two weeks over twenty factories and forty-five thousand workers had downed tools for a pay increase. In the following weeks, the stoppage spread to Osasco and São Paulo, before all the auto companies agreed to make pay increases of 11 to 13.5 percent.

The Odéon Théâtre in Paris during the May 1968 strike *(Photo by Eric Koch/Anefo, courtesy of Nationaal Archief)*

13 **May 13, 1968** Up to ten million workers launched a general strike in France during the May 68 rebellion, as hundreds of thousands took to the streets in Paris following violent student riots.

May 13, 1985 Philadelphia police attacked the home of Black liberation and environmentalist group MOVE with automatic weapons, then dropped a bomb on it, killing five adults and six children, and destroying sixty-one homes in the predominantly Black neighborhood when the fire spread, making 250 people homeless.

A force of close to five hundred police officers fired over ten thousand rounds of ammunition into the house, in which there were numerous women and children, while other officers blew holes in the walls with explosives. The police commissioner then ordered that the house be bombed with an improvised explosive device made from C4 provided by the FBI. Only two people survived the blast and ensuing fire: Ramona Africa and Michael Ward, aged thirteen. While no officials were prosecuted, Africa was subsequently jailed for seven years on riot and conspiracy charges. The incident occurred during the tenure of Philadelphia's first Black mayor, a Democrat named Wilson Goode.

14 **May 14, 1913** Philadelphia longshoremen walked out on strike. Around half of the four thousand strikers were African American. The strikers met and decided to join the Industrial Workers of the World union (IWW)—one of the earliest examples of effective, multiracial unionism in the US. Two weeks later the workers won the strike. 🎙 **6**

May 14, 1931 In Ådalen, Sweden, troops opened fire with a heavy machine gun on a peaceful demonstration of striking sulfate factory workers, killing four demonstrators and one bystander and wounding several other people.

15 **May 15, 1831** In London, a jury found the stabbing to death of a police officer "justifiable homicide," despite the coroner locking the jury in a room to get them to change their mind. The recently formed Metropolitan Police had violently attacked a demonstration of the National Union of the Working Classes, and defending themselves the workers stabbed three policemen, killing one.

Police were widely hated by Londoners, who largely saw them as a violent gang set up to protect the property of the rich and keep the working class in abject poverty. Officers were routinely mocked in the street and given nicknames like "raw lobsters," "blue devils," and "Peel's bloody gang," after Robert Peel, the politician who established the force. They were also frequently attacked, with some early recruits being stabbed, others blinded, and one even held down while someone ran him over.

May 15, 1950 A general strike broke out in Nairobi, Kenya, then part of the British Empire. Union leaders planned to declare a strike the following day, but workers themselves had already walked out, demanding the freedom of two jailed union leaders, big minimum wage increases, annual pay increases, subsidized housing, sick pay, fourteen days paid vacation per year, unemployment insurance, and more rights for taxi drivers. The unions later called for "freedom for all workers and all the East African territories." British authorities declared the strike illegal and attacked mass meetings of workers with tear gas. Meanwhile strikers shaved the heads of scabs. Women organized logistics and the distribution of food supplies. With around one hundred thousand firmly committed workers out on strike, for some reason union leaders ordered a return to work, despite only a small increase in the minimum wage in some townships being agreed to. Hundreds of strikers were dismissed in the wake of the dispute.

Striking truck drivers battle police, Minneapolis, 1934 *(Courtesy of the National Archives at College Park/Wikimedia Commons)*

16 **May 16, 1934** Minneapolis truck drivers in the Teamsters union went on strike, shutting down almost all commercial transport in the city. The dispute lasted over three months, ending with most of the workers' demands being met and opening the way for more workers' organization in Minneapolis. With its months of fierce battles between striking workers and scabs, protected by police and private guards, it also became a central labor dispute in twentieth-century US history.

May 16, 1967 The All Circles Struggle Committee (ACSC) was established in Hong Kong in the wake of violent police repression of a strike of plastic flower factory workers.

On May 6, British colonial police violently beat picketing workers and bystanders, causing mass outrage. Protests against—and clashes with—police began breaking out across the city.

In the two days following the establishment of the ACSC to coordinate a movement against colonialism, 126 struggle committees were formed to share experiences and plan action. A week later, wildcat strikes began to break out, with widespread rioting. In June, a general strike was called.

It eventually faltered, although strikes in some industries continued until late July.

As the strike collapsed, many protesters began resorting to bomb attacks—both real and fake—targeting British authorities, to cause chaos and disrupt business as usual. What became known as the Hong Kong Riots lasted until December, before being called off after secret talks between British authorities and

British police beat up people submitting a petition at the government house *(Photo by and courtesy of Chau Yick)*

the Communist Party of China (CPC). The CPC was nominally opposed to British colonialism, but, in reality, the Chinese economy benefited from having access to international markets through British Hong Kong, so the CPC eventually decided not to push for British withdrawal.

While the protests ended, in their wake British authorities implemented numerous reforms that significantly improved the lives of working class Hong Kongers. These included UK-style social benefits for the unemployed, the disabled, and the elderly, construction of new hospitals and homes, abolition of some sexist laws, and the far-reaching eradication of rampant police corruption. 🎧 **30–31**

17 **May 17, 1949** Brick factory worker and former Italian resistance member Maria Margotti was killed in Molinella by Carabinieri—domestic paramilitary police. The previous day she had stood on a picket line of agricultural workers, along with other women attempting to stop scabs from replacing the strikers. Police attacked them particularly violently. So, on May 17, there was a demonstration protesting against police violence. The Carabinieri opened fire on the crowd with machine guns, killing

Maria Margotti *(Courtesy of Wikimedia Commons)*

Margotti. She was thirty-four years old. Her death caused mass outrage and spurred an escalation in opposition and resistance to the postwar state and its anti–working class policies.

May 17, 1965 In reaction to a general strike the right-wing Bolivian military dictatorship declared a state of siege and launched an all-out war on the organized working class. They also passed a series of laws dismantling labor unions and calling up all Bolivians aged nineteen to fifty into military service.

18 **May 18, 1968** The Senegalese May 68 began in earnest, with students launching a national strike following a government cut to student grants. Despite violent police repression, the movement grew over the next few days and eventually culminated in a workers' general strike, with many concessions being won.

May 18, 1980 After robbing local armories and police stations, the workers of Gwangju, South Korea, rose up against the brutal US-backed dictator, Chun Doo-hwan. The uprising took place after peaceful anti-government protesters had been fired upon and killed by government troops. Though it was bloodily suppressed, it helped ignite a chain of similar rebellions across Asia, winning people many democratic rights.

19 **May 19, 1918** During World War I, the Hungarian 6th Infantry Regiment of Ujvideck at Pecs mutinied and refused to go to the trenches. Instead they cut telephone wires and attacked municipal buildings and barracks, then occupied the local railway station. Surrounded by loyal military forces, they resisted for three days before surrendering. One in ten was shot at random. All higher-ranking officers involved were shot, and noncommissioned officers were jailed.

May 19, 1935 Two hundred banana loaders employed by the United Fruit Company at the port in Kingston, Jamaica, went on strike. On the second day of the stoppage, British colonial police opened fire on the workers, wounding one woman. Nonetheless, the strike spread, becoming a general strike in the city within a few days. It took weeks for security forces to regain control.

20 **May 20, 1910** The Japanese High Treason Incident began to unfold when police searched the room of lumber worker Miyashita Takichi and found bomb-making materials, prompting the mass

Kōtoku Shūsui, one of those executed as part of the High Treason Incident *(Courtesy of Wikimedia Commons)*

arrest of socialists and anarchists for conspiring to assassinate the emperor, with twenty-four of them sentenced to death after a show trial, even though only a handful were actually responsible.

May 20, 1936 The first issue of *Mujeres Libres* (Free Women), a Spanish anarchist-feminist magazine by the group of the same name aimed at ending the "triple enslavement of women to ignorance, to capital, and to men" was published. The group went on to play an important role in the Spanish Revolution, which broke out later that year. 🎧 **39–40**

21 **May 21, 1941** An actors' strike began in Norway against Nazi occupation. Many actors who were unwilling to perform after the Nazis took over broadcasting had previously signed a secret pledge to go on strike if any artist was fired for political reasons. Six actors, including Tore Segelcke, Lillemor von Hanno, Gerda Ring, and Elisabeth Gording, refused to work on the radio when ordered to by Nazi authorities. On May 21, they were

Tore Segelcke, 1959 *(Photo by Leif Ørnelund, courtesy of the Oslo Museum, CC by SA 4.0)*

summoned to Oslo police headquarters for interrogation, and all had their work permits revoked. That evening, workers walked out, shutting down every theater in the capital. By the following day, the strike had spread to Bergen and Trondheim. The Gestapo began threatening the actors, but they voted overwhelmingly to continue the strike. On May 24, German authorities gave an ultimatum to the workers and began arresting union representatives. But in spite of this and of being threatened with the death penalty, the strike continued for five weeks.

In the wake of the dispute, the Nazis decided to take complete control of theaters, but the general public had no interest in fascist "entertainment" and boycotted it.

May 21, 1979 In what would become known as the White Night riots, LGBT+ people in San Francisco reacted angrily when the killer of Harvey Milk was not convicted of murder. Milk, one of the first openly gay elected officials in the US, was shot and killed, along with the mayor George Moscone, by former police officer Dan White, who used his service revolver.

Burning police cars and rioters on the San Francisco Civic Center Plaza
(Photo by Daniel Nicoletta, courtesy of Wikimedia Commons)

Numerous San Francisco police officers wore t-shirts emblazoned with the slogan "Free Dan White," while others contributed to White's legal fund, which reportedly raised $100,000. Despite later admitting that the murders were premeditated, in court White used his now-infamous "Twinkie defense," claiming that the fact that he was eating junk food showed he was in a poor mental state. Rather than murder, he was only convicted of voluntary manslaughter.

Upon hearing the verdict, a crowd of five hundred mostly LGBT+ people began marching down Castro Street, calling others to join them, as they headed to City Hall. By the time they arrived, the crowd had grown to include thousands of people, and they attacked the building, smashing windows. Police waded into the crowd, beating people with batons, and the crowd began burning police cars. As one man set light to a vehicle, he told a reporter, "Make sure you put in the paper that I ate too many Twinkies."

In retaliation for their humiliating defeat, police attacked a gay bar later that night, screaming homophobic abuse, shattering windows, and beating drinkers and passersby, injuring numerous people. By the end of the night, sixty-one police officers and over one hundred members of the public had been hospitalized.

Dan White ended up only serving five years in prison. He killed himself shortly after his release.

22 **May 22, 1968** During the May 68 uprising, footballers in Paris occupied the headquarters of the French Football Association and issued a statement demanding the immediate dismissal of football "profiteers" and the establishment of football without profits, declaring, "United, we will make football once again what it ought never to have ceased to be—the sport of joy, the sport of the world of tomorrow that all the workers have started building."

May 22, 2006 Teachers in Oaxaca, Mexico, walked out on strike for the twenty-fifth consecutive year when the government refused to respond to their demands. What made this year unique was that they set up camp in the city center and urged students and their families to join them, defied orders to return to work, and even set up their own radio station. Tens of thousands joined the rebellion, which lasted for five months and faced massive repression from local police, federal police, and paramilitaries, who killed as many as twenty-seven people, including our friend Brad Will, activist journalist from New York.

23 **May 23, 1946** The largest mass arrest in the history of Rochester, New York, took place when three hundred police rounded up 208 municipal workers who were on strike for reinstatement to their jobs and union recognition. In addition to picketers, they arrested a teacher on her way to work, a plumber who was walking by, and even one of the strikers' dogs. The repression did not deter the workers, however, and the strike spread and was won the following week.

May 23, 1969 Workers launched a massive strike in the Industrial Corridor near Rosario, Argentina, as part of the prolonged Rosariazo rebellion against the military dictatorship.

Protesters during the Rosariazo rebellion *(Photo by Carlos Saldi, courtesy of Wikimedia Commons)*

24 **May 24, 1919** Thousands of coal miners in Alberta, Canada, walked off the job in a dispute over pay, the cost of living, and working conditions. They were organized in the One Big Union (OBU): a revolutionary union that planned to organize all workers into a single union to take control of society and run it collectively. Thirteen mine companies in Drumheller refused to negotiate and hired returning war veterans, arming them with clubs and iron bars, giving them free alcohol, and encouraging them to terrorize the workers and beat and torture the organizers, while the police turned a blind eye. By August the strike was broken.

May 24, 1990 The car of revolutionary construction worker and environmentalist Judi Bari was bombed, severely injuring her and wounding her colleague Darryl Cherney. They had been campaigning to protect ancient redwood forests in California from logging companies, had received death threats, and had previously had their car rammed by a logging truck.

Despite it being a clear attempt to murder them, FBI agents, who arrived on the scene almost immediately, attempted to frame them for their own attempted assassination.

Bari died of breast cancer in 1997, having lived in constant pain after the attack, but several years later Cherney and Bari's family won a civil rights case against the FBI for the frame job and were awarded $4.4 million.

25 **May 25, 1978** Police in Aotearoa/New Zealand attacked a Māori land occupation at Bastion Point, near Auckland, demanding the return of the stolen land. The Ōrākei Māori Action Committee (OMAC) had been occupying the land for 506 days when police moved in to evict them, arresting 222 people and demolishing buildings. However, protests continued, and in 1988 the government agreed to return the land to the Ngāti Whātua people.

May 25, 2020 George Floyd, forty-six, an African American security guard and father of two, was killed by Minneapolis police officer Derek Chauvin, who knelt on his neck for more than eight minutes. The killer, who had had eighteen previous complaints filed against him, ignored Floyd's desperate calls that he could not breathe and killed him. He continued to kneel on Floyd's neck after he lost consciousness. Even after paramedics arrived, he kept kneeling on his neck for a further minute and twenty seconds. Meanwhile, three of his colleagues stood by and protected him while onlookers filmed and called for help. With a spate of other killings of unarmed Black people by police and vigilantes, including Breonna Taylor, Ahmaud

Arbery, and Rayshard Brooks, the Black Lives Matter movement reemerged, swept the US, and spread internationally. At the time of writing (July 2020) over 4,700 protests have taken place in some 2,500 towns and cities around the US with between seven and twenty-six million participants, which would make it the largest protest movement in the country's history—this despite violent attacks on demonstrators by police, National Guard, and armed white supremacists.

The full scope of the movement cannot yet be known, but so far it has resulted in murder charges being filed against George Floyd's killers and has sparked growing calls for the defunding or even abolition of police forces. In Minneapolis, this has resulted in the city council pledging to dismantle its police department.

26 **May 26, 1824** The first recorded factory strike in US history took place when 102 girls and women working at the Slater Mill in Pawtucket, Rhode Island, picketed their factory. Two days prior, the mill owners in the town had decided to increase working hours by one hour a day for everyone, with no additional pay, and cut the pay of power loom weavers by 25 percent. The weavers affected were all girls and women aged fifteen to thirty, who were previously being paid "extravagant wages for young women," according to the employers. Something occurred that the owners did not expect, something that had never happened before in the infant textile industry or, indeed, any factory in the country: the women organized themselves and went on strike. They were joined by other workers and members of the local community, who blockaded the mills, protested, and hurled rocks at the mansions of the owners. One prominent local politician, George F. Jenckes, wrote in his journal during the dispute:

> I have just returned from one of the moste gloomy assemblage of people I have ever witnessed, from the street . . . across the bridge to Josiah Mill's shop is literally filled with Men Women and Children— making a mob of very daring aspect, insulting the managers of cotton mills in every shape—pulling and hauling—screaming and shouting thro the streets.

On the final day of the week-long strike, one of the mills was set ablaze. The day after the fire, the mill owners moved to negotiate with the workers, and they reached a compromise. In the wake of the dispute, other groups of workers began organizing themselves, and other strikes would break out across the New England textile industry in the coming years. 🏴 **32**

May 26, 1944 A general strike broke out in Marseille, in Vichy France. Metalworkers, public servants, and transport workers joined a stoppage of shipyard workers that had begun the previous day, demonstrating in front of the city hall, demanding "bread!" The strike held out until the Gestapo arrested fifteen thousand workers, but the crackdown was short-lived, as Marseille was liberated soon after.

27 **May 27, 1919** Workers in Lima, Peru, declared a general strike in protest against the high cost of living, shutting down economic activity in the area. The government eventually crushed the strike by killing at least one hundred protesters and wounding and jailing hundreds more.

May 27, 2004 Six people, including one woman, were killed and dozens wounded by the Lebanese Army during a trade union demonstration in the Al-Salam neighborhood of Beirut's southern suburb. The Confédération Générale des Travailleurs Libanais (General Confederation of Lebanese Workers; CGTL) had called on workers to strike and take to the streets across the country to protest high fuel prices and the high cost of living. Angry demonstrators torched the five-story Ministry of Labor building, and security forces arrested more than 130 protesters in one of Lebanon's deadliest worker protests since the civil war. The army was using live ammunition in the residential neighborhood of Al-Salam at the same time as the Lebanese government, headed by Rafic Hariri, was making preparations to receive international delegations to the Organization of Petroleum Exporting Countries (OPEC) meeting in Beirut less than a week later.

28 **May 28, 1913** Thousands of dockworkers in Philadelphia won their two-week strike for a pay increase and union recognition. They were organized in Local 8 of the Industrial Workers of the World (IWW), led by the Black dockworker Ben Fletcher.

Local 8, with a membership that included African Americans, Irish Americans, East European immigrants, and other ethnic groups, was probably the most racially and ethnically integrated union local in the United States during the World War I era. It was also among the most durable branches of the IWW, dominating the waterfront for almost a decade, despite massive employer and government repression. 🔊 **6**

May 28, 1936 Thirty-two thousand workers occupied the Renault plant in Paris. One hundred thousand more workers soon occupied every major engineering factory around the city. Over the following month, a strike wave swept the country from the factories to nonunionized shops, involving two million workers in twelve thousand strikes and occupations. To stop the upheaval, employers and the government had to agree to wage increases of 7 to 15 percent, a forty-hour workweek, paid vacation, and collective bargaining rights.

Strikers protest in Córdoba, May 29, 1969 *(Courtesy Wikimedia Commons)*

29 **May 29, 1969** Car factory worker Máximo Mena was shot and killed by police during a strike in Córdoba, Argentina. The result was a wave of riots and demonstrations throughout the city by workers and students, in what would become known as the "Córdobazo," the legendary revolt of the Córdoban working class, spelling the beginning of the end for the military government of General Juan Carlos Onganía.

May 29, 1972 The Dalit Panthers organization, modelled on the US Black Panthers, was formed in Maharashtra, India, to combat caste discrimination. Dalit means "oppressed" and refers to members of lower castes in India. The socialist group was most active during the 1970s and 1980s.

30 **May 30, 1925** British-led police in Shanghai massacred twelve workers and students who were supporting a strike at a Japanese-owned cotton mill. The working class responded with a massive strike: within a couple of weeks Shanghai, Guangzhou, and Hong Kong were shut down, with Hong Kong largely taken over by the workers, until the strike was broken the following year by Chinese nationalists.

May 30, 1969 A workers' uprising that would bring down the government began in Curaçao, a Caribbean island and part of the Dutch Empire. A mass strike was underway, and widespread rioting broke out against low pay and discrimination against the Black population. The rebellion was a key turning point in Curaçao's history.

31 **May 31, 1831** The Merthyr Tydfil uprising in Wales was sparked when bailiffs from the court of requests attempted to seize goods from the home of Lewis Lewis, known as Lewsyn yr Heliwr (Lewis the Huntsman). With the help of his neighbors, Lewis managed to prevent them from entering his home. The following day a demonstration by ironworkers began ransacking the houses of bailiffs and returning property to the original owners. The rebellion spread and lasted until mid-June.

May 31, 1921 Following a false allegation that a Black man attacked a white woman, the Tulsa massacre, one of the single worst incidents of racial violence in US, left three hundred dead. The *Tulsa Tribune* newspaper included a front-page article titled "Nab Negro for Attacking Girl in Elevator"

Little Africa section of Tulsa in flames, May 31, 1921
(Courtesy of Wikimedia Commons)

and a back-page editorial titled "To Lynch Negro Tonight."

Local whites were inflamed, and they attacked the Black community of Greenwood, at the time the most prosperous African American community in the US, commonly known as the Black Wall Street. Mobs were backed up by private planes that reportedly dropped incendiary devices and fired on Black residents. Hundreds were killed, and the entire thirty-five-block area was razed to the ground, leaving up to ten thousand people homeless. At the time of writing (early 2020) there are still a few survivors awaiting justice and reparations.

JUNE

1 **June 1, 1926** A police patrol in Wyndham, Australia, headed out to search for an Aboriginal man who had killed a white man for assaulting and whipping him. They returned on June 19. Over this period the Forrest River massacre took place, with the officers murdering and burning anywhere from eleven to three hundred Indigenous people. A Royal Commission confirmed the massacre took place, but no officers were convicted of any offences.

June 1, 1971 Dozens of homeless families occupied empty homes in Via Tibaldi, Milan. Supported by local factory workers, construction workers, and the unemployed, they resisted two violent police attempts at eviction, before eventually forcing the local government to rehouse them and 140 other families.

2 **June 2, 1863** The Combahee River Raid took place, with formerly enslaved Underground Railroad activist Harriet Tubman leading 150 Black Union soldiers. The only woman-led military operation during the American Civil War, it was a major success, with 750 enslaved people freed and the estates of several wealthy secessionist landowners looted and burned.

June 2, 1975 One hundred sex workers occupied the Church of Saint Nizier, in Lyon, refusing to leave unless their convictions for soliciting were rescinded. They were evicted after a week, but a precedent-setting legal judgment cancelled the workers' imminent prison sentences shortly thereafter.

3 **June 3, 1943** The Zoot Suit Riots began when some fifty white sailors in the US Navy left their armory, headed to Alpine Street in Los Angeles, and attacked young Mexican American children wearing zoot suits. They began by clubbing a group of twelve- and thirteen-year-old boys, stripping them of their clothes and burning them in a pile. The mob was soon detained by the local shore patrol, but after the arrival of a senior naval officer, they were released without charge.

The following day, young Chicano men drove past the armory hurling abuse at guards. Come nightfall, white sailors again headed out, this time to the Mexican American area of East Los Angeles, attacking people in the streets and in bars and theaters.

Over the next few days, many other servicemen joined the attacks. The vigilantes were praised by the press, while police arrested the victims of the

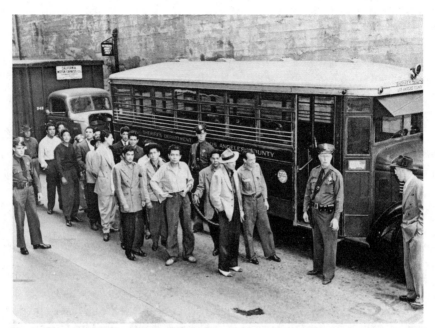

Zoot suiters outside Los Angeles jail, June 9, 1943 *(Courtesy of the Library of Congress, Prints & Photographs Division, New York World-Telegram and the Sun Newspaper Photograph Collection, reproduction number, LC-USZ62-113319)*

attacks rather than the perpetrators. Los Angeles city council even tried to ban the wearing of the suits.

Meanwhile, Black and Mexican zoot suit wearers, including groups of women known as Pachucas, like the Slick Chicks and Black Widows, organized and fought back. As clashes in Los Angeles faded, they began to break out in New York, Philadelphia, and Detroit, the latter after attacks on Black zoot suiters. Within weeks, Detroit exploded in its worst race riots up to that point. Zoot suits were, in the end, a symbol of Black and Mexican working class pride, defiance, and rebellion.

June 3, 2016 A federal judge in the United States ruled that women's soccer players could not go on strike, despite their collective bargaining agreement

US women's national soccer team with President Barack Obama, October 2015 *(Photo by Lawrence Jackson, courtesy of the White House/Wikimedia Commons)*

(which included a no-strike clause) having expired. The women were in a dispute over pay discrimination, as their male equivalents made up to four times more money, despite the women's team being much more successful and generating more revenue than the men's.

4 **June 4, 1950** The 43 Group of militant anti-fascist Jewish ex-service-men and women voted to disband itself at an extraordinary general meeting in London, England. The group had been formed four years prior by Jewish people who had fought in the British Army against the Nazis during World War II, who had seen the horrors of the concentration camps, and who returned home to see fascists organizing openly on UK streets. They resolved to continue their fight against fascism, racism, and anti-Semitism by any means necessary.

The group included decorated war hero Gerry Flamberg, apprentice hairdresser Vidal Sassoon, gay former officer Harry Bidney, and women like Doris Kaye, who infiltrated fascist groups, and Julie Sloggan, who was one of its most ardent street fighters. They disrupted and broke up fascist meetings, usually after breaking through the fascists' police guard, and harassed fascist aristocrat Oswald Mosley and his followers in towns and cities up and down the country. Eventually Mosley went into exile, and fascist organizing dwindled to the degree that the 43 Group dissolved itself, although veterans of the group would throw themselves back into the movement when Mosley attempted a comeback in the 1960s. 🔊 **35–37**

June 4, 1976 An eighteen-year-old Sikh schoolboy, Gurdip Singh Chaggar, was fatally stabbed in a racist attack outside the Dominion Theatre in Southall, London. When a passerby asked a police officer who had been killed, he responded, "Just an Asian." His murder triggered riots in the area and prompted local Asian and Black youths to form the Southall Youth Movement (SYM), which took the fight against racists into the streets. 🔊 **33–34**

5 **June 5, 1981** Workers in the Philippines held their first general strike after the end of martial law in the Bataan Export Processing Zone—something that the government had said would never happen. The strike lasted until June 7 and led to the establishment of the Alyansa ng Manggagawa sa Bataan (Bataan Labor Alliance; AMBA), which, in 1983, helped organize a wave of thirty-one strikes against twenty-two different firms.

June 5, 1996 Texas border community group Save Sierra Blanca (SSB) stepped up its campaign to oppose a nuclear waste disposal site in its community. It allied with many other environmental groups in the United States and Mexico. The disposal site was supported by, among others, Governor George W. Bush, President Bill Clinton, and Senator Bernie Sanders of Vermont. The campaign lasted for over two years, until the plan was officially shelved on October 22, 1998.

James Meredith walking to class at University of Mississippi accompanied by US marshals *(Courtesy of the Library of Congress Prints and Photographs Division, U.S. News & World Report Magazine Collection)*

6 **June 6, 1966** Anti-racist activist and war veteran James Meredith began a solitary march of over two hundred miles from Memphis, Tennessee, to Jackson, Mississippi, to protest against racism and to encourage Black voter registration. While doing so, he was shot by a white man in an attempted assassination, but others continued in his place. Meredith himself rejoined the march while still recovering. When Meredith arrived in Jackson, he was accompanied by some fifteen thousand people. In its later stages the march was protected by the Deacons for Defense and Justice, an African American civil rights group that was armed for self-defense.

Meredith had first come to prominence as the first African American to attend the all-white University of Mississippi. White supremacists rioted in protest at his admission, burning cars, destroying property, and attacking federal agents and US troops with rocks, bricks, and guns. After the violence subsided, many white students reportedly shunned and harassed him. Meredith is now eighty-six and has written numerous books.

June 6, 1988 A general strike was declared in South Africa by Black unions and anti-apartheid groups. Up to three million took part in the stoppage, protesting against the two-year-old state of emergency and further proposed restrictions on the right to strike. The strikers held out until June 8 against police, who opened fire on crowds in townships.

7 **June 7, 1968** Women workers at Ford's Dagenham plant in England walked out on strike for equal pay with male workers. They agreed to return to work after three weeks, when they were offered 92 percent of the men's wages. The strike was the key reason for the Equal Pay Act of 1970, although nominal pay equality at Ford was only achieved after a later strike, in 1984.

June 7, 1972 Police opened fire into a crowd of strikers demanding back pay in Karachi, Pakistan, killing three and injuring dozens. The funeral procession the next day was also attacked by police, and workers responded with a mass strike across the city. The police were under the control of the People's Party, the populist government elected with working class and radical left support.

8 **June 8, 1961** A group of Freedom Riders, including Kwame Ture (still known as Stokely Carmichael at this time), Gwendolyn Greene, and Joan Mulholland, were arrested in Jackson, Mississippi. Ture became a central organizer in the Student Nonviolent Coordinating Committee (SNCC), and later the Black Panther Party. He was a target of the FBI's COINTELPRO program and was "bad jacketed"—falsely portrayed as a CIA agent—which led to his expulsion from SNCC.

Greene (who later changed her name to Britt) had also been arrested in 1960 for refusing to leave the whites-only Glen Echo Amusement Park in Maryland. With others, she confronted counterprotesters from the American Nazi Party and continued picketing until the end of summer. The park then agreed to abolish segregation before reopening the following year.

Mulholland, then nineteen, had participated in numerous civil rights sit-ins, for which she was disowned by her family. In 1963, she was travelling in Mississippi with four other activists when their car was attacked by the Ku Klux Klan, who had orders to kill them, but they managed to escape. Mulholland remains active to this day.

June 8, 2017 After a ten-month-long campaign, including seven strike days and two occupations, cleaners at the London School of Economics became the first outsourced workforce in the UK to make a university bring them back in-house. The workers, all migrants and people

Striking cleaners picket the LSE *(Courtesy of United Voices of the World uvwunion.org.uk)*

of color, organized themselves in the grassroots United Voices of the World union (UVW), which also achieved numerous other victories for similar subcontracted workers across London by taking sustained strike action.

9 **June 9, 1910** Military forces of the Mexican dictator Porfirio Díaz attacked the city of Valladolid, in Yucatan, which had been liberated five days previously, following an insurrection. Two hundred rebels were killed, with five hundred injured and six hundred taken prisoner.

Three accused ringleaders, Maximiliano Bonilla, Atilano Albertos, and José E. Kantún, were executed, while the others were sentenced to long periods of hard labor. However, some of the rebels managed to escape and took refuge among the Maya population.

Though the Valladolid insurrection was crushed, it spurred further resistance to the dictatorship and is commonly referred to as the "first spark" of the revolution that began in earnest that November.

June 9, 1944 German socialist and member of the anti-fascist resistance Johanna Kirchner was beheaded by the Nazis in Berlin.

When Hitler came to power, she went underground and later moved to France. In 1942, she was arrested by the collaborationist Vichy regime and handed over to the Gestapo. She was sentenced to ten years of hard labor.

Later her case was brought back to court, and she was sentenced to death for "Marxist high-treason propaganda." On the day of her execution, she wrote to her children: "Don't cry for me. I believe in a better future for you."

On the same day, ninety-nine civilians were hanged from lampposts and balconies by Nazi troops in Tulle, France, in reprisal for an attack by resistance maquis that killed forty Nazi soldiers. Others were sent to the concentration camps. In total, 213 died.

The following day German troops destroyed the entire nearby town of Oradour-sur-Glane, killing 642 people, including women, children, and babies, leaving only seven survivors, six men and one woman, Marguerite Rouffanche, who was shot but survived by hiding in bushes until she was rescued the next day.

10 **June 10, 1918** A mass rally of African workers took place in Johannesburg. They were protesting against the jailing of 152 African municipal workers who had gone on strike for a shilling a day increase in pay. Radicals attempted to organize a general strike the following month. It was called off, but thousands of miners did not hear about the cancellation and walked out.

June 10, 1973 A strike of gravediggers at three cemeteries in the New York metropolitan area was expanded to include forty-four others. On June 21, the courts issued an order for strikers to return to work, which they ignored. The president of the striking Local 365 of the Cemetery Workers and Greens Attendants was subsequently found guilty of contempt of court, jailed, and fined. After twenty-seven days of strike action, the employers, from Jewish, Roman Catholic, and nonsectarian cemeteries, collectively agreed to most of the workers' demands, including annual wage increases of twelve dollars per week for the next three years and an employer-funded pension scheme. During the dispute some bodies were buried by relatives and friends of the deceased, but a backlog of at least 1,400 unburied bodies remained.

11 **June 11, 1914** London's Westminster Abbey, built in 1090, one of the world's most famous churches, was bombed by the suffragettes in an attack described as "dastardly" by the right-wing *Daily Telegraph*. The violence of the movement for women's suffrage in the UK is often forgotten by liberal commentators.

June 11, 1972 Women in Tokyo, Japan, marched in protest against a eugenics amendment bill before Parliament. Thousands of people, mostly women and girls, many of them disabled, would be forcibly sterilized under the program.

12 **June 12, 1963** Medgar Wiley Evers, an African American civil rights activist from Mississippi involved in efforts to overturn segregation at the University of Mississippi was shot in the back and killed by Byron De La Beckwith, as he pulled into his driveway after returning from a meeting in the early morning.

Beckwith, a white supremacist and member of the White Citizens' Council, was arrested. He was later put on trial twice, in both cases before all-white juries that had been illegally screened and investigated by the state beforehand. The former governor of the state interrupted the second trial to shake Beckwith's hand while Evers's widow Myrlie was testifying. He walked free and for years boasted about the murder at Ku Klux Klan rallies. He also unsuccessfully sought the Democratic Party nomination as a gubernatorial candidate.

After years of campaigning, Myrlie succeeded in getting the case reopened, and, in 1994, Beckwith was eventually convicted and sent to prison, where he died a few years later.

June 12, 1966 Following the Puerto Rican Day Parade, a youth was shot in the leg by police, causing two days of riots in Chicago, known as the Division Street riots.

13 **June 13, 1953** The events leading to the Chuka massacre began when a British military unit was sent to the Chuka area of Kenya to flush out suspected Mau Mau rebels. Over the next five days, twenty unarmed Kenyan civilians were murdered, and some of them were beaten, tortured, and mutilated. British forces cut off six of the victims' hands and put them in their bags before returning to camp. No British soldiers were charged for the killings.

June 13, 1973 Thousands of mostly migrant workers at the Broadmeadows Ford plant in Australia walked off the job, smashed up their factory, fought off police attacks, and forced their union to endorse their stoppage. In retaliation, the company threatened to relocate production to Malaysia. Nonetheless, the strike continued and received strong support from the local community. The Greek Orthodox Church donated to the strike fund, while doctors set up free clinics for strikers' families, and glaziers refused to fix windows broken in the riot. After ten weeks, Ford gave in, agreeing to numerous demands from the workers, including hiring women, hiring more workers, slowing production, increasing the number of toilet breaks, and increasing pay.

14 **June 14, 1381** During the peasants' revolt in England, Wat Tyler's rebel army of some fifty to one hundred thousand people captured London Bridge and the Tower of London. There they killed the chancellor, Archbishop Simon of Sudbury, and the treasurer, Sir Robert Hales.

The rebellion had broken out in May in protest at the imposition of a poll tax on every-one aged fifteen and over, which exacerbated the economic hard-ship of workers and the poor. People were also enraged by the brutality of tax inspectors, who

Illustration of the Chancellor and Treasurer being killed *(Published c.1470 in Chroniques de France et d'Angleterre, vol. 2)*

measured people's pubic hair to determine their age, which was seen as state-sanctioned sexual assault, particularly in the case of girls and women. The rebellion soon developed into a deep and sophisticated social movement demanding radical changes to feudal society and peaked with the taking of the Tower.

On June 15, Wat Tyler attended a parley with King Richard II, where he was murdered. Realizing his weak position, Richard promised the rebels that he would implement many of their demands, including the abolition of the tax, and even the abolition of forced labor and serfdom, but, while the poll tax was ended, once the rebels had dispersed and returned home, they were no longer a threat, so Richard reneged on all of his other pledges and hanged 1,500 of them. It was a brutal but important lesson not to trust the promises of the powerful.

June 14, 1991 Up to half a million women in Switzerland took part in a nation-wide women's strike, demanding legal enforcement of gender equality, which was incorporated into the federal constitution on June 14, 1981. Of primary concern was the continuing pay differential between men and women. Women walked out again on the same date in 2011, and, in 2019, women in Switzerland walked out once more demanding better recognition and remuneration for care work, an end to sexual harassment, and action against wage inequality.

Women in Switzerland earn around 20 percent less than men on average, and 40 percent of this pay differential cannot be explained by factors like men and women working different jobs.

15 **June 15, 1960** Twenty-two-year-old student Michiko Kanba was killed by police during a demonstration at the Diet building in Tokyo. She was one of hundreds of thousands of people participating in daily protests in opposition to the terms of the Japan-US security treaty, which would permanently station US troops in the country.

June 15, 1990 The Battle of Century City took place when police in Los Angeles attacked some five hundred janitors and their supporters during a peaceful Service Employees International Union (SEIU) demonstration against cleaning contractor ISS. The event generated public outrage that resulted in recognition of the workers' union and spurred the creation of an annual June 15 Justice for Janitors Day.

16 **June 16, 1531** Henry VIII modified the vagrancy laws he had brought in the previous year, laws which had been key in creating the working class. People kicked off communal land by enclosures who were not in wage labor were designated as vaga-bonds. For their first offence, vaga-bonds were to be whipped. For a

Etching of a vagrant, sixteenth century
(Courtesy of libcom.org)

second offence, they were whipped and had half an ear sliced off. For a third offence, they were to be executed.

Laws like this introduced in England and elsewhere in Europe were how we—a working class who have nothing to sell but our labor—were first created. This dispossession of the vast majority of the population was then spread around the globe by colonialism.

Rather than capitalism and wage labor being a natural state of affairs, as is often assumed, it is actually a system that was created over an extended period of time with massive state violence.

June 16, 1976 Pupils at schools in Soweto, South Africa, who were boycotting class to protest against the use of Afrikaans, took to the streets. After police opened fire on the crowd, rioting quickly spread across the country, and the resulting uprising helped spur on the anti-apartheid struggle.

Two years prior, the government had made Afrikaans mandatory in schools alongside English, but, while it was widely spoken by white settlers, especially those of Dutch heritage, almost no Black South Africans knew the language. Organizing against its imposition began almost immediately and developed in the run-up to the Soweto riots.

17 **June 17, 1937** Austrian anti-fascist Katia Landau, who had travelled to Spain with her husband to fight the nationalists during the civil war, was arrested by the Soviet secret police, the NKVD. She was brutally tortured in an attempt to make her sign a confession that she was a foreign agent or counterrevolutionary.

Upon learning that her husband had disappeared, she went on a hunger strike, with five hundred other women joining her in solidarity. When the prison was visited by foreign representatives of workers' organizations, they were greeted by the women singing the popular socialist anthem "The Internationale"—all "fascist agents," according to the Partido Comunista de España (Communist Party of Spain; PCE).

While her husband was murdered by PCE forces, Katia survived the war, moving to Mexico, where she lived into her nineties, at least. 🎙 **39–40**

June 17, 1971 Construction workers in New South Wales, Australia, initiated a "green ban," refusing to build luxury houses over Kelly's Bush, the last open space in the suburb of Hunters Hill. Local women had been campaigning to save the park. Despite a management threat to use scabs, the builders and residents won, and Kelly's Bush remains an open public reserve today. A wave of green bans subsequently began, stopping billions of dollars of harmful development over the next four years.

18 **June 18, 1935** Around a thousand locked out dockers and their supporters were violently attacked by hundreds of armed police and Royal Canadian Mounted Police (RCMP), generally known as Mounties, in

Vancouver, British Columbia, as they went to picket scabs unloading ships at Ballantyne Pier. Several workers were hospitalized, including one who was shot in the legs while attempting to flee. After the attack, the strike faltered. However, it cleared the way for the founding of a new, independent union, whose members won many strikes in subsequent years.

June 18, 1943 Eighteen-year-old Ukrainian anti-Nazi fighter Maria Kislyak was executed alongside her two friends Fedor Rudenko and Vasiliy Bugrimenko. She had lured two Nazi officers into the woods for her friends to kill. The first time she was arrested by the Gestapo, she did not confess and was released. But the second time the Gestapo rounded up one hundred civilians and said they would kill them all unless the killers came forward. Maria and her friends confessed, and she claimed to be the leader of the group.

19 **June 19, 1937** After employers failed to agree to oil workers' pay demands, workers at one of Trinidad's oilfields went on strike. British colonial authorities attempted to arrest Uriah Butler, a former oil worker turned preacher, who was helping to lead the dispute, but he was defended by a crowd of workers, who killed two policemen, soaking one of them with paraffin and burning them both. Butler went into hiding, as the strike quickly spread across all of the oilfields, and then to the rest of the economy. A state of emergency was declared, and two British warships rushed to the island, arriving on June 22 and 23, bringing marines and additional police from England and Ireland. Two local military units were also mobilized against the workers. The arrest and imprisonment of numerous workers finally quashed the rebellion. Butler was captured in September and jailed for two years for sedition.

June 19, 1937 The Women's Day massacre took place in Youngstown, Ohio, with police killing sixteen people and injuring nearly three hundred when striking steelworkers' wives and children demonstrated their support for the workers at Republic Steel, who had gone on strike after one thousand union supporters were fired.

Strikers' wives organized a Women's Day to support the men. The presence of women angered the police captain, who ordered the women to leave. When they refused and instead spat on and cursed at the officers, police fired tear gas at the crowd of women, children, and even babies, which outraged the workers, who rushed to the scene to defend their families. At that point, police opened fire, killing and wounding hundreds, many of whom were shot in the back as they fled.

20 **June 20, 1905** King of Sweden Oscar II publicly and formally called off plans to invade the recently independent Norway. The announcement was prompted by the threat of a nationwide general strike by Swedish unions if mobilization for war went ahead.

June 20, 1967 Boxing legend Muhammad Ali was convicted for refusing the Vietnam War draft in Houston, Texas. Ali was a vocal opponent of the US war, saying, "Why should they ask me to put on a uniform and go 10,000 miles from home and drop bombs and bullets on brown people in Vietnam while so-called Negro people in Louisville are treated like dogs?"

To try to quell the escalating resistance to the war, Ali was given the maximum sentence of five years in prison and a $10,000 fine. But this effort proved unsuccessful, and the anti-war movement continued to grow.

Despite the Nation of Islam beginning to distance themselves from Ali, demonstrations supporting him took place around the world, from Egypt to Guyana to London to Ghana. Four years later his conviction was overturned by the Supreme Court. Ali had no regrets:

> I wasn't trying to be a leader. I just wanted to be free. And I made a stand all people, not just Black people, should have thought about making, because it wasn't just Black people being drafted. The government had a system where the rich man's son went to college, and the poor man's son went to war. Then, after the rich man's son got out of college, he did other things to keep him out of the Army until he was too old to be drafted.

🔊 10–11, 14

21 **June 21, 1919** Bloody Saturday occurred during Canada's best-known general strike—the Winnipeg General Strike. When thirty thousand strikers assembled for a demonstration, the Winnipeg mayor read the riot act to scare the strikers, and police on horseback charged into the crowd, beating them with clubs and firing weapons. The violent attack resulted in the death of two strikers. Mike Sokowolski was shot in the heart, and Mike Schezerbanowicz was shot in the legs and later died of gangrene. Up to forty-five others were injured, and there were numerous arrests. Four Eastern European immigrants were rounded up at the time, two of whom were deported. The day ended with Winnipeg effectively under military occupation. Later, the police shut down the strikers' paper, the *Western Labour News*, and arrested the editors for penning commentaries about the Bloody Saturday events. Eventually, the repression broke the strike.

Mounted police charge strikers in Winnipeg, June 21, 1919
(Courtesy of Wikimedia Commons)

June 21, 1964 Three civil rights workers, James Earl Chaney, a twenty-one-year-old Black unionized plasterer and organizer with the Congress of Racial Equality (CORE) from nearby Meridian, Mississippi, Andrew Goodman, a twenty-year-old white Jewish anthropology student from New York, and Michael "Mickey" Schwerner, a twenty-four-year-old white Jewish CORE organizer and former social worker from New York, were lynched on the night of June 21 by members of the Mississippi White Knights of the Ku Klux Klan, the Neshoba County sheriff's office, and the Philadelphia, Mississippi, police department. The three had been working on the Freedom Summer campaign, attempting to register African Americans to vote.

22 **June 22, 1908** The Red Flag Incident, the opening move of the imperial government to crush the socialist movement, took place in Tokyo, Japan. Celebrated anarchist Koken Yamaguchi was released from prison and was met by crowds waving red flags adorned with anarchist, communist, and revolutionary slogans and singing communist songs. Police violently attacked and broke up the demonstration, arresting fourteen prominent activists, who were later sentenced to lengthy prison terms.

June 22, 1941 The Sisak People's Liberation Partisan Detachment, the first Yugoslav partisan unit, was founded in response to the Nazi occupation of the country. Its seventy-nine members were mostly Croats, although there was one Serb woman, Nada Dimić. Today, June 22 is commemorated in Croatia as a public holiday called "Anti-Fascist Struggle Day."

23 **June 23, 1950** Delivery drivers for Smithfield meat market in London went on wildcat strike. The strike, which lasted into July, was condemned by the Labour government, which brought in troops as scabs to break the strike—just one of many occasions when the postwar Labour government used soldiers against the working class.

June 23, 1980 One hundred paint sprayers at the British Leyland Longbridge plant in Birmingham walked out on strike after being told that their two daily tea breaks would be shortened and staggered. The strike spread and completely shut down production at the factory, which was estimated to have cost the firm at least £10 million (approximately US$23.3 million) in lost production of Mini and Allegro cars. After ten days, unions agreed to accept an element of the troubled company's "recovery plan" regarding breaks in return for British Leyland conducting a study to determine if there were genuine grounds for changing them.

24 **June 24, 1976** The Polish government announced enormous staple food price rises, and in response there were strikes, public protests, and rioting countrywide. In Radom, demonstrators burned the Communist Party headquarters, built barricades, and fought the police, injuring seventy-five officers. After less than twenty-four hours, the proposed price increases were withdrawn.

June 24, 1980 A two-day general strike protesting against the US-backed military dictatorship and its counterinsurgency death squads began in El Salvador. Eighty-five percent of the economy was shut down, and eighty thousand people took to the streets. Police and soldiers killed two people who were building barricades in the suburb of Delgado.

25 **June 25, 1876** The Battle of the Little Bighorn, in which a combined force of Lakota, Arapaho, and Northern Cheyenne tribes routed Lieutenant Colonel

Painting of the Battle of Little Bighorn, 1903 *(By Charles Marion Russell, courtesy of Wikimedia Commons)*

George Armstrong Custer's army, began. It was the biggest engagement of the Great Sioux War of 1876, during which the US military attempted to force Native Americans off their land and onto reservations in order to mine newly discovered gold in the Black Hills. On June 25–26, Native American warriors fought the seven-hundred-strong US 7th Cavalry, destroying five of its twelve companies, and killing its commanding officer, Custer, along with four of his relatives.

June 25, 1878 The Kanak rebellion in New Caledonia began when Indigenous Melanesian warriors killed four French colonial policemen and most European settlers in the La Foa region. As attacks escalated and spread, the French Army moved to aggressively crush the rebellion, which it succeeded in doing by December, having killed as much as 5 percent of the Kanak population, with many chiefs executed without trial and many tribes deported to other islands. Nonetheless, the colonization project was nearly halted for twenty years.

Anarchist Louise Michel, who was imprisoned on New Caledonia, along with thousands of other Paris Commune deportees, was one of the few white people to support the rising. She gave two Melanesian fighters her prized red scarf from the Paris uprising.

June 26, 1950 The international arts organization the Congress for Cultural Freedom (CCF) was set up by the US Central Intelligence Agency (CIA) as part of the "cultural cold war." The congress was one of the many ways the CIA tried to promote art to rival the growing popularity of socialist realism. Abstract expressionism was one of the main art movements to benefit from this support. When news of the CIA backing was revealed in 1966, the project collapsed.

June 26, 1993 Four thousand workers took to the streets in Decatur, Illinois, in a protest that included workers from A.E. Staley, who had been working to rule to oppose the imposition of a new inferior contract, joining striking coal miners and Caterpillar workers, who were on a go-slow across the Midwest.

The following day, Staley locked out its nearly eight hundred production workers in an attempt to force them to switch from eight- to twelve-hour shifts, setting in motion a mammoth struggle that would only end in December 1995, when, after betrayal by the leadership of the United Paperworkers International Union (UPIU), a majority of strikers voted to accept the contract. Some union members were so angry at the result that company security and police were required to protect union local president Jim Shinall.

Meanwhile, workers at Caterpillar also walked out on strike for seventeen months, until the United Auto Workers (UAW) called off the action in defeat. Bridgestone-Firestone workers in Decatur and at four other plants were also forced to accept twelve-hour shifts following the defeat of their ten-month strike.

27 **June 27, 1905** The Industrial Workers of the World union (IWW) was founded in the United States at a convention in Chicago. Among the founders were Eugene V. Debs, Mother Jones, Lucy Parsons, and Big Bill Haywood.

One of the first multiracial unions in the country, the IWW advocated all workers uniting into one big union and taking control of society. It organized large swathes of previously unorganized workers in the US and won big improvements for hundreds of thousands of workers, facing savage repression from employers, with many organizers beaten, jailed, and murdered. It also spread to other countries, including Chile, Australia, and South Africa. Although it is much smaller than it was, it still exists today, and its members are active in many projects. 🎧 **6, 9, 16, 19**

IWW protest in New York City, 1914 *(Courtesy of Wikimedia Commons)*

June 27, 1936 The Soviet Union reversed the 1920 Bolshevik "decree on the protection of women's health," which had legalized abortion and granted women numerous reproductive rights. The new law forbade all abortions, apart from cases where the life of the mother was at risk or where there was a serious hereditary disease. Both doctors providing abortions and women seeking them were criminalized by the new law. While arguing that the earlier decision to legalize abortions was right, the Communist Party claimed that "only under conditions of socialism . . . where woman is an equal member of society . . . is it possible seriously to organize the struggle against abortions by prohibitive laws as well as by other means."

Following a series of famines, the government was keen to increase population growth, and the party had begun to place more emphasis on the importance of the family unit. The ban remained in place until after the death of Joseph Stalin in 1953.

28 **June 28, 1969** The Stonewall riots began in the early hours. The New York Police Department, as part of its policy of closing gay bars, raided the Stonewall Inn, which had a substantial poor and working class LGBT+ clientele. However, for the first time in the city, rather than submitting to arrest, a crowd began to gather around the police. Inside the bar, gender nonconforming people, trans women, and lesbians began resisting invasive body searches. And outside a "butch" lesbian fought back against police when they arrested her, calling on the crowd that had formed to "do something." According to some eyewitnesses and her own account, this indi-

The Stonewall Inn, 1969 *(Courtesy of the New York Public Library/Wikimedia Commons)*

vidual was Stormé DeLarverie, a biracial lesbian and drag performer, who was known as a "guardian of lesbians" in the Village, although this is disputed by others who point out that the only police record for a lesbian arrested that night was of a Marilyn Fowler.

The crowd, which included a significant number of Black, Latine, and white LGBT+ patrons and passersby, then began to physically fight the

police, triggering riots that lasted for six days. Those involved in the disturbances included Marsha P. Johnson, John O'Brien, and popular folk musician Dave Van Ronk.

In the aftermath, participants and other LGBT+ radicals, including
O'Brien, as well as Martha Shelley, set up the Gay Liberation Front, which
revolutionized the gay rights movement. They organized anniversary protests on June 28 the following year in New York, Los Angeles, San Francisco,
and elsewhere. This became the annual Pride celebration that continues to
this day all over the world. 📻 **25–26**

June 28, 1976 Elena Quinteros, Uruguayan teacher, anarchist, and opponent of the military dictatorship, was kidnapped from the grounds of the
Venezuelan embassy, having escaped military custody. A member of the
Federación Anarquista Uruguaya (Uruguayan Anarchist Federation; FAU),
she escaped her army escort and jumped over the wall of the embassy,
asking for sanctuary. Embassy staff tried to help her, but soldiers grabbed
her and a tug-of-war ensued, in which her leg was broken. Finally, the troops
managed to drag her off and transport her to a military torture center, where
she was "disappeared." The Venezuelan ambassador demanded her return,
but it was refused, leading to a major diplomatic incident and resulting in
Venezuela cutting off diplomatic ties with Uruguay.

29 **June 29, 1892** Workers at the Homestead Carnegie steel plant in
Pennsylvania were locked out after refusing to accept new production demands. Andrew Carnegie was determined to break the Amalgamated
Association of Iron and Steel Workers (AA), in which skilled workers at the
plant were organized. His plant manager Henry Clay Frick locked out the
union workers, then fired them on July 2. The unskilled nonunion workers
then walked out in protest.

Frick brought in three hundred armed Pinkerton detectives to break
the strike. They killed nine strikers, but eventually a crowd of ten thousand
workers, many of them armed, repelled the attack. The workers held out
until November, when the governor brought in eight thousand militia to
escort strikebreakers into the plant. The dispute basically destroyed the
union and enabled Carnegie to implement pay cuts and longer working
hours.

June 29, 1936 One hundred Mexican American mineworkers, including Jesús
Pallares, were deported as "undesirable aliens" following a strike in Gallup,

New Mexico. Pallares had helped organize eight thousand miners into the Liga Obrera de Habla Espanola (League of Spanish-Speaking Workers).

In 1935, miners in Gallup, including members of the League of Spanish-Speaking Workers, went on strike. To break the strike, martial law was declared for six months. Hundreds of miners and their families were evicted from their homes, two miners were killed by police, and many others arrested, including Pallares, dozens of whom were later deported from the United States.

30 **June 30, 1977** A riot and mass strike took place against police repression in Faridabad, India. Thousands of factory workers downed tools, shutting down local industry to protest the death in police custody of Harnam Singh, a maintenance foreman at one of the leading companies of Faridabad. Violence had erupted in many parts of Faridabad, and vehicles proceeding to the capital were stoned, looted, and burned. According to coworkers, Singh had been tortured to death by the police on the factory premises in the presence of the managing director, a sub-inspector of police, and some other senior company officials.

June 30, 2013 Over two hundred workers at the Zhongji Pile factory in Huizhou, in China's Guangdong Province, surrounded the company's office, trapping five executives inside, demanding unpaid wages and protesting against proposed layoffs. After four days of the occupation, the bosses caved in, agreeing to back pay and backtracking on the layoffs.

JULY

1 **July 1, 1944** A general strike forced Guatemalan dictator Jorge Ubico to step down, and a social democratic government was established.

July 1, 2012 Thousands of people in the Chinese city of Shifang took part in often violent protests against the construction of a copper plant, which residents feared would cause environmental and health problems. Residents stormed government buildings, smashed windows and vehicles, and attacked police. The protest ended on July 3, when the government announced it had terminated the construction of the copper plant and released the vast majority of those arrested.

2 **July 2, 1902** The Philippine-American War officially ended with victory for the United States. The US had taken over the newly independent republic following a vicious campaign that left up to a quarter of a million civilians dead.

July 2, 1986 Workers in Chile began a two-day general strike to protest against the military rule of General Augusto Pinochet. The US- and UK-backed dictator tortured and murdered tens of thousands of workers and opponents during his rule.

Relatives of the "disappeared" demonstrate in front of the Chilean presidential palace
(Courtesy of the Museum of Memory and Human Rights/Wikimedia Commons)

3 **July 3, 1981** In Southall, an area of London with a large South Asian population, riots broke out when racist skinheads attending a gig at the Hambrough Tavern began attacking Asian people. They assaulted an Asian woman, smashed the windows of Asian shops, and looked for Asian homes to attack. Police failed to act, so the Asian community took the fight to the racists to defend themselves. They ended up having to battle both the fascists and the police. By the end of the night, the tavern had been burned to the ground, some sixty police officers had been injured, and thirty-three arrests had been made. 🎧 **33–34**

July 3, 1988 The US Navy shot down Iran Air Flight 655, a civilian passenger plane with 290 people on board, all of whom were killed. The victims included sixty-six children and an entire family of sixteen who were on their way to a wedding in Dubai. The incident took place during the war between Iran and Iraq, which was launched by Saddam Hussein, with US backing. It followed a catalogue of errors, including the naval officer in charge of firing the missile aboard the USS *Vincennes* hitting the wrong key no fewer than twenty-three times before eventually firing it. The US military then claimed that the *Vincennes* was rushing to defend a merchant vessel under attack from Iran, when an aircraft outside the commercial air corridor descended toward the ship in "attack mode," which was later proven false on all counts. The US military also tried to claim the ship was in international waters, with naval officials going as far as to delete an Iranian island from the map they showed Congress. In fact, the ship was in Iranian waters, in clear violation of international law. Meanwhile, the US media backed the official line, with the *New York Times* apportioning blame between the pilot Mohsen Rezaian and Iran.

In the aftermath, officers and crew of the *Vincennes* were welcomed home and decorated as heroes, receiving combat action ribbons and, in one case, a commendation medal for "heroic achievement" for "quickly and precisely complet[ing] the firing procedure." The captain was later awarded the Legion of Merit for "exceptionally meritorious conduct as a commanding officer." Donations from the public to construct a monument honoring the USS *Vincennes* in Indiana also shot up following the incident, and the monument was constructed and dedicated the following year.

4 **July 4, 1776** The Continental Congress of thirteen American colonies declared independence from Britain in the American Revolution. Despite the fiery rhetoric of the Declaration of Independence about all "men" being "equal" and possessing certain "inalienable rights," the new freedoms didn't apply to everyone. Chattel slavery continued for nearly another century, the almost total genocidal annihilation of Native Americans accelerated, and the new US government would invade, conquer, or overthrow elected governments in many other countries, just like the British before them.

July 4, 1998 Best friends Lin Newborn, twenty-four, an African American skinhead, and Daniel Shersty, twenty, a white US Air Force serviceman, both members of Anti-Racist Action, were murdered in the desert outside Las Vegas by a gang of white supremacists. One neo-Nazi was swiftly jailed, and others were convicted in 2012 for the murders.

Lin "Spit" Newborn, 1993 *(Courtesy of Wikimedia Commons)*

5 **July 5, 1888** Fourteen hundred women and girls working at the Bryant & May match factory in East London walked out on strike in solidarity with a worker who had been fired for criticizing the appalling conditions at the plant. Management quickly offered to reinstate the worker, but the strikers refused to return

Bryant & May strike committee, with local activists Herbert Burrows and Annie Besant (back center) *(Courtesy of Wikimedia Commons)*

to work until management agreed to a number of other concessions, including ending unfair wage deductions.

July 5, 1934 San Francisco's Bloody Thursday occurred when police killed two striking longshoremen and a bystander and hospitalized 115 people. Workers had been on strike against casual hiring methods on the docks. Within two weeks, workers across the city launched a general strike against the wishes of the unions, and while the American Federation of Labor (AFL) disowned them, effectively ending the strike, the longshoremen won the establishment of jointly operated hiring halls.

6 **July 6, 1934** Eight hundred workers from two plantations in Couva, Trinidad, demonstrated in front of the warden's office, complaining at the lack of work. Violence erupted when police attempted to keep protesters away from businesses and workers responded by looting. Unrest spread to other plantations. Two bosses were attacked, and one company headquarters stoned and set on fire. British colonial police arrested twelve demonstrators.

July 6, 1992 Pioneering Black trans activist and sex worker Marsha P. Johnson's body was found in the Hudson River. She is most famous for participating in the Stonewall rebellion, which sparked a global movement for LGBT+ liberation, but she also spent years doing radical organizing on the ground. She took part in the Gay Liberation Front and the demonstration on the anniversary of the beginning of the Stonewall riots, which became Pride. She also cofounded Street Transvestites Action Revolutionaries (STAR) with her friend, Latina trans activist Sylvia Rivera. STAR was a radical campaigning group that also provided housing and support for gay, gender nonconforming, and trans youth. Later she threw herself into AIDS activism, becoming an organizer in ACT UP. All the while, Johnson engaged in survival sex work and was constantly harassed by police, being arrested over one hundred times. Police ruled her death a suicide, despite a massive head wound. Friends and activists insisted that Johnson wasn't suicidal and highlighted evidence that she may have been murdered. In late 2012, the NYPD reopened the case as a possible homicide. It remains unsolved.

7 **July 7, 1912** The Grabow massacre took place in Louisiana, leaving four dead and fifty injured. During a strike by the Brotherhood of Timber Workers (BTW), part of the Industrial Workers of the World (IWW), a few dozen timber workers demonstrated outside the mill owned by the Galloway family in Grabow. When union organizer A.L. Emerson began speaking, a man emerged from the office and fired at him, clipping the brim of Emerson's hat. Then more shooting broke out, lasting fifteen minutes, during which some three hundred shots were fired.

While none of the bosses were charged, most of the strikers were arrested and tried on serious charges, including riot and murder. All of the workers were acquitted in a significant victory for the union. One of the union gunmen, Leather Britches Smith, was murdered by vigilantes later that year. 🎙 6

July 7, 1999 When one hundred workers found that their payment for the previous three weeks of work had not come through, three hundred construction workers picketed a building site in Central London, shutting work down. The strike saw British workers build solidarity with workmates from countries across Eastern and Western Europe, as they won back most of their unpaid wages.

8 **July 8, 1876** The Hamburg massacre began when an armed white mob—the Red Shirts—marched on a majority Black Republican district in Hamburg, South Carolina. In the small hours of the following morning, they killed six Black National Guard militiamen, murdering four of them after they had surrendered. It was part of a campaign by the Democrats to suppress African American voting and disrupt the Republican Party. It was successful. The Democrats managed to retake the state in the election later that year, then passed laws to establish single-party white supremacist rule, impose legal segregation (Jim Crow), and eventually disenfranchise African Americans with a new constitution in 1895.

July 8, 1968 The Dodge Revolutionary Union Movement (DRUM), a new group of Black workers, picketed out thousands of workers at the Detroit Dodge auto plant in opposition to the racial discrimination accommodated by the United Auto Workers union (UAW). 🎙 12

9 **July 9, 1919** Bartenders in Allentown, Pennsylvania, went on strike to impress on citizens the "horrors" of prohibition, which was due to be introduced. There was a working class movement of hundreds of thousands under the rubric "no beer, no work" that aimed to stop prohibition with strike action. However, this was the only actual strike that took place, as far as we have been able to determine.

July 9, 1959 The Wadi Salib riots were sparked in Haifa, Israel when police shot and wounded Yaakov Elkarif, a Mizrahi Jewish immigrant. Originally an affluent Palestinian neighborhood, it was largely destroyed in 1949 by the Israeli government, and the vast majority of the Arab population had been forced to flee. Poor Jewish people of North African and Middle Eastern origin were moved into the derelict and overcrowded homes and were told they would be temporary, until they could be relocated, but that never happened. The Ashkenazi Jewish establishment, which saw them as inferior, neglected them, leaving them in poverty, facing high levels of crime. On July 10, the day after the killing, years of simmering anger exploded. Local residents protested outside the police station, and eventually began fighting police, burning cars, and looting shops. The following day, rioting broke out in other cities with significant North African populations, including in Tiberias. At least one of the protest organizers, David Ben-Haroush, was subsequently imprisoned.

10 **July 10, 1914** Twenty-seven-year-old suffragette Rhoda Fleming leaped onto the footboard of the king and queen's limousine in Perth, Scotland, and tried to break its windows. The attempt was described in the press as "perhaps the most daring that has occurred in the history of the women's suffrage agitation."

July 10, 1985 The French intelligence service blew up the Greenpeace ship *Rainbow Warrior* at the Port of Auckland, in Aotearoa/New Zealand, killing Fernando Pereira, a photographer. The ship was headed to protest against French nuclear testing. France initially denied responsibility, but New Zealand police arrested two of its agents and charged them with murder. Eventually, they were sentenced to ten years in prison for manslaughter, but the French government won their freedom after just two years.

11 **July 11, 1917** In São Paulo, police beat to death José Martínez (referred to as Antonio Martínez in some sources), a twenty-one-year-old shoemaker who happened to be a bystander to a workers' demonstration against the high cost of living. Police then attacked his large funeral procession with swords. The working class responded with riots across the city, and the next day 12,500 people went on strike, joined by a further 5,000 the following day, the stoppage subsequently growing into a general strike. Workers only agreed to return to work for a widespread 10 percent pay increase.

July 11, 1937 Jack Shirai, a Japanese American cook who went to Spain to fight the fascists in the civil war was killed in combat. A volunteer in the American Abraham Lincoln Brigade, he was shot dead after volunteering to fetch supplies for his starving unit. He was buried that night beside Oliver Law, an African American volunteer.

Jack Shirai in Spain *(Courtesy of the Abraham Lincoln Brigade Archives)*

Deportation of striking miners from Bisbee, July 12, 1917 *(Courtesy of the Arizona Historical Society/Wikimedia Commons)*

12 **July 12, 1917** Over a thousand copper miners in the Industrial Workers of the World union (IWW) who were on strike were illegally deported by armed vigilantes from Bisbee, Arizona, to New Mexico. 🎙 **6**

July 12, 1921 The funeral of Tommaso Pesci, an innocent farmer who was murdered by fascists two days earlier, took place in Viterbo, Italy. His funeral procession was led by a column of the Arditi del Popolo, Italy's first militant anti-fascist group, which marched armed with knives, bayonets, and walking sticks. The killing prompted the first action of the Arditi outside Rome, during which they successfully prevented fascists from entering Viterbo for three days.

13 **July 13, 1948** Japan introduced the Eugenics Protection Act into law. The bill had been submitted by the Socialist Party and legalized abortion and some types of contraception, but its main provision was to greatly expand sterilizations of disabled people, to prevent the birth of supposedly "poor-quality" children.

Over the next half-century, nearly seventeen thousand people, mostly women and girls—some as young as nine—were forcibly sterilized. Another eight thousand were sterilized with "consent," although in reality they were probably pressured by authorities to agree. Many of those sterilized had been diagnosed with mental health problems or with things like "hereditary feeblemindedness." Nearly sixty thousand women had abortions because of illnesses that were allegedly "hereditary."

The law was only overturned in 1996, with paltry compensation paid to surviving victims in 2019. While more recently eugenics has been associated with the far right, in the past figures on the left had also advocated for it.

July 13, 1976 A team of Uruguayan and Argentinian soldiers kidnapped Uruguayan anarchist Sara Méndez and a friend. She woke up in a torture camp run by the US-backed dictatorship and was unable to track down her infant son, who had been taken from her and put up for adoption. They were not reunited until 2002.

14 **July 14, 1970** Puerto Rican activist group the Young Lords occupied Lincoln Hospital's major administrative building in response to New York City's indifference to the health needs of Puerto Ricans and African Americans in the South Bronx and the deplorable conditions of health care delivery at Lincoln Hospital.

The Young Lords' actions at Lincoln were an extension of the group's activism around issues of public health in East Harlem. Their health activism included the Garbage Offensive, protesting against irregular sanitation services; breakfast programs for poor children; the Lead Offensive, during which they conducted door-to-door medical home visits in collaboration with progressive nurses, medical technicians, and doctors to test local children for lead poisoning and adults for tuberculosis; and the takeover of a city-operated tuberculosis truck.

July 14, 2011 The Israeli tent protest movement began when Daphni Leef pitched a tent in central Tel Aviv after discovering that she could not afford a flat. Within twenty-four hours, dozens joined her, and over the subsequent two weeks a nationwide protest movement against housing prices, the high cost of living, and social inequality emerged. It was the largest predominantly Jewish protest movement in Israel's history, although some Arab communities also established protest camps. Israeli nationalism effectively dampened the movement, which was anxious to avoid any association with the "left," which one activist described as being "all but synonymous with 'traitors,'" and voiced support for the state in its war against Palestinians.

15 **July 15, 1971** A left-wing group called the United Red Army was formed in Japan, purporting to espouse the ideology of Chinese communist leader Mao Zedong. Its name turned out to be unintentionally ironic, as within a year fourteen of its twenty-nine members, considered not revolutionary enough, had been murdered in internal purges.

July 15, 2009 Construction workers in South Africa building stadiums for the 2010 World Cup won their strike for a pay increase. Seventy thousand workers had walked out more than a week earlier on indefinite strike for a 13 percent increase, claiming they would strike until 2011, if necessary. They settled for 12 percent.

16 **July 16, 1977** House worker Rita Ward began a lie-in at Northampton General Hospital, in England. In pain from gallstones, she had been waiting eighteen months for an operation and had been told she would need to wait another year, unless she could pay £500 (approximately US$875) for private treatment, in which case it could be done the following day. So Rita, with support from hospital workers, got into bed and refused to leave until she was treated. Hospital management caved in and operated on her a few days later, without delaying any other operations.

July 16, 1978 A mass anti-racist sit-down protest occurred on the corner of Brick Lane and Bethnal Green Road, in London's biggest Bengali community, in an attempt to prevent fascist National Front literature from being sold.

17 **July 17, 1936** A Spanish military uprising began in Morocco when right-wing generals declared war on the new republican government. In Barcelona, workers began to respond, with members of the Confederación Nacional del Trabajo (National Confederation of Labor; CNT) union seizing two hundred rifles from the holds of two ships docked in the harbor and distributing them to union activists.

Anti-fascist militia fighters in Spain, 1936 *(Courtesy of Wikimedia Commons)*

Two days later, workers across Spain took up arms and launched a far-reaching social revolution. The ensuing civil war pitted the working class against the Spanish capitalists, who were backed by Nazi Germany and fascist Italy.

In the revolutionary areas, anarchist and socialist workers and peasants took over workplaces and land and began to run them collectively.

At that point, the Western democracies, including Britain and France, abandoned the republic and enforced a blockade on Spain that stopped the flow of aid and weapons to the anti-fascists. Meanwhile, Italy and Germany openly flouted the ban, and the US oil giant Texaco supplied the nationalists with oil and other supplies without even demanding payment, while stopping any supplies to the republic.

Thousands of mostly working class people came from all over the world to aid the workers and peasants of Spain in their battle against the nationalists, but, ultimately, after nearly three years of bitter and bloody warfare, the nationalists, with their superior weaponry and equipment, were victorious. 🎧 **39–40**

July 17, 1978 The Hackney and Tower Hamlets Defense Committee organized a day-long strike against racist attacks, which brought the London Borough of Tower Hamlets to a standstill. They were joined by four hundred pupils from the predominantly British Asian Robert Montefiore School, who protested against the racist violence in and around their school.

18 **July 18, 1917** A furniture worker in Rio de Janeiro learned of a strike in São Paulo and walked off the job. Two of his colleagues joined him. By the afternoon, 150 workers had walked out, and, by the next day, workers at five factories were on strike, with the stoppage continuing to mushroom. On July 22, a general strike was called, demanding a maximum eight-hour workday and a 20 percent pay increase. Tens of thousands of metal and factory workers joined the strike, shutting down industry. The government declared martial law but failed to break the workers, and the employers settled the following month.

July 18, 1969 The Black Panthers held a common conference in Oakland, California, with the white anti-racist Young Patriots Organization and the Puerto Rican radical group the Young Lords.

The Young Patriots were a group of poor mostly Appalachian migrants in Chicago. Although they opposed racism, they originally sported the Confederate flag, which they believed was a symbol of rebellion. As they worked more with communities of color, the flag was abandoned as an irredeemable symbol of white supremacy.

Before he was assassinated by the police, leading Panther Fred Hampton played a key role in building links with the Young Patriots and other white working class youth.

19 **July 19, 1958** A key early successful sit-in protest of the US civil rights movement began in Wichita, Kansas. A group of Black students began to sit silently at the whites-only counter of the Dockum Drug Store to protest segregation. The aim was to prevent sales and inflict enough economic damage that segregation would be dropped. They faced repeated harassment by police and white racists, and they brought clubs, knives, and a gun to protect themselves, although they did not end up needing to use them. After twenty-three days, the owner caved in and desegregated his entire chain.

While the National Association for the Advancement of Colored People (NAACP) did not initially support the sit-in, after the success in Wichita, it adopted the tactic, which led to desegregation of lunch counters in a number of states.

July 19, 1984 The Dunnes Stores anti-apartheid strike began in Dublin, Ireland. Shopworker Mary Manning refused to check out a customer's South African fruit, as members of her union, the Irish Distributive and Administrative Union (IDATU), had voted to not handle South African goods. Manning was suspended, and she and eleven of her colleagues went on strike in protest. The stoppage went on for an incredible three years, ending when the Irish government introduced a ban on South African products.

20 **July 20, 1943** Two Jewish members of the Waldkommando work unit at the Sobibor extermination camp attacked their Ukrainian guard and encouraged other members of the unit to escape. The Waldkommando was composed of twenty Polish and twenty Dutch Jews, and it supplied wood for the crematorium by cutting down trees and digging out the stumps. Szlomo Podchlebnik and Josef Kopf initiated the breakout with a knife Podchlebnik had in his boot. Several Polish prisoners—Podchlebnik, Kopf, Zyndel Honigman, Chaim Korenfeld, Abram Wang, and Aron Licht—were able to successfully escape. Kopf and Licht were murdered by Polish anti-Semites in separate incidents after their escape. The others survived the war.

After the breakout, only Dutch Jews who were unable to speak Polish and did not know the countryside were allocated to the Waldkommando at the camp.

July 20, 1979 Native American political prisoner Leonard Peltier escaped from Lompoc Federal Correctional Institution, in California, with two other detainees, one of whom, Bobby Gene Garcia, was shot to death by a guard. Peltier, a leading member of the American Indian Movement, had been sentenced to two consecutive

Leonard Peltier wanted poster
(Courtesy of the Federal Bureau of Investigation/Wikimedia Commons)

life sentences for the deaths of two Federal Bureau of Investigation (FBI) agents. He had been warned by fellow Native American prisoner Standing Deer (aka Robert Wilson) that there was a contract on his life in the prison.

Peltier's original trial was riddled with inconsistencies and distortions. For example, an FBI ballistics expert claimed during the trial that a shell case found near the bodies matched Peltier's rifle, but his report stating that the cartridge did not match was withheld from the jury. And three witnesses who placed Peltier near the scene of the crime later recanted, stating that the FBI had tied them to chairs and coerced their testimony. The legal misconduct was so severe that Peltier has received support from individuals and groups as diverse as Nelson Mandela, Archbishop Desmond Tutu, the European Parliament, and the United Nations Commissioner for Human Rights.

Peltier was recaptured three days later.

21 **July 21, 1921** Anti-fascists in Sarzana, Italy, fought back against six hundred fascists who had gathered in the town to demand the release of a fascist squad who had been arrested for an attack three days prior. While negotiations between officials and the fascists was ongoing, some of the fascists opened fire, killing a soldier and injuring a policeman. The military returned fire, and then the local population gave chase after the fleeing fascists. Local people, many of them organized in the anti-fascist Arditi del Popolo, pursued the fascists into the surrounding countryside, killing eighteen and wounding thirty. It was the first major setback suffered by the growing and violent fascist movement in the country.

July 21, 1945 Members of the Irish Women Workers' Union (IWWU) staged a laundry strike that affected many of Dublin's hotels, demanding a second week of paid holiday. Hospital laundry workers were exempt from the strike action. The strike lasted fourteen weeks and ended in victory for the women. The following year the government conceded to two-week paid holidays for all workers.

22 **July 22, 1920** Government forces raided the Santiago headquarters of the Industrial Workers of the World union (IWW). It was trying to break a three-month long IWW strike of maritime workers aimed at preventing the export of cereals during a domestic famine. A general campaign of repression against anarchists in Chile followed, which did not, however, stop the IWW from organizing a further maritime strike in 1923.

July 22, 2005 Civil servants in the Kingdom of Tonga went on strike for a 60 to 90 percent pay increase. The strike effectively brought the government to a standstill and grew to include many other public sector employees, ending up being the most significant challenge to the island's monarchy in its history. The striking workers won their pay increase and forced the government to begin reforming itself.

23 **July 23, 1918** The Japanese rice riots against high prices began, a revolt up to then unparalleled in the country's history in terms of scope, size, and violence. It eventually led to the fall of Prime Minister Terauchi Masatake's government.

July 23, 1967 One of the biggest rebellions in US history occurred in Detroit, following a police raid on a bar in a poor African American majority area in the early hours of the morning. Black and white residents fought police in the streets and looted goods, while snipers took potshots at officers from windows. It ended with over forty deaths, more than seven thousand arrests, and over two thousand buildings destroyed. 🔊 **12**

24 **July 24, 1777** A crowd of working class women in Boston seized coffee from a seller named Thomas Boylston. It was one of dozens of food riots that occurred during the American Revolution, primarily in the North but also in Maryland and possibly Virginia. Around a third of them were organized by women.

July 24, 2009 Thirty thousand steel workers in China rioted and beat their chief executive to death when they heard their plant was being privatized. The sale was subsequently scrapped.

25 **July 25, 1867** German communist Karl Marx wrote the preface to the first German edition of his masterwork, *Das Kapital* (Capital). It remains the most decisive and insightful critique of the capitalist system ever written. While the first three chapters can be slow going, we highly recommend reading the work at some point.

July 25, 1972 The US government admitted its role in the Tuskegee syphilis experiment: a horrific forty-year study of poor Black agricultural workers in Alabama who had syphilis but were not informed. Numerous people died as a result, and women and children were infected with the disease. The government owned up following leaks to the media about the program. The resulting public outrage forced the introduction of federal regulation to protect human subjects in medical trials.

A doctor drawing blood from a patient as part of the study, 1932 *(Courtesy of the National Archives Atlanta/Wikimedia Commons)*

26 **July 26, 1937** British authorities in Barbados secretly deported Clement Payne, a worker who was trying to start a trade union, to Trinidad, where police were waiting to arrest him for possessing prohibited literature. He was originally charged with knowingly making a false declaration for stating he had been born in Barbados, whereas, unknown to him, he had actually been born in Trinidad of Barbadian parents. He appealed his conviction, and, although his appeal was successful, he was expelled from the island. In response, workers rioted and strikes spread for several days.

July 26, 1950 The No Gun Ri massacre took place, with US ground troops murdering one hundred to three hundred South Korean civilians, in one of the biggest mass killings by American soldiers.

27 **July 27, 1816** A fort on the Apalachicola River in Florida was firebombed by the US Army. The fort had provided home and safety to more than three hundred Black and Choctaw families. This marked the beginning of the Seminole Wars and the eventual US conquest of Florida.

July 27, 1933 Bus drivers in Havana went on strike, and other drivers soon walked out in sympathy. This was the start of the unrest that culminated in a general strike of Cuban workers and students that paralyzed the nation and forced the brutal dictator Gerardo Machado from power.

Machado made a last-minute deal with trade union leaders and the central committee of the Cuban Communist Party, claiming that they would be legalized and given government support if they ended the strike, but the agreement was rejected by workers, and the strike continued, even after police killed twenty demonstrators. On August 9, the military decided to stop supporting Machado, and two days later his government collapsed.

28 **July 28, 1915** The United States invaded Haiti, crushing opposition and setting up a dictatorship that governed the country for the next two decades.

July 28, 1932 When World War I veterans marched demanding the wartime bonuses they had been promised, the US government sent the army with tanks, fixed bayonets, teargas, and sabers to attack them and their families, killing three.

The bonus payments were due to be paid in 1945, but when the Great Depression hit, leaving many veterans destitute, they decided to demand earlier payment. Up to twenty-five thousand vets, Black and white, formed a "Bonus Army" and set up camp in Washington, DC. Major George Patton, whose life had been saved by one of the protesters, advised his troops to bayonet and kill a large number of protesters as "an object lesson." Generals Douglas MacArthur and Dwight D. Eisenhower were the other officers in charge of this operation, which killed two veterans and an eleven-week-old baby, partially blinded an eight-year-old boy, and injured a thousand others.

29 **July 29, 1910** The predominantly African American citizens of Slocum, Texas, were massacred in an act of terror designed to preserve economic white supremacy. Hundreds of armed white racists attacked the town, gunning down Black people as they hid in their homes, worked, or tried to flee. Official accounts range from eight and twenty-five victims, but many believe the figure to be much higher. After the massacre and the exodus of Black residents, the racists stole their homes and property. The town remains overwhelmingly white to this day. None of the perpetrators were punished and none of the victims compensated.

July 29, 1962 When British fascist aristocrat Oswald Mosley attempted to march through Manchester, he was attacked and knocked to the ground by anti-fascists. He had to be rescued and escorted away by 250 police, who were unable to prevent the fascist from being pelted with tomatoes, eggs, coins, and stones. Following the march, Mosley attempted to speak, but he was drowned out by a crowd of five thousand anti-fascists, forcing police to end the meeting after just seven minutes. Clashes between local residents and blackshirts continued for some time, with the police arresting forty-seven people. 🔊 **35–37**

30 **July 30, 1766** Silver miners in Real del Monte, Mexico, went on strike against a 25 percent pay cut in the first recorded strike against an employer in North American history. They faced down repression from the Spanish colonial bosses' private army and held out until September, when the employers caved in.

July 30, 1913 Twenty thousand textile workers in Barcelona, mostly women and children, went on strike against low wages and long hours. Women strikers cut the hair of scabs, marking them as traitors. The strike continued until September 15, when the governor introduced a maximum sixty-hour workweek.

31 **July 31, 1922** Workers in Italy declared an indefinite general strike against fascism. However, the nationalist unions did not join it, and the middle class and capitalists supported the fascists breaking the strike. After two days, the superior military organization of the fascists broke the strike across most of Italy, with workers in Bari and Parma holding out until August 7.

July 31, 1945 The UK's newly elected Labour government sent six hundred conscript troops into the Surrey docks in London to try to break a go-slow of dockworkers fighting for better pay. A *Telegraph* journalist described the go-slow:

> In everything they did the men were unhurried in a way that looked deliberate. There was evidence that their actions were planned. True, the cranes were working and goods were passing from the dockside to the ship, but there was a leisureliness about the proceedings that made everything seem half-hearted. I soon learned the reason. At the moment bags of sugar were going aboard in slings. But it was pointed out that the slings were carrying only 4 at a time instead of the normal 12.

AUGUST

1 **August 1, 1917** Frank Little, a biracial Cherokee organizer for the Industrial Workers of the World union (IWW), was brutally murdered during a miners' strike in Butte, Montana. Little had travelled to Montana from Arizona to support a strike of seventeen thousand copper miners against the mine owners, including the Anaconda mining company. After threats were published in the local press, six masked men abducted Little from

Frank Little *(Courtesy of Wikimedia Commons)*

his boarding house, tied and dragged him behind their car, then beat him and hanged him from a railway bridge. Most historians believe Anaconda hired his killers. Little's funeral was attended by 6,800 people. 🎙 6

August 1, 1938 The event known as the Hilo massacre took place in Hawaii when police opened fire at an unarmed group of striking dockworkers. Longshoremen in different unions and of many different ethnicities had united and staged a series of walkouts for equal pay with dockworkers on the West Coast of the US. On August 1, two hundred workers gathered to protest against the arrival of a steamship. Police attacked and started shooting, wounding a quarter of those present.

2 **August 2, 1944** Some four thousand Roma and Sinti people in the Auschwitz-Birkenau concentration camp resisted being taken to the gas chambers. The SS swarmed into the Roma camp, but prisoners, who had armed themselves with sticks and crowbars and barricaded themselves indoors, fought the Nazis tooth and nail. A non-Roma prisoner who survived said that everyone was fighting, and that "women [were] the fiercest in their fight," as they were "younger and stronger" than the other detainees and were "protecting their children." Inevitably, they were overcome and murdered in the gas chambers. This act of resistance was initially reported to have taken place on May 16 that year, and that date has been adopted as the annual Romani Resistance Day.

August 2, 1980 A timebomb exploded in a waiting room in the Bologna train station, killing eighty-five people and injuring over two hundred. Carried out by neo-fascists, it is one of the worst terrorist attacks in European history, and was undertaken during the *strategia della tensione* (strategy of tension): a state

Bologna train station immediately after the bombing *(Courtesy of Wikimedia Commons)*

security operation in which attacks were carried out by the far right or security services and blamed on anarchists and communists.

3 **August 3, 1492** Columbus set sail from Palos, Spain, for the "Indies," with disastrous consequences for the people who already lived there. There are popular myths that he discovered the United States and proved the earth was round. However, he never set foot in what is now the mainland US, and the fact that the earth was a sphere had been known since the days of the ancient Greeks. Columbus himself believed the earth to be pear-shaped. He landed in what is now known as the Bahamas, where he and his crew were greeted by the Indigenous Taíno people, who lived in village communes and held all property in common.

Columbus began immediately imprisoning and murdering the Indigenous people and enslaving them in the search for gold. The Taíno began fighting back but couldn't defeat the Spanish, with their advanced weaponry and armor, so many began to kill themselves and their children to avoid a worse fate. Within just two years, half of the 250,000 Indigenous people on nearby Haiti were dead. More colonizers came, and the genocide of the native population continued across the Caribbean and the Americas. Despite all of this, today, in many places across the region, Indigenous communities survive and continue to resist.

August 3, 1929 A children's summer camp run by socialists just outside Los Angeles was raided, and six mostly young women and one man were arrested. The raid was conducted by members of the American Legion, led by the district attorney. Nineteen-year-old communist Yetta Stromberg, one of those arrested, was later convicted and jailed, along with five other women, for having a red flag. Stromberg was sentenced to one to ten years in prison, with the other defendants receiving sentences ranging from six months to five years in San Quentin State Prison. The one man who was convicted, World War I veteran Isadore Berkowitz, hanged himself after the verdict.

California was one of twenty-four states that banned the flying of red socialist or black anarchist flags in 1919: a crime often punishable by a sentence of ten years or more. Stromberg eventually took her case to the Supreme Court, and, in 1931, the court overturned the ban as a violation of the First Amendment, which guaranteed the right to free speech.

4 **August 4, 2011** Violent clashes erupted between protesters and security forces in a significant escalation of a popular movement demanding education reform in Chile. Protests had begun in May, primarily demanding better state support for education and improved schools to enable more poorer Chileans to access higher education and to meet the needs of Indigenous Mapuche students.

On August 4, striking pupils attempting to march on the presidential palace in the capital Santiago were attacked by riot police. In response, rioting broke out around the city, with road blockades and widespread violence, including a retail outlet, La Polar, which charged excessive interest rates, being set on fire.

By the end of the day, 874 people had been arrested. Nonetheless, protests escalated significantly over the coming months, and while the government did offer to make certain concessions, like bringing in low-interest student loans, discontent continued.

August 4, 2011 Mark Duggan, a twenty-nine-year-old Black father of six, was shot and killed by the London Metropolitan Police. At the time of the incident, the Independent Police Complaints Commission (IPCC), the supposedly independent body tasked with investigating police misconduct, claimed that Duggan had opened fire on a police officer, who was only saved by the bullet hitting his police radio. It later became clear that the IPCC was lying, that Duggan never fired, and that the police officer was shot by one of his colleagues. In spite of this, the IPCC was still put in charge of investigating Duggan's death. In response to the killing, days of rioting broke out across England, in a British precursor to the Black Lives Matter movement.

5 **August 5, 1964** The US began bombing North Vietnam in Operation Pierce Arrow, after "intelligence" reported a North Vietnamese attack on US ships. These reports later turned out to be false.

Over the course of the Vietnam War, US forces would drop hundreds of millions of bombs on Vietnam, Cambodia, and Laos, killing huge numbers of people. Unexploded ordnance continues to kill and maim people in the region every year. 🎧 **14**

August 5, 1981 After just two days on strike, 11,345 federal air traffic controllers were fired by US president Ronald Reagan, himself a former union leader, for refusing his order to return to work. The workers were banned from federal service for life (although this was lifted over a decade later), their union was legally dissolved later in October, and military air traffic controllers were used as replacements until new hires could be trained.

6 **August 6, 1945** The US dropped an atomic bomb on Hiroshima, slaughtering tens of thousands of civilians, despite officials believing that Japan was about to surrender. Numerous senior US military officials confirmed that the bombing was unnecessary to defeat Japan. However, at the end of World War II, the US wanted to issue a warning to its Eastern Bloc "allies."

Mushroom cloud over Hiroshima *(Courtesy of US 509th Operations Group/Wikimedia Commons)*

General Dwight D. Eisenhower explained: "Japan was at the moment seeking some way to surrender with minimum loss of 'face.' It wasn't necessary to hit them with that awful thing." For his part, Admiral William D. Leahy, former chair of the Joint Chiefs of Staff, stated, "The use of this barbarous weapon at Hiroshima and Nagasaki was of no material assistance in our war against Japan. The Japanese were already defeated and ready to surrender. My own feeling was that in being the first to use it, we had adopted an ethical standard common to the barbarians of the Dark Ages. I was taught not to make war in that fashion, and wars cannot be won by destroying women and children." And the US Strategic Bombing Survey determined that "Japan would have surrendered even if the atomic bombs had not been dropped, even if Russia had not entered the war, and even if no invasion had been planned or contemplated."

August 6, 1970 Some three hundred members of the Youth International Party, or Yippies—countercultural radical youth—invaded Disneyland, protesting against the Vietnam War and calling for the liberation of Minnie Mouse from patriarchal captivity. Disney brought in extra security and 150 armed riot police in preparation for the event: a theatrical "convention." The youth engaged in a few provocative actions, including commandeering a raft to invade Fort Wilderness, openly smoking pot, snake dancing down Main Street, U.S.A., and demonstrating outside the Bank of America branch in the park, before some of them were arrested and the rest expelled from the park. 🎧 **14**

7 **August 7, 1842** A mass meeting of eighteen thousand workers organized by the Chartist movement took place in the UK. They decided to call a general strike beginning the following day, demanding universal male suffrage.

A Chartist mass meeting, 1848 *(Photo by William Edward Kilburn, courtesy of Wikimedia Commons)*

August 7, 1900 The first issue of Mexican radical newspaper *Regeneración*, cofounded by Ricardo Flores Magón, was published. Despite being frequently suppressed in Mexico and the US, the paper would exist in numerous different incarnations over the next two decades and would become quite influential during the Mexican Revolution.

8 **August 8, 1845** Britain's Parliament passed an Enclosure Act, taking away common land and appointing enclosure commissioners, who could enclose more land without submitting a request to Parliament. From the seventeenth to twentieth century, the British government passed

Issue of *Regeneración*, **1910** *(Courtesy of Wikimedia Commons)*

over five thousand Enclosure Acts, enclosing 6.8 million acres of common land that the public previously had the right to use.

Often military force was used to crush any resistance. The enclosures were a vital part of the development of capitalism, as they created a whole class of landless people who had no way of surviving other than by selling their labor power—i.e., the working class.

August 8, 1936 The French government closed the border with revolutionary Spain, forcing people who wanted to volunteer to fight against the fascists to cross the Pyrenees mountains on foot. The nationalists, on the other hand, had no problem shipping in fascist volunteers from around Europe, as well as troops from Italy and Nazi Germany. Despite this, tens of thousands of

African American volunteers Edward Johnson and Claude Pringle in Spain *(Photo courtesy of Kevin Buyers/Abraham Lincoln Brigade Archives)*

working class people from all around the world came to join the Spanish workers' and peasants' struggle against fascism, many of them joining the International Brigades.

9 **August 9, 1956** Twenty thousand women in Pretoria, South Africa, marched against pass laws: apartheid laws curtailing freedom of movement for Black and Indian people. The demonstration, organized by the Federation of South African Women (FEDSAW) delivered a petition against the laws with one hundred thousand signatures, and the participants sang "*Wathint'Abafazi Wathint'imbokodo*," meaning, "Now that you have touched the women, you have struck a rock." The protest kickstarted a wave of over two years of civil disobedience across the country, during which thousands of women were arrested, before the leadership of the African National Congress panicked and called it off. Today, August 9 is commemorated in South Africa as Women's Day.

August 9, 1970 One hundred fifty people, including the British Black Panthers, marched on local police stations to demand an end to police raids on the Mangrove Caribbean restaurant in Notting Hill. Nine people, including writer Darcus Howe, were arrested

Protest against the Mangrove restaurant raids *(Courtesy of the National Archives catalogue reference MEPO 31/21 [A22])*

and charged with conspiracy to incite a riot. All were later acquitted. Home Office documents later revealed the raids were part of a plot to destroy the emerging Black power movement in the UK.

10 **August 10, 1956** Working with the Union Française Nord-Africaine (UFNA) terrorist group, André Achiary, a former French military intelligence officer, planted a bomb in the Casbah of Algiers, which exploded killing seventy-three people. The attack was part of a brutal counterinsurgency campaign waged by France against the Algerian independence movement.

August 10, 2005 The Gate Gourmet dispute began in London. British Airways had outsourced its airline meal production to Gate Gourmet, staffed primarily by Asian women workers. The company cut wages, and working conditions worsened. Planning on further undermining working conditions, the company brought in hundreds of temporary agency workers to do the work of the permanent employees.

Seeing agency workers in their usual posts, the workers assembled in their canteen to discuss and protest against what was happening. Gate Gourmet responded by firing more than seven hundred of the workers. In a gesture of solidarity unusual in these times, British Airways baggage handlers walked out on a wildcat sympathy strike, shutting Heathrow Airport completely for forty-eight hours. But their union, the Transport and General Workers' Union (TGWU), ordered them back to work.

Although the fired workers set up picket lines, TGWU officials reached an agreement with bosses for some of the workers to be reinstated with terms and working conditions that were worse than those the workers had opposed in the first place. Many of the workers fought on until April of the following year, but the union refused to make their action official, and they were defeated.

11 **August 11, 1965** After an altercation during the arrest of a young Black motorist by Los Angeles police officers, LA's Watts neighborhood exploded into six days of rioting, with mass looting and anti-police violence. This rebellion played a role in shifting elements of the civil rights movement away from a commitment to pacifism.

August 11, 1984 During the great miners' strike, as many as twenty-five thousand women marched in London against pit closures. Miners' wives and others set up Women Against Pit Closures (WAPC), which played a crucial role in helping the miners stay out for as long as they did. 🎙 **13**

12 **August 12, 1937** One hundred forty-four socialists, communists, and anarchists were executed en masse at the Tobolsk prison in the Soviet Union. By the end of the following year, 2,500 people had been shot at the prison. The killings occurred during the purge trials of the late 1930s, in which many critics or potential critics of the government were executed or jailed, including many of the Bolsheviks who took part in the 1917 revolution.

August 12, 2017 Thirty-two-year-old anti-racist Heather Heyer was killed and dozens injured in a white supremacist terrorist attack in Charlottesville, Virginia. Heather was one of thousands of people protesting against a Unite the Right rally of neo-Nazis, Ku Klux Klan activists, and other white nationalists and anti-Semites, when she was hit by a car deliberately driven at high speed into the crowd by twenty-year-old neo-Nazi James Alex Fields

Jr., who was pictured at the earlier Unite the Right protest holding a shield emblazoned with the logo of Vanguard America, a far-right group.

Elsewhere in the city, another group of fascists attacked and viciously beat DeAndre Harris, a young African American education worker, leaving him with a number of injuries, including a spinal injury. President Donald Trump said some of the neo-Nazi demonstrators were "very fine people."

13 **August 13, 1973** Five Black pro-independence activists were sentenced to eight consecutive life sentences in the US Virgin Islands.

After the killing of eight American tourists on the Rockefeller-owned Fountain Valley golf course, US colonial authorities rounded up dozens of Black people and viciously tortured five of them in an attempt to extract confessions.

Although the jury was deadlocked following the trial, nine jurors testified that during deliberation they were threatened with FBI investigations of themselves and family members. The judge, formerly the Rockefeller family's private attorney and the lawyer for the golf course, refused to declare a mistrial, compelling the jurors to deliver guilty verdicts.

One of those convicted, Ishmael LaBeet, later hijacked a plane while being transferred to a different prison and flew it to Cuba. He was jailed for a period but is now free.

August 13, 1977 In what would come to be known as the Battle of Lewisham, South London residents and anti-fascists staged running battles with police and National Front members to stop a fascist demonstration.

14 **August 14, 1889** The great London dock strike began when workers at West India Dock walked out and called on others to join them. Within two weeks, 130,000 were out, and dockers' wives organized a rent strike for the duration of the stoppage. Other workers, Jewish tailors among them, walked out with their own demands.

Mass meeting of strikers (*Courtesy of Wikimedia Commons*)

Australian dockers donated money to support their British colleagues, and after four weeks the employers caved in and agreed to nearly all the workers' demands.

The men had been inspired by the strike of "match girls" at Bryant & May the previous year. The dispute marked a turning point in British working class history, as disorganized casual workers like the dockers were inspired to organize themselves and start to win.

August 14, 1943 Vietnamese revolutionary Nguyễn An Ninh died in prison after being jailed for promoting a working class and peasant revolt against the French colonial regime. He had been jailed by the French on four previous occasions, but his final sentence of five years in prison and ten years of exile was effectively a death sentence.

Nguyễn An Ninh *(Courtesy of Wikimedia Commons)*

15 **August 15, 1947** India became independent from British rule. While the standard narrative is that the movement for independence was a peaceful one led by Mohandas Gandhi, the reality is very different. There had been decades of often intensely violent struggle against British occupation involving mutinies, uprisings, riots, assassinations, and bomb attacks before the colonial power agreed to withdraw.

In addition to leaving India, Britain divided the country into two separate states: India, with a majority Hindu population, and Pakistan, with a majority Muslim population. Arbitrary lines drawn on a map by a British official in secret caused panic and confusion. The conflict that would result left up to sixteen million people displaced, between two hundred thousand and two million dead, and up to one hundred thousand women abducted and/or raped.

August 15, 1961 A local group of the National Association for the Advancement of Colored People (NAACP) in Monroe, North Carolina, presented a ten-point program for racial equality to the town aldermen.

Faced with massive racist violence occurring with police collusion, many Black residents took up arms to defend themselves. One of them was Marine Corps veteran and local NAACP chapter head Robert F. Williams, who was an advocate for self-defense against white racists. Williams set up a local National Rifle Association club called the Black Armed Guard, which defended the local Black community from Ku Klux Klan attacks. He was eventually falsely accused of kidnapping by the FBI, which forced him and his wife Mabel to flee to Cuba, in 1961. In Cuba, he hosted a radical radio show broadcast to African Americans in the US South. In 1965, he and his wife relocated again, this time to China.

He returned to the US in 1969 and was promptly arrested, but in 1975 all charges against him were dropped.

Robert F. Williams wanted poster (Courtesy of the Federal Bureau of Investigation/Wikimedia Commons)

When he died in 1996, legendary civil rights activist Rosa Parks delivered the eulogy at his funeral, where she paid testament to "his courage and . . . his commitment to freedom," adding, "What he did should go down in history and never be forgotten."

16 **August 16, 1819** The Peterloo massacre took place, with British cavalry charging into a crowd of between sixty and eighty thousand working class people gathered in Saint Peter's Fields, in Manchester, to demand the right to vote. Fifteen people were killed and up to seven hundred injured, with women protesters who were dressed in white being particularly targeted. In the aftermath of the killings, Percy Bysshe Shelley penned one of his most powerful poems, "The Mask of Anarchy," which ends with this stirring call to arms:

> Rise like Lions after slumber
> In unvanquishable number—
> Shake your chains to earth like dew
> Which in sleep had fallen on you—
> Ye are many—they are few.

 15

August 16, 2012 Police in South Africa massacred thirty-four miners who were on a wildcat strike fighting for a pay increase at the Marikana mine operated by the British platinum company Lonmin. Seventy-eight others were injured in a violent attack by security forces, which the African National Congress government falsely claimed was an act of self-defense on the part of the police. It was the worst violence by security forces in the country since the days of apartheid. A few days prior, officials in the National Union of Mineworkers (NUM) had opened fire on the striking workers—mostly their own members—leaving two critically injured.

Sculpture commemorating the 1795 slave revolt in Curaçao *(Photo by Charles Hoffman, CC by SA 2.0 https://www.flickr.com/photos/23088289@N02/4383339615)*

17 **August 17, 1795** A group of around forty enslaved Black people in the Dutch colony of Curaçao rebelled and kickstarted a slave revolt on the island. They informed their "owner" they would no longer be his slaves, then they left and began freeing other enslaved people and gathering weapons. The rebellion lasted just over a month before the leaders were captured and killed. Nonetheless, it won new rights for the enslaved.

August 17, 1987 Workers in South Korea occupied factories and the shipyard of the Hyundai Corporation in the city of Ulsan. Meanwhile, upwards of three hundred thousand workers battled riot police in the city, in one of the biggest confrontations to date between workers and the US-backed dictatorship. The strikes spread, and the Great Workers' Struggle, as the movement would come to be known, would, at its height, involve around 1.2 million workers—one-third of the regular workforce—with 3,749 strikes taking place by the end of the year.

18 **August 18, 1812** Food riots, primarily led by women, broke out in Leeds and Sheffield, England. In Leeds, the local paper described the group of women and boys who were seizing corn and wheat and assaulting sellers as being "dignified with the title of Lady Ludd." In Sheffield flour dealers were forced to reduce their prices to three shillings per stone.

August 18, 1823 The Demerara slave revolt in the British colony of Demerara-Essequibo, present-day Guyana, saw over ten thousand enslaved, mainly Creole people, go from plantation to plantation stealing weapons and locking up their masters, even putting some of them in stocks. The rebellion was crushed by colonial troops and an armed civilian militia. Despite the fact that white prisoners reported that they had been treated humanely, hundreds of the participants were hunted down and put to death in the aftermath of the rebellion, with others sentenced to one thousand lashes.

Word of the revolt spread across the Caribbean and back to England, where it spurred the abolitionist movement. Following an even bigger rebellion in Jamaica, slavery was largely abolished in the British Caribbean over the following decade.

19 **August 19, 1936** The gay socialist poet Federico García Lorca was taken from his jail cell and executed on the order of General Franco's military authorities. The Spanish Civil War had broken out a month previously, and his sympathies were clear: "I will always be on the side of those who have nothing and who are not even allowed to enjoy the nothing they have in peace." To date, his remains have not been found. 🔊 **39–40**

Federico García Lorca, 1919 (Courtesy of the Colección Fundación Federico García Lorca/ Wikimedia Commons)

August 19, 1953 Prime Minister Mohammad Mosaddegh of Iran was overthrown in a coup organized by the CIA on behalf of the British and American governments. Mosaddegh's government had instituted a number of social reforms in the country, including unemployment benefits, compensation for injured workers, and the abolition of forced labor in the countryside. He planned to nationalize the British-owned oil fields to fund things like rural housing, public baths, and pest control, so the British intelligence agency MI6 asked the CIA to remove him.

20 **August 20, 1948** Workers for the African Wharfage Company in Zanzibar City, present-day Tanzania, went on strike for higher wages. Intimidation by the British colonial authorities won the strike the sympathy of many other workers on the island. A general strike developed that shut down the city and much of the island's economy. The strike lasted until September 13, when the company gave in on wage increases and improved working conditions.

August 20, 1976 The Grunwick strike began in North West London when Devshi Bhudia was dismissed from his job at a photo processing plant for working too slowly, and three colleagues walked out in his support. Three days later, the predominantly East African Asian women workers began picketing in a dispute that would last nearly two years. Although it would ultimately end in defeat, it was a key event in the British working class movement. The incredible fight put up by the workers, as well as the solidarity received from around Britain, pushed the predominantly white trade union organizations to see Asian and migrant workers as fellow workers they should organize alongside rather than as competitors for jobs. 🎙 1

21 **August 21, 1831** The Nat Turner rebellion threw Southern enslavers into a panic, as around seventy enslaved people rose up in Southampton County, Virginia. Turner, who was literate and deeply religious, began the rebellion with a few trusted colleagues who travelled from plantation to plantation, freeing the enslaved people and killing all of the whites they came across. The rebellion was suppressed by US troops within a few days. Although Turner managed to evade capture for several weeks, when he was arrested he was sentenced to the medieval punishment of being hanged and drawn and quartered.

In the aftermath of the uprising, dozens of enslaved people, as well as free African Americans, were murdered by white racist mobs seeking vengeance. Many Southern slave states introduced new laws banning teaching enslaved people to read and further restricting their freedoms.

August 21, 1981 One hundred and forty mostly women workers at the Lee Jeans factory in Greenock, Scotland, returned to work after a seven-month occupation, having blocked the closure of the plant and secured their jobs.

22 **August 22, 1943** The *Statesman* magazine published the photograph at right
of starving people during the Bengal famine
in British colonial India during World War II.
The governor of Bengal had ordered the
removal or destruction of rice across much of
Bengal in 1942 to prevent it getting into enemy
hands, also confiscating forty-six thousand
boats from local people and devastating the

**Dead or dying children in
Calcutta, 1943** *(Courtesy of the
Statesman/Wikimedia Commons)*

fishing industry. Authorities then began diverting food from rural areas,
where there were already shortages, to people deemed a "priority," namely
wealthier and better-educated people and those working in war industries
and the civil service.

Flooding damaged farmland, putting food supplies at risk. The government of British prime minister Winston Churchill did not, however, act on
the warnings it received. When the famine began, instead of providing relief,
the government forbade the colony from using its own financial reserves
or ships to import food and continued to export thousands of tons of rice
to Europe, while putting excess food from elsewhere in the British Empire
into storage.

In all, two to four million people died, in what most historians consider an entirely human-caused famine. India had previously suffered
much bigger reductions in food supply without mass deaths—in 1873–1874,
for example. But Winston Churchill was a white supremacist and an anti-
Semite, who cared nothing for the local population. He believed that "the
starvation of anyhow underfed Bengalis is less serious than that of sturdy
Greeks," and, during the famine, he proudly exclaimed, "I hate Indians. They
are a beastly people with a beastly religion."

August 22, 1947 Chege Kibachia, leader of the African Workers Federation,
was arrested in Nakuru, Kenya, by British colonial police amid strikes and
working class protests against a racist system of identity cards. Five days
later, labor leader Makhan Singh was arrested as well. Meanwhile, the president, independence leader Jomo Kenyatta, worked with the British Labour
government and Trades Union Congress (TUC) to bring over an "expert,"
James Patrick, to help the government establish pliant unions. Patrick
advised the Kenyan government to set up unions as purely workplace
bodies with no political remit, dividing workers by trade. The stated aim
was not to advance the interests of workers but to improve productivity.

Kibachia was internally exiled for ten years and Singh was deported to India.

23 **August 23, 1851** A violent riot broke out in Sydney, Australia, when police tried to arrest a sailor, Michael Knight, who was wearing women's clothing. To cheers of the locals, Knight decked the officer who attempted the arrest and headed to a church. Knight then disturbed the service and began abusing the parishioners, until more police arrived and managed to make the arrest. On hearing of Knight being taken into custody, hundreds of sailors assembled and began attacking police officers and police stations, freeing all the prisoners along the way.

Illustration of Michael Knight decking the police officer *(By Agustin Huarte, 2019)*

August 23, 1966 Two hundred Aboriginal workers at the Wave Hill pastoral station in Australia walked out on strike for equal pay with white workers. They remained out for an incredible nine years, and what began as a wage dispute became the demand that the British aristocrat Lord Samuel Vestey return the land to them. They were eventually successful in gaining the return of some of the land.

Dexter Daniels, one of those involved in the strike, 1970 *(Courtesy of Northern Territory Library/Wikimedia Commons)*

24 **August 24, 1800** A group of enslaved people led by Gabriel, an enslaved blacksmith, gathered in central Virginia, intending to recruit others for an insurrection planned for August 30. They had hatched an extremely ambitious plan to march on Richmond, capture the capitol, and hold the governor hostage to negotiate freedom for enslaved people. Unfortunately, the plot was betrayed, and twenty-six of the participants executed. But the struggle against slavery continued.

August 24, 2011 Against the background of a militant student movement, the Central Unitaria de Trabajadores de Chile (Workers United Center of Chile; CUT) called a nationwide two-day strike. As many as six hundred thousand people took to the streets, and police responded by arresting 750, injuring many more and killing one sixteen-year-old boy. A few days later, the government caved in to a key demand of the movement and prohibited state funding for for-profit educational institutions.

25 **August 25, 1921** The Battle of Blair Mountain began. It was the largest armed rebellion in the US since the Civil War. For five days in late August and early September 1921, following the killing of miners and their supporters in Welch and Sharples, ten thousand striking coal miners in Logan County, West Virginia, battled armed strikebreakers and deputies. Faced with the over-

Miners surrender arms after the battle *(Courtesy of Wikimedia Commons)*

whelming firepower of US federal troops and even the air force, the miners eventually surrendered or returned to their homes. 📡 **7**

August 25, 1944 A group of thirty-two Spanish and eight French resistance fighters in La Madeleine, France, tackled an entire German column, consisting of 1,300 men in sixty trucks, with six tanks and two self-propelled guns. The maquis blew up the road and rail bridges and positioned themselves on surrounding hills with machine guns. The battle raged from 3:00

Free French Black soldiers, c.1942 *(Courtesy of the Library of Congress/Wikimedia Commons)*

p.m. until noon the following day. Three maquisards were injured, while eight Germans were killed, nearly two hundred wounded, and the rest surrendered. After this humiliating defeat, the Nazi commander killed himself before he could be captured.

That same day, the Forces françaises libres (Free French Forces) liberated Paris, and the occupying German troops surrendered. The Free French unit that recaptured the city had been ethnically cleansed of Black soldiers—who made up a significant proportion of the Free French Army—as US and UK military commanders were only willing to allow the French to liberate the city if they excluded Black troops. Black servicemen were also excluded from the liberation celebrations. For example, resistance hero Georges Dukson, who had been shot and wounded in action, was removed from the event at gunpoint.

26 **August 26, 1919** Former garment worker Fannie Sellins, who had become an organizer with the United Mine Workers of America (UMWA), was murdered by company thugs and sheriff's deputies during a coal strike in Pennsylvania. She attempted to intervene when a miner was being beaten and was shot and killed. Her killers were never punished.

August 26, 1930 Strikebreaking dockworkers at Port Adelaide, Australia, were attacked around the town by mobs of locals, including one group of women demonstrators. During this protracted industrial dispute, scabs were kicked and beaten as they left the train station. One who escaped by diving into the river and swimming toward a ship had to be rescued by police, while mounted police protected another group at Princes Wharf. A group of women attempted to attack scabs as they left work, forcing them to flee to the railway station under police escort.

27 **August 27, 1889** The great strike of East End Jewish tailors in London began during a dockers' strike. Eight thousand workers, mostly Jewish immigrants from Russia, elected a strike committee and walked out, demanding a maximum twelve-hour workday (they were working fourteen to eighteen hours). Despite the antipathy of the dockers' union leader, predominantly Irish Catholic dockers donated to the strike fund and helped the tailors hold out until October, when the employers caved in.

August 27, 1974 African American prisoner Joan Little killed a white prison guard in self-defense and escaped from the Beaufort County jail in North Carolina. The guard had threatened her with an ice pick and forced her to perform a sex act, at which point, she managed to grab the pick and kill him.

Illustration of Joan Little (*dignidadrebelde, 2016, CC by SA 2.0* *https://flickr.com/photos/28987073@N08/30539190706*)

She handed herself in to police the following week and was charged with first-degree murder, which carried an automatic death sentence. Her case rallied support from civil rights activists, including Rosa Parks, as well as feminists and anti–death penalty activists. She became the first woman in the US to successfully use resisting sexual assault as a defense for using deadly force.

28 **August 28, 1830** In Kent, England, a threshing machine was destroyed by angry laborers—the start of the Swing rebellion. Farmworkers sent demand letters to bosses signed by "Captain Swing," and if they did not comply, mobs would attack the farms, set them aflame, and smash the machines.

August 28, 1968 In Chicago, Black bus drivers went on a wildcat strike against their racist union. While 80 percent of drivers were Black, the union leadership was white and did not heed the concerns of Black workers. White scab drivers kept services running in the wealthier neighborhoods. 🎙 **8**

29 **August 29, 1979** After years of fruitless campaigning, thirty to forty LGBT+ activists took direct action and occupied the Swedish national health board to protest homosexuality being classified as a mental illness. The board agreed with protesters and removed the designation in October.

August 29, 1997 Workers at the Lusty Lady Club in San Francisco voted to join the Exotic Dancers Union, part of a local branch of the Service Employees International Union (SEIU). The women undertook an extended organizing campaign, and later took on-the-job direct action, pointedly dancing with their legs closed. The workers eventually won guaranteed work shifts, pay increases, removal of one-way mirrors, abolition

Exotic Dancers Union members, including Cinnamon Maxxine, left, and Stephany Joy Ashley, right, May Day 2008 *(Photo by Matthew Roth, CC by SA 2.0 https://www.flickr.com/photos/ matthewalmonroth/2478956762)*

of racist scheduling, and protection from arbitrary discipline and firing. The women later took over the club and ran it as a workers' cooperative, with an elected management. 👤 **20**

30 **August 30, 1908** Following a violent campaign of repression, union leaders called off a strike by Black and white coal miners in Birmingham, Alabama, four days after the governor sent in the army to evict the strikers' tent colony. Despite this, workers attempted to continue the stoppage but were defeated. Armed thugs terrorized the strikers, lynching one Black miner, while the press generated hysteria about the race-mixing workers. The *Birmingham Age-Herald* denounced a union meeting where "a negro ... embrace[d] a white speaker ... in the very presence of gentle white women and innocent little girls." The defeat was a blow to mineworkers and working class racial unity in the South.

August 30, 1979 Screen icon and Black Panther supporter Jean Seberg died by suicide following a campaign of harassment by the FBI, which had tragically resulted in the death of her premature baby nine years prior. She had provided significant financial support to the National Association for the Advancement of

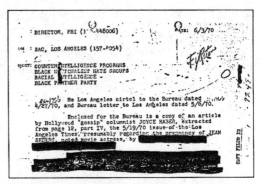

FBI memo on Jean Seberg *(Courtesy of the Federal Bureau of Investigation/Wikimedia Commons)*

Colored People, Native American education groups, and the Black Panthers, including to their free breakfast for schoolchildren program.

As part of the FBI's COINTELPRO operation directed against radical movements, they were already tapping Seberg's phone. Upon learning that Seberg was pregnant, under the supervision of FBI Director J. Edgar Hoover, the agency concocted a false story that the father of her baby was a prominent Black Panther, not her husband. The story was first reported by gossip columnist Joyce Haber in the *Los Angeles Times* and syndicated in some one hundred other newspapers, before spreading even more widely. A few weeks after the story was published, Seberg overdosed on sleeping pills and subsequently delivered a premature baby who died two days later. At her daughter's funeral, Seberg opened the casket to prove that the story was a lie, and that the baby was her husband's. According to those who knew her, the story caused a downward spiral for Seberg, culminating in her suicide.

31 **August 31, 1942** A wildcat general strike broke out in Luxembourg against the occupying Nazi regime's order to conscript young people into the German Army. Steelworkers and primary school teachers walked out, and postal workers began a go-slow before walking out the following day, refusing to deliver telegrams from the German trade union ordering a return to work under pain of execution. The strike was broken by Nazi terror after about a week. Hundreds of workers were arrested, with some sent to concentration camps or executed. Hundreds of schoolchildren were arrested and sent to reeducation camps. Despite the collapse of the strike, resistance to the draft continued, with around 40 percent of all those being conscripted deserting and going into hiding.

August 31, 1944 Maria Dimadi, Greek interpreter and anti-Nazi resistance activist, was executed by members of the Greek collaborationist Security Battalions. She had been working as a spy in the German garrison headquarters and passing information to the resistance.

SEPTEMBER

September 1, 1939 The first fighting of World War II in Europe took place, as fifty-six workers at the post office in Gdańsk (aka Danzig), Poland, took up arms and attempted to repel the Nazi takeover. The workers beat back the first two attacks by German troops, which were backed

Captured defenders of the post office in Gdańsk
(Courtesy of Wikimedia Commons)

up by police, SS and SA volunteers, and local pro-Nazi Germans. After fifteen hours of fighting, the surviving employees surrendered to escape the building, which by this point was on fire. As none of them were soldiers, they were tried as bandits and executed. The workers who died and the ones who were executed afterward were posthumously relieved of their charges of banditry and rehabilitated. In 1979, a monument was built in Gdańsk in their honor.

September 1, 2007 The *Guardian* newspaper published an article revealing that Indian soldiers based in what is now Pakistan had chemical weapons tested on them by the British colonial administration from the 1930s onward. Large numbers of the troops suffered burns in the tests carried out by scientists from Porton Down, apparently to see if mustard gas did greater damage to South Asian skin than to white skin.

September 2, 1962 Oswald Mosley and his fascist blackshirts attempted to hold a meeting in Ridley Road, East London, while the British National Party attempted to assemble in nearby Dalston. Anti-fascists from the Yellow Star Movement, an organization launched in July 1962 in response to an anti-Semitic rally held in Trafalgar Square by the National Socialist Movement, held a nonstop meeting to keep Mosley off his favorite pitch. Mosley was forced to relocate to Victoria Park Square, Bethnal Green, where his meeting collapsed under a hail of stones, eggs, and fruit, causing him to flee, as protesters hammered on his car windows with their fists. It was the fourth of his meetings broken up by crowds in just a few weeks. 🎙 35–37

September 2, 2005 Just after Hurricane Katrina, New Orleans police officer David Warren gunned down Henry Glover, an unarmed African American man who was picking up baby clothes. Some members of the public tried to assist Glover, but they were physically attacked by police officers. Another officer, Gregory McRae, then drove Glover away in a civilian's car, setting the car containing the body on fire. He was observed by a fellow officer laughing while he did this. Five police officers were subsequently charged. Warren was originally convicted of manslaughter and jailed but later won an appeal and was acquitted. This was just one of many racist police murders and abuses in the wake of Hurricane Katrina.

3 **September 3, 1791** Postrevolutionary France completed its new penal code. It became the first Western European country to decriminalize homosexuality, no longer making any mention of prohibitions against sodomy in private.

September 3, 1934 Sixty-five thousand textile workers in North Carolina joined the strike of workers in Alabama against reduced work hours accompanied by reduced pay.

Workers in Alabama had walked out in July when employers reduced working hours from forty to thirty per week, reducing pay by 25 percent. The Union of Textile Workers (UTW) had withdrawn their threat of a national strike in return for a seat on the industrial relations board and a government study, so the Alabama workers initially fought alone.

When workers in North Carolina walked out, the strikers drove to working mills and spread the strike. Within two days 325,000 workers were on strike. In response, authorities declared martial law in different areas across the country, and police and National Guard troops shot, bayoneted, and killed numerous workers.

In the end the UTW called off the strike, declaring "an overwhelming victory," despite not having achieved any concessions from the employers.

4 **September 4, 1919** Four thousand miners from the Kanawha coalfields, many of them armed, marched on Logan County, West Virginia, after hearing rumors of women and children being killed and beaten by mine guards. They were stopped by Governor John J. Cornwell, with threats of an army intervention and promises to investigate the miners' grievances. 🎙 7

September 4, 2005 The Danziger Bridge shootings took place in the wake of Hurricane Katrina when several New Orleans police officers opened fire with assault weapons on an unarmed African American family. The

Bartholomews were on their way to a grocery store when plainclothes police with machine guns shot six of them, killing two and stomping on one of the victims. Some of the victims were shot up to seven times and lost limbs. One man was shot five times in the back and a teenage girl was shot four times. The police then fabricated a story, claiming that they had been fired on by four suspects, that an officer had been shot, and that they had to return fire. They even arrested one of the survivors and charged him with eight counts of attempted murder against the police. The officer in charge of investigating the shootings helped fabricate evidence to support the shooters' lies. Guilty verdicts for the killers were handed down in 2011, six years after the crimes.

5 **September 5, 1911** A UK nationwide strike wave of schoolchildren was sparked when pupils in Llanelli, Wales, walked out in sympathy with a boy who had been disciplined by a deputy headmaster. Beginning with this one school, walkouts spread across the country to at least sixty-two towns and cities, with pupils demanding shorter hours and an end to corporal punishment. The schoolchildren's strikes followed a summer of workers' industrial disputes.

September 5, 1917 Mass arrests of radical workers took place in the US, with US marshals raiding the national offices of the Socialist Party and of the Industrial Workers of the World union (IWW), as well as some twenty branch offices of the IWW in different states. 🎙 **6**

6 **September 6, 1921** To protest against the refusal of the Cork Harbour Board to increase wages, workers at Cork Harbour took over the Harbour Board's offices, hoisted a red flag, and established a soviet (workers' council). Their plan was to collect dues from shipping agents directly. The labor minister intervened, and the soviet was ended through negotiations within hours. However, a contemporary article in the *Irish Times* observed:

> Short-lived as was this outbreak of Irish Bolshevism, it was highly ominous. To-day Irish Labour is permeated with a spirit of revolt against all the principles and conventions of ordered society. The country's lawless state in recent months is partly responsible for this sinister development, and the wild teachings of the Russian Revolution have fallen on willing ears. It is small consolation for thoughtful Irishmen that the first experiments in practical Communism—like this affair at Cork and like the seizure of Messrs. Cleeve's premises at

Bruree—have collapsed in a few days or hours. Their real significance lies in the temper and aspirations which they reveal.

September 6, 1966 Mozambican-Greek revolutionary Dimitri Tsafendas assassinated the architect of apartheid, South African Prime Minister Hendrik Verwoerd, by stabbing him during a parliamentary session. Tsafendas was at the time working in the parliament building. Despite the bravery of his act, anti-apartheid leaders and his family distanced themselves from Tsafendas after the assassination. In his statement to police he was clear about his motives, saying that he "did believe that with the disappearance of the South African prime minister a change of policy would take place. . . . I was so disgusted with the racial policy that I went through with my plan to kill the prime minister." To avoid admitting their security had failed, the authorities decided to claim he was mentally ill. Under torture and facing the death penalty, Tsafendas eventually agreed to plead insanity. He was subsequently found not guilty of murder by reason of insanity and sent to a secure psychiatric hospital. He survived to see the end of the apartheid regime, but the new African National Congress government did not order his release. He died in custody in 1999.

7 **September 7, 1934** Anti-fascists hung a banner atop the British Broadcasting Corporation (BBC) headquarters advertising a demonstration against a rally by Oswald Mosley and his British Union of Fascists (BUF) that weekend. While Mosley had been invited on the BBC to promote his Nazi views and advertise his demonstration, the BBC, like the rest of the British press, refused to give a platform to anti-fascists or to mention the counterprotest. Despite this, on the day, over one hundred thousand Londoners overwhelmed the fascists and their police guard and drove them out of Hyde Park.

September 7, 1977 Violent clashes took place between workers and bosses' thugs at a machine tool factory in Mohan Nagar, India. Workers protesting outside the plant against unfair wage deductions were attacked by armed security guards. Local workers and passersby joined the demonstration, and the guards opened fire, triggering a violent response from the crowd, which burned down the factory, killing the two shooters. Workers in neighboring factories went on wildcat strike in solidarity, with twenty thousand people gathering in protest the next day.

8 **September 8, 1941** The Norwegian Melkestreiken (milk strike) against the occupying Nazi authorities took place. Workers arriving for work on Monday found that their already reduced milk ration had been cut completely. Workers at a shipyard and a steelworks spontaneously walked out after breakfast, and over the next two days the stoppage spread to some fifty workplaces, involving twenty to twenty-five thousand workers. The Nazis responded by declaring martial law, executing two union leaders, and jailing several others.

September 8, 1972 Sixty Black sailors aboard the USS *Constellation* during the Vietnam War gathered in a secluded barbershop on board. They shared stories of the endemic racism in the navy: being denied promotions and being stuck in lower paid positions and subjected to harsher discipline than white sailors. They would later form an organization called the Black Fraction, which, fifty-six days later, would be responsible for the first mass mutiny in the history of the United States Navy. 🔊 **10–11**

9 **September 9, 1739** The Stono Rebellion in South Carolina, the largest uprising of enslaved people in the mainland British colonies, began. A literate enslaved man named Jemmy (or Cato) marched with twenty-two others, mostly from Central Africa, brandishing a banner bearing the word "Liberty!" and attacked a store, seizing weapons and ammunition. They planned to head to Florida, where Spanish colonial authorities offered escaped slaves freedom, in an effort to undermine British rule. On their way, they burned plantations, freed other enslaved people, and killed whites, until a well-armed mounted militia attacked them. While the rebels managed to kill twenty-three militiamen, they lost forty-seven of their number, whose severed heads were displayed on stakes to serve as a warning to others. Many of those who escaped were later captured and executed or sold to enslavers in the Caribbean.

In response to the rebellion, authorities enacted strict laws to try to prevent a recurrence: banning the enslaved from assembling in groups and learning to read, but also prohibiting importation of enslaved people from Africa for ten years and introducing penalties for masters who overworked their slaves or were excessively brutal.

September 9, 1945 In the wake of World War II, the US occupation administration in Korea announced that the Japanese colonial government would remain intact. After massive outcry, they replaced some Japanese bureaucrats with Americans but enlisted the deposed Japanese officials as advisers.

10 **September 10, 1897** Nineteen unarmed striking coal miners and mine workers were killed and thirty-six injured near Lattimer, Pennsylvania, by a posse organized by the Luzerne County sheriff, for refusing to disperse. The strikers, most of whom were shot in the back, were migrant workers originally brought in as strikebreakers, who had later organized themselves. The killers were put on trial, but all were acquitted. However, the massacre marked a turning point in mine workers' organization in the United States, and miners, particularly migrant workers, flooded into the United Mine Workers (UMW) union and won major improvements.

September 10, 1962 White supremacists attempted to assassinate civil rights activist Fannie Lou Hamer in Mississippi. She was staying with her friend Mary Tucker, when racists drove by, firing sixteen shots at her, all of which missed. Hamer (born Townsend) had been attempting to register to vote but had been denied the right to do so by a racist registration test that had been designed to prevent Black people and Native Americans from registering. Hamer failed the registration test when she was unable to answer a question asking her to explain "de facto laws."

Illustration of Fannie Lou Hamer *(dignidadrebelde, CC by SA 2.0 https://www.flickr.com/photos/dignidadrebelde/29822833790)*

11 **September 11, 1973** The right-wing General Augusto Pinochet launched a coup against the elected left-wing government of Salvador Allende in Chile. Allende had appointed Pinochet as head of his armed forces the previous month, and Pinochet had used the position to orchestrate the coup.

On day one, the new government began rounding up thousands of people—mostly working class activists and left-wingers—holding them in the national stadium and killing many. The brutal military dictatorship, which was backed by Western powers, including the US and UK, implemented the harsh right-wing economic ideology of the neoliberal Chicago Boys. While international observers heralded the resultant "economic miracle," in reality living standards declined for the vast majority of the population, with wages falling and spending on health care, education, and housing being cut. Any workers who attempted to resist were murdered, tortured, imprisoned, or "disappeared." A popular method of execution was to throw civilians from helicopters into the ocean or over the Andes mountains. Many members of the alt-right today celebrate these murders with "helicopter memes."

Chilean soldiers burning socialist literature
(Courtesy of the Central Intelligence Agency/Wikimedia Commons)

Over the next seventeen years, more than three thousand people were murdered by the regime, with more than thirty-seven thousand others illegally imprisoned and/or tortured. Many prisoners were systematically raped and sexually abused by guards, with women a particular target. In addition to being violated by guards, some women were sexually assaulted using dogs, rats, and spiders and were forced to have sex with male family members. Many children of those killed were turned over to the Catholic Church or put up for adoption, with the children either receiving no information or being told their parents had died in accidents.

September 11, 2017 In Nairobi, Kenya, drivers for rideshare services Taxify, Little, and Mondo-Ride joined Uber drivers on an indefinite strike they had begun the previous month, demanding a cut in commission rates.

Earlier in the year, Uber had been forced to increase fares by 20 percent after a series of protests and strikes by drivers, but the increases failed to make up for a 30 percent reduction the firm made to try to undercut regular taxis. Uber also increased its commission rate from 20 to 25 percent. Drivers demanded that it be reduced to 10 percent.

Subsequent strikes also took place in 2018 and 2019, winning some concessions from the bosses.

12 **September 12, 1945** Following the defeat of the Japanese colonial authorities, the People's Republic of Korea was declared (not to be confused with the Democratic People's Republic of Korea, aka North Korea). It had a twenty-seven-point program, including land redistribution, rent control, nationalization of major industries, guaranteed human rights, universal suffrage, equality for women, a ban on child labor, and workers' rights, including a maximum eight-hour workday.

These reforms were not to the liking of US authorities, who were supposedly committed to "national self-determination," so they decided to abolish the republic in their southern zone and set up a military dictatorship. Thousands of those who opposed the dictatorship were massacred, including roughly 10 percent of the population on Jeju Island.

September 12, 1969 The Gay Liberation Front (GLF) protested in New York City against the homophobic advertising policy of the *Village Voice* newspaper. The GLF had been established following the Stonewall rebellion and marked a qualitative shift in the movement for LGBT+ rights. It was a complete departure from the previously moderate, assimilationist attitude of what was known as the "homophile" movement, instead advocating for militant action, gay liberation, and the rights of all oppressed people. 🎙️ **25–26**

13 **September 13, 1911** Twelve pupils at St Mary's Roman Catholic School in Hull, England, called fellow pupils out on strike to protest corporal punishment and excessive workloads. They marched to nearby schools, pulling out hundreds of schoolchildren, then went for a swim in the River Humber.

September 13, 1971 The Attica Prison uprising, which had begun on September 9, was crushed. Prisoners in appalling conditions had united across racial lines and taken control of the prison, demanding better treatment. Talks with authorities had broken down, and when the desperate prisoners threatened their unharmed hostages, Governor Nelson Rockefeller (of the absurdly rich Rockefeller family) ordered that the prison be retaken. The New York State Police launched tear gas into the yard and fired nonstop into the smoke for two minutes, using weapons that included shotguns and personal firearms loaded with ammunition outlawed under the Geneva Convention. Many hostages and inmates (most of whom were not resisting, as they stumbled and choked in the smoke) were wounded, and by the time the facility was retaken, twenty-nine inmates and nine hostages had been killed. Afterward, in celebration of the massacre police troopers were heard cheering "white power." But despite the repression, a wave of rebellion swept America's prisons.

14 **September 14, 1960** A US-backed coup took place in Congo against the first democratically elected prime minister in the country's history, socialist independence leader Patrice Lumumba. The CIA initially planned to assassinate him—one plot involved poisoning his toothpaste—but instead he was arrested, beaten, tortured, and then shot. Soldiers from the former ruling Belgian authorities then dug up his body, dismembered it, and dissolved it in sulfuric acid, grinding what was left to powder and scattering it.

September 14, 1989 Seven members of AIDS campaign group ACT UP infiltrated the New York Stock Exchange and chained themselves to the VIP balcony to protest against the high cost of the only approved AIDS drug, AZT. Shortly after the protest, Wellcome, its manufacturer, cut the price by 20 percent.

15 **September 15, 1845** Five thousand women cotton mill workers in and around Pittsburgh went on strike for a maximum ten-hour workday and for an end to child labor. Months into the strike, hundreds marched on the Blackstock mill, one of the largest in the area. The women broke down the factory's gates and forcibly expelled the scabs, while the men who accompanied them kept the police at bay. Although the women's demands were not met, the strike drew national attention. On Independence Day, 1848, the Pennsylvania legislature passed a ten-hour workday law. However, the law had numerous loopholes and was never really enforced. The struggle for better working conditions and a shorter workday would have to wait for the next generation of worker activists to pick up where the cotton workers had left off.

September 15, 1954 US veterans of the Abraham Lincoln Brigade—antifascist volunteers during the Spanish Civil War—were brought before the Subversive Activities Control Board (SACB) to respond to attempts to classify them as a subversive organization.

This is some of what Crawford Morgan, one of its members, said:

> Being a Negro, and all of the stuff that I have had to take in this country, I had a pretty good idea of what fascism was and I didn't

want no part of it. I got a chance to fight it there with bullets and I went there and fought it with bullets. If I get a chance to fight it with bullets again, I will fight it with bullets again.... I felt that if we didn't lick Franco and stop fascism there, it would spread over lots of the world. And it is bad enough for white people to live under fascism, those of the white people that like freedom and democracy. But Negroes couldn't live under it. They would be wiped out.... From the time I arrived in Spain I felt like a human being, like a man. People didn't look at me with hatred in their eyes because I was Black, and I wasn't refused this or refused that because I was Black. I was treated like all the rest of the people were treated, and when you have been in the world for quite a long time and have been treated worse than people treat their dogs, it is quite a nice feeling to go someplace and feel like a human being.

Crawford Morgan
(Courtesy of the Abraham Lincoln Brigade Archives)

16 **September 16, 1923** Itō Noe and her lover Ōsugi Sakae, both worker activists, anarchists, and free love advocates, were arrested by police in Tokyo, Japan. Police blamed radicals for starting fires, which in reality were caused by the Great Kantō Earthquake, and killed many militants. Itō and Ōsugi were beaten and strangled to death in their cells, then dumped in a well.

Itō Noe *(Courtesy of Wikimedia Commons)*

September 16, 1973 Chilean communist folk singer and musician Victor Jara was murdered by General Augusto Pinochet's troops, following his US-backed coup a few days earlier. Jara was taken prisoner, along with thousands of others, and held in in Chile's national stadium, where guards tortured him, broke his fingers and smashed his hands, and then told him to try playing his guitar. He was then shot over forty times.

In the wave of working class rebellion that erupted across Chile in 2019, his songs, including "El Derecho de Vivir en Paz" (The Right to Live in Peace), echoed in the streets as they were sung by huge crowds of protesters.

17 **September 17, 1849** Legendary abolitionist Harriet Tubman and her brothers Ben and Henry escaped from slavery in Maryland. After the escape, Ben and Henry decided to go back, which essentially forced Harriet to return as well. But, shortly after, she escaped again and travelled to Philadelphia.

In the years following her escape, Tubman worked tirelessly to save money to return and free other enslaved people. Tubman later helped John Brown recruit fighters for an insurrection at Harpers Ferry. Later in life, Tubman was active in the women's rights movement until her death in 1913.

September 17, 1922 One of the most serious clashes in the postal workers' strike against the new Irish Free State occurred in Dublin when soldiers opened fire on one of the men and three of women striking. One of the workers, Olive Flood, was hit, but fortunately the bullet deflected off her garter belt, and she escaped with a minor flesh wound. A journalist reported that the incident "had no effect whatsoever on the determination of the girls to carry on."

18 **September 18, 1963** A crowd of thousands burned down the British embassy in Jakarta, Indonesia, protesting against the colonial creation of Malaysia two days earlier. They also attacked the official residence of the British ambassador and burned British cars.

September 18, 1974 Flora Sanhueza Rebolledo, Chilean teacher and revolutionary, died at the age of sixty-three, as a result of the torture she suffered at the hands of General Augusto Pinochet's right-wing regime.

Flora travelled to Spain in 1935 and took part in the social revolution during the civil war. Following the fascist victory, she fled to France, where she was interned as a political prisoner until 1942, after which she returned to Chile and, inspired by working class cultural associations of the earlier part of the century, founded Ateneo Libertario Luisa Michel in Iquique for women weavers. Given that this was during the dictatorship of Gabriel González Videla and the fascist persecution of anarchists and communists, much of her work was effectively clandestine. In 1953, the Ateneo Libertario Luisa Michel opened its door to children of working women, changing its name to the Escuela Libertaria Luisa Michel. At its peak, it had more than seventy regular students, but it closed its doors in 1957.

Flora was arrested and tortured following the Pinochet coup. Placed under house arrest, she subsequently died as a result of the injuries she had sustained.

19 **September 19, 1793** During the Haitian Revolution, six hundred British soldiers sent from Jamaica landed at Jérémie, Haiti. They were welcomed by the white French property owners, who had signed a secret accommodation with Britain. In exchange for their support, Saint-Domingue would become a British colony, slavery would be reinstated, people of color would be stripped of citizenship, and the conditions of Britain's economic policies would favor the colonists. Soldiers fought for five years before finally being defeated by the Haitian revolutionary forces.

September 19, 2007 Workers in Nordhausen, Germany, who had been occupying their bicycle factory to oppose closure, relaunched production under workers' control, making "strike bikes."

20 **September 20, 1763** Filipina revolutionary anti-colonial leader Gabriela Silang was executed by Spanish authorities. The previous week, she had attempted to besiege Vigan, but she was forced back to Abra, where she was later captured. She and her troops were hanged in Vigan's central plaza.

September 20, 1898 Migrant anarchist worker Polenice Mattei was murdered by police in São Paulo. At the time, anarchists in Brazil were at the center of the working class movement, fighting for a reduction in the length of the workday, for health insurance, and against war. They published some one hundred magazines and newspapers, including four dailies. The government fought back by jailing and deporting hundreds and murdering dozens.

21 **September 21, 1945** Two hundred thousand coal miners in the US went on strike in support of supervisory employees' demand for collective bargaining. This was part of a wave of strikes in the wake of World War II.

September 21, 1976 Chilean socialist refugee Orlando Letelier and think tank worker Ronni Moffitt were murdered in Washington, DC, by a car bomb planted by General Augusto Pinochet's secret police. The killings by agents

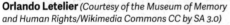

Orlando Letelier *(Courtesy of the Museum of Memory and Human Rights/Wikimedia Commons CC by SA 3.0)*

Ronni Moffitt *(Courtesy of the Moffitt family/Wikimedia Commons CC by SA 3.0)*

of the US-backed dictator were part of Operation Condor, a Latin American anti-communist program supported by the US, which killed up to sixty thousand working class militants, socialists, and anarchists.

22 **September 22, 1912** The syndicalist union Casa del Obrero Mundial (House of the World Worker; COM) was formed in Mexico.

However, during the upheaval of the Mexican Revolution, the union began supporting a capitalist faction involved in the conflict—the constitutionalist forces of Venustiano Carranza—and wound up fighting against the revolutionary peasant army of Emiliano Zapata. After it had outlived its usefulness, the Carranza government turned on the union and shut it down.

September 22, 1918 A mass mutiny and uprising of Bulgarian troops during World War I began. Soldiers deserting at Dobro Pole formed their own army, electing officers, and turned their weapons on their leaders. Their rebellion was only suppressed in December, with ten thousand soldiers subsequently imprisoned.

23 **September 23, 1945** The Saigon commune came into being when workers rose up, independently of the Việt Minh, in response to French and Japanese troops, supported by Gurkhas under British command, entering the city. Centered in poor suburbs, the rebels cut down trees and flipped over cars and trucks to build makeshift barricades. The insurgents shot colonial police and officials, and in some areas popular resentment at years of racism and abuse exploded in mass killings of French civilians.

Meanwhile, the official independence movement, the Việt Minh, avoided direct conflict, instead supporting a food blockade of the foreign troops. Although, as one participant in the uprising commented, this was "a futile hope, as the British ships controlled the access to the harbour." On October 5, additional French forces arrived under the command of General Leclerc, and by the following week the uprising had essentially been defeated.

September 23, 1969 After management imported tires from Greece, striking Pirelli workers in Milan, Italy, set truckloads of the tires on fire, causing management to lock the workers out. Though the lockout was soon revoked, Pirelli bosses tried to fire one militant, resulting in a spontaneous strike and demonstration in which the worker was carried back into the factory.

24 **September 24, 1934** The month-old Salinas lettuce strike ended when workers won concessions. The strike of agricultural workers in the Filipino Labor Union (FLU) faced massive repression from racist mobs and armed vigilantes; however, they held out and won a pay increase and union recognition.

September 24, 2003 A group of twenty-seven pilots in the Israeli Air Force sent a letter to the head commander refusing to participate in assassination missions in the West Bank and Gaza. They stated these attacks were "illegal and immoral" and were "harming innocent civilians."

25 **September 25, 1968** The Seattle city council brought in a gun control law at the behest of Republican mayor James Braman, to prevent Black Panther self-defense patrols. In particular, council members were alarmed when armed Panthers appeared at Rainier Beach High School to defend Black students who had been attacked and threatened by whites. The city passed an emergency measure to prohibit the display of a "dangerous weapon" to "intimidate others."

September 25, 2005 Sex workers in Gyeonggi Province, South Korea, organized in the Democratic Coalition of Sex Workers and signed the first collective bargaining agreement with brothel owners in the country's history.

26 **September 26, 1919** During the Russian Revolution, the anarchist Revolutionary Insurrectionary Army of Ukraine, nicknamed "the Makhnovists" after its commander Nestor Makhno, ended months of retreat and turned on their pursuers: General Anton Denikin's counterrevolutionary "White" army. The Mahhnovists took Denikin's forces by surprise, routing them and ending Denikin's march on Moscow.

September 26, 1955 During a visit by dictator General Francisco Franco to Barcelona, underground resistance activist Francesc Sabaté Llopart hailed a cab and had it drive around the Catalan capital. During the journey he fired anti-regime leaflets through the sunroof from a mortar he had assembled and had inside a suitcase on the back seat. He reassured the worried driver, saying, "Don't worry, I work for the government, and I am distributing informational materials." He later left the driver with a generous tip.

27 **September 27, 1915** A strike of five thousand garment workers in Chicago was called by the Amalgamated Clothing Workers of America (ACWA), demanding better pay, shorter hours, and the abolition of blacklisting. In retaliation, employers called in large numbers of police and fired hundreds of strikers. Workers responded by calling a further twenty-five thousand people out on strike, in a dispute that lasted for months.

September 27, 1917 Study groups of African and white radicals in South Africa formed the Industrial Workers of Africa (IWA), a revolutionary, multiracial union with an all-African committee and a simple slogan: *Sifuna Zonke!* (We Want Everything!).

28 **September 28, 1975** Three Black liberation activists held up the Knightsbridge branch of the Spaghetti House chain in London at the end of a Saturday evening, hoping to steal the weekly takings. The robbery went wrong and police arrived, so the men, calling themselves the Black Liberation Army, took staff members hostage and demanded safe passage out of the country. After a five-day siege by hundreds of police, they surrendered.

September 28, 1991 Leading labor organizer Shankar Guha Niyogi was assassinated in his sleep at midnight in Bhilai, India. Niyogi, who had successfully led efforts to organize cement factory workers and contract coal miners, as well as to establish health care and cultural programs for poor workers and peasants, had angered many local industrialists, whose profits had suffered as a result.

He was murdered by a hired gunman, Paltan Mallah. In 1997, several capitalists were convicted, along with Mallah, of conspiracy to murder. In 2005, in a judgment that caused widespread dismay in India, the industrialists' convictions were overturned by the Supreme Court.

29 **September 29, 1920** Chilean anarchist poet and Industrial Workers of the World union (IWW) member José Domingo Gómez Rojas died at just twenty-four years of age after being arrested, tortured, and allegedly losing his sanity. More than forty thousand people attended his funeral, at which his poem "Protestas de Piedad," written while in confinement, was read. Thereafter, the poem became a symbol for anarchist and pacifist groups opposing the oligarchy that dominated the country.

September 29, 2007 Tens of thousands of textile workers in Ghazl El-Mahalla, Egypt, won their week-long illegal wildcat strike after achieving most of their demands. Concessions by management included a 7 percent increase in basic salary, additional bonuses, pay for the strike days, no victimization of strikers, and the impeachment of the chairman of the board and his assistants.

30 **September 30, 1918** Amid growing unrest over the rising cost of living, bank employees in Zürich walked out in their first ever strike. A local general strike then broke out in support of the bank workers' demand for pay increases, leading to an outright success.

Strikers and cavalry in Zürich, 1918 *(Courtesy of Wikimedia Commons)*

September 30, 1919 The Elaine massacre, in Arkansas, one of the worst incidents of racial violence in US history, occurred. Around one hundred Black workers, mostly sharecroppers employed by white plantation owners, attended a meeting of the Progressive Farmers and Household Union of America (PFHUA) to try to organize for better pay. The union placed armed guards outside the church where the meeting was held to protect it from attack.

The exact cause of the incident is disputed, but a shootout broke out, leaving a white sheriff's deputy injured and a white railroad security officer dead. In the aftermath, up to one thousand armed white racists descended on the town and began murdering Black people, while US troops locked up hundreds of African Americans in makeshift stockades, torturing many of them. They remained locked up until they could be questioned by their white employers, who could then have them released.

Authorities completely denied the massacre took place, and instead charged 122 African Americans with various crimes, with twelve swiftly convicted and sentenced to death by electric chair. This sentence was later reduced on appeal, but seventy-seven Black people ended up serving prison sentences, some quite lengthy.

The exact number of victims is unknown, but estimates of African Americans killed ranges from one hundred to several hundred. None of the white perpetrators of the massacre were charged with any crime, despite some admitting to participating in torture.

OCTOBER

1 **October 1, 1935** Antonio Soberanis Gómez, a barber and worker organizer, spoke at a public meeting in Corozal, Belize, and was subsequently prosecuted by British colonial authorities for using "seditious language." He had played a key role in organizing among the unemployed and in recent strikes of stevedores and rail workers. To avoid the appearance of a "Black versus white affair," the governor selected a Black magistrate to try the case, expressing his wish that Soberanis be "put away for a good long sentence." The trial aroused nationwide interest, and workers contributed to Soberanis's defense fund, while authorities banned all public meetings. Eventually Soberanis was acquitted and fined a mere eighty-five dollars for using "insulting words."

October 1, 1946 Police in Daegu attacked Koreans demonstrating against post–World War II US and Japanese domination, killing three and injuring many more. The people responded with a mass counterattack, killing thirty-eight officers. This marked the beginning of the Autumn Uprising.

2 **October 2, 1937** Under the orders of US-backed Dominican dictator President Rafael Trujillo, the genocide of more than twenty thousand Haitians began, in what is now known as the Parsley massacre.

October 2, 1968 Just prior to the start of the Olympic Games, the Tlatelolco massacre took place in Mexico City, with police murdering hundreds of students who were demonstrating peacefully. At the time, many workers and poor farmers were fighting for better working conditions, and the government responded with violent repression during what is known as the "dirty war."

People were angry at the huge cost of staging the Olympics, as well as about police repression. On October 2, around ten thousand school pupils and university students gathered in protest at the Plaza de las Tres Culturas, in Mexico City, chanting, "We don't want Olympics, we want revolution!" A little after 6:00 p.m., five thousand troops surrounded the square and began firing into the crowd and into nearby buildings. Throughout the night, soldiers and police officers went on a rampage, rounding people up, and beating and killing protesters, bystanders, and local residents. Authorities and the media claimed that troops were defending themselves from sniper fire, but much later it was revealed that the snipers who began the shooting were members of the Presidential Guard.

Troops on the streets of Mexico City, 1968 *(Courtesy of Cel·lí/Wikimedia Commons)*

The CIA, concerned about protests against the Olympic Games, had been in close contact with Mexican authorities, and the US military provided equipment, weapons, and ammunition. Six days before the massacre, Mexican federal security told the CIA that "the situation will be under complete control very shortly."

3 **October 3, 1935** Ethiopia, formerly Abyssinia, and the only African country to remain independent of colonial powers, was invaded by fascist Italy under Benito Mussolini. The Italians committed countless atrocities, including using poison gas, conducting aerial bombardment, and holding people in concentration camps. Black people around the world were outraged, and many Black men and women volunteered to fight against the fascist colonizers.

October 3, 1952 The Mau Mau campaign against British colonialism in Kenya escalated when the rebels stabbed to death the first white European victim of the uprising in the town of Thika. The British media used the killings of whites to justify the repression of poor Kenyans, killing tens of thousands and throwing hundreds of thousands into concentration camps. However, the fact is that only thirty-two whites were killed in the course of the conflict.

Battle of Cable Street mural in East London *(Photo by tpholland, CC by SA 2.0 https://www.flickr.com/photos/tpholland/4161095925)*

4 **October 4, 1936** Oswald Mosley's British Union of Fascists planned to march through a predominantly Jewish section of East London; instead the Battle of Cable Street occurred. The fascists were met by over one hundred thousand local residents and workers who—insistent that "They shall not pass!"—fought both the blackshirts and the police protecting them, forcing the march to be abandoned. 🎧 **35–37**

October 4, 1939 Four Italian immigrant anarchists, Arthur Bortolotti (aka Attilio Bortolotti and Arthur Bartell), Ruggero Benvenuti, Ernest Gava (some sources state that the third was a Cuban named Marco Joachim), and Vittorio Valopi were arrested under Canada's new War Measures Act for possession of anti-fascist "subversive literature" and, in Bortolotti's case, a triggerless handgun. They were threatened with deportation to Mussolini's fascist Italy, which would have effectively been a death sentence.

Luckily for the group, famous anarchist Emma Goldman threw herself into helping them with their case, organizing a support committee to exert pressure for their release and to raise money for their legal defense. Goldman contacted a progressive lawyer known for defending workers and got all of them but Bortolotti freed in two to three weeks. Bortolotti took the burden upon himself and insisted he alone was responsible.

Bortolotti was released on bail three-and-a-half months later and sentenced to deportation on February 13, 1940 (just days before Goldman had a stroke). His sentence was reversed before Goldman died in May.

Contemporary illustration of the March on Versailles (*Courtesy of Wikimedia Commons*)

5 **October 5, 1789** Thousands of women in Paris, angry over the high price and scarcity of bread, ransacked the city armory for weapons and besieged the Palace of Versailles in one of the opening salvos of the French Revolution.

October 5, 1945 A six-month strike by set decorators turned into a bloody riot at the gates of Warner Brothers Studios in Burbank, California, when scabs tried to cross the picket line. The incident is still identified as Hollywood Black Friday and the Battle of Burbank. By the end of the day, some three hundred police and deputy sheriffs had been called to the scene and over forty injuries were reported. Partly in response to this dispute, the government passed the Taft-Hartley Act in 1947 to break up workers' organizations.

6 **October 6, 1976** The Thammasat University massacre (aka the October 6 event) occurred in Thailand when state forces and far-right royalist mobs attacked student protesters, after four to five thousand students from various universities had demonstrated for more than a week against the return of former military dictator Thanom Kittikachorn from Singapore.

After years of workers, peasants, and students fighting for democracy, social justice, and even in some cases an end to capitalism itself, the Thai ruling class responded with the utmost brutality and installed a new dictatorship over the mutilated bodies of those struggling for freedom. Dozens of demonstrators were killed, many of them hanged from trees and then beaten with sticks and chairs.

October 6, 1985 Tottenham, London, went up in flames as residents of the Broadwater Farm estate rose up against police after the death of Cynthia Jarrett, an innocent Afro-Caribbean mother, during a police search of her home only days after police had shot Dorothy "Cherry" Groce in Brixton. Police tried to frame several men and boys for the killing of a police officer during the disturbances, and three were jailed for several years before being released on appeal.

October 7, 1944 An armed rebellion broke out in the Auschwitz concentration camp. Resistance members in the camp found out the Sonderkommando (the Jewish prisoners tasked with working in the crematoria and disposing of bodies) were due to be murdered on that day. The group fought back with knives and improvised weapons, including handmade grenades made from smuggled gunpowder and sardine cans. They burned down Crematorium IV, killed three SS officers, even cremating one, and injured others.

October 7, 1985 Nurses across the state of Victoria, Australia, started a work-to-rule campaign that eventually turned into an all-out strike when managers tried to break the action. The workers were demanding pay increases and action on staff/patient ratios. Ending in a partial victory, the dispute would lay the groundwork for the even bigger, victorious 1986 nurses' strike.

October 8, 1967 Yamasaki Hiroaki was killed by police and around six hundred people injured during an anti-war demonstration near Haneda airport, in Japan. Students demonstrating against the Vietnam War had fought riot police on a bridge, forcing them back and commandeering a police van and water cannon truck. They had been driving the truck toward the airport when a cry went up that a Kyoto University student had been killed. Fighting stopped until his body was removed, then police used tear gas, batons, and a water cannon to disperse protesters, sweeping some off the bridge into the river. The battle and the police repression constituted a significant milestone in the student movement, resulting in an increase in militancy.

October 8, 1970 A bomb exploded at the Chelsea home of the UK's Conservative Party attorney general Peter Rawlinson for the second time in just a few weeks. Planted by the Angry Brigade urban guerrilla group, it was a protest against the increasingly repressive state tactics being used against the workers' movement and the Irish civil rights movement. Like all of the Angry Brigade bombings, it was designed to avoid any injuries. The communiqué declared:

> We are no mercenaries.
> We attack property not people.
> [Employment Minister Robert] Carr, Rawlinson, [Metropolitan Police Commissioner John] Waldron, would all be dead if we had wished.
> Fascists and government agents are the only ones who attack the public. . . . We have started to fight back and the war will be won by the organised working class, with bombs.

 2–3

9 **October 9, 1912** The mostly women workforce at the Phoenix Mill in Little Falls, New York, walked out on wildcat strike to force their employer to follow a new state law limiting working hours to fifty-four per week, down from sixty. Two thousand other workers from the Phoenix and Gilberts Mills joined them on strike, and the workers joined the Industrial Workers of the World union (IWW). The IWW sent in organizers, including Matilda Robbins (née Tatiana Gitel Rabinowitz) and Big Bill Haywood, among others. Fellow IWW member Helen Keller also supported the strike.

The police chief declared: "We have a strike on our hands and a foreign element to deal with. We have in the past kept them in subjugation and mean to hold them where they belong." He sent police to attack the workers and raid the strike headquarters, but the strikers held out, and, by January, they won shorter hours with no loss of pay.

October 9, 1945 The UK Labour government defended its imprisonment of 226 Spanish Civil War and anti-Nazi resistance fighters, describing them as "serving members of an enemy para-military organisation." The men had been interned in France but escaped and joined the resistance. They were then captured by the Germans, and, upon "liberation," they were rounded up and sent to a concentration camp in Lancashire, England.

One internee, Agustin Soler, killed himself and others like Eustagio Bustos were driven mad by the persecution.

A hunger strike by detainees, along with public protests, led to the men being transferred to a single camp in Chorley, Lancashire, where they were at least allowed to identify themselves as republicans. There, they took strike action the

Interned Spanish refugees *(Photo by Marie Louise Berneri)*

following January and, in 1946, were either released or deported.

10 **October 10, 1947** A strike was launched by Black African railway workers across the whole of French West Africa—Senegal, Benin, Ivory Coast, and Guinea. The stoppage lasted until March 19 the following year, when workers returned to work, having gained numerous concessions from their employer.

During the dispute, working class women sustained their families financially and contributed to the solidarity of the community by writing pro-strike songs and taunting strikebreakers.

October 10, 1971 At 11:00 a.m., the men of Bravo Company, 1/12, First Cavalry Division of the United States Army near the Cambodian border declared a private unofficial ceasefire with the North Vietnamese. The move followed a mutiny shortly before, with six men refusing to go on a dangerous mission. These men were facing a court-martial. A petition was circulated in support of the mutineers and was signed by two-thirds of the company. A journalist leaked the petition to the French press, and the army dropped the courts-martial and shipped Bravo Company out to safety, replacing them with Delta Company.

A few days later, twenty men in Delta Company refused to head out, and the army pulled them and the artillery company they were supporting out, abandoning the position. 🎙 **10–11**

11 **October 11, 1972** Approximately fifty people detained in the Washington, DC, jail seized control of a cellblock and held twelve prison officials hostage, demanding improved conditions and reductions in overcrowding.

October 11, 1972 Chicane activists occupied the abandoned Beacon Hill Elementary School in Seattle and founded El Centro de la Raza (Center for People of All Races), a Chicane/Latine civil rights community organization that still exists today.

12 **October 12, 1925** Amid a mass rent and workers' strike in Panama, police killed two organizers, and President Rodolfo Chiari requested US troops to help put down the rebellion. The following day, three US infantry battalions and a machine-gun battery arrived and took control of Panama City, banning all gatherings of more than five people and arresting any strikers who attempted to meet.

Tenants in Panama City had begun withholding rent to protest against rising rents and unsanitary conditions. After police violently suppressed the tenants, killing several, wounding dozens, and arresting and deporting others, the strike spread to Colón, and workers launched a general strike.

October 12, 1972 Simmering racial tensions aboard the USS *Kitty Hawk* during the Vietnam War exploded into a race riot, following multiple racist incidents against Black sailors. A number of Black sailors armed themselves with makeshift weapons, including broom handles, wrenches, and lengths of pipe, and began vandalizing the ship and attacking white sailors. Fighting continued until the early hours of the morning, when the men were persuaded to put down their weapons by biracial Black and Native American officer Ben Cloud. A mob of white sailors then armed themselves for a fight. When Cloud ordered them to disperse, they dismissed him as a "n——r." Six weeks later, twenty-seven Black sailors were arrested and charged, while no white sailors were. However, news of the rebellion spread and inspired unrest elsewhere in the fleet. 🎙 **10–11**

13 **October 13, 1157 BCE** The earliest recorded strike was reported as having occurred on a date that most likely translates to October 13, 1157 BCE in our current calendar. The dispute is recounted in a papyrus written by a scribe in the ancient Egyptian town that is now called Deir el-Medina.

Gangs of skilled construction workers in the employ of Pharaoh Ramses III stopped work when, eighteen days after their payday, they had still not received their wages, which would have been paid in food and other goods. The workers shouted that they were hungry and sat down by a temple. Officials gave them some pastries, and they returned home, but the following day they protested once more, demanding their pay at the central grain storehouse in Thebes. Eventually, they received their back pay, but the pattern of workers needing to go on strike to be paid what they were owed was repeated multiple times.

October 13, 1970 Twenty-six-year-old Black communist Angela Davis was arrested by the FBI in New York City. She had fled California after a warrant for her arrest was issued in August in connection with an attempted jail-break. Notorious FBI director J. Edgar Hoover had listed Davis on the FBI's Ten Most Wanted Fugitives list, and with her arrest President Richard Nixon congratulated the FBI on its "capture of the dangerous terrorist." Davis was eventually acquitted of all charges.

14 **October 14, 1973** A mass uprising involving student demonstrations and workers' strikes took place in Thailand, overthrowing the military dictatorship and demanding more democratic freedoms. The overthrow of the dictatorship occurred on the crest of a rising wave of wildcat strikes, increasing the confidence of workers, peasants, and students, who continued in subsequent years to fight for more than just parliamentary democracy.

October 14, 1977 Anti-gay crusader Anita Bryant was "pied" by Tom Higgins, a gay rights activist. Bryant, who was already well-known as a singer, led Save Our Children, a homophobic campaigning group that successfully overturned legal protections for LGBT+ people in Dade County, Florida. Declaring her opposition to homosexuality, Bryant said: "I will lead such a crusade to stop it as this country has not seen before." After being pied, Bryant burst into tears and began praying.

Bryant was also brand ambassador for Florida orange juice, which was subjected to a mass boycott campaign. Gay bars replaced screwdrivers (vodka and orange juice cocktails) with "Anita Bryants"—made with vodka and apple juice, with the profits donated to the campaign. Bryant's lucrative Florida Citrus Commission contract subsequently lapsed, and her marriage failed, which caused her to be ostracized by some Christian fundamentalists who did not approve of divorce.

Later in life, Bryant's homophobic views softened, and she said she was "more inclined to say live and let live." In 1998, Dade County reintroduced legal protections for LGBT+ people, and efforts by Christian groups to overturn them failed.

15 **October 15, 1964** Labour leader Harold Wilson becomes Prime Minister after his party's victory in the general election. One of his acts while in power was to send British troops to Oman to defend the medieval puppet rule of Sultan Said bin Taimur against a popular insurgency. Oman was one of the only countries in the world where slavery was legal, and the country had only one hospital and three schools. It had an infant mortality rate of over 30 percent, and radios, bicycles, football, sunglasses, and trousers were all illegal. Said's reign had been propped up by the British for years, and the Labour government continued the pattern, massacring civilians, poisoning wells, torching villages, torturing rebels, and shooting livestock.

October 15, 1966 Bobby Seale and Huey P. Newton met in Oakland, California, where they set up the Black Panther Party for Self-Defense. Despite heavy repression, the party would exist until 1982, running a variety of programs, from free breakfasts for schoolchildren and community health clinics to armed citizen patrols and monitoring the police. A seldom-mentioned fact

Bobby Seale, center, addressing a rally, 1971 *(Courtesy of Michiganensian/Wikimedia Commons)*

about the group is that in the 1970s a majority of its members were women and girls.

16 **October 16, 1859** Abolitionist John Brown and a small band of Black and white followers raided a federal armory in Harpers Ferry, West Virginia, with the intention of using the weapons to arm enslaved people. The rebellion was crushed the following day by US marines under the command of General Robert E. Lee, with seven killed and ten wounded. Brown and some of the other survivors were captured and tried for treason. Unsurprisingly, with the judge and all twelve jurors being slaveowners, they were convicted and sentenced to death.

One of those who managed to escape, an African American man named Osborne Perry Anderson, eventually sought refuge in Canada. He was the only participant to write an account of the events, *A Voice from Harper's Ferry*. He later served in the Union Army with other survivors of the raid.

October 16, 1968 African American sprinters Tommie Smith and John Carlos raised their gloved fists in a Black power salute during the playing of the US national anthem when they were awarded gold and bronze medals at the Olympics. Smith would later clarify: "I wore a black glove to represent social power or Black power; I wore socks, not shoes, to represent poverty; I wore a black scarf around my neck to symbolize the lynching, the hangings that Black folks went through while building this country."

Following the protest, they were largely ostracized by the American sporting establishment. While *Time* magazine now consid-

Left to right: Peter Norman, Tommie Smith, and John Carlos *(Photo by Angelo Cozzi, courtesy of Wikimedia Commons)*

ers its picture of the event as the most iconic photograph of all time, back then an article in the magazine read, in part: "'Faster, Higher, Stronger' is the motto of the Olympic Games. 'Angrier, nastier, uglier' better describes the scene in Mexico City last week." Back home, both Smith and Carlos were subject to abuse, and they and their families received death threats.

The Australian athlete Peter Norman, the other man on the podium, also showed solidarity with the protest, wearing an "Olympic Project for Human Rights" badge in protest of his government's "White Australia" policy. He too would be reprimanded by his nation's Olympic authorities and was not picked for the following Olympic Games—although it is disputed whether this was as a consequence of his stand in Mexico. When Norman died suddenly in 2006, Smith and Carlos helped carry his coffin and delivered eulogies at his funeral.

17 **October 17, 1950** Miners in the International Union of Mine, Mill, and Smelter Workers union (IUMMSW) went on strike against the Empire Zinc Company in New Mexico. Their initial demands were for an end to discriminatory pay, which paid white workers more than Mexican workers, and to segregated housing. Later, they added indoor plumbing and hot water for Mexican American homes to their list of demands. The company fought back, sending police to harass picketers, posting eviction notices on company houses, cutting off credit to strikers at the company grocery store, and sending in scabs. In time, however, miners from other companies in the area joined the picket line.

Eight months into the strike, the company got a court injunction forbidding the strikers to return to the picket line, so the wives of the workers took up the picket line to get around the company's legal tactic. The women faced sexism, police violence, and mass arrest but stayed strong. After fifteen months the company gave in to nearly every demand, agreeing to improve wages and benefits and provide hot water to homes in the town.

The strike drew national attention and was dramatized in the 1954 film *Salt of the Earth*, directed and produced by filmmakers blacklisted by Hollywood, with most roles played by workers rather than professional actors.

October 17, 1961 Scores of Algerian demonstrators were massacred by police in Paris after an 8:30 p.m. to 5:30 a.m. curfew was ordered for "Algerian Muslim workers," "French Muslims," and "French Muslims of Algeria." Some thirty to forty thousand were marching in the demonstration called by the Algerian Front de Libération Nationale (National Liberation Front; FLN), which was fighting for independence from France. Eleven thousand people of various nationalities and religions were arrested and more than two hundred demonstrators were beaten to death, robbed by police, and thrown in the Seine River.

The chief of police had been a prominent Nazi collaborator. At the time, the French media hardly covered the killings, and the government only acknowledged the events in 1998, claiming that only forty people had been killed.

18 **October 18, 1931** German workers in Braunschweig went on strike to show their opposition to the Nazis. In the latter half of 1931, there were twenty-five political strikes by a total of thirty thousand workers to protest fascism, with many more the following year. However, they remained mostly short stoppages in small and medium-size enterprises and were insufficient to damage the state.

October 18, 1948 Three United Brewery Workers officials in New York City were booed off stage when they tried to address a meeting of wildcat striking brewery workers at the Brooklyn Labor Lyceum. Union members had insisted they would not listen to union representatives unless they agreed to speak with the steering committee set up by the strikers themselves. Nearly three thousand workers at twelve of the city's fourteen breweries had walked out five days previously to protest the union-sanctioned dismissal of twenty-one drivers. Seventy taverns in Manhattan had by this point run out of beer.

19 **October 19, 1920** The battle of Ch'ing-Shan-Li began in Manchuria, with the Korean Independence Army, under the command of anarchist General Kim Chwa-chin, wiping out an entire division of the Japanese Imperial Army.

October 19, 1920 Sylvia Pankhurst was arrested and charged under Regulation 42 of the Defense of the Realm Act with attempting to cause sedition in the navy by editing and publishing two articles in the October 16 issue of the newspaper *Workers Dreadnought*: "Discontent on the Lower Deck," which was based on a letter from a young navy rating named Springhill and published under the pseudonym S.000 (Gunner), and an article on racism titled "The Yellow Peril and the Dockers," written by Claude McKay, under the pseudonym Leon Lopez. The latter article urged dockers not to load ships supplying arms to anti-communist forces, just a few months after the successful May 10 boycott of the SS *Jolly George*.

20 **October 20, 1877** This drawing at right depicting starving people awaiting famine relief in Bangalore, India, was published in *Illustrated London News*. During the famine of 1873–1874, there were few or even no deaths, as the British governor, Richard Temple, organized a swift relief effort. Temple was strongly criticized by British officials afterward for spending too much. So when the famine of 1876 struck, he did not repeat his earlier "mistake." While Indians were starving, hundreds of thousands of tons of food were exported to England, and only meager relief was pro-

Illustration of people awaiting famine relief *(Courtesy of the Illustrated London News/ Wikimedia Commons)*

vided. Around 5.5 million people died in what many historians describe as an act of genocide.

October 20, 1952 Governor Baring of Kenya signed an order declaring a state of emergency to crush the Mau Mau rebellion against British colonial rule. Early the next morning, British authorities carried out a mass arrest of over 180 alleged Mau Mau leaders in Nairobi. Over the coming years the British would murder tens of thousands of civilians. They also dropped over six million bombs on the country and carried out a mass campaign of torture, rape of women, and castration of men to suppress the movement.

21 **October 21, 1935** The Saint Vincent labor rebellion began on the British-occupied Caribbean island, when workers protesting against the high prices in the capital, Kingstown, were fired on by police. People were also protesting against plans to maintain sugar tariffs that helped producers at the expense of consumers. They held an angry rally outside the courthouse, where they smashed windows and damaged the cars of officials. The governor and attorney general were attacked, and the crowd ransacked the office of a councilor and plantation owner, and some protesters broke into the prison, liberating ten prisoners. Armed police read the Riot Act and then began firing into the crowd, killing one person and injuring several others. Rioting then spread to Georgetown and Chateaubelair, with protesters cutting telephone wires and destroying bridges. At midnight that night, a British warship arrived. Authorities declared a state of emergency the next day that lasted for three weeks.

October 21, 1970 The first women's liberation demonstration in Japan took place in Tokyo, kickstarting the feminist movement in the country. The women demanded the legalization of the contraceptive pill and opposed any prohibition of abortion.

After the failure of the mass movement against the Japan-US security treaty, women student activists finally felt able to express their demands as women. Until then they had held their peace so as not to be seen as "undermining" the struggle against the treaty.

Sexual liberation and free love also exploded at that time and, without contraceptives, millions of women were having to have abortions. The pill was only legalized in 1999.

22 **October 22, 1905** Thirty thousand workers in Chile rose up against poor working conditions and the rising cost of living. Butchers, shoemakers, cigar makers, tapestry makers, telegraph workers, and others took part in the revolt, which saw rail workers blow up railway tracks. The police were overwhelmed, so the rich formed a "white guard" to begin massacring workers. After 250 were killed, the rebellion subsided, but the working class movement nonetheless continued to grow in strength.

October 22, 1972 Feminists in Vancouver, British Columbia, Canada, founded the Service, Office and Retail Workers' Union of Canada (SORWUC). They sought to represent workers in marginalized, low-paying, largely women-dominated sectors that weren't high priorities for the big business unions. No union officials were paid more than the highest wage in a SORWUC contract, and rank-and-file members directly decided what they wanted in their collective agreements. The union was also committed to the rights of Indigenous women, sex workers, and single mothers, campaigned for daycare, and defended abortion rights. Due to their radicalism, they were targeted by both the bosses and the labor movement bureaucrats. They disbanded in 1986.

23 **October 23, 1901** A general strike broke out in Rosario, Argentina, in response to the police killing of anarchist migrant worker Cosme Budislavich during a sugar refinery strike.

A destroyed Soviet tank in Budapest *(Courtesy of FORTEPAN/Nagy Gyula/Wikimedia Commons CC by SA 3.0)*

October 23, 1956 A nationwide revolt in Hungary saw thousands organize themselves into workers' councils and militias, demanding not a transition to capitalism but rather a socialism controlled by the working class itself.

Peter Fryer, a member of the British Communist Party and a journalist for the Party newspaper the *Daily Worker* wrote in his first dispatch:

> After eleven years the incessant mistakes of the Communist leaders, the brutality of the State Security Police, the widespread bureaucracy and mismanagement, the bungling, the arbitrary methods and the lies have led to total collapse. This was no counter-revolution, organised by fascists and reactionaries. It was the upsurge of a whole people, in which rank-and-file Communists took part, against a police dictatorship dressed up as a Socialist society—a police dictatorship backed up by Soviet armed might.
>
> And I have no hesitation in placing the blame for these terrible events squarely on the shoulders of those who led the Hungarian Communist Party for eleven years. . . . They turned what could have been the outstanding example of people's democracy in Europe into a grisly caricature of Socialism. They reared and trained a secret police which tortured all—Communists as well as non-Communists—who dared to open their mouths against injustices. It was a secret police

which in these last few dreadful days turned its guns on the people whose defenders it was supposed to be.

Fryer's article went unpublished, and the rebellion was soon crushed by Russian tanks, leaving around 20,000 Hungarians and 3,500 Russians dead.

24 **October 24, 1975** Ninety percent of women in Iceland went on general strike for equality with men. Working women stayed home, and houseworkers refused to cook, clean, and look after children. Today Iceland has the lowest gender inequality in the world, although women still earn only 80 percent of men's wages, so discrimination and the struggle against it continues.

October 24, 2007 *Time* magazine reported that some thirty-five thousand sex workers were on strike in Bolivia to protest police harassment. The women, organized in the National Organization for the Emancipation of Women in a State of Prostitution—a union for sex workers—also refused mandatory STD testing until police stopped the harassment.

25 **October 25, 1983** The Hayes Cottage Hospital in England was occupied by its workers to protest a proposed closure the following week. The workers ran the hospital themselves until the government caved in. The hospital remained open until the 1990s, when it was turned into a private nursing home.

October 25, 1983 The US invaded the Caribbean island of Grenada, ostensibly to protect US citizens but really to assert its dominance over the region.

26 **October 26, 1977** Eight thousand workers at the Swadeshi Cotton Mills in Kanpur, India, surrounded their factory, locking the bosses inside, because they had not been paid in several weeks. The unions offered no help, so workers beat up the union leaders. They then placed gas cylinders and acid bottles on the roof of the factory and threatened to start blowing things up. After a fifty-four-hour siege, the workers' back wages were paid.

October 26, 1983 The Northwood and Pinner Cottage Hospital in England was occupied by its workers to protest against its proposed closure. Beginning the following day, October 27, they collectively ran the hospital themselves, eventually winning their struggle. The hospital remained open for a further twenty-five years.

27 **October 27, 1962** At the height of the Cuban Missile Crisis, second-in-command Vasily Arkhipov of the Soviet submarine B-59 refused to agree with his captain's order to launch nuclear torpedoes against US warships and set off what might well have been a terminal superpower nuclear war.

The US had been dropping depth charges near the submarine in an attempt to force it to surface, unaware it was carrying nuclear arms. The Soviet officers, who had lost radio contact with Moscow, concluded that World War III had begun, and two of the officers

Vasily Arkhipov, 1960 *(Courtesy of Wikimedia Commons)*

agreed to "blast the warships out of the water." Arkhipov disagreed and, as unanimous consent of the three officers was required for launch, it is thanks to his dissent that we are able to write about it today.

October 27, 1970 The Republican administration of President Richard Nixon passed the Comprehensive Drug Abuse Prevention and Control Act, as part of their "war on drugs." A Nixon adviser, John Ehrlichman, later admitted in an interview with Dan Baum published in *Harper's Magazine*:

> The Nixon campaign in 1968, and the Nixon White House after that, had two enemies: the anti-war left and Black people. You understand what I'm saying? We knew we couldn't make it illegal to be either against the war or Black, but by getting the public to associate the hippies with marijuana and Blacks with heroin, and then criminalizing both heavily, we could disrupt those communities. We could arrest their leaders, raid their homes, break up their meetings, and vilify them night after night on the evening news. Did we know we were lying about the drugs? Of course we did.

28 **October 28, 1916** Conscription to the Australian Army during World War I was narrowly defeated in a referendum by 51 percent to 49 percent. Labor prime minister Billy Hughes, a former union leader, had vigorously attempted to introduce conscription. He blamed the Industrial

Workers of the World union (IWW) for the defeat.

The IWW had been extremely active in opposing conscription and the war. Hughes responded by banning the organization and arresting and jailing many of its members and activists. But when a second referendum was held the following year, it

IWW mass meeting in Sydney, 1916 *(Courtesy of the University of Washington Industrial Workers of the World Photograph Collection)*

was defeated by an even bigger margin. 🎙 **19**

October 28, 2016 A young fish seller in the Rif region of Morocco, Mouhcine Fikri, was crushed by a dumpster while police were confiscating his fish. His horrific death was filmed by witnesses and posted online, sparking outrage across the region. Thousands of people attended his funeral two days later, and protest marches took place in Casablanca, Marrakesh, and Rabat. Over the next few months, an extensive and sophisticated social movement grew, demanding an end to the permanent state of emergency in the Rif and numerous reforms, including improvements to education, particularly for women, better health care, lower prices, land reform, and more.

29 **October 29, 1918** During the night, sailors in the German Navy refused an order to attack the British in the North Sea. The order was given five times, but each time the sailors resisted, despite one thousand mutineers being arrested. Over the coming nights the rebellion spread, paralyzing the imperial fleet and leading to a revolution and the end of

Rebel sailors demonstrate in Germany, November 1918 *(Courtesy of the Bundesarchiv, Bild 146-1976-067-10A/CC-BY-SA 3.0)*

World War I—something that is usually ignored in official narratives of the conflict.

October 29, 1940 In France, Iranian Muslim diplomat Abdol Hossein Sardari wrote to Vichy government officials to try to persuade them that Jews from

Central Asia (Jugutis) were not technically Jewish under Nazi race laws. In 1943, as a result of his arguments, the Nazis agreed and exempted them. Without the consent of his bosses, Sardari began issuing Iranian passports to Jews, helping some two thousand escape the Vichy regime.

30 **October 30, 1919** Residents of the Pennsylvania Working Home for Blind Men demanded higher wages for their work, threatening to strike the following week. The visually impaired men made brooms, whisks, carpets, and other goods, and their home had increased their rent with no increase in their wages. They formed a union and affiliated with the American Federation of Labor (AFL). The boss told the *New York Times* that the men, "like the rest of the world, have got strike fever."

October 30, 1944 The left-wing Greek People's Liberation Army (GPLA) liberated Thessaloniki from Nazi occupation. At dawn, some GPLA units stopped the Nazis from blowing up power plants and food factories, while

Partisans in Greece *(Courtesy Φωτογραφική έκθεση υπηρεσίας Διπλωματικού και Ιστορικού Αρχείου. Diplomatic and Historical Archive Department/Wikimedia Commons CC by SA 2.0)*

others attacked retreating German units. By 2:00 p.m., liberation was complete, and the partisans began parading through the streets. The population then gathered and elected representatives for self-government. The city remained under the control of the local community until February of the following year, when it was taken over by the right-wing Greek state. Over the course of the occupation, Thessaloniki lost 10 percent of its total population, 96 percent of its Jewish population, and 90 percent of its industry.

31 **October 31, 1978** Thirty thousand oil workers went on strike in Iran, marking one of the early actions of the Iranian Revolution. The oil workers, as well as the workers' and women's movements in general, would play a major role in the revolution, until they were crushed by followers of the religious fundamentalist Ayatollah Khomeini.

October 31, 1986 Five thousand nurses in Victoria, Australia, stopped work, held a mass meeting, and voted for an indefinite strike against pay cuts to begin the next day. The strike continued to grow, and the government finally caved in on December 19.

NOVEMBER

1 **November 1, 1954** The Algerian War began, with Algerians revolting against French colonial rule. The French military responded to the rebellion with extreme brutality, using widespread torture and killing hundreds of thousands of people, mostly civilians. Later, French paramilitaries joined the conflict, carrying out terrorist attacks and murdering Algerian civilians. Back at home, French police murdered scores of people who demonstrated against French colonialism, mostly French Muslims and French Algerians, as well as several French communists. But the anti-colonial struggle continued, achieving independence in 1962.

November 1, 1972 Indian workers at the Mansfield Hosiery Mills in Loughborough, England, were on strike for higher wages and the right to promotion to jobs reserved for white workers. When the men and women first walked out in October, the National Union of Hosiery and Knitwear Workers (NUHKW) refused to back the strike. It was eventually forced to do so when strikers occupied its offices. But the union still refused to call out its white members, who, in any case, benefited from the discrimination against Indians. Asian textile workers in the area did, however, walk out in sympathy. The dispute ended in December, with the workers winning concessions. Subsequently, a commission of inquiry wrote a report detailing union complicity in racist practices, and warned that if unions did not desist in their racism, then Black and Asian workers would form their own union. 🎙 **1**

2 **November 2, 1912** Dozens of striking timber workers, who had been on trial on charges arising from the Grabow massacre, including riot and murder, were acquitted of all charges. The massacre occurred after timber bosses opened fire on strikers organized in the Brotherhood of Timber Workers (BTW) outside the Grabow mill in Louisiana, causing a shootout that left four dead and fifty injured. Four days after the acquittal, the mill was burned to the ground. The official report determined that the fire was an accident.

November 2, 1970 Actor and Vietnam GI resistance supporter Jane Fonda was arrested at the Cleveland airport as she returned from a Vietnam Veterans Against the War (VVAW) event held in Canada and charged with drug smuggling. The following day Fonda was also charged with kicking a police officer, when a famous mugshot was taken of her, with her fist raised in defiance. Both charges were bogus—the "drugs" were vitamins—and both were later dismissed. Fonda is clear that the intention was to discredit her, because of her valuable support for the GI anti-war movement.

In addition to being a patron of VVAW, Fonda was a leading organizer of and participant in the Fuck The Army (FTA) tour, an anti-war alternative to the United Service Organizations (USO) shows which are put on to entertain the troops. 🎙 **10–11**

3 **November 3, 1970** A regional office of the United Farm Workers union (UFW) in California was bombed. The UFW—largely made up of Latine and Filipine workers—had been on strike for weeks in a jurisdictional dispute with the Teamsters union.

November 3, 1979 The Greensboro massacre took place in North Carolina. Five anti-racists, four of them members of the Communist Workers' Party (CWP), at an anti–Ku Klux Klan (KKK) demonstration were killed by members of the KKK and the American Nazi Party (ANP). Police had cooperated with the Nazis, giving them a map of the anti-racists' demonstration route. The killers were later acquitted by all-white juries.

4 **November 4, 1910** In France, in a prelude to the Champagne Riots of the following year, several grape growing communes decided to stop paying taxes. Growers were angry at champagne producers driving down prices and importing cheaper grapes from elsewhere in Europe to make their "champagne." They wanted the government to legislate that champagne had to be made primarily from grapes from the Champagne region.

A few months later, on January 17, simmering discontent erupted into violence when growers in the village of Damery intercepted a wagonload of imported grapes and threw it into the Marne River. Growers then raided the warehouses of a producer they considered "fraudulent" and raised a red flag at the town hall. Protests, including singing the "Internationale," escalated into a full-blown insurrection. The government responded by initiating a nine-month occupation of the area by forty thousand troops, but they also implemented the law the protesters were demanding.

November 4, 1913 The East London Federation of Suffragettes (ELFS) which was fighting for women's rights and working class emancipation had its first paramilitary assembly and gun drill in Victoria Park, London. The following day, the group formally inaugurated their People's Army, a community militia to resist police repression. Sylvia Pankhurst, a left communist and

Illustration of the People's Army drill *(By Hester Reeve, hesterreeve.com)*

daughter of famous suffragette Emmeline, was a key organizer of both ELFS and the People's Army.

5 **November 5, 1843** An enslaved woman named Carlota led an uprising in Matanzas, Cuba. Brandishing machetes, Carlota and her coconspirators summoned other enslaved people with a kettle drum, then killed the cane plantation slave owners before heading to neighboring plantations and farms to free other slaves. The rebellion lasted until the following year, when authorities succeeded in violently repressing it. Carlota herself was tied to four horses and torn apart. The abolition of slavery in Cuba was finally achieved in 1886.

November 5, 1916 At least five members of the Industrial Workers of the World union (IWW) were massacred by police and bosses' thugs after about three hundred IWW members travelled from Seattle on two steamships to support striking workers and the right to free speech in Everett, Washington.

Only one of the steamships, the *Verona*, which carried over two hundred IWW members, got to the dock in Everett, where more than two hundred police and anti-union vigilantes were waiting. When asked by the Sheriff Don McRae who their leader was, the IWW members on the boat replied, "We're all leaders." Moments later the boat, which was also carrying non-IWW passengers and crew, came under intense gunfire (two vigilantes were even accidentally shot from behind by their fellow vigilantes). In the chaos, the steamship reversed direction and headed back to Seattle, advising the *Calista* to do the same. Upon arriving back in Seattle, seventy-four Wobblies were arrested and put on trial. They were all acquitted some six months later, a significant victory for the union. 🔊 **16**

Funeral of IWW member Felix Baran *(Courtesy of the University of Washington Social Issue Files Dc/i neg #11504/ Wikimedia Commons)*

6 **November 6, 1913** Against the background of a mass direct-action campaign against racist pass laws, striking Indian mine workers in South Africa demonstrated against a new tax on former indentured laborers. Around two thousand miners marched, as did some women and children. The mine workers were also joined by Mohandas Gandhi, who was arrested at the demonstration. Gandhi did not initially support the movement against the tax, as he feared it would alienate the white population; however, he was swept up by the working class discontent. The tax was soon scrapped.

November 6, 1986 The Iran-Contra scandal—the US sale of arms to Iran to raise funds for right-wing paramilitaries in Nicaragua—first came to light. President Ronald Reagan said, "The speculation [that the US had sold arms to Iran] has no foundation," which was, of course, a lie. The fact of the matter is that the US wanted to overthrow the left-wing Sandinista government and had been providing arms and support to the right-wing Contra death squads. Eventually, public opposition to the policy forced Congress to cut off funding, so the Reagan administration continued it illegally by selling weapons to Iran, technically a hostile power, through the Israeli government. They then used those funds to purchase weapons that the CIA delivered to the Contras.

7 **November 7, 1917** The October Revolution, one of the most momentous events in world history, began in Russia. Bolsheviks, anarchists, and Left-Socialist Revolutionaries overthrew the government formed by

Socialist Revolutionary Party leader Alexander Kerensky, which was committed to continuing Russia's disastrous participation in World War I. They seized control of key locations in Petrograd, culminating in the storming of the Winter Palace.

It is known as the "October" Revolution, because it took place during that month on the Old Style calendar Russia used at the time.

November 7, 1968 Police in Rawalpindi, Pakistan, opened fire on a student rally against the Mohammad Ayub Khan dictatorship, killing three people. The repression backfired, triggering protests against the regime across the country. Working class people began to refuse to pay bus and railway fares, peasant revolts were launched, and industrial workers went out on strike. By March of the following year, the government had collapsed, agreeing to hold elections in 1970.

8 **November 8, 1965** Harold Wilson, the UK Labour prime minister, authorized the establishment of the British Indian Ocean Territory. This was the first act in the ethnic cleansing of the Chagos Archipelago. Over the next few years, the entire Chagossian population was forcibly removed from their homes, never to return. One foreign office official wrote to diplomat Dennis Greenhill: "We must surely be very tough about this. The object of the exercise was to get some rocks which will remain ours. There will be no Indigenous population except seagulls." Greenhill replied: "Along with the birds go some few Tarzans or Men Fridays." The residents were only allowed to take one suitcase each, before being forcibly transferred to the Seychelles, and all pets were destroyed. The aim of the ethnic cleansing was to allow the government to lease the largest island to the US for a military base at a dollar per year.

November 8, 2004 Nickel smelter workers in New Caledonia went on strike to protest the firing of two coworkers for previous strike activity. The strike lasted twenty-two days and ended when both workers were rehired. The strike cost the company over $40 million.

9 **November 9, 1918** As revolution swept the country and the Kaiser abdicated, German workers fought to end World War I. Berlin was gripped by an anti-war general strike, with rebel sailors, soldiers, and workers taking to the streets. The deputy chairman of the Sozialdemokratische Partei Deutschlands (Social Democratic Party; SPD) Philipp

Schneidermann learned that revolutionary socialist Karl Liebknecht, fresh out of prison, planned to declare a socialist republic. To avoid being outmaneuvered, he defied the party leader and took to a balcony at the Reichstag, where he declared a republic. That evening, dozens of workers from large Berlin factories, mistrusting the SPD leadership, occupied the Reichstag and announced elections to factory and army regiment councils the following day to form a revolutionary government.

November 9, 1988 Brazilian security forces murdered three striking workers and injured dozens. Workers at the Companhia Siderúrgica Nacional (National Iron Metallurgy Company) of Brazil had been on strike for a pay increase and for the reinstatement of workers fired for their political beliefs. Those killed were Carlos Augusto Barroso, nineteen, William Fernandes Leite, twenty-two, and Valmir Freitas Monteiro, twenty-seven. Despite the repression, the workers continued their sit-in strike for over two more weeks. The massacre was orchestrated by the new "democratic" government after the fall of the military dictatorship.

10 **November 10, 1970** Puerto Rican radicals from the Young Lords took over Lincoln Hospital, in New York City's South Bronx. More than six hundred people, including clerical workers, nurses, and doctors, joined them in occupying the nurses' residence to publicize the flagrant disregard for human life in New York City hospitals.

November 10, 1995 Ken Saro-Wiwa, Ogoni Indigenous author, activist, and environmentalist, and eight other people were hanged by the Nigerian state. Saro-Wiwa advocated for Ogoni rights and helped organize nonviolent resistance to the destruction of Indigenous lands by the Royal Dutch Shell oil company. Many witnesses who testified against Saro-Wiwa later recanted, admitting that they had been bribed either by the government or by Shell to lie. Saro-Wiwa was the first of

Illustration of Ken Saro-Wiwa *(dignidadrebelde, CC by SA 2.0 https://www.flickr.com/photos/dignidadrebelde/30541935515)*

the nine activists to be murdered. It took five attempts to kill him. The other victims were Baribor Bera, Saturday Dobee, Nordu Eawo, Daniel Gbooko, Paul Levera, Felix Nuate, Barinem Kiobel, and John Kpuine. Saro-Wiwa's final words were: "Lord take my soul, but the struggle continues."

11 **November 11, 1918** Two hundred fifty thousand men and women began a general strike across Switzerland. Compared to revolutionary actions elsewhere at the time, the demands were relatively moderate, including: immediate new elections on the basis of proportional representation; the introduction of women's suffrage; a general duty to work; the forty-eight-hour workweek; democratic reform of the army; an adequate food supply; state pensions for the elderly and disabled people; state monopolies in export and import; and coverage of the national debt by the rich. The following day ninety-five thousand troops were brought in to crush the strike, and, on November 13, the government issued an ultimatum. The next day strike leaders decided to end the general strike to prevent further escalation of the situation. After the strike ended that day, three people in Grenchen were killed by troops. In the aftermath of the strike, military tribunals sentenced 127 people, mainly railway workers. Women did not get the right to vote until 1971.

November 11, 1948 Wildcat striking brewery workers in New York City won a month-long walkout demanding the scrapping of excessively short drivers' schedules that did not give them enough time to load and unload their vehicles. A mass meeting of the remaining three thousand strikers (five small breweries having already conceded to the demands) agreed to end their strike at midnight that night and return to work the following day.

Bosses were also forced to drop their multimillion-dollar lawsuit against the United Brewery Workers' union, which had, in any case, denounced the walkout and tried first to order and then manipulate the strikers back to work. Edward Hughlett, a union official who tried to address the meeting was booed so loudly he was forced to surrender the microphone twice, and the *New York Times* reported that the "hostility toward the international union official took on such menacing proportions that six uniformed patrolmen rushed out of a side room to protect him."

12 **November 12, 1977** The first Reclaim the Night marches in the UK took place in Leeds, York, Bristol, Manchester, Newcastle, Brighton, and London. They were called by the Leeds Revolutionary Feminist Group, which was inspired by news of coordinated women-only Take Back the Night marches against sexual harassment held in towns and cities across West Germany on April 30, 1977.

This was particularly significant to women in the area, because serial murderer Peter Sutcliffe, dubbed by the press the "Yorkshire Ripper," had sexually attacked and murdered thirteen women across Yorkshire, including in Leeds, from 1975 to 1980. Women in the area were angry that the police response to these murders seemed slow, and that the press barely reported on them, because it was mainly sex workers who were killed. When a young student was murdered, the press and the police seemed to take more notice.

Official police advice was that women not go out at night, effectively putting them under a curfew. This was not a helpful suggestion, especially for women working late shifts or night shifts or for sex workers, who often had no choice but to go out at night.

November 12, 1984 A group of anti–nuclear weapon activists damaged a nuclear missile silo in Missouri, taking a pneumatic drill to the silo. Four, including Helen Woodson, a mother of eleven, were arrested and jailed with extremely harsh sentences. Woodson ended up serving twenty-seven years.

13 **November 13, 1909** Suffragette Theresa Garnett attacked Home Secretary Winston Churchill with a horsewhip in Bristol, shouting, "Take that in the name of the insulted women of England!" Garnett was arrested for assault, but Churchill did not want to appear in court, so he did not press charges. Instead she was jailed for one month for "disturbing the peace." In prison, Garnett joined other suffragettes on hunger strike and was force-fed. She set fire to her cell in protest and was moved to a solitary confinement punishment cell.

Theresa Garnett, 1909 *(Photo by Linley Blathwayt, courtesy of Wikimedia Commons)*

November 13, 1974 Plutonium plant worker and Oil, Chemical and Atomic Workers Union (OCAW) activist Karen Silkwood was mysteriously killed in a car crash while on her way to meet a *New York Times* reporter with a bundle of evidence on health and safety violations at her workplace. The bundle of evidence was never found, and although she was killed in a head-on collision, the rear of her car had been damaged and contained paint chips, leading her supporters to believe she was rammed off the road. She and her apartment were also heavily contaminated with plutonium, which the company claimed she did herself to smear the firm. Her family sued the company after her death and was awarded nearly $1.4 million.

14 **November 14, 1917** The "Night of Terror" began at the Occoquan Workhouse in Virginia. A group of women, mostly members of the National Women's Party (NWP), had been arrested while protesting outside the White House in support of voting rights for women earlier that day. Guards were ordered to torture them while they were in detention, and just after midnight, early on November 15, the thirty-three suffragist prisoners were brutally beaten and abused.

November 14, 1973 Students at the Athens Polytechnic went on strike to protest the military dictatorship. They barricaded themselves inside the university, set up a radio station, and began broadcasting to the city, calling on others to join their struggle.

On November 17, in the early hours of the morning, an army tank smashed through the university gates intent upon evicting the students but ended up triggering a wider uprising.

The number of people killed in the repression is still debated in Greece, but it was at least twenty-four, with hundreds of others injured.

To this day November 17 is observed as a holiday by the Greek educational system and recognized as the central milestone in the restoration of democracy in 1974.

15 **November 15, 1922** Between three hundred and one thousand people were massacred by the state during a general strike in Guayaquil, Ecuador. Power company and trolley workers had walked out on strike to protest worsening economic conditions and were joined by every other worker in the city. Strikers and their families assembled for a peaceful rally on November 15. Completely unprovoked, the armed forces and police opened fire on the crowd, killing hundreds.

November 15, 2011 In Trinidad, Bolivia, a group of disabled Bolivians began a march to capital La Paz meant to encourage the government to increase support for disabled people and to tackle societal stigma about disability. The march grew to two hundred, including children, with a thousand supporters gathering in La Paz. When the march entered La Paz in February 2012, riot police attacked the marchers. In the aftermath, an embarrassed President Evo Morales conceded to several of the marchers' demands.

16 **November 16, 1984** Two thousand Black residents in Johannesburg, South Africa, were arrested for nonpayment of rent. They claimed, truthfully, that they were unable to pay rent, because they had burned down the rent office. Apparently, the police did not consider this a valid excuse.

November 16, 1989 Six Jesuit priests, their housekeeper, and her daughter were murdered by the US-backed military in El Salvador. The regime considered the priests to be "subversives." After the soldiers killed them, they tried to make the murders look like the work of left-wing guerrillas.

17 **November 17, 1915** Thousands of housewives and workers in Glasgow marched on the sheriff's court in support of twenty thousand rent strikers, in a dispute that led to the introduction of rent control throughout Britain. One observer, Willie Gallacher, wrote:

> From early morning the women were marching to the centre of the city where the sheriff's court is situated.... But even as they marched, mighty reinforcements were coming from the workshops and the yards. From far away Dalmuir in the West, from Parkhead in the East, from Cathcart in the South and Hydepark in the North, the dungareed army of the proletariat invaded the centre of the city.

November 17, 1983 The Zapatista Army of National Liberation (EZLN) was founded in Chiapas, Mexico, by six people, some from the urban North and others from rural Indigenous communities in the mountains of Chiapas, Mexico. Eleven years later, around three thousand predominantly Indigenous armed EZLN members launched an uprising taking control of a considerable amount of land in the region, freeing prisoners, and destroying police and army barracks. In a counterattack by the Mexican Army, the guerrillas lost control of many towns and cities and retreated into the Lacandon jungle.

Subsequently the Zapatistas established a number of self-governing autonomous communities, with a total population of over three hundred thousand people. Other than personal property, private ownership was abolished, with collective ownership of land and collectively owned and run workplaces. Radical, democratic schools, where pupils are not graded, were established, as was a universal health care service, massively improving public health and reducing infant mortality. The communities also have a strong commitment to Indigenous, women's, and LGBT+ rights.

18 **November 18, 1965** The term "sexism" was probably coined by Pauline M. Leet during a student-faculty forum at Franklin and Marshall College. Specifically, the word sexism appears in Leet's forum contribution "Women and the Undergraduate," and she defines it by comparing it to racism, stating:

> When you argue . . . that since fewer women write good poetry this justifies their total exclusion, you are taking a position analogous to that of the racist—I might call you in this case a "sexist." . . . Both the racist and the sexist are acting as if all that has happened had never happened, and both of them are making decisions and coming to conclusions about someone's value by referring to factors which are in both cases irrelevant.

November 18, 1967 Korean workers employed by the United States Army in Vietnam rioted to show their dissatisfaction with their food, overturning tables, attacking Americans, and forcing an American project manager to eat some of their food to show him how bad it was. An American civilian shot three Koreans, and military police stormed the area, but the Korean workers counterattacked with bulldozers and trucks, which they rammed into trailers and buildings, and hijacked boats. The strike and riots were only suppressed four days later. 🎙 **14**

19 **November 19, 1915** Joe Hill, a Swedish American Industrial Workers of the World union (IWW) member and songwriter, was executed by firing squad for the killing of a grocery store owner and his son. Not only did Hill have no motive for the double murder, there was no direct evidence linking him to the crime, which most historians believe he did not commit. His union membership was, however, frequently raised during the trial.

Joe Hill, 1915 *(Courtesy of the Library of Congress/Wikimedia Commons)*

During his lifetime, Hill wrote many songs, including "There Is Power in a Union," "Casey Jones—the Union Scab," and "The Preacher and the Slave" (the origin of the expression "pie in the sky").

In his final letter to IWW leader Big Bill Haywood, he wrote, "Goodbye Bill. I die like a true blue rebel. Don't waste any time in mourning. Organize." 🎙 6

November 19, 1984 One of the world's worst industrial disasters occurred when tanks in a PEMEX petroleum storage facility in San Juanico, Mexico, exploded, killing more than five hundred people and burning an additional five thousand. The plant's safety features were woefully inadequate, but fixing them would have cut into company profits.

20 **November 20, 1913** Margarita Ortega, a Mexican schoolteacher, sharpshooter, and anarchist was arrested and imprisoned by the government of Victoriano Huerta. She and her daughter had thrown themselves into organizing and fighting in the Mexican Revolution. After her arrest by government forces, she was tortured but refused to name any of her comrades, shouting "Cowards! Tear my skin to pieces, break my bones, drink all of my blood, and I will never denounce one of my friends." She was shot three days later.

November 20, 1969 A group of seventy-eight Native Americans occupied Alcatraz Island, demanding more rights, including a Native American university. The occupiers elected a council, set up a school, and distributed tasks among themselves, voting on all major decisions. They held out until June 1971, when authorities evicted the protesters without agreeing to any of their demands. But the action was reported around the

Sign on occupied Alcatraz Island *(Courtesy of the National Park Service/Wikimedia Commons)*

world and helped galvanize a new wave of Native American activism.

21 **November 21, 1920** Soldiers of the Irish Republican Army (IRA) assassinated fifteen suspected British intelligence officers. In retaliation, British colonial police raided Croke Park stadium, where a Gaelic football

match was being played before thousands of spectators, opening fire indis-
criminately and killing fourteen people, including one of the players.

November 21, 1922 Mexican anarchist communist of Zapotec mestizo
descent Ricardo Flores Magón died after months of illness and neglect
in Leavenworth Prison, in Kansas. He was one of the major thinkers of
the Mexican Revolution and the Mexican revolutionary movement and a
member of the anarchist Partido Liberal Mexicano (Mexican Liberal Party;
PLM). He also organized with the Industrial Workers of the World (IWW)
and edited the anarchist newspaper *Regeneración*, which aroused workers
against the dictatorship of Porfirio Díaz. While in prison, he described the
persecution of the US government: "I am caught by the formidable mecha-
nism of a monstrous machine, and my flesh may get ripped open, and my
bones crushed, and my moans fill the space and make the very infinite
shudder, but the machine will not stop grinding, grinding, grinding."

22 **November 22, 1919** The Bogalusa labor massacre took place in
Louisiana. African American worker organizer Sol Dacus was threatened by agents of the Great Southern Lumber Company. White union
members, including the American Federation of Labor (AFL) district repre-
sentative, came to his defense, and four people were murdered by racist
paramilitaries.

November 22, 1968 A mass demonstration was held outside the occupied
Yasuda auditorium, where students at the University of Tokyo had been on
strike since October, in a long-running dispute over unpaid internships for
medical students and a host of other issues.

23 **November 23, 1887** The Thibodaux massacre occurred. Black Louisiana
sugarcane workers, in cooperation with the racially integrated
Knights of Labor union (K of L), had gone on strike at the beginning of the
month over their meager pay, issued in scrip rather than money. The scrip
was redeemable only at the company store, where excessive prices were
charged.

Plantation owners were angry when the first freeze of the season
arrived and damaged crops. After two white strike breakers were shot and
injured, the Louisiana militia, aided by bands of "prominent citizens," shot
and killed at least fifty unarmed Black sugar workers striking for a dollar
per day wage and lynched two strike leaders.

November 23, 1969 Leading Black Panther Fred Hampton spoke at a meeting organized by the Women's International League for Peace and Freedom (WILPF), at the University of Illinois. Among those in attendance was Luis Kutner, a lawyer and cofounder of Amnesty International. Unknown to Hampton, Kutner was an informant for the FBI and reported on the meeting to his handler, claiming that Hampton was "ranting and raving," claiming that President Nixon was "a member of the 'capitalistic establishment'" and asserting that "Nixon must die." Kutner said that he was telling the FBI this because of Hampton's "possible violation of federal law." Just days later, the FBI had Hampton, aged just twenty-one, killed.

24 **November 24, 1995** French workers took part in a massive general strike against welfare and pension reforms. A movement arose in October to oppose measures by the right-wing government of Prime Minister Alain Juppé that aimed to reduce France's budget deficit to the 3 percent limit set by the Maastricht Treaty on European Union. The most controversial proposals were cuts to public sector pensions and an increase of the minimum retirement age to sixty. Some schemes allowed employees to retire at fifty or fifty-five. Huge strikes hit transport, utilities, mining, banking, insurance, and the post office, while clashes with police took place across the country. By December, the government was forced to scrap its pension plans.

November 24, 2010 Much of Portugal ground to a halt in the country's first general strike in more than twenty years, opposing austerity cutbacks. Transport, manufacturing, and public services were particularly hard hit. Austerity measures proposed by the governing Socialist Party included a freeze on public sector pay and widespread privatization.

25 **November 25, 1941** Three young Austrian boys, members of the Schlurf movement, were arrested by the Gestapo for destroying a Hitler Youth noticeboard. The Schlurfs were working class Austrian youths who rejected Nazism, militarism, racism, and the work ethic. They had long hair and listened to jazz and swing music. The boys wore sharp double-breasted suits and the girls, or "Schlurf kittens," wore colored dresses with knee-length hemlines. The Nazis campaigned against the "Schlurf menace," and many Schlurfs fought Hitler Youth in the streets.

After the Allied victory, the new "democratic" authorities continued to denounce young workers who rejected work discipline and authority as "Schlurfs." 🔊 **4**

November 25, 1960 Three sisters—Patria Mercedes Mirabal Reyes, Minerva Mirabal Reyes, and Antonia María Teresa Mirabal Reyes—were assassinated for their opposition to the US-backed Dominican dictatorship of Rafael Trujillo. They had started a group called the Agrupación Política 14 de Junio (14th of June Movement), named after the date of a massacre Patria had witnessed. Two of the sisters, Minerva and Maria Teresa, were imprisoned, raped, and tortured on several occasions, and their husbands were also arrested and tortured. However, they persisted in their resistance, and Trujillo decided to put an end to them once and for all.

On May 18, 1960, Minerva and Maria Teresa, along with their husbands, were convicted and sentenced to three years in prison for undermining the security of the Dominican state. In a strange gesture, on August 9, Minerva and Maria Teresa Mirabal were released by express provision of Trujillo. Their husbands, however, remained in prison. Purportedly a show of mercy, it was, however, part of a plan by which they would be assassinated by the Servicio de Inteligencia Militar secret police.

On November 25, the sisters and Rufino de la Cruz, who was driving their jeep, were stopped by Trujillo's henchmen. They were separated and clubbed to death. The bodies were then gathered and put in the jeep, which was run off the mountain road in an attempt to make their deaths look like an accident. In honor of the women, the UN later designated November 25 International Day for the Elimination of Violence against Women.

26 **November 26, 1926** The national British coal strike ended in defeat, with miners' delegates advising the remaining strikers to return to work. The strike had begun on May 1 to protest wage cuts, increased work hours, and the elimination of their union from pay negotiations.

Striking miners in Tyldesley, 1926 *(Courtesy of Wikimedia Commons)*

The Trades Union Congress (TUC) initially called a general strike in support of the miners, but despite its success they panicked and called it off without gaining any concessions, leaving the miners to struggle on alone. By October, hunger and hardship were forcing a significant number of the strikers to return to work.

November 26, 1938 A football team of Basque boys who were refugees from the Spanish Civil War played a friendly match in Pontypridd, Wales. Wales welcomed many working class children who were fleeing the conflict between workers and peasants and General Francisco Franco's nationalist forces. Tickets to the game were sold to raise funds to support the children.

27 **November 27, 1835** James Pratt, a groom, and John Smith, a laborer, were executed by hanging in London for having sex. They were the last men to be formally executed in Britain for homosexuality.

November 27, 1868 A detachment of US troops under the command of General George Custer attacked an encampment of sleeping Cheyenne people, who were on a reservation, flying a white flag, and had a guarantee of safety from the commander of the local fort. In the so-

Illustration of Custer's attack at Washita *(Courtesy of Harper's Weekly/Wikimedia Commons)*

called "Battle of the Washita," the village was destroyed and 103 Native Americans were massacred, including the peace-seeking chief Black Kettle.

28 **November 28, 1971** Members of the 62 Group of militant Jewish anti-fascists broke up a meeting of the far-right Northern League at the Royal Pavilion Hotel in Brighton, England. The meeting included former German SS officers, as well as members of the National Front. Several of the fascists were hospitalized, and the anti-fascists set off smoke bombs to enable their escape. 🎙 **35–37**

November 28, 1985 An internal document circulated within the Shell Oil Company stated that

> there has been a global warming over the last 100 years, that the 0.5 degrees increase is a result of CO_2 [carbon dioxide] buildup, that we will see a further 1–2 degree warming over the next 40 years. . . . Such a rise would be greater than any change in the last 1000 years. . . . The global mean sea level has risen by some 15 cm over the last 100 years. . . . By 2050, the range of uncertainty of the rise in global mean sea level is 20–120 cm.

It formed part of an extensive confidential 1988 internal company report on the greenhouse effect, which definitively showed that from at least 1981

Shell had been aware of climate change, that it was the result of human behavior, that burning fossil fuels was its primary cause, and that it would have catastrophic effects. Despite this, for decades the company covered up its findings, sponsored fake public studies to try to deny climate change, and fought any government attempts to limit CO_2 emissions.

29 **November 29, 1830** "Captain Swing" farmworkers fighting for better pay and more jobs attacked a farmer and constable in Stour Provost, Dorset. Some of them were arrested and taken to Shaftesbury, but local Swing sympathizers released the prisoners. Before the night was over further rioting broke out in five other towns.

"Captain Swing" was the fictional rebel leader in whose name workers' demand letters were sent.

November 29, 1864 The Sand Creek massacre took place, with US troops attacking a peaceful gathering of Cheyenne and Arapaho people camping under a US flag.

The United States had recognized that the Cheyenne and Arapaho possessed large swathes of land covering parts of present-day Colorado, Nebraska, Wyoming, and Kansas. But after the discovery of gold in the area, settlers invaded the land to mine it, and eventually the government forced the Indigenous people to sign a new treaty and give up over 90 percent of their land. Some chiefs considered the new treaty a betrayal and ignored it, but Black Kettle and his band of Cheyenne and Arapaho wanted peace above all and signed.

They first moved to Fort Lyon, then relocated to Big Sandy Creek, both times at the direction of government. Despite doing everything they were told, even flying a US flag and a white surrender flag above their designated US camp, up to nine hundred troops attacked them while the warriors were out hunting. The soldiers butchered 170 or more unarmed people, mostly women and children, torturing them, then scalping and mutilating the victims and cutting out women's genitals and attaching them to their hats. Between nine and twenty-four of the attackers were killed.

Robert Bent reported in the *New-York Tribune* that he "saw one squaw lying on the bank, whose leg had been broken. A soldier came up to her with a drawn sabre. She raised her arm to protect herself; he struck, breaking her arm. She rolled over, and raised her other arm; he struck, breaking that, and then left her without killing her. I saw one squaw cut open, with an unborn child lying by her side."

Meanwhile, a local newspaper praised the "brilliant feat of arms" and stated the soldiers had "covered themselves with glory."

30 **November 30, 1961** A covert CIA operation known as the Cuban Project or Operation Mongoose that aimed to overthrow the Cuban Communist Party government led by Fidel Castro was authorized by President John F. Kennedy. As a result, the CIA orchestrated multiple terrorist attacks in Cuba, including against railways, oil and food storage, a powerplant, a sawmill, and other targets. While Operation Mongoose was officially terminated in late 1962, sabotage of the Cuban economy by the US government continues to this day.

November 30, 1966 Barbados declared independence from Britain. In 1625, following the Spanish eradication of the native population of Barbados, the British laid claim to the island. After sugarcane was introduced in 1640, tens of thousands of enslaved people of African descent were brought in to work on the plantations, and they soon became a large majority of the population. Rebellions of the enslaved people forced the eventual abolition of slavery; however, British rule remained. In the twentieth century, waves of working class unrest that colonial authorities struggled to crush swept the country.

DECEMBER

December 1, 1919 During a strike by dockworkers in Trinidad and Tobago, strikers attacked working warehouses, ran off the scabs, and marched on the city, forcing working enterprises to close. Public sector workers, coal carriers, and Indian rural laborers walked out on strike as well, leading to an effective general strike. Britain, the colonial power, responded by sending troops and rounding up dozens of strikers, eventually imprisoning eighty-two and deporting four key organizers. The government also introduced strict new laws to stop strikes and protests. But the dockers were successful in winning a 25 percent pay increase, with workers in other enterprises also gaining concessions.

December 1, 1955 Rosa Parks, a Black civil rights activist, was arrested in Montgomery, Alabama, for refusing a bus driver's order to give up her seat in the "colored" section for a white passenger, because the white section was full. Contrary to the popular myth that Parks was simply a woman who was tired at the end of the workday and refused to

Rosa Parks arrested during the bus boycott (*Courtesy of Wikimedia Commons*)

stand up, she was actually an activist dedicated to fighting segregation, had attended direct-action training, and had undertaken fundraising work to support other Black women who had been arrested for refusing to vacate their seats for white people. Parks later declared, "The only tired I was was tired of giving in." Anti-racist organizations decided to take on her case and organize a widespread bus boycott across the city that became a key struggle in the civil rights movement.

December 2, 1980 Four Catholic nuns from the US were kidnapped, raped, and murdered by government-backed and US-trained right-wing death squads during the civil war in El Salvador. This war raged on for some twenty years and involved brutal violence against workers' and peasants' organizations, as well as left-wing religious groups.

December 2, 1984 The world's worst industrial disaster took place in Bhopal, India, when the Union Carbide chemical plant leaked poisonous gases that affected five million people, killing, blinding, and disabling tens of thousands. The crumbling plant had no health and safety measures.

The chief executive responsible, Warren Anderson, went unpunished, and of the $470 million compensation paid to the Indian government, only a small fraction made its way to the victims and their families: an average of $500 each.

Those exposed continue to die prematurely today, and children continue to be born with disproportionately high incidences of birth defects, cancers, and chronic illnesses.

3 **December 3, 1944** British-trained and -equipped Greek police, alongside Nazi collaborators, fired on an anti-Nazi demonstration in Athens, killing twenty-eight people, while US and British troops watched. Previously, British forces had attempted to disperse the crowd and shot tracer ammunition over the heads of demonstrators, to no avail. The rationale behind the move was to weaken the anti-Nazi partisans, who had been allied with Britain for the previous three years, as British prime minister Winston Churchill felt they had been overly influenced by communists.

December 3, 1946 One hundred forty-two American Federation of Labor (AFL) union branches downed tools in support of a strike of four hundred women employees, resulting in over one hundred thousand walking out, in what would become known as the Oakland general strike.

Stan Weir, a merchant mariner who was there, described the scene:

> By nightfall the strikers had instructed all stores except pharmacies and food markets to shut down. Bars were allowed to stay open, but they could serve only beer and had to put their juke boxes out on the sidewalk to play at full volume and no charge. "Pistol Packin' Mama, Lay That Pistol Down," the number one hit, echoed off all the buildings. That first 24-hour period of the 54-hour strike had a carnival spirit. A mass of couples danced in the streets. The participants were making history, knew it, and were having fun.

Despite solid strike action, the AFL central labor council called off the action on the morning of December 5 without consulting the workers and without achieving any concessions for the striking women.

4 **December 4, 1956** Thirty thousand women demonstrated in Budapest as part of the wider working class uprising for a socialist society with genuine workers' control. The protest commemorated those who were killed exactly one month prior during the second attack on the city by the Red Army, which effectively put an end to the insurrection. One woman at the demonstration was shot and injured by Russian troops, while another was rescued from arrest by fellow demonstrators. Men who attempted to join the march were repelled by the women protesting.

December 4, 1969 Chicago Black Panther leader Fred Hampton was murdered while asleep in his bed during a raid on his apartment by Chicago Police in conjunction with the FBI. Hampton had been drugged earlier in the evening by an FBI informant, who also told agents the location of Hampton's bed, where he slept alongside his nine-month pregnant fiancée Deborah Johnson. Fellow Panther activist Mark Clark was also killed in the attack, and several others were injured.

Just twenty-one, Hampton was an active, charismatic, and effective organizer, who had been making significant inroads in establishing links with working class whites and building a "Rainbow Coalition" that included Puerto Rican, Native American, Chicane, Chinese American, and white radicals.

Hampton and Clark are among the most well-known victims of the FBI director J. Edgar Hoover's COINTELPRO program, which, among other things, was meant to "prevent the rise of a Black Messiah" who could unite African American resistance.

5 **December 5, 1955** Four days after the arrest of Rosa Parks for refusing to vacate her seat in the "colored" section of a segregated bus for a white passenger, the Montgomery bus boycott began. It was a seminal moment in the civil rights movement, not just for racial equality but also as part of Black women's struggles against sexual violence. Sexual harassment and assault of African American women, predominantly domestic workers, was rife on the city's buses. In the lead-up to the boycott, dozens of women had lodged complaints about nasty, sexualized insults, inappropriate touching, and physical abuse by drivers.

December 5, 2008 Workers at the Republic Windows and Doors manufacturer in Chicago began a sit-down strike against layoffs without compensation. The strike was one of the first to occur in the fallout of the 2008 financial crisis and won widespread support. The strike ended with compensation and all staff keeping their jobs.

6 **December 6, 1918** Black soldiers in the British West Indies Regiment stationed in Taranto, Italy, mutinied against appalling racist treatment and attacked their officers. Though violently suppressed, many of the mutineers later returned home to the Caribbean and joined worker and anti-colonial unrest.

December 6, 1989 Fourteen women, most of whom were training in engineering fields, were murdered in a mass shooting at the École Polytechnique in Montreal. The twenty-five-year-old shooter specifically targeted women, claiming he was "fighting feminism," and killed himself after shooting twenty-eight people, only four of them men. Those killed were: Geneviève Bergeron, Hélène Colgan, Nathalie Croteau, Barbara Daigneault, Anne-Marie Edward, Maud Haviernick, Maryse Laganière, Maryse Leclair, Anne-Marie Lemay, Sonia Pelletier, Michèle Richard, Annie St-Arneault, Annie Turcotte, and Barbara Klucznik-Widajewicz. The day is commemorated annually across Canada as the National Day of Remembrance and Action on Violence against Women.

7 **December 7, 1959** Oil workers on the island of Fiji went on strike. The strike by the Wholesale and Retail Workers General Union (WRWGU) was notable for being the first strike to unite several ethnic groups of workers, mainly Fijian and Indian. The strike threatened both the British colonial government and the traditional Fijian chiefs, who collaborated in opposition to the strike.

December 7, 2006 Three thousand women working at the Misr Spinning and Weaving complex in El-Mahalla El-Kubra, Egypt, left their workstations in protest against non-payment of a bonus. They marched through the plant chanting, "Where are the men? Here are the women!" shaming the men into joining the strike. While thousands of workers gathered in a nearby square, seventy workers remained in the factory, occupying it to prevent production being restarted. They resisted eviction by riot police and remained inside, until, on the fourth day, the government conceded defeat and agreed both to pay the bonus and to commit to not privatizing the plant. The strike triggered a wave of walkouts across the country.

8 **December 8, 1949** A conference of dockworkers in France agreed to prevent all cargo destined for Indochina from being transported from multiple ports during the colonial war in the region. France had been at war with the anti-colonial movement in Vietnam since 1946, a conflict that had spread to the neighboring French protectorates of Cambodia and Laos.

The Mediterranean coastal ports of Marseille, Sète, Nice, Port-de-Bouc, Port-Saint-Louis, Port-Vendres, and Toulon were all blocked. The move followed a refusal of dockers the previous month to load two ships headed for Indochina: the *Montbeliard* and the *Cap Tourane*.

December 8, 2008 Two days after police killed fifteen-year-old Alexis Grigoropoulos, protests across Greece escalated into a full-blown revolt. The rebellion was so militant and extensive that it resulted in the jailing of the officers responsible for the killing. One commentator noted:

> The anarchists themselves were surprised by the level of violence coming from many parts of society. They felt anxious. These were the people who before were very active and very violent, and now they felt surprised and even a little anxious about society. They felt that society had surpassed them.

9 **December 9, 1959** The British government circulated a secret memo as part of Operation Legacy: a plan to destroy official records of the British Empire's crimes in its colonies. The memo ordered the burning of files, although subsequently the government also allowed "for documents to be packed in weighted crates and dumped in very deep and current-free water at maximum practicable distance from the coast." Operation Legacy proved highly successful, and Britain's appalling colonial legacy is not at all well-known in the UK.

December 9, 1987 The uprising of Palestinians against Israeli occupation that became known as the First Intifada began. Palestinians took part in a general strike, refused to pay Israeli taxes, boycotted Israeli institutions, and rioted, in disturbances that would last into the early 1990s.

10 **December 10, 1924** The first gay rights organization in the US, the Society for Human Rights, was founded in Chicago by postal worker and former soldier Henry Gerber. A few months later, police arrested several leading members, including Gerber, and the group ceased to exist.

December 10, 1984 A group called Lesbians and Gays Support the Miners (LGSM) put on a benefit show called Pits & Perverts at Camden's Electric Ballroom, featuring pop group Bronski Beat, to support miners, who had been on strike for several months against mass pit closures. The gig raised

LGSM members in the Onllwyn Miners' Welfare Hall
(Courtesy of LGSM)

over £5,000 (approximately US$6,700) for strikers in South Wales.

LGSM had been set up following the London Pride demonstration the previous summer and began raising desperately needed money for mining communities, as the government was essentially attempting to starve striking coal miners back to work.

The organization played a crucial role in Britain in bringing together the workers' and LGBT+ movements and in garnering support from the trade union movement for LGBT+ rights. 🎧 **27–29**

11 **December 11, 1981** A death squad backed by the administration of US president Ronald Reagan massacred about one thousand people in El Mozote, El Salvador. Prior to being killed, many of the victims—half of them children—were tortured, and girls as young as ten were raped by the US-trained soldiers. The death squad was fighting against a left-wing insurgency, but the villagers of El Mozote had remained largely neutral.

December 11, 1983 Three weeks after cruise missiles arrived at Greenham military base in the UK, fifty thousand women protested by encircling the base, holding mirrors, symbolically reflecting the military's image back on itself. Toward the end of the day, women began tearing down large sections of the fence around the facility, and police made hundreds of arrests.

12 **December 12, 1948** The Batang Kali massacre took place in Malaya, with British troops massacring twenty-four unarmed villagers, as part of the campaign against a communist insurgency in the British imperial colony. None of the murderers were charged with any offences.

December 12, 1969 After months of workers' and students' strikes, a bomb exploded at a bank in central Milan, killing sixteen people and wounding eighty-eight. It was initially blamed on the extraparliamentary left, leading to numerous arrests and the police murder of anarchist rail worker Giuseppe Pinelli. It was later discovered that the bombing had been carried out by the far right in concert with the state, as part of what would become known as the *strategia della tensione* (strategy of tension) counterinsurgency campaign. Three fascists were eventually jailed in 2001.

13 **December 13, 1905** Radical farmhand Sándor Csizmadia and some friends set up the Union of Rural Workers in Hungary. It grew rapidly, and in less than two years it had seventy-five thousand members in 625 groups. Having reached this level of strength, day laborers and farm domestics went on strike. The government tried to crush the strike by arresting four thousand people, imposing huge fines on strikers, and eventually banning the union.

December 13, 1971 Six thousand Indigenous Ovambo workers in what is now Namibia went on strike and began a boycott of food from work kitchens in opposition to an exploitative apartheid forced contract work system. The government called in white students and non-Ovambo Black workers as scabs and sent police to attack the strikers, but the stoppage spread.

By January 3, many workplaces and every major mine was on strike. At that point, the South African government agreed to reform the contract system, but the strike continued until January 21, when the system was officially abolished and major concessions, including freedom for workers to choose and leave jobs and free medical care, were granted.

14 **December 14, 1914** General Roberto Silva Renard, the officer responsible for Chile's bloodiest massacre, the Santa Maria School massacre, the killing of more than two thousand striking miners and their wives and children, was stabbed seven times in the street by Antonio Ramón Ramón, a Spanish anarchist whose brother was killed in the massacre. He survived

Mugshot of Antonio Ramón Ramón
(Courtesy of Wikimedia Commons)

the attack but suffered permanent injuries. Ramón was detained, but workers held public campaigns for his defense, and he was only jailed for five years.

December 14, 1951 Bagel bakers in New York City went on strike, shutting thirty-two of the city's thirty-four bagel bakeries. This left shelves bare of bagels and almost entirely cut off the weekly supply of 1.2 million bagels to the city, causing what the *New York Times* described as a "bagel famine." The bakers came to an agreement with the employers in January, but bagel drivers remained out until seven weeks after the start of the dispute, when they reached a deal to compensate them for wages lost during the strike.

15 **December 15, 1890** The Sioux chief Sitting Bull was killed by Indian police at the Standing Rock Reservation in South Dakota. Fearing the growth of the spiritual Ghost Dance movement, which foresaw an end to white expansionism, Indian agent James McLaughlin sent thirty-nine officers and four volunteers to arrest Sitting Bull. Sitting Bull refused to cooperate with police, so they used force, which outraged the crowd that had gathered, one of whom shot a policeman. Police retaliated by shooting Sitting Bull in the chest and head, killing him. A battle then erupted, leaving seven additional villagers and eight police officers dead.

Sitting Bull, c.1883 *(Photograph by David F Barry, courtesy of Wikimedia Commons)*

December 15, 1912 The Federación Obrera Regional del Perú (Regional Workers' Federation of Peru; FORP) held its second assembly, at which it adopted the demand for a maximum eight-hour workday. The union had been formed in October and was subsequently joined by numerous other unions, including electricians', textile workers', and day laborers' unions, as well as anarchist workers' groups.

16 **December 16, 1871** In France, teacher and revolutionary Louise Michel was put on trial following the crushing of the Paris Commune, a three-month period earlier in the year when workers and soldiers had controlled the city. She was charged with trying to overthrow the government, encouraging citizens to arm themselves, and possession and use of weapons, among other offences. Exiled to New Caledonia, she spent four months in a cage on a prison ship. She became a national hero and was granted amnesty in 1880. When a man tried to assassinate her, Michel defended him in court, claiming "he was misled by an evil society."

December 16, 1910 The Houndsditch murders took place in London's East End: three policemen were shot dead and two others seriously injured by a gang of Latvian revolutionaries who had bungled a jewelry store burglary. Investigators focused on the Anarchist Club in Jubilee Street, and Italian anarchist Errico Malatesta was wrongly implicated.

The events were the prelude to the famous Siege of Sidney Street, in which hundreds of police and soldiers battled the radicals. A Latvian revolutionary named Peter the Painter eluded capture and became an East End working class anti-hero.

Peter the Painter, c.1910 *(Courtesy of the Dundee Courier/Wikimedia Commons)*

17 **December 17, 1933** Sexual contact between men was recriminalized in the Soviet Union, after being decriminalized in 1922 in the wake of the 1917 revolution. Authorities claimed that homosexuality was the result of Western bourgeois and German fascist influences, and the official Soviet newspaper *Pravda* published an article that ended with the slogan: "Destroy homosexuality and fascism will disappear!" In early 1934, gay men began to be arrested in large numbers in major Russian cities and sent to the gulags.

One of those imprisoned under the law, Valery Klimov, wrote about the treatment they received:

> There were about ten occasions when gays were murdered before my eyes. One was beaten to death in a prison in Sverdlovsk. There were one hundred men in our cell; three or four raped him every day and then chucked him under the bunks. It was bestial, a nightmare. Once ten of them raped him and then jumped on his head. I nearly went mad there; my hair turned grey. That's how people lose their sanity; many never recover even after they leave.

While lesbianism was never prohibited, and some stereotypically "masculine" lesbians were valued in the military, many lesbians still suffered persecution, including termination of studies or jobs, bullying, threats to strip them of custody of their children, and being committed to psychiatric facilities.

December 17, 1970 In an attempt to crush protests against price rises, the government ordered soldiers to fire on dockworkers in Gdynia, Poland. Dozens were killed and then buried during the night to try to prevent rioting. However, the repression was unsuccessful, and strikes, workplace occupations, and riots swept the country, forcing the government to back down shortly afterward.

18 **December 18, 2010** Following the self-immolation of street vendor Mohamed Bouazizi, protesters took to the streets in Tunisia, eventually toppling the dictator Zine El Abidine Ben Ali and sparking what later became known as the Arab Spring.

December 18, 2012 Armed forces in Sierra Leone shot several striking miners, killing two of them. The miners had walked out to protest nonpayment of bonuses and racism and for better working conditions at the foreign-owned diamond mine. In the wake of the shootings, a police station was set on fire and local taxi drivers joined the strike in solidarity.

19 **December 19, 1996** Following a massive nonpayment campaign, Ireland's minister for the environment announced that additional charges for water introduced in Dublin in 1994 would be scrapped. Working class residents organized themselves in local groups federated together to resist the charges, with over 50 percent of residents not paying. Local authorities attempted to force people to pay by taking residents to court and by shutting off people's water; however, the campaign resisted cutoffs and fought in the courts as well, eventually forcing the government to back down.

December 19, 2001 Workers and the unemployed in Argentina reacted to an economic crisis with a wave of often violent demonstrations, street blockades, and workplace takeovers. The slogan of the movement was "¡Que se vayan todos!" (They all must go!), in reference to politicians and the government. Thirty-nine people died in the repressive government response, but finally President Fernando de la Rúa resigned.

20 **December 20, 1960** Municipal workers across Belgium came out on official strike against a new law that reduced workers' purchasing power. While the other unions discussed what to do, an unparalleled wildcat strike movement swept the country. The result was a general strike that lasted until January 21.

Damage after the Koza riot (Photo by Larry Gray, courtesy of Wikimedia Commons)

December 20, 1970 The Koza riot took place in Okinawa, Japan, when, after nightfall, five thousand residents clashed with hundreds of American military police as they protested against the continuing US occupation. Locals injured dozens of US troops, burned cars, and destroyed several buildings in the Kadena Air Base.

21 **December 21, 1848** Escaped enslaved people Ellen and William Craft boarded a steamship in Savannah, Georgia, heading to Philadelphia, arriving on Christmas morning. Ellen, who was light-skinned, disguised herself as a white male slaveowner, wearing a top hat and cravat, with William as her slave.

Ellen and William Craft (Courtesy of the Liberator newspaper/ Wikimedia Commons)

After the passing of the Fugitive Slave Act of 1850, escaped slaves in the North had to be returned to the South, so the Crafts fled to England, where they lived for nineteen years, having five children and getting involved in the abolitionist movement and struggles for women's suffrage, before returning to the US after the Civil War.

December 21, 1907 The Santa Maria School massacre, possibly the worst massacre of striking workers in history, took place, with the Chilean Army killing over two thousand people: striking nitrate miners and their wives and children, who were camped at a school in Santa María, Iquique. An anarchist later attempted to assassinate the military officer responsible.

22 **December 22, 1988** Brazilian rubber worker activist, environmentalist, and Indigenous rights advocate Chico Mendes was assassinated by a rancher.

To try to protect the Amazon rainforest, rubber workers and Mendes, a senior official in their union, asked the government to set up reserves to prevent deforestation. Rubber workers in Cachoeira set up roadblocks to keep out a rancher named Darly Alves da Silva, who had bought part of a reserve. Later, Mendes launched a campaign

Chico Mendes at home with his son Sandino, 1988 *(Courtesy of Miranda Smith, Miranda Productions/Wikimedia Commons CC by SA 3.0)*

that stopped da Silva from logging in another area, as well as succeeding in getting a warrant issued for a murder allegedly committed by da Silva elsewhere. Mendes delivered the warrant to police, but they failed to act on it.

On the evening of Thursday, December 22, Mendes was assassinated in his home by da Silva's son. He was the nineteenth rural activist to be murdered in Brazil that year.

Da Silva, his son, and one of their employees were jailed for nineteen years for the killing, and following a global outpouring of support, the Chico Mendes Extractive Reserve was set up. It and other reserves that were subsequently established now cover over thirty-three million acres.

> At first I thought I was fighting to save rubber trees, then I thought I was fighting to save the Amazon rainforest. Now I realize I am fighting for humanity.
>
> —Chico Mendes

December 22, 1997 Forty-five Indigenous supporters of the Zapatista rebel movement in Chiapas, Mexico, were massacred by paramilitaries at a pacifist prayer meeting, with atrocities that included shooting pregnant women and stabbing them in the stomach. Government troops nearby failed to intervene to prevent the attack, instead they tried to cover up the killings, cleaning up the blood in the church where the Catholics had been killed.

23 **December 23, 1928** Australian judge Lionel Oscar Lukin ruled that timber workers should increase their working hours from forty-four to forty-eight per week, with a decrease in wages. On January 3, timber workers collectively decided they would refuse to work the additional four hours. Employers retaliated four weeks later by locking out thousands of workers at seventy timber mills in New South Wales. Workers responded by calling a strike that lasted for nearly nine months.

Employers tried to appeal to the wives of strikers to get them to exert pressure on their husbands. The Industrial Peace Association organized a meeting and called on women to attend and "register their protest against the cruel wrong which is being done to helpless children by the policy of strikes." At the meeting, speakers were drowned out by women singing "Solidarity Forever." The meeting ended after a young woman climbed on her chair and declared, "We don't scab on our men, and we don't want to."

Eventually, facing increasing police and government repression, the strike was called off in defeat, with the hope that a Labor government would be elected and would reverse the decision. Labor did win a landslide victory, but most strikers fired during the dispute were not reinstated following the return to work.

December 23, 2013 After an unfavorable job review from a manager, Citibank worker Lennon Ray Brown downed 90 percent of the bank's networks by erasing configuration files. He said he did it so that management could "see what the guys on the floor [are] capable of doing when they keep getting mistreated." Citibank reported him to police, and he was jailed for twenty-one months.

24 **December 24, 1913** A tragedy known as the Italian Hall disaster, or the 1913 massacre, occurred in Calumet, Michigan. The wives of copper miners who had been on strike since July organized a Christmas party at the Italian Hall. Exactly what happened next is disputed, but by the end of the night seventy-three people, fifty-nine of them miners' children, were dead: crushed to death in the stairway as they tried to flee the crowded building.

Eight of the eyewitnesses who testified in front of a House of Representatives subcommittee reported that a man wearing a Citizens' Alliance button yelled "fire," leading to a crush on the stairs. Some people believe that the doors were held shut. The Citizens' Alliance was an anti-union vigilante organization that worked with employers to break strikes.

December 24, 1983 It was announced that the pop group the Flying Pickets, made up of actors who had supported the miners' strikes in 1972 and 1974, had the UK Christmas number one single with their a cappella cover of Yazoo's (known as Yaz in the US) song "Only You."

Flying pickets were groups of strikers who travelled around the country to picket out other workers in solidarity, a tactic that had helped bring down the Conservative government in 1974. The band, who were militant socialists, later got into conflict with their record label for picketing the Drax power station during the 1984 miners' strike, and some stores refused to sell their records.

25 **December 25, 1522, 1831, and 1837** On Christmas Day in 1522, a Muslim-led revolt occurred on the sugar plantation of Christopher Columbus's son Diego, in Santo Domingo, in present-day Dominican Republic. Armed with the machetes they used to cut cane, the rebels, including enslaved West Africans, succeeded in killing a number of colonial settlers before the insurrection was quelled. Of the fifteen bodies recovered, nine were Europeans. Many of the insurgents managed to escape to the mountains, where they formed independent communities among the Taíno people.

On the same date just over three centuries later, in 1831, enslaved people in Jamaica went on strike to demand emancipation. They launched an armed revolt that eventually forced the British Empire to outlaw slavery in the region.

Then, again, on Christmas Day, six years later, in 1837, the Africans and Native Americans who made up Florida's Seminole nation defeated a vastly superior US invading army bent on cracking this early rainbow coalition and returning the Africans to slavery.

December 25, 1914 One hundred thousand troops on the Western Front during World War I called an unofficial truce, refusing to fight one another. German soldiers began singing "Silent Night" and other Christmas carols in English, French, and

British and German troops fraternizing during the truce
(Courtesy of the Imperial War Museum/Wikimedia Commons)

German. They were joined by British soldiers. Then they slowly emerged from the trenches and met in no man's land, exchanging gifts and in some places playing football. 🎙 **38**

26 **December 26, 1862** The largest mass execution in US history took place during the US-Dakota War of 1862, when thirty-eight Dakota people were hanged. Some of the trials of the Native Americans lasted less than five minutes, and President Abraham Lincoln personally reviewed the trial paperwork and approved the death penalties.

December 26, 1904 Metalworkers went out on strike in Baku, in what is now Azerbaijan, with numerous demands, including an eight-hour workday, pay increases, and Sundays off. Within five days most enterprises in the city were shut down, including the crucial oil industry, with regular protests and clashes with security forces.

In contrast to an unsuccessful strike the previous year, this time workers held out until January 12, when the first collective agreement in the history of the Russian Empire was signed. In particular, the workers achieved a nine-hour workday, with four paid days off each month, a pay increase, and better living and working conditions.

27 **December 27, 1797** The crew of the Royal Navy ship the *Marie Antoinette* murdered their officers and took the ship into a French port in the Caribbean. It was part of a wave of mutinies in the British fleet caused by poor working conditions and a growing sense of working class consciousness among sailors.

December 27, 1923 Japanese revolutionary, Daisuke Nanba, attempted to assassinate the crown prince to avenge the deaths of his comrades Kōtoku Shūsui, Ōsugi Sakae, and Itō Noe at the hands of the state. He was unsuccessful and was arrested, sentenced to death, and executed two days later.

Namba Daisuke, 1923 *(Courtesy of Wikimedia Commons)*

28 **December 28, 1907** Ten thousand households in New York City went on rent strike against rent price hikes. The action was sparked by sixteen-year-old textile worker Pauline Newman, who enlisted four hundred other young women factory workers to help persuade families to join.

Landlords fought back with water shutoffs and revenge evictions, but the families stood firm, and by early January around two thousand households won reduced rents.

December 28, 1973 What some historians have referred to as the first strike in space took place on the Skylab 4 space station. The workers had a punishing schedule, and mission commander Jerry Carr complained to ground control, "We would never work sixteen hours a day for eighty-four straight days on the ground, and we should not be expected to do it here in space." Pilot William Pogue said they wanted to have more time for contemplating the universe and "studying the stars, the Earth below, and ourselves." Carr eventually sent a wire to ground control stating, "We need more time to rest. We need a schedule that is not so packed. We don't want to exercise after a meal. We need to get things under control." On December 28, the astronauts turned off their radios and spent the day relaxing, working on personal projects, and doing experiments at their own pace. After twenty-four hours, the controllers agreed to a compromise that made the workload and mood of the last six weeks of the mission much more pleasant.

29 **December 29, 1890** Near Wounded Knee Creek, in South Dakota, US troops in the 7th Cavalry Regiment massacred over two hundred Lakota men, women, and children, many of them unarmed and fleeing, as well as killing some of their own colleagues. For these "brave" deeds, some twenty servicemen were awarded the Medal of Honor.

December 29, 1968 The University of Tokyo was forced to cancel its 1969 entrance exams, as it had been completely disrupted by a student strike and wave of occupations, which had been ongoing since October. Striking students battled anti-strike Communist Party students and riot police in an ongoing conflict over unpaid internships and faculty collaboration with the police.

30 **December 30, 1930** Indigenous workers on the Pesillo hacienda in the northern Ecuadorian highlands went on strike for better pay and conditions and were joined by others working nearby. They attacked the main hacienda house and forced local officials to flee. The government sent in troops to arrest strike leaders and destroy their houses, but the workers held firm and won concessions. More importantly, their actions helped spark a wave of rural protest in the country.

December 30, 1936 Fifty workers at the Flint General Motors plant sat down on wildcat strike against the forcible transfer of three inspectors who had been ordered to quit the union but had refused. When workers noticed management making preparations to transfer production elsewhere, the mostly nonunion workforce occupied the plant and defied court injunctions and violent attacks from guards and police, holding out till February, when the company caved in, granting union recognition and decisively changing the balance of power between workers and bosses. Despite the militancy of the strikers and the participation of Black workers like Roscoe Van Zandt and J.D. Dotson, the strict Jim Crow segregation of the workplace was maintained under the resulting contract with the United Auto Workers union (UAW).

31 **December 31, 1912** A strike of New York City hotel workers and wait staff organized by the Industrial Workers of the World union (IWW) began. The strike initially only targeted some hotels with particularly bad working conditions. Just after 11:00 p.m., fighting broke out outside the Hotel Astor, when twenty-five private detectives and armed police confronted thirty striking waiters, who fought back with bricks. The stoppage became a general strike in January, demanding, among other things, that tipping be abolished and replaced with decent wages. The strike ended later that month without winning concessions from the employers. However, several subsequent strikes succeeded in winning much better pay and conditions, which to some extent persist today. 🎙 **6**

December 31, 1969 Dwight and Karl Armstrong stole a twin-engine Cessna plane from an airport outside Madison, Wisconsin, flew fifty-three miles north and dropped three bombs on the Badger Army Ammunition Plant to protest the Vietnam War. The brothers' uncle had previously worked at the plant and had been killed in a workplace accident. The bombs failed to explode, but the attack was one of many violent anti-war acts that rocked the US as the Vietnam War dragged on. 🎙 **14**

Postscript

You have now reached the end of *Working Class History: Everyday Acts of Resistance & Rebellion*. We really hope you have enjoyed it and learned something new. Researching and promoting people's history is never over. And we always need help. So if you have any little-known events to share with us, or if you would like to get involved in Working Class History in some capacity, please get in touch.

All of our work is funded by our readers and listeners on Patreon. Supporters get access to exclusive content and benefits, including early access to podcast episodes, exclusive bonus episodes, free and discounted books and merchandise, and more. You can get more information and sign up at patreon.com/workingclasshistory.

You can also support our work by using our online store, where we have a range of radical history books and merchandise, at shop. workingclasshistory.com.

Email: info@workingclasshistory.com
Instagram: @workingclasshistory
Twitter: @wrkclasshistory
Facebook: facebook.com/workingclasshistory

References

January

January 1, 1804 "Haitian independence 1804–1805," History of Haiti, 1492–1805, accessed April 14, 2020, https://library.brown.edu/haitihistory/11.html; CLR James, *The Black Jacobins: Toussaint L'Ouverture and the San Domingo Revolution* (London: Secker & Warburg, 1938), accessed April 14, 2020, https://libcom.org/library/black-jacobins-toussaint-louverture-san-domingo-revolution; Peter Hallward, "Haitian Inspiration: On the bicentenary of Haiti's Independence," *Radical Philosophy* 123 (January–February 2004), accessed April 14, 2020, https://libcom.org/library/haitian-inspiration-on-bicentenary-haiti%E2%80%99s-independence; "US Invasion and Occupation of Haiti, 1915–34," Office of the Historian, accessed April 14, 2020, https://history.state.gov/milestones/1914-1920/haiti; "France Urged to Repay Haiti's Huge 'Independence Debt,'" BBC News, August 16, 2010, accessed April 14, 2020, https://www.bbc.com/news/world-europe-10988938.

January 1, 1994 Editors, "Zapatista National Liberation Army," Encyclopaedia Britannica, accessed April 14, 2020, https://www.britannica.com/topic/Zapatista-National-Liberation-Army; John Vidal, "Mexico's Zapatista Rebels, 24 Years on and Defiant in Mountain Strongholds," *Guardian*, February 17, 2018, accessed April 14, 2020, https://bit.ly/35ncIAj.

January 2, 1858 and 1904 Robert F. Grimmett, *Instances of Use of United States Armed Forces Abroad, 1798–2008* (Collingdale, PA: Diane Publishing, 2010), 5, 8; "Revolution in Montevideo," *New York Times*, March 3, 1858, 1.

January 2, 1920 Gregory Dehler, "Palmer Raids," Encyclopaedia Britannica, accessed April 14, 2020, https://www.britannica.com/topic/Palmer-Raids; Aleksandr Vladimirovich Avakov, *Plato's Dreams Realized: Surveillance and Citizen Rights from KGB to FBI* (New York: Algora, 2006), 36.

January 3, 1913 Brendan Maslauskas Dunn, "In November We Remember: The Centennial of the 1912 Little Falls Textile Strike," libcom.org, accessed April 14, 2020, https://bit.ly/3aQLHqo; "The Red Sweater Girls of 1912," *Little Falls Evening Times*, June 20, 2011, accessed April 14, 2020, https://upstateearth.blogspot.ca/2013/01/the-red-sweater-girls-of-1912.html; Robert E. Snyder, "Women, Wobblies, and Workers' Rights: The 1912 Textile Strike in Little Falls, New York," *New York History* 60, no. 1 (1979): 29–57, accessed April 14, 2020, www.jstor.org/stable/23169970.

January 3, 1966 "Jan. 3, 1966: Sammy Younge Jr. Murdered," Zinn Education Project, accessed April 14, 2020, https://www.zinnedproject.org/news/tdih/sammy-younge-jr-murdered; "Samuel Younge Jr.," Encyclopedia of Alabama, accessed March 14, 2020, http://www.encyclopediaofalabama.org/article/h-1669.

January 4, 1917 "Mass Strikes in Guyana, 1917," Guyana News and Information, accessed April 14, 2020, https://libcom.org/history/mass-strikes-guyana-1917.

January 4, 1938 Richard Hart, "Labour Rebellions in the 1930s in the British Caribbean Region Colonies," libcom.org, accessed April 14, 2020, https://bit.ly/2Yor3Lj.

January 5, 1939 Nick Heath, "Samuel Kaplan: Another Mysterious Disappearance in Spain," libcom.org, accessed April 14, 2020, https://libcom.org/history/samuel-kaplan-another-mysterious-disappearance-spain; Nathalio Kaplan, emails to Working Class History, January 25, 2017.

January 5, 1960 "Sabate Llopart, Francisco, 'El Quico,' 1915–1960," libcom.org, accessed April 14, 2020, https://libcom.org/history/articles/1915-1960-francisco-sabate-llopart; Pedro Costa, "Sabaté, guerrillero de película," *El País*, January 17, 2010, accessed April 14, 2020, https://elpais.com/diario/2010/01/17/eps/1263713210_850215.html.

January 6, 1945 Sybille Steinbacher, *Auschwitz: A History* (New York: HarperCollins, 2005), 155; Harry Borden, *Survivor: A Portrait of the Survivors of the Holocaust* (New York: Hachette Book Group, 2017), 272; Auschwitz Museum, tweets to Working Class History, January 5, 2020; Auschwitz Museum tweet, accessed April 14, 2020, https://twitter.com/auschwitzmuseum/status/1048962485016035335?lang=en; "The Revolt at Auschwitz Birkenau," Jewish Virtual Library, accessed April 14, 2020, http://www.jewishvirtuallibrary.org/the-revolt-at-auschwitz-birkenau. Some sources say the events occurred on January 5, but the Auschwitz Museum confirmed it was January 6.

January 6, 2005 "What 'Appen to South Africa? 1976–2005. Defiance to Apartheid, Neoliberalism, and Recuperators of Defiance," accessed April 14, 2020, https://bit.ly/2KPQEF3; K.R. Gupta, Gunnar Lind Haase Svendsen and Prasenjit Maiti, eds., *Social Capital*, vol. 2 (New Delhi: Atlantic Publishers & Distributors, 2008), 190; Patrick Bond, "Municipal Elections Won't Appease Furious South Africans," Z Commentaries, February 13, 2006, accessed April 14, 2020, https://bit.ly/3bYxSXW; Reena Parikh, "The Commodification of Water in South Africa: A Case Study of Westcliff" (senior honors thesis, Durban Boston College, 2006), accessed April 14, 2020, https://dlib.bc.edu/islandora/object/bc-ir:102232/datastream/PDF/view.

January 7, 1913 Franz Garcia, "A 100 años del logro de las 8 horas en el Callao (1913–2013)," anarkismo.net, February 27, 2013, accessed April 14, 2020, https://www.anarkismo.net/article/24972.

January 7, 1919 John Raymond Hébert, "The Tragic Week of January, 1919, in Buenos Aires: Background, Events, Aftermath" (PhD diss., Georgetown University, 1972); Norberto Galasso, *Perón: Formación, ascenso y caída (1893–1955)* (Buenos Aires: Colihue, 2006), 56–59; Dana Ward, "Timeline of Anarchism in Argentina," Anarchy Archives, accessed April 14, 2020, http://dwardmac.pitzer.edu/Anarchist_Archives/worldwidemovements/argtimeline.html; "Bolsheviki Invade Argentina," *Los Angeles Times*, January 11, 1919; "Acts of Anarchy Continue," *News and Courier*, January 13, 1919.

January 8, 1811 "Dictionary of Louisiana Biography," Louisiana Historical Association, accessed April 14, 2020, https://web.archive.org/web/20170421215417/http://www.lahistory.org/site18.php.

January 8, 1896 Maxine Molyneux, "No God, No Boss, No Husband: The World's First Anarcha-Feminist Group," *Latin American Perspective* 13, no 1 (Winter 1986): 119–45, accessed April 14, 2020, https://libcom.org/files/2633723.pdf.

January 9, 1907 "Río Blanco Strike," David G. LaFrance, Encyclopedia.com, updated March 5, 2020, accessed April 14, 2020, https://bit.ly/3d6fzQL.

January 9, 1973 "Timeline of the 1973 Durban Strikes," South African History Online, accessed April 14, 2020, https://www.sahistory.org.za/article/timeline-1973-durban-strikes.

January 10, 1918 Temma Kaplan, "Female Consciousness and Collective Action in Barcelona," *Signs* 7, no. 3 (Spring 1982): 545–66, accessed April 14, 2020, https://libcom.org/files/Barcelona%20Women's%20Protests_0.pdf.

January 10, 1966 "Jan. 10, 1966: Voting Rights Activist Vernon Dahmer Murdered," Zinn Education Project, accessed April 15, 2020, https://www.zinnedproject.org/news/tdih/vernon-dahmer.

January 11, 1912 "Lawrence, MA Factory Workers Strike 'for Bread and Roses,' U.S. 1912," Global Nonviolent Action Database, accessed April 15, 2020, https://bit.ly/2SsdEOD.

January 11 1998 Chittaroopa Palit and Achin Vanaik, "Monsoon Risings," *New Left Review* 21, (May–June 2003), accessed May 26, 2020, https://newleftreview.org/issues/II21.

January 12, 1922 Kit-ching Chan Lau, *China, Britain, and Hong Kong* (Hong Kong: Chinese University Press, 1990), 169–72; "1922: The Hong Kong Strike," libcom.org, accessed April 15, 2020, https://libcom.org/history/1922-the-hong-kong-strike.

January 12, 1964 Don Petterson, *Revolution in Zanzibar: An American's Cold War Tale* (New York: Basic Books, 2009); Ian Speller, "An African Cuba? Britain and the Zanzibar Revolution, 1964," *Journal of Imperial and Commonwealth History* 35, no. 2 (2007): 1–35, accessed April 15, 2020, https://bit.ly/35wXhWk; Timothy Parsons, *The 1964 Army Mutinies and the Making of Modern East Africa* (Santa Barbara, CA: Praeger Publishers, 2003), 107–10.

January 13, 1943 "ГРОМОВА УЛЬЯНА МАТВЕЕВНА": Герой Советского Союза," accessed April 15, 2020, http://moypolk.ru/soldiers/gromova-ulyana-matveevna/story. Some sources incorrectly refer to 14 January as date of Ulyana Matveevna Gromova's death.

January 13, 1947 Emily Kluver, "1947 Mombasa General Strike," libcom.org, accessed April 15, 2020, https://libcom.org/history/1947-mombasa-general-strike.

January 14, 1929 "Riot at Port Adelaide," *Register News-Pictorial*, January 15, 1929, 9, accessed April 15, 2020, http://trove.nla.gov.au/newspaper/article/54251637.

January 14, 1930 Nigel Jones, "The Making of a Nazi Hero," *History Today* 63, no. 6 (June 2013), accessed April 15, 2020, https://bit.ly/2YyjhPb; Daniel Siemens, *The Making of a Nazi Hero: The Murder and Myth of Horst Wessel* (London: I.B. Tauris, 2013), 3.

January 15, 1919 Helmut Dietmar Starke, "Rosa Luxemburg," Encyclopaedia Britannica, accessed April 15, 2020, https://www.britannica.com/biography/Rosa-Luxemburg.

January 15, 1934 Viscount Rothemere, "Hurrah for the Blackshirts!" *Daily Mail*, January 15, 1934; "Daily Mail," Media Bias/Fact Check, accessed April 15, 2020, https://mediabiasfactcheck.com/daily-mail.

January 16, 1973 Ed Goddard, "Change Begins at Home: Student Struggles Around Living Conditions," libcom.org, February 6, 2011, accessed April 15, 2020, https://libcom.org/library/change-begins-home-student-struggles-around-living-conditions.

January 16, 1997 Saira Menezes, "A Fatal Strike," *Outlook*, January 29, 1997, accessed April 15, 2020, https://www.outlookindia.com/magazine/story/a-fatal-strike/202922; "3 Held for Dutta Samant's Murder," Rediff India Abroad, April 2005, accessed April 15, 2020, https://www.rediff.com/news/2005/apr/10samant.htm.

January 17, 1961 Georges Nzongola-Ntalaja, "Patrice Lumumba: The Most Important Assassination of the 20th Century," *Guardian*, January 17, 2011, accessed April 15, 2020, https://bit.ly/3bXU7gD.

January 17, 1969 Bruce A Dixon, "Why I Don't do Kwaanza," accessed April 15, 2020, https://libcom.org/news/why-i-dont-do-kwaanza-bruce-dixon-23122014; Bob Pool, "Witness to 1969 UCLA Shootings Speaks at Rally," *Los Angeles Times*, January 18, 2008, accessed April 15, 2020, https://www.latimes.com/archives/la-xpm-2008-jan-18-me-panthers18-story.html.

January 18, 1958 Chick Jacobs and Venita Jenkins, "The Night the Klan Met Its Match," *Fayetteville Observer*, January 18, 2008, accessed April 15, 2020, https://charlotteaction.blogspot.com/2008/01/night-klan-met-its-match.html; Jefferson Currie II, "The Ku Klux Klan in North Carolina and the Battle of Maxton Field," *Tar Heel Junior Historian* 44, no. 1 (Fall 2004), accessed April 15, 2020, https://bit.ly/2Ypvplc; "Bad Medicine for the Klan: North Carolina Indians Break up Kluxers' Anti-Indian Meeting," *Life*, April 15, 1958, 26–28.

January 18, 1977 Sam Lowry, "1977: Egypt's Bread Intifada," libcom.org, December 29, 2009, accessed April 15, 2020, https://libcom.org/history/1977-egypts-bread-intifada; Heba Abdel-Sattar, "36 Years After the 'Bread Uprising': Egypt's Struggle for Social Justice Lives On," January 18, 2013, accessed April 15, 2020, https://bit.ly/2yZIsiT.

January 19, 1915 JayRaye, "We Never Forget: The Roosevelt Massacre of January 19, 1915," *Daily Kos*, January 26, 2015, accessed April 15, 2020, https://bit.ly/2YtvjZY.

January 19, 1984 Nadir Bouhmouch, "The Rif and the Moroccan State's Economic Pressure Cooker," Counterpunch, July 14, 2017, accessed April 15, 2020, https://bit.ly/2Yqzfup.

January 20, 1900 "Chinatown Fire of 1900," Hawaii History, accessed March 12, 2020, http://www.hawaiihistory.org/index.cfm?fuseaction=ig.page&PageID=548; Rebecca Onion, "The Disastrous Cordon Sanitaire Used on Honolulu Chinatown in 1900," Slate, August 15, 2014, accessed March 12, 2020, https://tinyurl.com/y93x6q6e; "The Chinatown Fires," Hawaii Digital Newspaper Project, accessed March 12, 2020, https://tinyurl.com/ybfpnkhh; "Fighting The Plague," *Honolulu Advertiser*, January 24, 1900; Steve Benen, "Joining the Far-Right, Trump Takes Steps To Rebrand Coronavirus," MSNBC, March 17, 2020, accessed April 5, 2020, https://tinyurl.com/y8alp7wp.

January 20, 1964 "British Troops Put Down Mutinies in Post-Colonial Kenya, Tanganyika and Uganda," libcom.org, July 8, 2018, accessed April 15, 2020, https://bit.ly/3aZfBZ2; John D. Gerhart, "Tanganyika Embarrassed by Need for British Assistance; Calls for Pan-African Force to Aid in Future Crises," Harvard Crimson, March 10, 1964, accessed April 15, 2020, https://www.thecrimson.com/article/1964/3/10/tanganyika-embarrassed-by-need-for-british; *Profile of the Labour Market and Trade Unions in Tanzania*, LO/FTF Council, April 2003, accessed April 15, 2020. https://bit.ly/2StLumg.

January 21, 1921 Osvaldo Bayer, *Rebellion in Patagonia* (Oakland: AK Press, 2016).

January 21, 1946 Jeremy Brecher, "The World War II and Post-War Strike Wave," libcom.org, accessed April 15, 2020, https://libcom.org/history/world-war-ii-post-war-strike-wave.

January 22, 1826 Richard Steven Street, *Beasts of the Field: A Narrative History of California Farmworkers, 1769–1913* (Palo Alto, CA: Stanford University Press, 2004), 81; "Proposed Finding against Acknowledgement of the Band of Juaneño Mission Indians Acjachemen Nation (Petitioner #84A)," Bureau of Indian Affairs, 132, accessed April 15, 2020, https://www.bia.gov/sites/bia.gov/files/assets/as-ia/ofa/petition/084A_juajba_CA/084a_pf.pdf.

January 22, 1969 Martin Glaberman, "Black Cats, White Cats, Wildcats: Auto Workers in Detroit, 1969," accessed April 15, 2020, https://libcom.org/library/black-cats-white-cats-wildcats-martin-glaberman.

January 23, 1913 "8000 Strike in Rochester," *New York Times*, January 24, 1913, 7, accessed April 15, 2020, https://nyti.ms/2Wg1Tf8; Joan M. Jensen, "The Great Uprising in Rochester," in Joan M. Jensen and Sue Davidson, eds., *A Needle, a Bobbin, a Strike: Women Needleworkers in America* (Philadelphia: Temple University Press, 1984), 94–113, accessed April 15, 2020, www.jstor.org/stable/j.ctv941x68.9.

January 23, 1982 "1982 South African Grand Prix Strike," libcom.org, accessed April 15, 2020, https://libcom.org/library/1982-south-african-grand-prix-strike; "Formula 1 Drivers Strike," Motorsport Retro, August 2014, accessed April 15, 2020, http://www.motorsportretro.com/2014/08/formula-1-drivers-strike.

January 24, 1964 "1964: British Troops Put Down Mutinies in Post-Colonial Kenya, Tanganyika and Uganda," libcom.org, accessed April 15, 2020, https://tinyurl.com/ya2wsdrg.

January 24, 1977 Guillermo Altares, "The Night Spain's Transition to Democracy Nearly Derailed," *El País*, February 3, 2016, accessed April 15, 2020, https://elpais.com/elpais/2016/02/03/inenglish/1454496288_346509.html; "María Luz Nájera murió alcanzada por un bote de humo antidisturbio," *El País*, January 25, 1977, accessed April 15, 2020, https://elpais.com/diario/1977/01/25/espana/222994831_850215.html; "Mari Luz Nájera, Estudiante Asesinada Hace 40 Años," Federación De Republicanos, January 24, 2017, accessed April 15, 2018, https://bit.ly/2WjeZIH.

January 25, 1911 "1911: Sugako Kanno, Radical Feminist," ExecutedToday. com, January 25, 2011, accessed April 15, 2020, http://www.executedtoday.com/2011/01/25/1911-sugako-kanno-radical-feminist; Kanno Sugako, "Reflections on the Way to the Gallows," libcom.org, accessed April 15, 2020, https://libcom.org/history/reflections-way-gallows.

January 25, 2011 Editors, "Egypt Uprising of 2011," Encyclopaedia Britannica, accessed April 15, 2020, https://www.britannica.com/event/Egypt-Uprising-of-2011.

January 26, 1932 "The Rent Strikes in New York," *Radical America* 1, no. 3 (November–December 1967): 13–14, accessed April 15, 2020, https://libcom.org/library/radical-america-13-new-york-rent-strike.

January 26, 1952 Anne-Claire Kerbœuf, "The Cairo Fire of 26 January of 1952 and the Interpretations of History," in Arthur Goldschmidt, Amy J. Johnson, and Barak A. Salmoni, eds., *Re-Envisioning Egypt 1919–1952* (Cairo: American University in Cairo Press, 2005), 194–216.

January 27, 1918 Victor Serge, "1918: The Proletariat's Democratic Revolution in Finland," libcom.org, accessed April 15, 2020, https://libcom.org/library/1917-proletariats-democratic-revolution-finland; Tuomas Tepora, "Finnish Civil War 1918," International Encyclopedia of the First World War, updated October 8, 2014, accessed May 29, 2020, https://encyclopedia.1914-1918-online.net/article/finnish_civil_war_1918.

January 27, 1923 Anarchist Federation, "Wilckens, Kurt Gustav, 1886–1923," libcom.org, accessed April 15, 2020, https://libcom.org/history/wilckens-kurt-gustav-1886-1923.

January 28 1917 "Jan. 28, 1917: The Bath Riots," Zinn Education Project, accessed April 15, 2020, https://www.zinnedproject.org/news/tdih/bath-riots; John Burnett, "The Bath Riots: Indignity along the Mexican Border," NPR, January 28, 2006, accessed April 3, 2020, https://www.npr.org/templates/story/story.php?storyId=5176177.

January 28, 1946 José Antonio Gutiérrez Danton, "1872–1995: Anarchism in Chile," libcom.org, accessed April 15, 2020, https://libcom.org/history/articles/anarchism-in-chile; "27 De Enero De 1946: Matanza De Trabajadores En Plaza Bulnes (Reportaje a los sucesos en el diario vespertino 'La Hora' del 27 de Enero de 1946)," El Sindical, accessed April 15, 2020, http://www.escuelasindical.org/blog/wp-content/uploads/2008/02/el-sindical-enero-2008.pdf.

January 29, 1911 Jim Miller, "The Magonista Revolt in Tijuana: A Prelude to the San Diego Free Speech Fight," libcom.org, accessed April 15, 2020, https://libcom.org/library/magonista-revolt-tijuana-prelude-san-diego-free-speech-fight; Richard Griswold del Castillo, "The Discredited Revolution: The Magonista Capture of Tijuana in 1911," *San Diego Historical Society Quarterly* 26, no. 4 (Fall 1980): accessed April 15, 2020, https://sandiegohistory.org/journal/1980/october/revolution.

January 29, 1935 Richard Hart, *Labour Rebellions in the 1930s in the British Caribbean* (London: Socialist History Society, 2002).

January 30, 1965 Simon Heffer, "The Dockers, Churchill and the War's Most Shameful Secret: Second World War Strikes Reveal Disgusting Lack of Patriotism," *Daily Mail*, January 29, 2015, accessed April 15, 2020, http://dailym.ai/2KSvNkv; Rob Ray, "The Peccadilloes of Winston Churchill," libcom.org, August 12, 2008, accessed April 15, 2020, https://libcom.org/blog/the-peccadillos-winston-churchill-12082008.

January 30, 1968 Julian E. Zelizer, "How the Tet Offensive Undermined American Faith in Government," *Atlantic*, January 2018, accessed April 15, 2020, https://bit.ly/3bYAHs2.

January 31, 1938 "Emma Tenayuca and the 1938 Pecan Shellers' Strike," libcom.org, accessed April 15, 2020, https://libcom.org/history/emma-tenayuca-1938-pecan-shellers-strike.

January 31, 1957 "Bagel Famine Threatens in City; Labor Dispute Puts Hole in Supply," *New York Times*, December 17, 1951, 1; "Lox Strike Expert Acts to End the Bagel Famine," *New York Times*, December 18, 1951, 27; "Return of the Bagel near As Drivers Settle Dispute," *New York Times*, February 7, 1952, 17.

February

February 1, 1960 Michael Ray, "Greensboro Sit-in," Encyclopaedia Britannica, accessed April 15, 2020, https://www.britannica.com/event/Greensboro-sit-in.

February 1, 2012 Brent Latham, "The Politics Behind Egypt's Football Riot," ESPN, February 3, 2012, accessed February 25, 2020, unavailable April 15, 2020, https://archive.is/20150204113316/http://espn.com/sports/soccer/story/_/id/7532975/-politics-egypt-football-riot-brent-latham; Mohamed Fadel Fahmy, "Eyewitnesses: Police Stood Idle in Egypt Football Massacre," CNN, February 2, 2012, accessed April 15, 2020, https://edition.cnn.com/2012/02/02/world/africa/egypt-soccer-deaths-color/index.html; "Egyptian Prosecutor Charges 75 Over Port Said Football Riot," *Guardian*, March 15, 2012, accessed April 15, 2012, https://www.theguardian.com/world/2012/mar/15/egyptian-football-riot-75-charged.

February 2, 1902 Melinda Tria Kerkvliet, *Manila Workers Unions, 1900–1950* (Quezon City, PH: New Day, 1992), 7; Dante G. Guevarra, *History of the Philippine Labor Movement* (Manila: Institute of Labor & Industrial Relations, Polytechnic University of the Philippines, 1991), 17–18.

February 2, 1988 Newsdesk, "Activists Take Over London's Landmarks to Reclaim LGBT+ History," thegayuk, accessed April 15, 2020, https://www.thegayuk.com/activists-take-over-londons-landmarks-to-reclaim-lgbt-history.

February 3, 1988 "1988: Nurses Protest for Better Pay," BBC Home, accessed April 15, 2018, http://news.bbc.co.uk/onthisday/hi/dates/stories/february/3/newsid_2525000/2525639.stm; "U.K. Inflation Rate, £100 from 1988 to 1997," UK Inflation Calculator, accessed April 15, 2020, https://www.officialdata.org/1988-GBP-in-1997.

February 3, 1994 "Guerra callejera en Ecuador," *El País*, February 2, 1994, accessed April 15, 2020, https://elpais.com/diario/1994/02/03/internacional/760230020_850215.html.

February 4, 1899 "The Philippine-American War, 1899–1902," Office of the Historian, accessed April 15, 2020, https://history.state.gov/milestones/1899-1913/war.

February 4, 1924 "KKK and IWW Wage Drawn Battle in Greenville," *Portland Press Herald*, February 5, 1924, accessed April 15, 2020, https://libcom.org/history/1924-kkk-iww-wage-drawn-battle-greenville.

February 5, 1885 "Feb 5, 1885 CE: Belgian King Establishes Congo Free State," *National Geographic*, accessed March 4, 2020, unavailable April 15, 2020, https://www.nationalgeographic.org/thisday/feb5/belgian-king-establishes-congo-free-state; Adam Hochschild "Leopold II," Encyclopaedia Britannica, accessed April 15, 2020, https://www.britannica.com/biography/Leopold-II-king-of-Belgium; "The Establishment of the Congo Free State," This Week in History, accessed April 15, 2020, https://sites.psu.edu/thisweekinhistory/2014/02/06/the-establishment-of-the-congo-free-state.

February 5, 1981 Susan Lochrie, "Greenock Jeans Factory Sit-in's Soundtrack," *Greenock Telegraph*, January 12, 2016, accessed April 15, 2020, https://www.greenocktelegraph.co.uk/news/14197832.greenock-jeans-factory-sit-ins-soundtrack; Andy Clarke, "And the Next Thing, the Chairs Barricaded the Door: The Lee Jeans Factory Occupation, Trade Unionism and Gender in Scotland in the 1980s," accessed April 15, 2020, https://bit.ly/2VW1BuN.

February 6, 1916 Alaister Sooke, "Cabaret Voltaire: A Night Out at History's Weirdest Nightclub," BBC Culture, accessed April 15, 2020, https://bbc.in/2KVDu9k.

February 6, 1919 History Committee of the General Strike Committee, "The Seattle General Strike of 1919," libcom.org, March 2019, accessed April 15, 2020, https://libcom.org/history/seattle-general-strike-1919; "Unionism in Butte Mines Contributes to City's Fascinating History," *Montana Standard*, accessed April 15, 2020, https://bit.ly/35rWN3r; George Everett, "When Toil Meant Trouble: Butte's Labor Heritage," accessed April 15, 2020, http://www.butteamerica.com/labor.htm.

February 7, 1919 Jay Brooks, "No Beer, No Work," Brookston Beer Bulletin, September 7, 2015, accessed April 14, 2020, http://brookstonbeerbulletin.com/no-beer-no-work; "Labor and Beer," *New York Times*, February 13, 1919, 14; "Allentown Bartenders Strike," *New York Times*, 10 July 1919, 36.

February 7, 1974 "This Day in History," Now Grenada, April 15, 2019, accessed April 15, 2020, http://www.nowgrenada.com/2019/01/this-day-in-history-34.

February 8, 1517 Marshall H. Saville, "The Discovery of Yucatan in 1517 by Francisco Hernandez De Cordoba," *Geographical Review* 6, no. 5 (November 1918): 436–48, accessed April 15, 2020, https://www.jstor.org/stable/207701.

February 8, 1968 "Feb. 8, 1968: Orangeburg Massacre," Zinn Education Project, accessed April 15, 2020, https://www.zinnedproject.org/news/tdih/orangeburg-massacre; Jim Morrill, "50 Years after 3 Students Died in SC Civil Rights Protest, Survivors Still Ask 'Why?'" *Charlotte Observer*, April 15, 2020, accessed April 15, 2020, https://www.charlotteobserver.com/news/local/article198943934.html.

February 9, 1912 Working Class History, "The Bridport Wildcat Strike, 1912," libcom.org, February 15, 2016, accessed April 15, 2020, https://libcom.org/history/bridport-wildcat-strike-1912.

February 9, 1995 "A Commune in Chiapas? Mexico and the Zapatista Rebellion, 1994–2000," *Aufheben* (Autumn 2000), accessed April 15, 2020, https://libcom.org/library/commune-chiapas-zapatista-mexico; "Chase Mexican Memo Fallout Continues," UPI, February 15, 1995, accessed April 15, 2020, https://bit.ly/2YqV5y3; Riordan Roett, "Mexico Political Update January 13, 1995: Chase Manhattan's Emerging Markets Group Memo," accessed April 15, 2020, http://www.realhistoryarchives.com/collections/hidden/chase-memo.htm.

February 10, 1960 Teresa Leonard, "February 1960 Sit-ins Move to Raleigh, NC," *News & Observer*, updated June 5, 2015 accessed April 15, 2020, https://www.mcclatchydc.com/news/special-reports/polygraph-files/article24744823.html.

February 10, 1979 Jocelyn Sherman, "Rufino Contreras Asked for 'a More Just Share' of What He Produced; 39 Years Ago the Company Answered Him with Bullets," United Farm Workers, February 9, 2018, accessed April 15, 2020, https://ufw.org/rufino.

February 11, 1967 Hailey Branson-Potts, "Before Stonewall, There Was the Black Cat; LGBTQ Leaders to Mark 50th Anniversary of Protests at Silver Lake Tavern," *Los Angeles Times*, February 8, 2017, accessed April 15, 2020, https://lat.ms/3f9loih; Mike Davis, "Riots Nights on Sunset Strip," *Labour/Le Travail* 59 (2007), 199–214, accessed May 29, 2020, http://www.lltjournal.ca/index.php/llt/article/view/5499.

February 11, 2004 "Slovakia's Unemployed Riots of 2004," libcom.org, February 21, 2017, accessed April 15, 2020, https://libcom.org/history/slovakias-unemployed-riots-2004.

February 12, 1920 "Recordando a Betsabé Espinoza," Revolucion Obrera, updated March 22, 2016, accessed April 15, 2020, https://www.revolucionobrera.com/emancipacion/recordando-a-betsabe-espinoza; Mireya Andrade, "Betsabé Espinosa: joven rebelde," Farianas, July 6, 2015, accessed April 15, 2020, https://bit.ly/3dal5Se.

February 12, 1978 Lydia Bailey, "Maori New Zealanders Occupy Golf Course in Struggle for Tribal Lands, 1975–83," Global Nonviolent Action Database, February 9, 2013, accessed April 19, 2020, https://bit.ly/2KQaTlZ.

February 13, 1913 "Mother Jones Biography," Biography.com, updated April 15, 2019, accessed April 15, 2020, https://www.biography.com/people/mother-jones-9357488.

February 13, 1951 "The 1951 Waterfront Dispute," Ministry for Culture and Heritage, accessed April 15, 2020, https://nzhistory.govt.nz/politics/the-1951-waterfront-dispute.

February 14, 1874 David Fieldhouse, "For Richer, for Poorer?" in P.J. Marshall, ed., *The Cambridge Illustrated History of the British Empire* (Cambridge: Cambridge University Press, 1996), 108–46, 400; David Hall-Matthews, "Historical Roots of Famine Relief Paradigms: Ideas on Dependency and Free Trade in India in the 1870s," *Disasters*, September 1996, 216–30; David Hall-Matthews, "Inaccurate Conceptions: Disputed Measures of Nutritional Needs and Famine Deaths in Colonial India," *Modern Asian Studies* 42, no. 6 (November 2008): 1–24.

February 14, 1939 Richard Hart, *Labour Rebellions in the 1930s in the British Caribbean* (London: Socialist History Society, 2002); "Leonora," *Guyana Chronicle*, May 10, 2014, accessed April 15, 2020, http://guyanachronicle.com/2014/05/10/leonora; "The Leonora Incident of 1939 Revisited," *Stabroek News*, February 25, 2010, accessed April 15, 2018, https://www.stabroeknews.com/2010/features/02/25/the-leonora-incident-of-1939-revisited; Von Marco Freyer, "The Demerara Distilleries 2.0," Barrel-Aged-Mind, accessed April 15, 2020, https://barrel-aged-mind.blogspot.com/p/blog-page_5.html; Rakesh Rampertab, "Kowsilla: A Leonora Woman," Guyana under Siege, February 27, 2005, accessed April 15, 2020, https://bit.ly/3feOBIA.

February 15, 1851 "Shadrach Minkins (d. 1875)," Encyclopedia of Virginia, accessed April 15, 2020, https://www.encyclopediavirginia.org/Minkins_Shadrach_d_1875#contrib.

February 15, 1913 "IWW Yearbook: 1913," IWW History Project, accessed April 15, 2020, http://depts.washington.edu/iww/yearbook1913.shtml.

February 16, 1924 Paul Williams, "Britain Facing Food Rationing as Dockers Strike," *Chicago Daily Tribune*, February 17, 1924, 3; "1924 Cabinet Conclusion on a Dock Strike," National Archives, Cabinet Papers, accessed April 15, 2020, https://tinyurl.com/yb2mxz92.

February 16, 1937 Martha Grevatt, "Immigrant Women Beat Cigar Company Bosses," libcom.org, accessed April 15, 2020, https://libcom.org/history/immigrant-women-beat-cigar-company-bosses-martha-grevatt.

February 17, 1964 Rakesh Rampertab, "Kowsilla: A Leonora Woman," Guyana under Siege, February 27, 2005, accessed April 15, 2020, http://www.guyanaundersiege.com/East%20Indian%20culture/Indian%20women/kowsilla/Kowsilla.htm.

February 17, 1977 Patrick Cuninghame, "'A Laughter That Will Bury You All': Irony as Protest and Language as Struggle in the Italian 1977 Movement," libcom.org, accessed April 15, 2020, https://bit.ly/2zSIysX; Claudio Gori Giorgi, *Antonio Ruberti* (Rome: Sapienza Università Editrice, 2015), 47.

February 18, 1946 John Meyer, "The Royal Indian Navy Mutiny of 1946: Nationalist Competition and Civil-Military Relations in Postwar India," *Journal of Imperial and Commonwealth History* 45, no. 1 (December 13, 2016).

February 18, 2010 Gregor Gall, "Sex Work Organisation in the Global South," libcom.org, accessed April 15, 2020, https://libcom.org/history/sex-work-organisation-global-south.

February 19, 1927 "Position at Shanghai," *Hansard*, February 21, 1927, accessed April 15, 2020, http://hansard.millbanksystems.com/commons/1927/feb/21/position-at-shanghai.

February 19, 1950 Richard Hart, *Labour Rebellions in the 1930s in the British Caribbean* (London: Socialist History Society, 2002); Fitzroy Baptiste, "Gairy and the General Strike of 1951: As Gleaned from British and US Sources," 2002, accessed April 15, 2020, http://www.open.uwi.edu/sites/default/files/bnccde/grenada/conference/papers/Baptiste.html; "Biography: Sir Eric Matthew Gairy," Government of Grenada, accessed April 15, 2020, https://bit.ly/2zV15oF.

February 20, 1834 Ian Schlom, "The Struggle of the 'Mill Girls': Class Consciousness in Early 19th-Century New England," libcom.org, accessed April 15, 2020, https://bit.ly/2StxYzo.

February 20, 1990 Elowyn Corby, "Coalminers Strike against Pittston Company in Virginia, 1989–1990," Global Nonviolent Action Database, accessed April 15, 2020, https://bit.ly/2Sv916m.

February 21, 1936 "Chae-ho, Shin: Korea's Kōtoku," *Libero International* 2 (1975), accessed April 15, 2020, https://libcom.org/library/shin-chae-ho-koreas-k%C3%B5toku.

February 21, 1965 "Biography," MalcolmX.com, accessed April 15, 2020, https://www.malcolmx.com/biography; "Malcolm X: from Nation of Islam to Black Power Movement," *Al Jazeera*, February 21, 2018, accessed April 15, 2020, https://bit.ly/2WyF5aP; "The Missing Malcolm: Manning Marable Interviewed by Simon J Black," *International Socialist Review* 63, accessed April 15, 2020, https://isreview.org/issue/63/missing-malcolm.

February 22, 1927 "Chronology: The Pre-War Korean Anarchist Movement, Part 1," *Libero International* 1 (January 1975), accessed April 15, 2020, https://libcom.org/library/chronology-pre-war-korean-anarchist-movement.

February 22, 2018 Michael Mochaidean, "How West Virginia Teachers Defied the State—and Their Unions," Organizing Work, libcom.org, accessed April 15, 2020, https://libcom.org/library/how-west-virginia-teachers-defied-state-their-unions; Jess Bidgood, "West Virginia Raises Teachers Pay to End Statewide Strike," *New York Times*, March 6, 2018, accessed April 15, 2020, https://www.nytimes.com/2018/03/06/us/west-virginia-teachers-strike-deal.html.

February 23, 1910 Angie Boehm, "Triangle Shirtwaist Factory Women Strike, Win Better Wages and Hours, New York, 1909," Global Nonviolent Action Database, March 9, 2013, accessed April 15, 2020, https://tinyurl.com/ybjvhpdc.

February 23, 2004 "Slovakia's Unemployed Riots of 2004," libcom.org, February 21, 2017, accessed April 15, 2020, https://libcom.org/history/slovakias-unemployed-riots-2004.

February 24, 1912 Danna Bell, "Children as Advocates: The Bread and Roses Strike of 1912," Library of Congress, December 2, 2014, accessed April 15, 2020, https://bit.ly/2VWC6cX; Christopher Klein, "The Strike That Shook America," History.com, updated November 26, 2019, accessed April 15, 2020, https://www.history.com/news/the-strike-that-shook-america-100-years-ago.

February 24, 1932 Ivonne Trías, *Gerardo Gatti: revolucionario* (Montevideo, UY: Ediciones Trilce, 2012), 15; "Atemptat contra Luis Pardeiro (24 de febrer de 1932)," ateneu llibertari estel negre, accessed April 15, 2020, http://www.estelnegre.org/documents/pardeiro/pardeiro.html.

February 25, 1941 Peter Cole, "Strike!!! Strike!!! Strike!!! On This Day in 1941 Dutch Workers Said No to the Nazi Persecution of Dutch Jews," History News Network, February 25, 2018, accessed April 15, 2020, https://historynewsnetwork.org/article/168353.

February 25, 1986 "The Fall of the Dictatorship," Philippines Official Gazette, accessed April 15, 2020, https://www.officialgazette.gov.ph/featured/the-fall-of-the-dictatorship.

February 26, 1860 Jerry Rohde, "Genocide and Extortion," *North Coast Journal*, February 25, 2010, accessed April 15, 2020, https://bit.ly/2YpOHXO; "From California.; The Humboldt Butchery of Indian Infants and Women-Jacob Elyea Hanged Bogus Mining Stories A Solid Ledge of Gold at Jacksonville Items About Town, & c.," *New York Times*, April 12, 1860, 8, accessed April 15, 2020, https://nyti.ms/2StOz5O; "California City Returns Island Taken from Native Tribe in 1860 Massacre," *Guardian*, October 21, 2019, accessed April 15, 2020, https://bit.ly/2xwY9O6; Benjamin Tarnoff, *The Bohemians: Mark Twain and the San Francisco Writers Who Reinvented American Literature* (New York: Penguin, 2014); Jack Norton, *Genocide in Northwestern California: When Our Worlds Cried* (San Francisco: Indian Historian Press, 1979), 82.

February 26, 1931 Alex Wagner, "America's Forgotten History of Illegal Deportations," *Atlantic*, March 6, 2017, accessed April 15, 2020, https://bit.ly/35x0SUk; "The Time a President Deported 1 Million Mexican-Americans for Stealing US Jobs," *Washington Post*, August 13, 2018, accessed April 15, 2020, https://wapo.st/2WhSMe1; "February 26, 1931: La Placita Raid," Zinn Education Project, accessed April 15, 2020, https://www.zinnedproject.org/news/tdih/la-placita-raid.

February 27, 1943 "The Rosenstrasse Demonstration, 1943," Holocaust Encyclopedia, accessed April 15, 2020, https://encyclopedia.ushmm.org/content/en/article/the-rosenstrasse-demonstration-1943.

February 27, 1973 "Siege at Wounded Knee, 1973," libcom.org, accessed April 15, 2020, https://libcom.org/history/1973-siege-at-wounded-knee; Emily Chertoff, "Occupy Wounded Knee: A 71-Day Siege and a Forgotten Civil Rights Movement," *Atlantic*, October 23, 2012, accessed April 15, 2020, https://bit.ly/2ydjBbk.

February 28, 1948 Amma Fosuah Poku, "This Day in History: 28th February 1948," GhanaWeb, February 28, 2012, accessed April 15, 2020, https://bit.ly/2VUVmHR; Nana Akwah, "Today in History—The Riots of 28th February 1948," GhanaWeb, February 28, 2013, accessed April 15, 2020, https://bit.ly/2zT4uUT; "Sgt Adjetey, Cpl Attipoe, Pte Odartey . . . February 28 Shooting Commemoration at Nationalism Park," February 26, 2012, Modern Ghana, accessed April 15, 2020, https://bit.ly/2z5taJa; Nii-Ashitei Ashitey, "Martyrs of X'borg Crossrodas: Sgt. Adjetey, Cpl. Lamptey & Cpl. Attipoe," GhanaWeb, February 28, 2014 accessed April 15, 2020, https://bit.ly/2KTIMSS.

February 28, 1969 Linda Holden Givens, "Seattle Black Panther Party Protests Gun-Control Bill in Olympia on February 28, 1969," History Link, October 16, 2018, accessed April 15, 2020, https://historylink.org/File/20649.

February 29, 1864 "Kate Mullany and the Collar Laundry Union," libcom.org, accessed April 15, 2020, https://libcom.org/history/kate-mullany-collar-laundry-union.

February 29, 2004 "France Sends Police Force to Haiti," CNN, February 29, 2004, accessed April 15, 2020, http://edition.cnn.com/2004/WORLD/europe/02/29/france.haiti.force.reut; Noam Chomsky, "Haiti: Democracy Restored," *Raven* 7, no, (Winter 1994): 295–320, accessed April 15, 2020, https://libcom.org/library/raven-28-chomsky-haiti.

March

March 1, 1919 Editors, "March First Movement," Encyclopaedia Britannica, accessed April 15, 2020, https://www.britannica.com/event/March-First-Movement; 박은식, 한국독립운동지혈사 (Seoul: 소명출판, 2012).

March 1, 1968 Kelly Simpson, "East L.A. Blowouts: Walking Out for Justice in the Classrooms," March 7, 2012, KCET, accessed April 15, 2020, https://bit.ly/35tUltA; "The Walkout—How a Student Movement in 1968 Changed Schools Forever (Part 1 of 3)," United Way, February 26, 2018, accessed April 15, 2020, https://bit.ly/2z7E8xK.

March 2, 1921 Steven Johns, "The Republic of Labin, 1921," libcom.org, accessed April 15, 2020, https://libcom.org/history/republic-labin-1921; Riccardo Celeghini, "Balcani: 'La miniera è nostra!' Storia della Repubblica di Albona," East Journal, March 23, 2016, accessed April 15, 2020, https://www.eastjournal.net/archives/71072.

March 2, 1955 Gary Younge, "She Would Not Be Moved," *Guardian*, December 15, 2000, accessed April 15, 2020, https://www.theguardian.com/theguardian/2000/dec/16/weekend7.weekend12.

March 3, 1816 "[3 de marzo] Un día como hoy en 1816, Juana Azurduy junto a su ejército derrotó a las tropas españolas," Colombia Informa, March 3, 2016, accessed April 15, 2020, https://bit.ly/3aZ97t8.

March 3, 1959 Wunyabari O. Maloba, *Mau Mau and Kenya: An Analysis of a Peasant Revolt* (Bloomington: Indiana University Press, 1993), 142–43; Richard Toye, "Rhetoric and Imperial Decline: Arguing the Hola Camp Massacre of 1959," Imperial & Global Forum, May 19, 2014, accessed April 15, 2020, https://bit.ly/2xpFjrY.

March 4, 1919 Phil Carradice, "The Kinmel Camp Riots of 1919," BBC Wales, March 4, 2012, accessed April 15, 2020, http://www.bbc.co.uk/blogs/wales/entries/cfb526c8-186d-3afe-b3e0-095c8898f868.

March 4, 1972 Ken Weller, *The Lordstown Struggle and the Real Crisis in Production*, Solidarity *Pamphlet* 45, c.1973, accessed April 15, 2020, https://libcom.org/library/lordstown-struggle-ken-weller; Agis Salpukas, "GM's Vega Plant Closed by Strike," *New York Times*, March 7, 1972, 42. The Weller article cites the incorrect start date.

March 5, 1943 Tim Mason, *Nazism, Fascism and the Working Class* (Cambridge: Cambridge University Press, 1995), chapter 8; David Broder, "The Strike against Fear," *Jacobin*, March 5, 2018, accessed April 15, 2020, https://www.jacobinmag.com/2018/03/italy-fascism-fiat-strike-pci.

March 5, 1984 Sam Lowry, "Notes on the Miners [sic] Strike, 1984–1985," libcom.org, accessed April 15, 2020, https://libcom.org/library/notes-on-the-miners-strike-1984-1985; Jonathan Winterton and Ruth Winterton, *Coal, Crisis, and Conflict: The 1984–85 Miners' Strike in Yorkshire* (Manchester: Manchester Press, 1989), 67; Mike Ironside and Roger V Seifert, *Facing Up to Thatcherism: The History of NALGO, 1979–1993* (Oxford: Oxford University Press, 2000), 171; Seamus Milne, "A Generation on, the Miners' Strike Can Speak to Our Time," *Guardian*, March 12, 2009, accessed April 15, 2020, https://www.theguardian.com/commentisfree/2009/mar/12/miners-strike. Due to the strike spreading gradually, other sources sometimes refer to the strike beginning on other dates, most commonly March 6.

March 6, 1922 Andrew Grant Wood, "Postrevolutionary Pioneer: Anarchist María Luisa Marín and the Veracruz Renters' Movement," libcom.org, accessed April 15, 2020, https://tinyurl.com/ya83nows.

March 6, 1974 "1974: Heath Calls Snap Election Over Miners," BBC Home, accessed April 15, 2020, http://news.bbc.co.uk/onthisday/hi/dates/stories/february/7/newsid_4054000/4054793.stm.

March 7, 1860 Howard Zinn, "The Lynn Shoe Strike—1860," libcom.org, accessed April 15, 2020, https://libcom.org/history/1860-the-lynn-shoe-strike; "The Great New England Shoe Strike of 1860," New England Historical Society, accessed April 15, 2020, http://www.newenglandhistoricalsociety.com/great-new-england-shoemakers-strike-1860; "1860 Showmakers [sic] Strike in Lynn," Massachusetts AFL-CIO, accessed April 15, 2020, https://tinyurl.com/y9sqwscp; "Labor and Labor Organizations," Pictorial Americana, Library of Congress, accessed April 15, 2020, https://www.loc.gov/rr/print/list/picamer/paLabor.html; "'We Are Not Slaves': Female Shoe and Textile Workers in Marblehead, Massachusetts, 1860," History Matters, accessed April 15, 2020, http://historymatters.gmu.edu/d/6590. Some sources give the incorrect date of March 8.

March 7, 1932 Fatimah Hameed, "Unemployed Detroit Auto Workers Conduct Hunger March to Protest Ford Motor Company's Policies, United States, 1932," Global Nonviolent Action Database, accessed April 15, 2020, https://bit.ly/2ybySJK; "1932 Ford Hunger March Massacre," libcom.org, accessed April 15, 2020, https://libcom.org/gallery/1932-ford-hunger-march-massacre.

March 8, 1917 and 1918 Barbara Engel, "Subsistence Riots in Russia during World War I," *Journal of Modern History* 69 (December 1997): 696–721, accessed April 15, 2020, https://libcom.

org/history/subsistence-riots-russia-during-world-war-i-barbara-engel; Temma Kaplan, "The Socialist Origins of International Women's Day," *Feminist Studies* 11, no. 1 (1985): 163–71, accessed April 15, 2020, https://libcom.org/files/International%20Women's%20Day.pdf.

March 8, 1926 "Police Wield Clubs on Fur Strike Mob," *New York Times*, March 9, 1926, 15, accessed April 15, 2020, https://timesmachine.nytimes.com/timesmachine/1926/03/09/99381113. html?pageNumber=15; "Agreement Reached to End Fur Strike," *New York Times*, June 11, 1926, 1, accessed April 15, 2020, https://nyti.ms/3c2qxGM; "Celebrate End of Fur Strike," *New York Times*, June 16, 1926, 52, accessed April 15, 2020, https://timesmachine.nytimes.com/timesmachine/1926/06/16/98482165.html?pageNumber=52.

March 9, 1883 Jayacintha Danaswamy, "Michel, Louise, 1830–1905," libcom.org, accessed April 15, 2020, https://libcom.org/history/articles/1830-louise-michel.

March 9, 1910 Judith McDonough, "The Westmoreland County Coal Miners' Strike, 1910–11," libcom.org, accessed April 15, 2020, https://libcom.org/history/westmoreland-county-coal-miners-strike-1910-11.

March 10, 1906 Véronique Laroche-Signorile, "Courrières: la catastrophe minière la plus meurtrière d'Europe (1906)," *Figaro*, March 9, 2016, accessed April 15, 2020, https://bit.ly/3fakQsd.

March 10, 1952 Sam Dolgoff, *The Cuban Revolution: A Critical Perspective* (Montréal: Black Rose Books, 1996), chapter 6, accessed April 15, 2020, https://libcom.org/library/chapter-6-batista-era; "Memorandum by the Secretary of State to the President," US Office of the Historian, March 24, 1952, accessed April 15, 2020, https://history.state.gov/historicaldocuments/frus1952-54v04/d327; "From the Archive, 11 March 1952: Batista's Revolution," *Guardian*, March 11, 2013, accessed April 15, 2020, https://www.theguardian.com/theguardian/2013/mar/11/cuba-batista-fifth-revolution-1952; "Speech of Senator John F. Kennedy, Cincinnati, Ohio, Democratic Dinner," American Presidency Project, October 6, 1960, accessed April 15, 2020, https://bit.ly/2KUK6Vu.

March 11, 1845 "Battle of Kororareka," Russell Museum, accessed April 15, 2020, http://www.russellmuseum.org.nz/Kororareka_battle.htm.

March 11, 1977 "11 March 1977: Francesco Lorusso Is Murdered by Police," InfoAut, March 11, 2016, accessed April 15, 2019, https://www.infoaut.org/english/11-march-1977-francesco-lorusso-is-murdered-by-police.

March 12, 1912 Sam Lowry, "The Lawrence Textile Strike, 1912," libcom.org, accessed April 15, 2020, https://libcom.org/history/articles/lawrence-textile-strike-1912; "March 12, 1912: Bread and Roses Strike Is Successful," Zinn Education Project, accessed April 15, 2020, https://www.zinnedproject.org/news/tdih/singing-strike.

March 12, 1951 Sam Lowry, "1951 Barcelona General Strike," libcom.org, accessed April 15, 2020, https://libcom.org/history/1951-barcelona-general-strike; "Strike Position in Barcelona," *Cairns Post*, March 14, 1951, 1, accessed April 15, 2020, https://trove.nla.gov.au/newspaper/article/42681500.

March 13, 1940 "13 March 1940: Udham Singh Shot and Killed Michael O'Dwyer in Britain," Maps of India, accessed April 15, 2020, https://bit.ly/3ffc1xd.

March 13, 1945 Vera Libera Arduino, Facebook, accessed April 15, 2020, https://www.facebook.com/vera.libera.arduino; Miriam Mafai, *Pane nero: donne e vita quotidiana nella seconda guerra mondiale* (Milan: A. Mondadori, 1987), 252–53; Tony De Nardo, "Una targa per ricordare la storia di Vera e Libera Arduino," CittAgora, July 17, 2018, accessed April 15, 2020, https://tinyurl.com/y76adfhs; "Vera Arduino (Torino, 1926–1945)," Museo Torino, accessed April 15, 2020, http://www.museotorino.it/view/s/f76a9a8d93fb4b77896e8bf26bc11269. Given that some sources date the execution of the Arduino sisters as March 12, we believe it occurred just after midnight.

March 14, 1970 Richard Linnett and Roberto Loiederman, *The Eagle Mutiny* (Annapolis, MD: Naval Institute Press, 2001); "E21–24: WCH Crime—The Columbia Eagle Mutiny" (podcast), *Working Class History*, accessed April 15, 2020, https://workingclasshistory.com/2019/04/09/wch-crime-columbia-eagle-mutiny.

March 14, 2018 "Suspects in Marielle Franco's Murder Have Ties to Bolsonaro Family," *Vice*, January 23, 2019, accessed April 15, 2020, https://bit.ly/35u3d27; "Marielle Franco Murder: Two

Rio Ex-Police Officers Held," BBC News, March 12, 2019, accessed April 15, 2020, https://www.bbc.com/news/world-latin-america-47538871; "Marielle Franco Murder: Suspect Shot Dead by Police," BBC News, February 9, 2020, accessed April 15, 2020, https://www.bbc.com/news/world-latin-america-51439016.

March 15, 1908 "Women Anarchists Have Become the Terror of World's Police," *Rochester Democrat and Chronicle*, March 15, 1908, 34.

March 15, 1917 Leon Trotsky, *The History of the Russian Revolution*, vols. 1–3, Max Eastman, trans. (New York: Simon & Schuster, 1932), accessed April 15, 2020, https://www.marxists.org/archive/trotsky/1930/hrr/index.htm; "The Centenary of the Abdication of Tsar Nicholas II of Russia," University of York, Department of History, March 27, 2017, accessed April 15, 2020, 2019, https://www.york.ac.uk/history/news/news/2017/tsar-nicholas-ii.

March 16, 1965 "Mounted Officers in 'Bama Charge, Flail Demonstrators; Man Who Gave Order Apologizes," *Waco News-Tribune*, March 17, 1965, 1; "Beat Alabama Marchers—Demonstrators Reach Capitol in Second Try," *Chicago Tribune*, March 17, 1965, 1.

March 16, 1979 Michael Mehigan, Witness Statement, July 12, 1994, accessed April 15, 2020, http://www.mcspotlight.org/people/witnesses/employment/mehigan.html.

March 17, 1876 Jerome A. Greene, *Lakota and Cheyenne: Indian Views of the Great Sioux War, 1876–1877* (Norman: University of Oklahoma Press, 1994); Brett French, "Battle of Powder River Was 1st of 3 That Cavalry Lost to the Indians in Montana," *Billings Gazette*, July 2, 2002, accessed April 15, 2020, https://bit.ly/2KPXRoB.

March 17, 1920 Richard J. Evans, "The Life and Death of a Capital," *New Republic*, September 27, 2012, accessed April 15, 2020, https://newrepublic.com/article/107689/abused-city-hitlers-berlin-thomas-friedrich; Gilles Dauvé and Denis Authier, *The Communist Left in Germany 1918–1921*, chapter 12, accessed April 15, 2020, https://libcom.org/library/communist-left-germany-1918-1921.

March 18, 1871 and 1911 Editors, "Commune of Paris 1871," Encyclopaedia Britannica, accessed April 15, 2020, https://www.britannica.com/event/Commune-of-Paris-1871; "1871: The Paris Commune," libcom.org, accessed April 15, 2020, https://libcom.org/history/articles/paris-commune-1871; Temma Kaplan, "The Socialist Origins of International Women's Day," *Feminist Studies* 11, no. 1 (1985): 163–71, accessed April 15, 2020, https://libcom.org/files/International%20Women's%20Day.pdf.

March 18, 1970 ShaKea Alston, "Feminist Sit-in at Ladies Home Journal, 1970," Global Nonviolent Action Database, May 25, 2015, accessed April 19, 2020, https://bit.ly/2KPGjZA.

March 19, 1969 Donald E. Westlake, "In Anguilla It's the Spirit of '71," *New York Times* May 23, 1971, accessed April 15, 2020, https://tinyurl.com/y5g4kuxq; Charles Doane, "The Invasion of Anguilla," Wave Train, May 25, 2016, accessed April 15, 2020, https://wavetrain.net/2016/05/25/the-invasion-of-anguilla-a-comedy-of-errors-caribbean-style; Taff Bowen, "Anguilla Police Unit 1969. . ." accessed April 15, 2020, https://www.anguilla-beaches.com/anguilla-history-british-invasion.html; Arleen Webster, comment on WCH photo, March 19, 2019 , accessed April 15, 2020, https://www.facebook.com/workingclasshistory/photos/a.296224173896073/1089756174542865.

March 19, 2019 Damian Carrington, "School Climate Strikes: 1.4 Million People Took Part, Say Campaigners," *Guardian*, March 19, 2019, accessed April 16, 2020, https://tinyurl.com/y38afccl; "Events List," Fridays for Future, accessed August 7, 2019, unavailable April 16, 2020, https://www.fridaysforfuture.org/events/list; David Crouch, "The Swedish 15-Year-Old Who's Cutting Class to Fight the Climate Crisis," *Guardian*, September 1, 2018, accessed April 16, 2020, https://tinyurl.com/yc8ys37g.

March 20, 1927 Siddharthya Swapan Roy, "The Lake of Liberation," *Outlook*, April 18, 2016, accessed April 16, 2020, https://www.outlookindia.com/magazine/story/the-lake-of-liberation/296954; Tejas Harad, "The Significance of Mahad Satyagraha: Ambedkar's Protest March to Claim Public Water," Feminism in India, March 20, 2017, accessed April 16, 2020, https://feminisminindia.com/2017/03/20/mahad-satyagraha; Swapna H. Samel, "Mahad Chawadar

Tank Satyagraha of 1927: Beginning of Dalit Liberation under B.R. Ambedkar," *Proceedings of The Indian History Congress* 60 (1999): 722–28.

March 20, 1975 "40 años del "Operativo Serpiente Colorada del Paraná," El Terrorismo de Estado antes del Golpe," la palabra caliente. . ., accessed April 16, 2020, https://tinyurl.com/ybojc8ca.

March 21, 1937 "The Ponce Massacre (1937)," Enciclopedia de Puerto Rico, accessed April 16, 2020, https://enciclopediapr.org/en/encyclopedia/the-ponce-massacre-1937; "The Ponce Massacre, 1937," libcom.org, accessed April 16, 2020, https://libcom.org/history/ponce-massacre-1937.

March 21, 1973 Past Tense, "The Mental Patients Union, 1973," libcom.org, accessed April 16, 2020, https://libcom.org/history/mental-patients-union-1973.

March 22, 1986 Clyde Haberman, "Filipino Strikers Picket US Bases," *New York Times*, March 23, 1986, accessed April 16, 2020, https://www.nytimes.com/1986/03/23/world/filipino-strikers-picket-us-bases.html; Mark Fineman, "Filipino Pickets Block Gates of US Naval Base," *Los Angeles Times*, March 23, 1986, accessed April 16, 2020, https://www.latimes.com/archives/la-xpm-1986-03-23-mn-5537-story.html.

March 22, 2009 Taxikipali, "Prisoner Activists Death Sparks Uprising in Women's Prison of Thebes, Greece," libcom.org, March 22, 2009, accessed April 16, 2020, https://tinyurl.com/y7qyk6em.

March 23, 1931 Abhishek Saksena, "12 Facts About Bhagat Singh That You Still Didn't Know," *India Times*, December 19, 2017, accessed April 16, 2020, https://tinyurl.com/ycqfj7op; Jain Narain Sharma, "Mahatma Gandhi and Bhagat Singh: A Clash of Ideology," accessed April 16, 2020, https://www.mkgandhi.org/articles/gandhi_bhagatsingh.html; "Remembering Shivaram Hari Rajguru on His Birthday," *India Today*, August 24, 2015, accessed April 16, 2020, https://tinyurl.com/ybre34kh; "The 24-Year-Old Martyr Who Gave Up His Life for India: Facts about Sukhdev Thapar You Must Know," *India Today*, May 15, 2017, accessed April 16, 2020, https://tinyurl.com/y9vat2hu.

March 23, 1944 "Via Rasella," Resistenza Italiana, accessed April 29, 2020, http://www.storiaxxisecolo.it/Resistenza/resistenza3.htm; "Ardeatine Caves Massacre," Holocaust Encyclopedia, accessed April 16, 2020, https://encyclopedia.ushmm.org/content/en/article/ardeatine-caves-massacre.

March 24, 1976 Paul Hoeffel, "Junta Takes Over in Argentina," *Guardian*, March 25, 1976, accessed April 16, 2020, https://tinyurl.com/y8rvlpb5.

March 24, 1987 "Homosexuals Arrested at AIDS Drug Protest," *New York Times*, March 25, 1987, 32; "No More Business as Usual!" ACT UP Historical Archive, accessed May 20, 2020, https://actupny.org/documents/1stFlyer.html.

March 25, 1911 "The 1911 Triangle Factory Fire," Cornell University, accessed April 16, 2020, https://trianglefire.ilr.cornell.edu.

March 25, 1969 Aileen Eisenberg, "Pakistani Students, Workers, and Peasants Bring Down a Dictator, 1968–1969," Global Nonviolent Action Database, February 22, 2013, accessed April 19, 2020, https://tinyurl.com/yab8ptnm.

March 26, 1953 "The Mau Mau Uprising, 1952–1956," South African History Online, accessed April 16, 2020, https://www.sahistory.org.za/article/mau-mau-uprising; "Kenya: Mau Mau Outrage," Hansard 181 (HL Deb 31 March 1953), 370–73, accessed April 16, 2020, https://api.parliament.uk/historic-hansard/lords/1953/mar/31/kenya-mau-mau-outrage.

March 26, 1978 Robert Crabbe, "Fighting Rages Over Tokyo Airport," *Nashua Telegraph*, May 20, 1978, accessed April 16, 2020, https://tinyurl.com/yaalky6s.

March 27, 1942 Larry Portis, *French Frenzies: A Social History of Popular Music in France* (College Station, TX: Virtualbookworm Publishing, 2004), 102.

March 27, 1943 "De aanslag op het Amsterdamse bevolkingsregister," Verzets Resistance Museum, accessed April 16, 2020, https://tinyurl.com/yxwvo39m; Chris Pasles, "O.C. Musical Pioneer Frieda Belinfante Dies at 90," *Los Angeles Times*, March 7, 1995, accessed April 16, 2020, https://www.latimes.com/archives/la-xpm-1995-03-07-me-39790-story.html; "Willem Arondeus," Holocaust Encyclopedia, accessed April 16, 2020, https://encyclopedia.ushmm.org/content/en/id-card/willem-arondeus.

March 28, 1919 "Red Scare (1919–1920)," Encyclopedia of Arkansas, accessed April 16, 2020, https://encyclopediaofarkansas.net/entries/red-scare-4600.

March 28, 1977 Jason Schultz, "A Disgrace Before God: Striking Black Sanitation Workers vs. Black Officialdom in 1977 Atlanta," libcom.org, accessed April 16, 2020, https://tinyurl.com/ybnemhkl.

March 29, 1986 "Weg met de Centrumpartij," Andere Tijden, accessed April 16, 2020, https://anderetijden.nl/aflevering/274/Weg-met-de-Centrumpartij.

March 29, 1988 International Communist Current, "A History of Trade Unionism in the Philippines," libcom.org, accessed April 16, 2020, https://libcom.org/history/history-trade-unionism-philippines.

March 30, 1919 Lucien van der Walt and the Bikisha Media Collective, "'Sifuna Zonke!': Revolutionary Syndicalism, the Industrial Workers of Africa and the Fight against Racial Capitalism, 1915–1921," SAASHA, February 24, 2012, accessed May 26, 2020, https://saasha.net/2012/02/24/sifuna-zonke-bmc-undated/#more-248; "Campaign against Passes in Transvaal," African National Congress, accessed March 30, 2018, unavailable April 16, 2020, http://www.anc.org.za/content/campaign-against-passes-transvaal-1919.

March 30, 1976 "Remembering Land Day," BBC News, March 30, 2001, accessed April 16, 2020, http://news.bbc.co.uk/2/hi/middle_east/1250290.stm; Daniel Byman, *Keeping the Peace: Lasting Solutions to Ethnic Conflicts* (Baltimore: Johns Hopkins University Press, 2002), 132; William Frankel, *Survey of Jewish Affairs* (Madison, NJ: Fairleigh Dickinson University Press, 1988), 40; Yifat Holzman-Gazit, *Land Expropriation in Israel: Law, Culture and Society* (Farnham, UK: Ashgate Publishing, 2007), 140.

March 31, 1979 Knight News Service, "San Francisco May Vote Out Vice Squad," *Lakeland Ledger*, October 29 1979, accessed April 16, 2020, https://tinyurl.com/ybywtddt; Josh Sides, *Erotic City: Sexual Revolutions and the Making of Modern San Francisco* (Oxford: Oxford University Press, 2009), 162–65; "SF Cops Who Assaulted Lesbians Are Suspended," *Advocate* 284 (January 1980): 9; Paul Grabowicz, "Anti-Gay Sentiments Turn Violent in Aftermath of Moscone-Milk Killings," *Washington Post*, May 12, 1979, accessed April 16, 2020, https://tinyurl.com/y9oqj6by.

March 31, 2009 Evan Johnston, "The Wonderful World of Bossnapping" (blog), May 1, 2016, accessed April 16 2020, https://evanjohnston.org/2016/05/01/the-wonderful-world-of-bossnapping.

April

April 1, 1649 John Simkin, "Gerrard Winstanley and the Failed Digger Revolution," updated January 2020, Spartacus Educational, accessed April 16, 2020, https://spartacus-educational.com/ExamECW6.htm.

April 1, 1982 "1982 Memo to Exxon Management About CO2 Greenhouse Effect," Climate Files, November 12, 1982, accessed April 16, 2020, https://tinyurl.com/yam3jn9a; Dana Nuccitelli, "Two-Faced Exxon: The Misinformation Campaign against Its Own Scientists," *Guardian*, November 25, 2015, accessed April 16, 2020, https://tinyurl.com/ybdlgu32; Benjamin Franta, "Shell and Exxon's Secret 1980s Climate Change Warnings," *Guardian*, September 19, 2018, accessed April 16, 2020, https://tinyurl.com/yaxg22sh.

April 2, 1920 "Chronik 1920," Deutsches Historisches Museum, accessed April 16, 2020, https://www.dhm.de/lemo/jahreschronik/1920.

April 2, 1980 "St Paul's Uprising, Bristol 1980," History Is Made at Night, December 17, 2020, accessed April 16, 2020, http://history-is-made-at-night.blogspot.com/2010/12/st-pauls-uprising-bristol-1980.html; Laura Churchill, "The St Paul's Riot 37 Years On," Bristol Live, April 3, 2017, accessed April 16, 2020, https://www.bristolpost.co.uk/news/bristol-news/st-pauls-riots-37-years-17634.

April 3, 1948 Governor of Jeju, "Jeju Uprising," April 3, 2001, New World Encyclopedia, accessed April 16, 2020, https://www.newworldencyclopedia.org/entry/Jeju_Uprising; Brittany M. Dixon, "A Riot, a Rebellion, a Massacre: Remembering the 1948 Jeju Uprising" (research paper, Eastern Illinois University, 2017), accessed April 16, 2020, https://www.eiu.edu/historia/Dixon2017.pdf.

April 3, 1974 "The Brockwell 3: A School Strike in 1974," Transpontine, November 29, 2010, accessed April 16, 2020, https://transpont.blogspot.com/2010/11/brockwell-three-school-strike-in-1974.html; citing Robert Moore, *Racism and Black Resistance in Britain* (London: Pluto Press, 1975).

April 4, 1935 John Haag, "Fabian, Dora (1901–1935)," Encyclopedia.com, updated April 4, 2020, accessed April 16, 2020, https://tinyurl.com/y8rff6pw; James J. Barnes and Patience P. Barnes, *Nazi Refugee Turned Gestapo Spy: The Life of Hans Wesemann, 1895–1971* (Santa Barbara, CA: Praeger Publishers, 2001), 93.

April 4, 1968 Jeff Wallenfeldt, "Assassination of Martin Luther King Jr.," Encyclopaedia Britannica, updated April 15, 2020, accessed April 16, 2020, https://www.britannica.com/topic/assassination-of-Martin-Luther-King-Jr; Bhaskar Sunkara, "Martin Luther King Was No Prophet of Unity. He Was a Radical," *Guardian*, January 21, 2019, accessed April 16, 2020, https://tinyurl.com/yd4yz6vo; Peter Dreier and E.P. Clapp, "Martin Luther King Was a Democratic Socialist," Huffpost, January 18, 2016, accessed April 16, 2020, https://tinyurl.com/yaav3n5e; Douglas Sturm, "Martin Luther King, Jr., as Democratic Socialist," *Journal of Religious Ethics* 18, no. 2 (Fall 1990): 79–105; "What an Uncensored Letter to MLK Reveals," *New York Times*, November 16, 2014, accessed April 16, 2020, https://tinyurl.com/ycl6gpqm.

April 5, 1932 Drew Brown, "Remembering the Time 10,000 Newfoundlanders Tried to Kill the Prime Minister," *Vice*, April 5, 2017, accessed April 16, 2020, https://tinyurl.com/y8bcgnh9.

April 5, 1971 *Ceylon: The JVP Uprising of April 1971, Solidarity London Pamphlet 42*, accessed April 16, 2020, https://libcom.org/files/Ceylon-solidarity-pamphlet.pdf; James P. Sterba, "Ceylon's Student Revolt: Years in the Planning Stage," *New York Times*, April 28, 1971, 14; A. Sivanandan, "Ethnic Cleansing in Sri Lanka," Institute of Race Relations, July 9, 2009, accessed April 8, 2020, http://www.irr.org.uk/news/ethnic-cleansing-in-sri-lanka; S. Arasaratnam, "The Ceylon Insurrection of April 1971: Some Causes and Consequences," *Pacific Affairs* 45, no. 3 (1972): 356–371; Fred Halliday, "The Ceylonese Insurrection," *New Left Review* 69 (September–October 1971), accessed April 9, 2020, https://newleftreview.org/issues/I69/articles/fred-halliday-the-ceylonese-insurrection; Rajesh Venugopal, "Sectarian Socialism: The Politics of Sri Lanka's Janatha Vimukthi Peramuna (JVP)," *Modern Asian Studies* 44, no. 3 (2010): 567–602.

April 6, 1871 "Against the Logic of the Guillotine: Why the Paris Commune Burned the Guillotine and We Should Too," CrimethInc, accessed April 16, 2020, https://tinyurl.com/yc8vebpr; Frank Jellinek, *The Paris Commune of 1871* (Vancouver, BC: Read Books, 2013), 227; Franklin E. Zimring, *The Contradictions of American Capital Punishment* (Oxford: Oxford University Press, 2004), 33; Robert Frederick Opie, *Guillotine: The Timbers of Justice* (Cheltenham, UK: History Press, 2013), 131; Jörg Osterloh and Clemens Vollnhals, *NS-Prozesse und deutsche Öffentlichkeit: Besatzungszeit, frühe Bundesrepublik und DDR* (Göttingen, DE: Vandenhoeck & Ruprecht, 2013), 368; John O. Koehler, *Stasi: The Untold Story of the East German Secret Police* (New York: Basic Books, 2008), 18.

April 6, 1968 Karen Grigsby Bates, "Bobby Hutton: The Killing That Catapulted the Black Panthers to Fame," NPR, April 6, 2018, accessed April 16, 2020, https://tinyurl.com/yayfwqko.

April 7, 1926 Debbie Foulkes, "Violet Gibson (1876–1956) Shot Mussolini," Forgotten Newsmakers, May 17, 2010, accessed April 16, 2020, https://tinyurl.com/y9b44u24; citing Frances Stonor Saunders, *The Woman Who Shot Mussolini* (New York: Metropolitan Books, 2010).

April 7, 2010 Jeewon Kim, "Danish Brewery (Carlsberg) Workers Strike for Beer Rights, 2010," December 9, 2010, Global Nonviolent Action Database, accessed April 16, 2020, https://tinyurl.com/yaxvfnzv.

April 8, 1929 "88 Years Ago, Bhagat Singh and Batukeshwar Dutt Did Something 'to Make the Deaf Hear,'" *India Today*, April 8, 2017, accessed April 16, 2020, https://tinyurl.com/ydf9c3xc.

April 8, 1958 Constance R. Sutton, "Continuing the Fight for Economic Justice: The Barbadian Sugar Workers' 1958 Wildcat Strike," libcom.org, accessed April 16, 2020, https://tinyurl.com/ybo597fp.

April 9, 1945 "Elser, Georg, 1903–1945," libcom.org, accessed April 16, 2020, https://libcom.org/history/elser-georg-1903-1945; "Georg Elser," Gedenkstätte Deutscher Widerstand, accessed April 16, 2020, https://tinyurl.com/y83gggne.

April 9, 1948 Benny Morris, *1948: A History of the First Arab-Israeli War* (New Haven, CT: Yale University Press, 2008); Sherif Kana'ana and Nihad Zeitawi, *The Village of Deir Yassin*, Monograph no. 4, Destroyed Village Series (West Bank, PS: Birzeit University Press, 1988); Stefan Brooks, "Deir Yassin Massacre," in Spencer C. Tucker, ed., *The Encyclopedia of the Arab-Israeli Conflict: A Political, Social, and Military History* (Santa Barbara, CA: ABC-CLIO, 2008), 297.

April 10, 1919 Peter E. Newell, *Zapata of Mexico* (Montréal: Black Rose Books, 1997 [1979]), accessed April 16, 2020, https://libcom.org/files/Zapata-Peter-Newell.pdf.

April 10, 1932 Jeffrey Rossman, "Strikes against Stalin in 1930s Russia," *Russian Review* 56, no. 1 (January 1997): 44–69, accessed April 16, 2020, https://libcom.org/history/strikes-against-stalin-1930s-russia-jeffrey-rossman.

April 11, 1945 "Persecution of Homosexuals," United States Holocaust Memorial Museum, accessed April 16, 2020, https://tinyurl.com/yaagxsxw; Emails between Working Class History and United States Holocaust Memorial Museum, April 23, 2019; *Handbook for Military Government in Germany*, Supreme Headquarters Allied Expeditionary Force Office of the Chief of Staff, accessed April 16, 2020, https://tinyurl.com/ybq4ndjx; Craig Kaczorowski, "Paragraph 175," GLBTQ Archive, 2004, accessed April 11, 2020, http://www.glbtqarchive.com/ssh/paragraph_175_S.pdf; W. Jake Newsome, "Homosexuals After the Holocaust: Sexual Citizenship and the Politics of Memory in Germany and the United States, 1945–2008" (PhD diss, University at Buffalo, 2016), accessed April 20, 2020, https://www.une.edu/sites/default/files/homosexuals_after_the_holocaust.pdf; Florence Tamagne, "La déportation des homo-sexuels durant la Seconde Guerre mondiale," *Revue d'éthique et de théologie morale* 239 (May 2006): 77–104, accessed April 20, 2020, https://www.cairn.info/revue-d-ethique-et-de-theologie-morale-2006-2-page-77.htm; Samuel Clowes Huneke, "Gay Liberation Behind the Iron Curtain," *Boston Review*, April 18, 2019, accessed April 20, 2020, https://bostonreview.net/gender-sexuality/samuel-clowes-huneke-gay-liberation-behind-iron-curtain.

April 11, 1972 "The Common Front Strikes," Canadian Encyclopedia, updated December 15, 2013, accessed April 16, 2020, https://www.thecanadianencyclopedia.ca/en/article/common-front-strikes; George "Mick" Sweetman, "1972: The Québec General Strike," libcom.org, accessed April 16, 2020, https://libcom.org/history/1972-the-quebec-general-strike.

April 12, 1920 John Dorney, "The General Strike and Irish Independence," libcom.org, June 6, 2013, accessed April 16, 2020, https://libcom.org/files/TheGeneralStrikeandIrishindependence.pdf.

April 12, 1927 International Communist Current, "The Chinese Revolution 1925–1927," libcom.org, accessed April 16, 2020, https://libcom.org/history/chinese-revolution-1925-1927; Arif Dirlik, *Anarchism in the Chinese Revolution* (Berkeley: University of California Press, 1991), chapter 7.

April 13, 1916 John Couzin, "The Fight for of Speech on Glasgow Green, 1916–1932," libcom.org, accessed April 16, 2020, https://libcom.org/history/articles/glasgow-green-free-speech-fight.

April 13, 1919 Kenneth Pletcher, "Jallianwala Bagh Massacre," Encyclopaedia Britannica, updated April 8, 2020, accessed April 16, 2020, https://www.britannica.com/event/Jallianwala-Bagh-Massacre; "1919 Jallianwala Bagh Massacre," Discover Sikhism, accessed April 16, 2020, http://www.discoversikhism.com/sikh_genocide/1919_jallianwalla_bagh_massacre.html.

April 14, 1816 "Harrow [Chamberlaine's]," Legacies of British Slave Ownership, UCL, accessed April 16, 2020, http://wwwdepts-live.ucl.ac.uk/lbs/estate/view/752; Donna Every, "The Bussa Rebellion and Vaucluse," July 28, 2016, accessed April 16, 2020, https://donnaevery.com/bussa-rebellion-vaucluse; "Bussa's Rebellion," National Archives, accessed April 16, 2020, http://www.nationalarchives.gov.uk/education/resources/bussas-rebellion; "The Emancipation Wars," National Library of Jamaica, accessed April 16, 2020, https://www.nlj.gov.jm/history-notes/The%20Emancipation%20Wars.pdf.

April 14, 1919 D.R. O'Connor Lysaght, "The Story of the Limerick Soviet, 1919," libcom.org, accessed April 16, 2020, https://libcom.org/library/1919-story-limerick-soviet.

April 15, 1916 "IWW Local Unions (Database)," IWW History Project, accessed April 16, 2020, http://depts.washington.edu/iww/locals.shtml; Jane Street, "Letter on the IWW Domestic Workers Union, 1917," accessed April 15, 2020, https://libcom.org/history/letter-iww-domestic-workers-union-1917-jane-street.

April 15, 1989 George Katsiaficas, "The Chinese Democratic Uprising, 1989," libcom.org, accessed April 16, 2020, https://libcom.org/history/chinese-democratic-uprising-1989; Anthony Tao, "No, 10,000 Were Not Killed in the 1989 Tiananmen Crackdown," SupChina, December 25, 2017, accessed April 16, 2020, https://supchina.com/2017/12/25/no-10000-not-killed-in-tiananmen-crackdown; Yueran Zhang, "The Forgotten Socialists of Tiananmen Square," *Jacobin*, June 4, 2019, accessed April 16, 2020, https://tinyurl.com/y2xr8vhk.

April 16, 1970 Martin Glaberman, "Black Cats, White Cats, Wildcats," libcom.org, accessed April 16, 2020, https://libcom.org/library/black-cats-white-cats-wildcats-martin-glaberman.

April 16, 1979 Margaret Randall, *Sandino's Daughters Revisited: Feminism in Nicaragua* (New Brunswick, NJ: Rutgers University Press, 1994), 243.

April 17, 1920 John Dorney, "The General Strike and Irish Independence," libcom.org, June 6, 2013, accessed April 16, 2020, https://libcom.org/files/TheGeneralStrikeandIrishindependence.pdf.

April 17, 1976 Kenan Malik, *From Fatwa to Jihad: The Rushdie Affair and Its Legacy* (London: Atlantic Books, 2017), 47–54, accessed April 16, 2020, https://libcom.org/history/here-stay-here-fight-kenan-malik; "E33–34: Asian Youth Movements in Bradford" (podcast), *Working Class History*, accessed April 16, 2020, https://workingclasshistory.com/2019/09/18/e28-29-asian-youth-movements-in-bradford.

April 18, 1888 Roland Oliver, "Some Factors in the British Occupation of East Africa, 1884–1894," *Uganda Journal* 15, no. 1 (March 1951): 49–64; Jacob Kushner, "The British Empire's Homophobia Lives on in Former Colonies," *Atlantic*, May 24, 2019, accessed April 16, 2020, https://www.theatlantic.com/international/archive/2019/05/kenya-supreme-court-lgbtq/590014.

April 18, 2001 Hassan Berber, "'Ulach Smah' ('No Forgiveness')—the Algeria Insurrection, 2001," libcom.org, June 22, 2001, accessed April 16, 2020, https://libcom.org/library/algeria-2001-ulach-smah-no-forgiveness.

April 19, 1943 "Warsaw Ghetto Uprising," Holocaust Encyclopedia, accessed April 16, 2019, https://encyclopedia.ushmm.org/content/en/article/warsaw-ghetto-uprising.

April 19, 1960 Kyung Moon Hwang, "Remembering April 19, 1960 Student Revolution," *Korea Times*, April 16, 2014, accessed April 16, 2020, http://www.koreatimes.co.kr/www/news/nation/2016/05/633_155532.html.

April 20, 1853 "Harriet Tubman Begins Working on the Underground Railroad," African American Registry, accessed April 16, 2020, https://aaregistry.org/story/harriet-tubman-starts-working-with-the-underground-railroad.

April 20, 1914 Sam Lowry, "The Ludlow Massacre, 1914," libcom.org, September 11, 2006, accessed April 16, 2020, https://libcom.org/history/articles/ludlow-massacre-1914; Gregory Deheler, "Ludlow Massacre," Encyclopaedia Britannica, updated April 13, 2020, accessed April 16, 2020, https://www.britannica.com/event/Ludlow-Massacre.

April 21, 1856 Terry Irving, Terence H. Irving, and Rowan J. Cahill, *Radical Sydney: Places, Portraits and Unruly Episodes* (Sydney, AU: University of New South Wales Press, 2010), 62; Editor, "History: First Eight-Hour Day with No Loss of Pay," *Socialist*, March 13, 2019, accessed April 16, 2020, https://thesocialist.org.au/8-hour-day; "Eight Hour Day Monument," Monument Australia, accessed April 16, 2020, https://tinyurl.com/ya8j37eu.

April 21, 2007 Joel Beinin, "Egyptian Workers and January 25th: A Social Movement in Historical Context," *Social Research* 79, no. 2 (Summer 2012): 323–48; Hossam el-Hamalawy, "Egypt: Garment Workers' Sit-in Reaches 26th Day," libcom.org, accessed April 16, 2020, https://tinyurl.com/yd8309at.

April 22, 1944 Sarah Azaransky, *The Dream Is Freedom: Pauli Murray and the American Democratic Faith* (New York: Oxford University Press, 2001); Charles E. Cobb Jr., *On the Road to*

Freedom: A Guided Tour of the Civil Rights Trail (Chapel Hill, NC: Algonquin Books of Chapel Hill, 2008), 2; Gregory Hunter, "Howard University: 'Capstone of Negro Education' during World War II," *Journal of Negro History* 79, no. 1 (Winter 1994); Pauli Murray, "A Blueprint for First Class Citizenship," *Crisis* (1944): 358–59; "Downtown, African-American Heritage Trail," Cultural Tourism DC, accessed April 16, 2020, https://www.culturaltourismdc.org/portal/downtown-african-american-heritage-trail; "Sit-in Challenges Restaurant Segregation in Washington DC," Today in Civil Liberties History, accessed April 16, 2020, http://todayinclh.com/?event=early-sit-in-washington-d-c-2; Kathryn Schulz, "The Many Lives of Pauli Murray," *New Yorker*, April 17, 2017, accessed April 16, 2020, https://www.newyorker.com/magazine/2017/04/17/the-many-lives-of-pauli-murray; Pam McAllister, "Black Women Led Sit-ins in the 1940s," Activists with Attitude, February 6, 2015, accessed April 16, 2020, http://activistswithattitude.com/black-women-led-sit-ins-in-the-1940s.

April 22, 1993 "Stephen Lawrence Murder: A Timeline of How the Story Unfolded," BBC News, April 13, 2018, accessed April 16, 2020, https://www.bbc.com/news/uk-26465916; Rob Evans and Paul Lewis, "Police 'Smear' Campaign Targeted Steven Lawrence's Friends And Family," *Guardian*, June 24, 2013, accessed May 19, 2020, https://www.theguardian.com/uk/2013/jun/23/stephen-lawrence-undercover-police-smears.

April 23, 1951 Lance Booth, "Overlooked No More: Barbara Johns, Who Defied Segregation in Schools," *New York Times*, May 8, 2019, accessed April 16, 2020, https://www.nytimes.com/2019/05/08/obituaries/barbara-johns-overlooked.html; "The Prince Edward County School Strike, 1951," libcom.org, accessed April 16, 2020, https://libcom.org/history/prince-edward-county-school-strike-1953.

April 23, 1971 "Veterans Discard Medals in War Protest at Capitol," *New York Times*, April 24, 1971, accessed April 16, 2020, https://tinyurl.com/yao2l43w; "E10–11: The GI Resistance in Vietnam" (podcast), *Working Class History*, accessed April 16, 2020, https://workingclasshistory.com/2018/08/06/e10-the-gi-resistance-in-vietnam-part-1.

April 24, 1912 Terry Randall, "RMS Olympic—Mutiny Over Titanic's Boat Situation," City of Southampton Society, accessed April 16, 2020, http://coss.org.uk/The-Olympic-Mutiny.php; Hugh Brewster and Laurie Coulter, *882 ½ Amazing Answers to Your Questions about the Titanic* (New York: Scholastic Paperbacks, 1999); Jason Ponic, "Whatever Happened to Olympic, Titanic's Sister?" Owlcation, updated January 29, 2020, accessed April 16, 2020, https://owlcation.com/humanities/Whatever-Happened-to-Olympic-Titanics-Sister-Ship.

April 24, 1954 Caroline Elkins, *Imperial Reckoning: The Untold Story of Britain's Gulag in Kenya* (New York: Henry Holt, 2010).

April 25, 1974 Phil Mailer, *Portugal: The Impossible Revolution?* (Oakland: PM Press, 2012); Kenneth Maxwell, "Portugal's Revolution Began in the Army," *New York Times*, May 18, 1975, accessed April 16, 2020, https://tinyurl.com/y9eokk63.

April 25, 2013 "The Legacy of the Dead—the Savar Collapse, Part 2," libcom.org, accessed April 16, 2020, https://libcom.org/news/legacy-dead-savar-collapse-part-2-24052013.

April 26, 1797 Alex Barker, "Mutiny in the Royal Navy at Spithead," *History Today* 47, no. 4 (April 1997), accessed April 16, 2020, https://www.historytoday.com/alex-barker/mutiny-royal-navy-spithead; "Research Guide B8: The Spithead and Nore Mutinies of 1797," Royal Museums Greenwich, accessed April 16, 2020, https://tinyurl.com/y8crwyc4; Conrad Gill, ed., *The Naval Mutinies of 1797* (Manchester: Manchester University Press, 1913); Ann Veronica Coats, *The Naval Mutinies of 1797: Unity and Perseverance* (Woodbridge, UK: Boydell & Brewer, 2011).

April 26, 1982 Anandi Ramamurthy, "Bradford 12: Self-Defense Is No Offence," libcom.org, accessed April 16, 2020, https://libcom.org/history/bradford-12-self-defense-no-offence; "E33–34: Asian Youth Movements in Bradford" (podcast), *Working Class History*, accessed April 16, 2020, https://workingclasshistory.com/2019/09/18/e28-29-asian-youth-movements-in-bradford.

April 27, 1934 José Antonio Gutiérrez Danton, "1872–1995: Anarchism in Chile," libcom.org, accessed April 16, 2020, https://libcom.org/history/articles/anarchism-in-chile.

April 27, 1981 Stewart Bell, *Bayou of Pigs: The True Story of an Audacious Plot to Turn a Tropical Island into a Criminal Paradise* (New York: HarperCollins, 2014); "Wolfgang Droege White

Supremacist Who Tried to Overthrow Dominica's Government Is Shot to Death," Dominican, April 5, 2005, accessed April 16, 2020, http://www.thedominican.net/articles/droege.htm.

April 28, 1945 "1945: Italian Partisans Kill Mussolini," BBC Home, accessed April 16, 2020, http://news.bbc.co.uk/onthisday/hi/dates/stories/april/28/newsid_3564000/3564529.stm; R.J.B. Bosworth, *Mussolini* (London: Arnold, 2002), 332–333; Ray Moseley, *Mussolini: The Last 600 Days of Il Duce* (Dallas: Taylor World Publishing, 2004); Peter Neville, *Mussolini* (Milton Park, UK: Routledge, 2003), 194–195.

April 28, 1965 "U.S. Troops Land in the Dominican Republic in Attempt to Forestall a 'Communist Dictatorship,'" History.com, accessed April 16, 2020, https://www.history.com/this-day-in-history/u-s-troops-land-in-the-dominican-republic; "April 28, 1965: 2nd Time the US Invades Dominican Republic," Dominican Today, April 28, 2014, accessed April 16, 2020, https://tinyurl.com/yap4zlsm.

April 29, 1992 Jeff Wallenfeldt, "Los Angeles Riots of 1992," Encyclopaedia Britannica, accessed April 16, 2020, https://www.britannica.com/event/Los-Angeles-Riots-of-1992.

April 29, 2020 Michael Sainato, "Strikes Erupt as US Essential Workers Demand Protection Amid Pandemic," *Guardian*, May 19, 2020, accessed May 19, 2020, https://tinyurl.com/ybjq93ee.

April 30, 1963 Madge Dresser, "Black and White on the Buses: The 1963 Colour Bar Dispute in Bristol," libcom.org, accessed April 16, 2020, https://libcom.org/history/black-white-buses-1963-colour-bar-dispute-bristol.

April 30, 1977 "Why Reclaim the Night?" Reclaim the Night, accessed April 16, 2020, http://www.reclaimthenight.co.uk/why.html.

May

May 1, 1886 "May Day Strike of 1886," Ohio History Central, accessed April 16, 2020, http://www.ohiohistorycentral.org/w/May_Day_Strike_of_1886; Jeremy Brecher, "Mayday, the 8-Hour Movement and the Knights of Labor," libcom.org, accessed April 16, 2020, https://libcom.org/history/mayday-8-hour-movement-knights-labor-jeremy-brecher; Christopher Thale, "Haymarket and May Day," Encyclopedia of Chicago, accessed April 16, 2020, http://www.encyclopedia.chicagohistory.org/pages/571.html; Sharon Smith, "The Legacy of Haymarket," *Socialist Worker*, January 28, 2011, accessed April 16, 2020, https://socialistworker.org/2011/01/28/the-legacy-of-haymarket; Ryan Kilpatrick, "Explainer: International Workers Day—China's Favourite American Holiday," that's, April 30, 2019, accessed April 16, 2020, https://tinyurl.com/yde2mnpt; "PBS Documentary on Haymarket Martyrs and the Origins of International Workers Day," Internet Archive, 2003, accessed April 16, 2020, https://archive.org/details/Haymarket-Documentary.

May 1, 1974 Ron Ramdin, "The Imperial Typewriters Strike, 1974," libcom.org, accessed April 16, 2020, https://libcom.org/history/imperial-typewriters-strike-1974-ron-ramdin.

May 2, 1967 Andrew Anthony, "Black Power's Coolest Radicals (but also a Gang of Ruthless Killers)," *Guardian*, October 18, 2015, accessed April 16, 2020, https://tinyurl.com/y7rh5mzv; David Emery, "Did the NRA Support a 1967 'Open Carry' Ban in California?" Snopes, accessed April 16, 2020, https://www.snopes.com/fact-check/nra-california-open-carry-ban; "State Capitol March," PBS, June 23, 1967, accessed April 16, 2020, http://www.pbs.org/hueypnewton/actions/actions_capitolmarch.html.

May 2, 1968 Dan Georgakas and Marvin Surkin, *Detroit, I Do Mind Dying: A Study in Urban Revolution* (Boston: South End Press, 1998).

May 3, 1926 libcom, "1926: British General Strike," libcom.org, accessed April 16, 2020, https://libcom.org/history/articles/british-general-strike; "What Was the General Strike of 1926?" BBC News, June 19, 2011, accessed April 16, 2020, https://www.bbc.com/news/uk-13828537.

May 3, 1953 Nick Heath, "After the Death of Stalin: The First Revolt—The Plovdiv Tobacco Workers' Strike, May 1953," libcom.org, accessed April 16, 2020, https://tinyurl.com/y9wr88rh; Christian F. Ostermann and Malcolm Byrne, *Uprising in East Germany 1953: The Cold War, the German Question, and the First Major Upheaval Behind the Iron Curtain* (Budapest: Central European University Press, 2001), 86–89.

May 4, 1919 Colin Everett, "Organised Labour in Brazil 1900–1937: From Anarchist Origins to Government Control," libcom.org, accessed April 16, 2020, https://tinyurl.com/y8bg3uq2.

May 4, 1961 "Freedom Rides," Stanford University: The Martin Luther King, Jr. Research and Education Institute, accessed April 16, 2020, https://kinginstitute.stanford.edu/encyclopedia/freedom-rides.

May 5, 1906 "1906 Cananea—Miners [sic] Strike," Historical Events of the International Revolutionary Movement, accessed April 16, 2020, http://ciml.250x.com/archive/events/english/1906_mexico/1906_cananea_strike.html.

May 5, 1970 Zoe Altaras, "The May 1970 Student Strike at UW," Antiwar and Radical History Project—Pacific Northwest, accessed April 16, 2020, https://depts.washington.edu/antiwar/may1970strike.shtml; Root & Branch, "No Class Today, No Ruling Class Tomorrow," libcom.org, accessed April 16, 2020, https://libcom.org/library/no-class-today-no-ruling-class-tomorrow-root-branch-1970.

May 6, 1933 Heike Bauer, *The Hirschfeld Archives: Violence, Death, and Modern Queer Culture* (Philadelphia: Temple University Press, 2017); "Institute for Sexual Science," Holocaust Teacher Resource Center, accessed April 16, 2020, https://www.holocaust-trc.org/homosexuals/institute-for-sexual-science; Lucy Diavolo, "LGBTQ Institute in Germany Was Burned Down by Nazis," *Teen Vogue*, September 20, 2017, accessed April 16, 2020, https://www.teenvogue.com/story/lgbtq-institute-in-germany-was-burned-down-by-nazis; Laura Darling, "Queer Women and AFAB People during the Holocaust," Making Queer History, April 22, 2016, accessed April 16, 2020, https://tinyurl.com/y6ukma62; "Lesbians and the Third Reich," United States Holocaust Memorial Museum, accessed April 16, 2020, https://encyclopedia.ushmm.org/content/en/article/lesbians-and-the-third-reich; Farah Naz Khan, "A History of Transgender Health Care," *Scientific American*, November 16, 2016, accessed May 20, 2020, https://blogs.scientificamerican.com/guest-blog/a-history-of-transgender-health-care; "Persecution of Homosexuals in the Third Reich," Holocaust Encyclopedia, accessed April 16, 2020, https://tinyurl.com/ycgsbeye; Email from the US Holocaust Memorial Museum, April 23, 2019.

May 6, 1937 Augusta V. Jackson, "A New Deal for Tobacco Workers," *Crisis*, October 1938, 322–23; Teresa Albano, "Today in Labor History: 400 Black Women Strike Over Wages, Conditions," People's World, May 6, 2013 accessed April 16, 2020, https://tinyurl.com/y8ap84y8.

May 7, 1912 "Waiters' Strike Ill-Timed; Just When High Cost of Living Ruins Restaurants" *New York Times*, June 1, 1912, accessed April 16, 2020, https://tinyurl.com/ybqbxwlr; "Waiters Out in 17 More Places," *New York Times*, June 1, 1912, accessed April 16, 2020, https://timesmachine.nytimes.com/timesmachine/1912/06/01/100536445.pdf; "The Waiters' Strike," *New York Times*, June 1, 1912, 10, accessed May 20, 2020, https://timesmachine.nytimes.com/timesmachine/1912/06/01/100536538.html?pageNumber=10; "The Collapsing Strike," *New York Times*, June 4, 1912, 10, accessed May 20, 2020, https://timesmachine.nytimes.com/timesmachine/1912/06/04/100536997.html?pageNumber=10; "The First Contract," Hotel Workers, accessed April 16, 2020, http://hotelworkers.org/about/history/the-story-of-the-first-contract?p=3.

May 7, 1980 Jun Sung Park, "사북, 부마항쟁과 광주민중항쟁을 잇는 징검다리," Hadream, August 11, 2005, accessed April 16, 2020, http://hadream.com/xe/history/42507?ckattempt=3.

May 8, 1928 Leónidas Noni Ceruti, "A 87 años del asesinato de la obrera Luisa Lallana," ANRed, May 10, 2015, accessed April 16, 2020, https://www.anred.org/2015/05/10/a-87-anos-del-asesinato-de-la-obrera-luisa-lallana; "Rosario Workmen Quit Long Strike," *New York Times*, August 24, 1929, 4, accessed April 16, 2020, https://timesmachine.nytimes.com/timesmachine/1929/08/24/91928120.html?pageNumber=4.

May 8, 1942 Ron Grossman, "The Birth of the Sit-in," *Chicago Tribune*, February 23, 2014, accessed April 16, 2020, https://tinyurl.com/yc3dlbgk; "Jack Spratt Coffee Shop Sit-in," Chicago Time Machine, accessed April 16, 2020, https://interactive.wttw.com/timemachine/jack-spratt-coffee-shop-sit; "CORE Leads Early Sit-in in Chicago," Today in Civil Liberties History, accessed April 16, 2020, http://todayinclh.com/?event=core-leads-early-sit-in-in-chicago.

May 9, 1914 Steven Johns, "Violence in the Women's Suffrage Movement," libcom.org, accessed April 16, 2020, https://libcom.org/history/violence-suffragette-movement.

May 9, 1936 WelcometoSpace, "The Bloody May of 1936 in Thessaloniki, Greece," libcom.org, accessed April 16, 2020, https://libcom.org/history/bloody-may-1936-thessaloniki-greece; Neni Panourgiá, *Dangerous Citizens: The Greek Left and the Terror of the State* (New York: Fordham University Press, 2009), chapter 2.

May 10, 1920 "Hands off Russia, 1919–1920," Hayes People's History, November 19, 2010, accessed May 20, 2020, https://ourhistory-hayes.blogspot.com/2010/11/hands-off-russia-1919-1920.html; "Dockers Boycott SS Jolly George, 1920," libcom.org, accessed April 16, 2020, https://libcom.org/history/dockers-boycott-ss-jolly-george-1920; "The Jolly George Protest 1920," TUC History Online, accessed April 16, 2020, https://tinyurl.com/y6whtz2o.

May 10, 1941 José Gotovitch and Paul Aron, eds., *Dictionnaire de la Seconde Guerre Mondiale en Belgique* (Brussels: André Versaille Éditeur, 2008), 220–21.

May 11, 1923 Andrew Grant Wood, "Postrevolutionary Pioneer: Anarchist María Luisa Marín and the Veracruz Renters' Movement," libcom.org, accessed April 15, 2020, https://tinyurl.com/ya83nows.

May 11, 1972 Paul Sharkey, ed., *The Federacion Anarquista Uruguaya: Crisis, Armed Struggle and Dictatorship, 1967–85,"* (London: Kate Sharpley Library, 2009), accessed April 16, 2020, https://libcom.org/files/FAU%20uruguay2.pdf.

May 12, 1916 Shane Hegarty and Fintan O'Toole, "Easter Rising 1916—the Aftermath: Arrests and Executions," *Irish Times*, March 24, 2016, accessed May 29, 2020, https://tinyurl.com/y6om4v3b; Dermot McEvoy, "1916 Easter Rising Leader James Connolly Born on This Day in 1868," Irish Central, June 5, 2019, accessed May 29, 2020, https://www.irishcentral.com/roots/history/easter-rising-leader-executed-in-1916-james-connolly.

May 12, 1978 David Vidal, "Thousands in Brazil Strike in Defiance of Military Regime," *New York Times*, May 24, 1978, accessed April 16, 2020, https://tinyurl.com/y9oxq7s2; John Humphrey, "Autoworkers and the Working Class in Brazil," libcom.org, accessed April 16, 2020, https://libcom.org/library/autoworkers-working-class-brazil-john-humphrey.

May 13, 1968 "General Strike Grips France," *Pittsburgh Post-Gazette*, May 13, 1968, 1.

May 13, 1985 William K. Stevens, "Police Drop Bomb on Radicals' Home in Philadelphia," *New York Times*, May 14, 1985, accessed April 16, 2020, https://tinyurl.com/y8x2xejl; "MOVE Bombing 1985," libcom.org, accessed April 16, 2020, https://libcom.org/library/move-bombing-1985.

May 14, 1913 Mouvement Communiste and Kolektivně proti Kapitálu, "100 Years Ago: The Philadelphia Dockers Strike and Local 8 of the IWW," accessed April 16, 2020, https://tinyurl.com/yaf9slsh.

May 14, 1931 Anders Sundstedt, "The Ådalen Shootings in Sweden, 1931," libcom.org, accessed April 16, 2020, https://libcom.org/history/adalen-shootings-sweden-1931; Max Rennebohm, "Swedish Workers General Strike for Economic Justice, Power Shift (Ådalen) 1931," Global Nonviolent Action Database, accessed April 16, 2020, https://tinyurl.com/ycp9dvnf.

May 15, 1831 "Heavy-Handed Policing: The Killing of Constable Culley," Open University, 2009, accessed April 16, 2020, https://tinyurl.com/yclxkb3t; Tony Moore, *The Killing of Constable Keith Blakelock: The Broadwater Farm Riot* (Hook, UK: Waterside Press, 2015), 19–21; "Today in London Legal History: A Jury Finds the Killing of a Copper to be 'Justifiable Homicide', 1833," Past Tense, May 15, 2017, accessed April 16, 2020, https://tinyurl.com/y8gtv76v.

May 15, 1950 "The Nairobi General Strike, 1950: From Protest to Insurgency," in Andrew Burton, ed., *The Urban Experience in Eastern Africa c.1750–2000* (Nairobi, KE: British Institute in Eastern Africa, 2002), accessed April 16, 2020, https://libcom.org/library/nairobi-general-strike-1950-protest-insurgency.

May 16, 1934 Jeremy Brecher, "The Minneapolis Teamsters Strike, 1934," libcom.org, accessed April 16, 2020, https://libcom.org/history/minneapolis-teamsters-strike-1934-jeremy-brecher.

May 16, 1967 E30–31: The Hong Kong riots, 1967 (podcast), *Working Class History*, accessed April 16, 2020, https://workingclasshistory.com/2019/07/15/e26-27-the-hong-kong-riots-1967; Benjamin Leung and Stephen Chiu, "A Social History of Industrial Strikes and the Labour Movement in Hong Kong, 1946–1989" (research paper, Social Sciences Research Centre, University of Hong Kong, 1991), accessed April 16, 2020, https://hub.hku.hk/bitstream/10722/42557/1/03.pdf.

May 17 1949 "Via Margotti Maria," Comune Ravenna, accessed April 16, 2020, http://extraweb. comune.ra.it/odonomastica/scheda.asp?CodTopon=1306; Flora Derounian, "How Women Rice Weeders in Italy Took on Fascism and Became Heroines of the Left," Conversation, March 7, 2018, accessed April 16, 2020, https://tinyurl.com/yamb67go.

May 17, 1965 "Bolivia DECRETO LEY No 7169 del 17 de Mayo de 1965," Derechoteca, accessed April 16, 2020, www.derechoteca.com/gacetabolivia/decreto-ley-7169-del-17-mayo-1965; "Bolivia DECRETO LEY No 7170 del 17 de Mayo de 1965," Derechoteca, accessed April 16, 2020, www.derechoteca.com/gacetabolivia/decreto-ley-7170-del-17-mayo-1965; "Bolivia DECRETO LEY No 7171 del 17 de Mayo de 1965," Derechoteca, accessed April 16, 2020, www.derechoteca. com/gacetabolivia/decreto-ley-7171-del-17-mayo-1965; "Bolivia DECRETO LEY No 7172 del 17 de Mayo de 1965," Derechoteca, accessed April 16, 2020, www.derechoteca.com/gacetabolivia/ decreto-ley-7172-del-17-mayo-1965.

May 18, 1968 Lassou, "May 1968 in Senegal," libcom.org, accessed April 16, 2020, https://libcom. org/library/may-1968-senegal.

May 18, 1980 George Katsiaficas, "The Gwangju Uprising, 1980," libcom.org, accessed April 16, 2020, https://libcom.org/history/1980-the-kwangju-uprising.

May 19, 1918 Nick Heath, "1890–1924: Anarchism in Hungary," accessed April 16, 2020, https:// libcom.org/history/articles/hungary-anarchism-1890-1924; "Public Holidays Calendar 1918," Kalendar 365, accessed April 16, 2020, https://kalender-365.de/public-holidays.php?yy=1918.

May 19, 1935 Richard Hart, *Labour Rebellions in the 1930s in the British Caribbean* (London: Socialist History Society, 2002); "Our History," Bustamante Industrial Trade Union, accessed February 1, 2018, unavailable April 16, 2020, http://bitujamaica.org/bitu-history.

May 20, 1910 Isaac Meyer, "The Great Treason Incident—Anarchism in Japan," libcom.org, accessed April 16, 2020, https://libcom.org/blog/great-treason-incident-anarchism-japan-16082018.

May 20, 1936 Martha A. Ackelsberg, *Free Women of Spain* (Oakland: AK Press, 2005), 128.

May 21, 1941 Anton Rønneberg, *Nationaltheatret gjennom femti år* (Oslo: Gyldendal, 1949) 382–87; Egil Hjort-Jenssen, *Norsk skuespillerforbund gjennom 50 år 1898–1948* (Oslo: Gyldendal, 1948), 143–49; Hans Fredrik Dahl, *Norsk krigsleksikon 1940–1945* (Oslo: Cappelen, 1995).

May 21, 1979 Kim Corsaro, "Remembering 'White Night'—San Francisco's Gay Riot," *San Francisco Bay Times*, May 18, 2006, accessed April 16, 2020, https://tinyurl.com/ybat2fq3; Randy Shilts, *The Mayor of Castro Street: The Life and Times of Harvey Milk* (New York: St. Martin's Press, 1982); Fred Rogers, "Elephant Walk Took Brunt of Police Attack in the Castro," Uncle Donald's Castro Street, accessed April 16, 2020, http://thecastro.net/milk/rogers.html; Mike Weiss, "Ex-Clerk Says He Destroyed White's Gun/Weapon Used in Assassinations Was Considered Missing," *San Francisco Gate*, January 24, 2003, accessed April 16, 2020, https:// tinyurl.com/y7rbf6ge; "Killer of Moscone, Milk Had Willie Brown on List," *San Jose Mercury News*, September 18, 1998, 1A; Wallace Turner, "Ex-Official Guilty of Manslaughter in Slayings on Coast; 3,000 Protest," *New York Times*, May 22, 1979, accessed April 16, 2020, https://tinyurl.com/ y6wbgx6p; Chester Hartman, *City for Sale: The Transformation of San Francisco* (Berkeley: University of California Press, 2002), 233–237; Cynthia Gorney, "The Legacy of Dan White," *Los Angeles Times*, January 4, 1984, accessed May 20, 2020, https://tinyurl.com/yag9hap9.

May 22, 1968 Footballers' Action Committee, "Football to the Footballers!" libcom.org, accessed April 17, 2020, https://libcom.org/library/football-footballers.

May 22, 2006 Kylin Navarro, "Oaxacan Teachers Strike against Governor, 2006," Global Nonviolent Action Database, November 1, 2010, accessed April 17, 2020, https://nvdatabase. swarthmore.edu/content/oaxacan-teachers-strike-against-governor-2006.

May 23, 1946 Jon Garlock, "The 1946 General Strike of Rochester, New York," libcom.org, accessed April 17, 2020, https://libcom.org/history/1946-general-strike-rochester-new-york.

May 23, 1969 Antonius C.G.M. Robben, *Political Violence and Trauma in Argentina* (Philadelphia: University of Pennsylvania Press, 2010), 40.

May 24, 1919 "Drumheller Coal Mining Strike of 1919," Alberta Culture and Tourism, accessed April 17, 2020, https://tinyurl.com/ya8yu8kj; "Strikes—The Drumheller Strike of 1919," When Coal Was King, accessed April 17, 2020, https://tinyurl.com/ya4qyh9t.

May 24, 1990 Ben Rosenfeld, "Federal Court Orders FBI To Turn Over Evidence for Independent Forensic Analysis in 1990 Judi Bari Car Bombing Case," Industrial Workers of the World, April 2, 2012, accessed April 17, 2020, https://tinyurl.com/ya53lls8; "Judi Bari 1949–1997," Industrial Workers of the World, accessed April 17, 2020, https://www.iww.org/history/biography/JudiBari/1.

May 25, 1978 "Occupation of Bastion Point Begins," New Zealand History, accessed April 17, 2020, https://nzhistory.govt.nz/occupation-of-bastion-point-begins.

May 25, 2020 Evan Hill, Ainara Tiefenthäler, Christiaan Triebert, Drew Jordan, Haley Willis, and Robin Stein, "How George Floyd Was Killed in Police Custody," New York Times, May 31, 2020, accessed July 3, 2020, https://www.nytimes.com/2020/05/31/us/george-floyd-investigation.html; Alisha Ebrahimji, "This Is How Loved Ones Want Us to Remember George Floyd," CNN, June 3, 2020, accessed July 3, 2020, https://www.cnn.com/2020/05/27/us/george-floyd-trnd/index.html; Scottie Andrew, "Derek Chauvin: What We Know About the Former Officer Charged in George Floyd's Death," CNN, June 1, 2020, accessed July 3, 2020, https://www.cnn.com/2020/06/01/us/derek-chauvin-what-we-know-trnd/index.html; Larry Buchanan, Quoctrung Bui, and Jugal K. Patel, "Black Lives Matter May Be the Largest Movement in US History," New York Times, July 3, 2020, accessed July 3, 2020, https://www.nytimes.com/interactive/2020/07/03/us/george-floyd-protests-crowd-size.html; Dionne Searcey and John Eligon, "Minneapolis Will Dismantle Its Police Force, Council Members Pledge," New York Times, June 7, 2020, accessed July 3, 2020, https://www.nytimes.com/2020/06/07/us/minneapolis-police-abolish.html.

May 26, 1824 "E32: The Pawtucket Mill Strike" (podcast), Working Class History, August 12, 2019, accessed April 17, 2020, https://workingclasshistory.com/2019/08/12/e28-the-pawtucket-mill-strike; Joey La Neve DeFrancesco, "Pawtucket, America's First Factory Strike," Jacobin, June 6, 2018, accessed April 17, 2020, https://www.jacobinmag.com/2018/06/factory-workers-strike-textile-mill-women.

May 26, 1944 Ludivine Broch, Ordinary Workers, Vichy and the Holocaust: French Railwaymen and the Second World War (Cambridge: Cambridge University Press, 2016), 197; "La grève générale à Marseille," Bulletin international de discussion de la Gauche Communiste Italienne 6 (June 1944), accessed April 17, 2020, http://archivesautonomies.org/spip.php?article2096.

May 27, 1919 Steven Hirsch, "Anarcho-Syndicalism in Peru, 1905–1930," accessed April 20, 2020, https://libcom.org/library/anarcho-syndicalism-peru-1905-1930-steven-hirsch.

May 27, 2004 "'Leaded/Unleaded'—the Story of the 2004 Beirut General Strike Now Online," libcom.org, accessed April 17, 2020, https://libcom.org/news/article.php/beirut-general-strike-2004-dvd-0106; "Lebanese Soldiers Surrounded the Burned Building of the Labour Ministry" (photo), Reuters, May 27, 2004, accessed April 17, 2020, https://pictures.reuters.com/archive/LEBANON-PROTEST-RP4DRIHVEKAA.html; Nada Raad, "Beirut Makes Final Preparations to Host OPEC Summit," Daily Star Lebanon, June 2, 2004, accessed April 17, 2020, https://tinyurl.com/yd2tgje3; "'Five Dead' in Lebanon Protests," BBC News, May 27, 2004, accessed April 17, 2020, http://news.bbc.co.uk/2/hi/middle_east/3753913.stm.

May 28, 1913 Mouvement Communiste and Kolektivně proti Kapitálu, "100 Years Ago: the Philadelphia Dockers Strike and Local 8 of the IWW," libcom.org, accessed April 16, 2020, https://tinyurl.com/yaf9slsh.

May 28, 1936 Shane Bentley, "France: 'Everything Is Possible': The June 1936 Strike Wave," Green Left 673 (November 1993), accessed April 17, 2020, https://www.greenleft.org.au/content/france-everything-possible-june-1936-strike-wave.

May 29, 1969 James P. Brennan, "Córdobazo," Encyclopedia.com, updated April 15, 2020, accessed April 17, 2020, https://www.encyclopedia.com/humanities/encyclopedias-almanacs-transcripts-and-maps/cordobazo-el; James P. Brennan, "Working Class Protest, Popular Revolt and Urban Insurrection in Argentina: The 1969 Cordobazo," libcom.org, accessed April 17, 2020, https://tinyurl.com/y7xseztw.

May 29, 1972 Mamta Rajawat, Encyclopaedia of Dalits in India (Bangaluru, IN: Anmol Publications, 2004), 325.

May 30, 1925 Editors, "May Thirtieth Incident," Encyclopaedia Britannica, accessed April 17, 2020, https://www.britannica.com/event/May-Thirtieth-Incident; International Communist Current, "The Chinese Revolution 1925–1927," libcom.org, accessed April 16, 2020, https://libcom.org/history/chinese-revolution-1925-1927.

May 30, 1969 Nelson M. Pierre, "Curaçao Uprising May 30th 1969," Colors, May 2014, accessed April 17, 2020, http://www.colorszine.com/2014_05/Curaçao-Uprising.html.

May 31, 1831 "1831: Merthyr Tydfil Uprising," libcom.org, accessed April 17, 2020, https://libcom.org/library/1831-merthyr-tydfil-uprising; "Merthyr Rising Marked in Town 183 Years after Historic Event," BBC News, May 31, 2014, accessed April 17, 2020, https://www.bbc.com/news/uk-wales-south-east-wales-27648283.

May 31, 1921 Tulsa Race Riot: A Report by the Oklahoma Commission to Study the Tulsa Race Riot of 1921, February 28, 2001, accessed April 17, 2020, https://tinyurl.com/y7qotkpt; B.C. Franklin, "The Tulsa Race Riot and Three of Its Victims," Smithsonian, August 22, 1931, accessed April 17, 2020, https://nmaahc.si.edu/object/nmaahc_2015.176.1; Tim Madigan, *The Burning: Massacre, Destruction, and the Tulsa Race Riot of 1921* (New York: St Martin's Press, 2001); "Survivors of Infamous 1921 Tulsa Race Riots Still Hope for Justice," Al Jazeera, July 19, 2014, accessed April 17, 2020, https://tinyurl.com/yaq85jj9.

June

June 1, 1926 Neville Green, *The Forrest River Massacres* (Fremantle, AU: Fremantle Arts Centre Press, 1995).

June 1, 1971 Ernest Dowson, "1971: Via Tibaldi Occupation," libcom.org, accessed April 17, 2020, https://libcom.org/history/articles/via-tibaldi-occupation; "1970 L'occupazione di via Tibaldi (fotografie di Walter Buonfino)," Radio Rock Revolution Anni 70, December 2, 2014, accessed April 17, 2020, https://tinyurl.com/yaufsoj2.

June 2, 1863 Earl Conrad, "Harriet Tubman," *Commonwealth*, July 10, 1863, accessed April 17, 2020, http://www.harriettubman.com/tubman2.html; "The Combahee Ferry Raid," Smithsonian, accessed April 17, 2020, https://nmaahc.si.edu/blog/combahee-ferry-raid.

June 2, 1975 Mathieu Lilian, "An Unlikely Mobilization: The Occupation of Saint-Nizier Church by the Prostitutes of Lyon," *Revue française de sociologie* 42, no. 1 (2001): 107–31, accessed April 17, 2020, https://libcom.org/files/article_rfsoc_0035-2969_2001_sup_42_1_5416.pdf.

June 3, 1943 Anarchist Federation, "The Zoot Suit as Rebellion," *Organise!* 82 (Summer 2014), accessed June 6, 2020, http://libcom.org/history/zoot-suit-rebellion; "June 3, 1943: The Zoot Suit Riots," Zinn Education Project, accessed June 6, 2020, https://www.zinnedproject.org/news/tdih/zoot-suit-riots; Marisa Gerber, "Zoot Suit Riots: After 75 Years, LA Looks Back on a Violent Summer," *Los Angeles Times*, June 4, 2019, accessed April 17, 2020, https://tinyurl.com/tznju6p.

June 3, 2016 Andrew Das, "Judge Rules US Women's Soccer Team Can't Strike Before Olympics," *New York Times*, June 4, 2016, accessed April 17, 2020, https://tinyurl.com/ydgnfguf.

June 4, 1950 "E35–37: The 43 Group" (podcast), Working Class History, February 17, 2020, accessed July 3, 2020, https://workingclasshistory.com/2020/02/17/e35-37-the-43-group; Steve Silver, "From Anti-Fascist to Cold War," *Searchlight*, February 2002, accessed July 3, 2020, http://stevesilver.org.uk/from-anti-fascist-war-to-cold-war.

June 4, 1976 Vivek Chaudhary, "How London's Southall Became 'Little Punjab,'" *Guardian*, April 4, 2018, accessed April 17, 2020, https://www.theguardian.com/cities/2018/apr/04/how-london-southall-became-little-punjab; Kavita Puri, "The Pool of Blood That Changed My Life," *Three Pounds in My Pocket*, BBC Radio 4, August 5, 2015, accessed April 17, 2020, http://www.bbc.com/news/magazine-33725217; Ken Roe, "Dominion Cinema," Cinema Treasures, accessed April 17, 2020, http://cinematreasures.org/theaters/21203.

June 5, 1981 Steven C. McKay, *Satanic Mills or Silicon Islands? The Politics of High-Tech Production in the Philippines* (Ithaca, NY: Cornell University Press, 2018), 135; Anil Verma, Thomas A. Kochan, and Russell D. Lansbury, *Employment Relations in the Growing Asian Economies* (New York: Routledge, 2005), 207; International Communist Current, "A History of Trade Unionism in the Philippines," libcom.org, accessed April 16, 2020, https://libcom.org/history/history-trade-unionism-philippines.

June 5, 1996 Lydia Bailey and Rebecca Contreras, "Texans Defend Sierra Blanca Community against Nuclear Waste Disposal 1996–1998," Global Nonviolent Action Database, accessed April 17, 2020, https://tinyurl.com/y963cmmm.

June 6, 1966 "James Meredith and the March against Fear," National Archives, accessed April 17, 2020, https://www.archives.gov/research/african-americans/black-power/sncc/march-against-fear.

June 6, 1988 Scott Kraft, "2 More Die as Blacks End S. Africa Strike," *Los Angeles Times*, June 9, 1988, accessed April 17, 2020, http://articles.latimes.com/1988-06-09/news/mn-6249_1_south-africa-s-economy; "7 Killed in S Africa during General Strike," *Chicago Tribune*, June 8, 1988, 4.

June 7 1968 Jessica Siegel, "Ford Female Employees Win Strike for Equal Pay, Dagenham, England, 1968," Global Nonviolent Action Database, March 15, 2013, accessed April 19, 2020, https://tinyurl.com/ybkz3ar7.

June 7, 1972 Kamran Asdar Ali, "Strength of the Street: Karachi 1972," libcom.org, accessed April 17, 2020, https://libcom.org/library/strength-street-karachi-1972.

June 8, 1961 Mark Trainer, "Joan Trumpauer Mulholland: Civil Rights Hero," Share America, February 9, 2017, accessed April 17, 2020, https://share.america.gov/joan-mulholland-civil-rights-hero.

June 8, 2017 United Voices of the World, Facebook, June 8, 2017, accessed April 17, 2020, https://tinyurl.com/y8kphwqx; Louisa Acciari and Davide Però, "On The Frontline: Confronting Precariousness, Outsourcing And Exploitation—Lessons From The LSE Cleaners," Discover Society, December 6, 2017, accessed April 17, 2020, https://tinyurl.com/y7oo2s65.

June 9, 1910 "Rebelion De Valladolid 'Primera Chispa De La Revolucion Mexicana' 4 De Junio De 1910," Yucatan Government General Archive, accessed April 17, 2020, https://tinyurl.com/y9pb5q4g.

June 9, 1944 Alan Riding, "Upheaval in the East; Where Nazis Took Fierce Revenge, French Hatred for Germans Recedes," *New York Times*, March 7, 1990, accessed April 17, 2020, https://tinyurl.com/y8zmj35l; Headsman, "1944 Johanna Kirchner," Executed Today, June 9, 2012, accessed April 17, 2020, http://www.executedtoday.com/2012/06/09/1944-johanna-kirchner.

June 10, 1918 Lucien van der Walt and the Bikisha Media Collective, "'Sifuna Zonke!': Revolutionary Syndicalism, the Industrial Workers of Africa and the Fight against Racial Capitalism, 1915–1921," SAASHA, February 24, 2012, accessed April 16, 2020, https://saasha.net/2012/02/24/sifuna-zonke-bmc-undated.

June 10, 1973 Edward Hudson, "Gravediggers Union Ends 27-Day Strike," *New York Times*, July 7, 1973, 1, accessed April 17, 2020, https://tinyurl.com/yc9tvgvx.

June 11, 1914 "Suffragettes in Abbey," *Argus (Melbourne)*, June 13, 1914, 21; "Suffragettes in Abbey," *Daily Telegraph*, June 12, 1914.

June 11, 1972 "Women's Liberation in Japan," Getty Images, accessed April 17, 2020, https://tinyurl.com/yc7xf8uo; Daniel Hurst, "'They Stole My Life Away': Women Forcibly Sterilised by Japan Speak Out," *Guardian*, April 3, 2018, accessed April 17, 2020, https://tinyurl.com/ydalgqdw.

June 12, 1963 David Stout, "Byron De La Beckwith Dies; Killer of Medgar Evers Was 80," *New York Times*, January 23, 2001, accessed April 17, 2020, https://tinyurl.com/y8fugozh.

June 12, 1966 Aaron Fountain, "US Latino Urban Riots," libcom.org, June 13, 2016, accessed April 17, 2020, https://libcom.org/history/us-latino-urban-riots.

June 13, 1953 Ben Fenton, "MoD 'Refusing to Release File on Massacre of Kenyans,'" *Telegraph*, July 10, 2006, accessed April 17, 2020, https://tinyurl.com/ydecyjpc; David Anderson, Huw Bennett, and Daniel Branch, "A Very British Massacre," *History Today* 56–58 (August 2006): 20–22, accessed April 17, 2020, https://www.historytoday.com/archive/very-british-massacre.

June 13, 1973 Iain McIntyre, "1973: Broadmeadows Ford Workers' Strike," in *Disturbing the Peace: Tales from Australia's Rebel History* (Melbourne: Homebrew Books, 2005), 35–41, accessed April 17, 2020, https://libcom.org/history/articles/broadmeadows-ford-workers-strike-1972.

June 14, 1381 Sylvia Federico, "The Imaginary Society: Women in 1381," *Journal of British Studies* 40, no. 2 (2001): 159–83; Ben Johnson, "Wat Tyler and the Peasants Revolt," Historic UK, accessed April 17, 2020, https://www.historic-uk.com/HistoryUK/HistoryofEngland/Wat-Tyler-the-Peasants-Revolt; Editors, "Peasants Revolt," Encyclopaedia Britannica, accessed April 17, 2020, https://www.britannica.com/event/Peasants-Revolt; Paul Foot, "'This Bright Day of Summer': The Peasants' Revolt of 1381," Marxist Internet Archive, June 1981, accessed April 17, 2020, https://www.marxists.org/archive/foot-paul/1981/06/1381.html; Editors, "Wat Tyler," Encyclopaedia Britannica, accessed April 17, 2020, https://www.britannica.com/biography/Wat-Tyler.

June 14, 1991 Noëmi Landolt and Anja Suter, "Frauenstreik 2011: Die Transparente könnten noch immer dieselben sein," *Wochenzeitung*, June 9, 2011, accessed April 17, 2020, https://www.woz.ch/-1c51; "Vor 25 Jahren: Der Frauenstreiktag vom 14. Juni 1991," Schweizerisches Sozialarchiv, accessed April 17, 2020, https://tinyurl.com/y966l9a3; "Zweiter landesweiter Frauenstreik am 14. Juni 2019," Eidgenössische Kommission für Frauenfragen, accessed April 17, 2020, https://tinyurl.com/yapk3qxc.

June 15, 1960 Keiji Hirano, "Legacy of 1960 Protest Movement Lives On," *Japan Times*, June 11, 2010, accessed April 17, 2020, https://tinyurl.com/yb39xn4e.

June 15, 1990 Jono Shaffer and Stephen Lerner, "25 Years Later: Lessons from the Organizers of Justice for Janitors," TalkPoverty, June 16, 2015, accessed April 17, 2020, https://tinyurl.com/y95no2fz.

June 16, 1531 Karl Marx, *Capital*, vol. 1, (Moscow: Progress Publishers, 1965), chapter 28, accessed April 17, 2020, https://libcom.org/history/bloody-legislation-against-expropriated; Frank Aydelotte, *Elizabethan Rogues and Vagabonds* (Oxford: Clarendon Press, 1913), accessed April 17, 2020, https://archive.org/details/cu31924027958150.

June 16, 1976 "1976: The Soweto Riots," libcom.org, accessed April 17, 2020, https://libcom.org/history/1976-the-soweto-riots; "The June 16 Soweto Youth Uprising," South African History Online, accessed April 17, 2020, https://www.sahistory.org.za/article/june-16-soweto-youth-uprising.

June 17, 1937 Katia Landau, "Stalinism in Spain (1938)," *Revolutionary History* 1, no. 2 (Summer 1988), accessed April 17, 2020, https://www.marxists.org/history/etol/document/spain/spain08.htm.

June 17, 1971 "The Kelly's Bush Green Ban, 1971," libcom.org, accessed April 17, 2020, https://libcom.org/history/articles/kellys-bush-green-ban; Verity Burgmann, "A Perspective on Sydney's Green Ban Campaign, 1970–74," IWW Environmental Unionism Caucus, June 7, 2013, accessed April 17, 2020, https://tinyurl.com/yaaoctpz.

June 18, 1935 Sam Lowry, "The Battle of Ballantyne Pier, 1935," libcom.org, accessed April 17, 2020, https://libcom.org/history/1935-battle-ballantyne-pier; John Mackie, "This Week in History: 1935—the Battle of Ballantyne Pier," *Vancouver Sun*, June 19, 2015, accessed April 17, 2020, https://tinyurl.com/yac4c5h4.

June 18, 1943 "1943: Maria Kislyak, Honeytrapper," Executed Today, June 18, 2017, accessed April 17, 2020, http://www.executedtoday.com/2017/06/18/1943-maria-kislyak-honeytrapper; "The Execution of Women by the Nazis during World War II," Capital Punishment UK, accessed April 17, 2020, http://www.capitalpunishmentuk.org/nazi.html.

June 19, 1937 Richard Hart, *Labour Rebellions in the 1930s in the British Caribbean* (London: Socialist History Society, 2002); "Trinidad Leaseholds," Grace's Guide to British Industrial History, accessed April 17, 2020, https://www.gracesguide.co.uk/Trinidad_Leaseholds.

June 19, 1937 Benjamin Blake, "The Women's Day Massacre," Western Reserve Historical Society, accessed April 17, 2020, https://academic.csuohio.edu/clevelandhistory/Issue3/articles/steelpage6content.htm; Benjamin St. Angelo, "How Labor Disputes Led to Violence: Personalities, Paternalism, and Power at Republic Steel in Youngstown, Ohio: 1937," (research paper, Ohio State University, December 2017), accessed April 17, 2020, https://tinyurl.com/ycuqd6ct.

June 20, 1905 Fatimah Hameed, "1905: Swedish Workers Threaten General Strike against War with Norway," Global Nonviolent Action Database, February 22, 2013, accessed April 17, 2020, https://bit.ly/2wMiwX1.

June 20, 1967 Dave Zirin, "June 20, 1967: Muhammad Ali Convicted for Refusing the Vietnam Draft," Zinn Education Project, accessed April 17, 2020, https://tinyurl.com/yaypkqgu; Martin Waldron, "Clay Guilty in Draft Case; Gets Five Years in Prison," *New York Times*, June 21, 1967, 1.

June 21, 1919 "Fighting the Good Fight: Winnipeg General of 1919," Canadian Public Health Association, accessed April 17, 2020, https://www.cpha.ca/fighting-good-fight-winnipeg-general-strike-1919.

June 21, 1964 "Murder in Mississippi," PBS, American Experience, accessed April 17, 2020, https://www.pbs.org/wgbh/americanexperience/features/freedomsummer-murder.

June 22, 1908 Janet Hunter, ed., *Concise Dictionary of Modern Japanese History* (Berkeley: University of California Press, 1984), 175.

June 22, 1941 Dragutin Pavličević, *Povijest Hrvatske* (Zagreb, HR: Naklada Pavičić, 2007), 441–42.

June 23, 1950 Paul Smith, *Unionization and Union Leadership: The Road Haulage Industry* (London: Routledge, 2016 [2001]); "London Meat Distribution (Strike)," Hansard 477, cc257–60, July 4, 1950, accessed April 17, 2017, http://hansard.millbanksystems.com/commons/1950/jul/04/london-meat-distribution-strike; "The Labour Government vs the Dockers 1945–1951," *Solidarity Pamphlet* 19, accessed April 17, 2020, https://libcom.org/library/labour-party-dockers-1945-1951-solidarity.

June 23, 1980 Keith Adams, "Archive: Tea-break Strike Ends," AROnline, July 3, 1980, accessed April 17, 2020, https://www.aronline.co.uk/archive/archive-tea-break-strike-ends.

June 24, 1976 Nick Palazzo, "Polish Workers Strike, Stop Price Increases, 1976," Global Nonviolent Action Database, February 24, 2013, accessed April 17, 2020, https://nvdatabase.swarthmore.edu/content/polish-workers-strike-stop-price-increases-1976; Radio Free Europe, "Poznan 1956 and Radom 1976," libcom.org, accessed April 17, 2020, https://libcom.org/library/poznan-1956-radom-1976.

June 24, 1980 "Amplio eco de la huelga general en El Salvador," *El País*, June 26, 1980, accessed April 17, 2020, http://elpais.com/diario/1980/06/26/internacional/330818419_850215.html.

June 25, 1876 Gregory J.W. Urwind, "Battle of the Little Bighorn," Encyclopaedia Britannica, accessed April 17, 2020, https://www.britannica.com/event/Battle-of-the-Little-Bighorn; "Battle of the Little Bighorn," History.com, accessed April 17, 2020, https://www.history.com/topics/native-american-history/battle-of-the-little-bighorn.

June 25, 1878 "1878: The Great Kanak Rebellion," Découvrir la Nouvelle-Calédonie, archived September 28, 2019, accessed March 4, 2020, https://tinyurl.com/ybkoqq7e; "The Rebel France Could Not Crush," *Guardian*, April 25, 2017, accessed April 17, 2020, https://tinyurl.com/lnyu9ya.

June 26, 1950 "Cultural Cold War: Origins of the Congress for Cultural Freedom, 1949–50," Central Intelligence Agency, archived June 16, 2006, accessed April 17, 2020, https://web.archive.org/web/20060616213245/http://cia.gov/csi/studies/95unclass/Warner.html.

June 26, 1993 C.J. Hawking, "Staley's Legacy of Struggle, Lessons of Defeat," Solidarity, accessed April 17, 2020, https://solidarity-us.org/atc/61/p774; Louis Uchitelle, "800 Workers Locked Out by Staley," *New York Times*, June 29, 1993, accessed April 17, 2020, https://tinyurl.com/y9cm5qou; "Union Leaders Give Up on Caterpillar Strike," *New York Times*, December 4, 1995, accessed April 17, 2020, https://www.nytimes.com/1995/12/04/us/union-leaders-give-up-on-caterpillar-strike.html; "Bridgestone-Firestone Strike Is Called Off," *New York Times*, May 24, 1995, accessed April 17, 2020, https://www.nytimes.com/1995/05/24/us/bridgestone-firestone-strike-is-called-off.html.

June 27, 1905 "Minutes of the IWW Founding Convention," Industrial Workers of the World, accessed April 17, 2020, https://www.iww.org/history/founding.

June 27, 1936 "Decree on the Prohibition of Abortions. June 27, 1936," in J. Meisel and E.S. Kozera, eds., *Materials for the Study of the Soviet System* (Ann Arbor: G. Wahr, 1953), accessed April 17, 2020, https://www.revolutionarydemocracy.org/archive/abort.htm.

June 28, 1969 "E25–26: The Stonewall Riots and Pride at 50" (podcast), *Working Class History*, April 17, 2020, accessed April 17, 2020, https://workingclasshistory.com/2019/05/13/e21-22-the-stonewall-riots-and-pride-at-50; Dennis Eskow, "Stonewall Inn Is Raided by the Police," *New York Daily News*, June 29, 1969, 1, accessed May 20, 2020, https://www.nydailynews.com/new-york/stonewall-riot-place-1969-article-1.2267954; David Carter, *Stonewall: The Riots That Sparked the Gay Revolution* (New York: Griffin Publishers, 2010); Jonathan Ned Katz, "Stonewall Riot Police Reports," Out History, updated June 11, 2019, accessed May 26, 2020, http://outhistory.org/exhibits/show/stonewall-riot-police-reports/contents/fowler.

June 28, 1976 Edgar Rodrigues, "Elena Quinteros, 1945–1976," libcom.org, accessed April 17, 2020, https://libcom.org/history/elena-quinteros-1945-1976; "¿Quién fue Elena Quinteros?" Telenoche, July 17, 2019, accessed April 17, 2020, https://www.telenoche.com.uy/nacionales/%C2%BFquien-fue-elena-quinteros.

June 29, 1892 Eric Foner and John A. Garraty, *The Reader's Companion to American History* (Boston: Houghton Mifflin Harcourt Publishing, 1991); "The Strike at Homestead Mill," PBS, American Experience, accessed April 17, 2020, https://www.pbs.org/wgbh/americanexperience/features/carnegie-strike-homestead-mill.

June 29, 1936 Rick Smith Show, "Organizing in the Mines," Daily Kos, June 29, 2015, accessed April 17, 2020, https://www.dailykos.com/stories/2015/6/29/1397574/-Organizing-in-the-Mines; Yolanda Alaniz and Megan Cornish, *Viva la Raza: A History of Chicano Identity and Resistance* (Seattle: Red Letter Press, 2008), 102.

June 30 1977 "The of Cycle of Struggle 1973 to 1979 in India," GurgaonWorkersNews 60 (November 2013), accessed April 17, 2020, https://libcom.org/history/cycle-struggle-1973-1979-india.

June 30, 2013 Evan Johnston, "The Wonderful World of Bossnapping" (blog), May 1, 2016, accessed April 16 2020, https://evanjohnston.org/2016/05/01/the-wonderful-world-of-bossnapping.

July

July 1, 1944 Piero Gleijeses, *Shattered Hope: The Guatemalan Revolution and the United States, 1944–1954* (Princeton, NJ: Princeton University Press, 1991), 25.

July 1, 2012 Adam Ford, "Huge Protests Force Chinese Government Retreat Over Pollution," Commune, accessed April 17, 2020, https://tinyurl.com/yb6du4gg; Tania Branigan, "Anti-Pollution Protesters Halt Construction of Copper Plant in China," *Guardian*, July 3, 2012, accessed April 17, 2020, https://www.theguardian.com/world/2012/jul/03/china-anti-pollution-protest-copper.

July 2, 1902 Stephen Kinzer, "The US Conquest of the Philippines, 1898–1902," libcom.org, accessed April 17, 2020, https://libcom.org/history/us-conquest-philippines-1898-1902; "Philippine-American War," Newspapers.com, accessed April 17, 2020, https://www.newspapers.com/topics/american-imperialism/philippine-american-war.

July 2, 1986 "5 Killed in Chile on the First Day of General Strike," *New York Times*, July 3, 1986, accessed April 17, 2020, https://tinyurl.com/y7zr7nzs.

July 3, 1981 Jay Dyer, "Skinheads, Asians Battle in London," UPI, July 3, 1981, accessed April 17, 2020, https://www.upi.com/Archives/1981/07/03/Skinheads-Asians-battle-in-London/3055362980800; R.W. Apple Jr., "Neo-Nazis Accused in London Riots," *New York Times*, July 5, 1981, 3, accessed April 17, 2020, https://www.nytimes.com/1981/07/05/world/neo-nazis-accused-in-london-riots.html; "Short Hot Summer 1981" (blog), History Is Made at Night, July 11, 2011, accessed April 17, 2020, https://tinyurl.com/y9035ljf.

July 3, 1988 "The Forgotten Story of Iran Air flight 655," *Washington Post*, October 16, 2013, accessed April 17, 2020, https://tinyurl.com/ya45ljt8; Soapy, "A Look at Lockerbie: Iran Flight 655," libcom.org, accessed April 17, 2020, https://libcom.org/blog/road-lockerbie-iran-flight-655-10012016.

July 4, 1776 Howard Zinn, "A People's History of the American Revolution," libcom.org, accessed April 17, 2020, https://libcom.org/history/peoples-history-american-revolution.

July 4, 1998 Lynda Edwards, "Death in the Desert," *Orlando Weekly*, June 17, 1999, accessed April 17, 2020, http://www.orlandoweekly.com/orlando/death-in-the-desert/Content?oid=2263332.

July 5, 1888 "Strike of Bryant and May's Match Girls," *Reynolds Newspaper*, July 8, 1888, accessed April 17, 2020, https://www.bl.uk/collection-items/newspaper-article-reporting-the-match-girls-strike; John Simkin, "The 1888 London Matchgirls Strike," accessed April 17, 2020, https://spartacus-educational.com/TUmatchgirls.htm.

July 5, 1934 Jeremy Brecher, "The Dock Workers Strike and San Francisco General Strike, 1934," libcom.org, accessed April 17, 2020, https://tinyurl.com/ycfyk2fv.

July 6, 1934 Richard Hart, *Labour Rebellions in the 1930s in the British Caribbean* (London: Socialist History Society, 2002).

July 6, 1992 "Marsha P. Johnson" (obituary), *New York Times*, March 8, 2018, accessed April 17, 2020, https://www.nytimes.com/interactive/2018/obituaries/overlooked-marsha-p-johnson.html; Gillian Brockwell, "The Transgender Women at the Heart of the Stonewall Riots Were Pushed Out of the Gay Rights Movement. Now They Are Getting a Statue in New York," *Washington Post*, June 12, 2019, accessed April 17, 2020, https://tinyurl.com/ybe9hjyp; Shayna Jacobs, "Exclusive: DA Reopens Unsolved 1992 Case Involving the 'Saint of Gay Life,'" *New York Daily News*, December 16, 2012, accessed April 17, 2020, https://tinyurl.com/yblq3fc8; *Frameline Voices—Pay It No Mind: The Life and Times of Marsha P. Johnson*, YouTube, November 29, 2012, accessed April 17, 2020, https://www.youtube.com/watch?v=Bo0nYv9QIj4; "Episode 11: Marsha P. Johnson & Randy Wicker" (podcast), accessed August 11, 2019, https://makinggayhistory.com/podcast/episode-11-johnson-wicker.

July 7, 1912 "Site of Grabow Riot/Beauregard Regional Airport," Clio, accessed April 17, 2020, https://www.theclio.com/web/entry?id=48463; "July 7, 2012:1912 Grabow Riot Centennial Observation," Friends of DeRidder Army Air Base, accessed April 17, 2020, https://tinyurl.com/y7wgrfcj; W.T. Block, "'Leather Britches' Smith and the Grabow Riot," Calcasieu Parish, accessed April 17, 2020, http://theusgenweb.org/la/calcasieu/block/leatherbritches.html.

July 7, 1999 Mark Metcalf, "The Dahl Jenson Strike, 1999," Revolutions per Minute, accessed April 17, 2020, https://libcom.org/history/articles/dahl-jenson-strike-1999.

July 8, 1876 "July 8, 1876: Hamburg Massacre," Zinn Education Project, accessed April 17, 2020, https://www.zinnedproject.org/news/tdih/hamburg-massacre; "After Slavery: Hamburg Massacre," Lowcountry Digital History Initiative, accessed April 17, 2020, http://ldhi.library.cofc.edu/neatline/show/after-slavery-hamburg-massacre.

July 8, 1968 Dan Georgakas and Marvin Surkin, *Detroit, I Do Mind Dying: A Study in Urban Revolution* (Boston: South End Press, 1998).

July 9, 1919 "Allentown Bartenders Strike," *New York Times*, July 10, 1919, 36; "No Beer, No Work," Brookston Beer Bulletin, September 7, 2015, accessed April 17, 2020, http://brookstonbeerbulletin.com/no-beer-no-work.

July 9, 1959 Asher Schechter, "Wadi Salib Riots," *Ha'aretz*, June 16, 2013, accessed April 17, 2020, https://www.haaretz.com/jewish/1.5280465; William Parry, "Palestinian Homes Abandoned in Nakba Attest to History of Haifa's Wadi Salib Neighborhood," *Washington Report on Middle East Affairs*, January–February 2016, 28–29, accessed April 17, 2020, https://tinyurl.com/ycl7dl8e.

July 10, 1914 "Daring Outrage at Perth," *Glasgow Herald*, July 11, 1914, 14.

July 10, 1985 "The Bombing of the Rainbow Warrior," Greenpeace International, accessed April 17, 2020, https://tinyurl.com/yas99d5m.

July 11, 1917 Colin Everett, "Organized Labor in Brazil 1900–1937: From Anarchist Origins to Government Control," libcom.org, accessed April 16, 2020, https://tinyurl.com/y8bg3uq2.

July 11, 1937 Miyamoto Masao, "The Japanese Man Who Died on the Spanish Front," *Sennaciulo* 57, no. 2 (February 1986), accessed April 17, 2020, https://libcom.org/library/japanese-who-died-spanish-front-miyamoto-masao.

July 12, 1917 Fred Watson, "Still on Strike! Recollections of a Bisbee Deportee," *Journal of Arizona History* 18 (Summer 1977): 171–84, accessed August 11, 2019, http://www.library.arizona.edu/exhibits/bisbee/docs/jahwats.html.

July 12, 1921 Silvio Antonini, *Faremo a fassela gli Arditi del Popolo* (Viterbo, IT: Edizioni Sette Città, 2010).

July 13, 1948 Justin McCurry, "Japan Apologises to Victims of Forced Sterilisation," *Guardian*, April 24, 2019, accessed April 17, 2020, https://tinyurl.com/y54p6ftt; Daniel Hurst, "Victims of Forced Sterilisation in Japan to Receive Compensation and Apology," *Guardian*, March 18, 2019, accessed April 17, 2020, https://tinyurl.com/y2hq2ent; Andrew Gordon, ed., *Postwar Japan as History* (Berkeley: University of California Press, 1993), 306; Yoshio Sugimoto, *An Introduction to Japanese Society* (Cambridge: Cambridge University Press, 2014), 167; Masae Kato, *Women's Rights? The Politics of Eugenic Abortion in Modern Japan* (Amsterdam: Amsterdam University Press, 2009), 243.

July 13, 1976 Paul Sharkey, ed., *The Federacion Anarquista Uruguaya: Crisis, Armed Struggle and Dictatorship, 1967–85*" (London: Kate Sharpley Library, 2009), accessed April 16, 2020, https://libcom.org/files/FAU%20uruguay2.pdf.

July 14, 1970 Alfonso A. Narvaez, "Young Lords Seize Lincoln Hospital Building," *New York Times*, July 15, 1970, accessed April 17, 2020, https://tinyurl.com/y7cdawe8; "July 14, 1970: Young Lords Occupied Lincoln Hospital," Zinn Education Project, accessed April 17, 2020, https://www.zinnedproject.org/news/tdih/young-lords.

July 14, 2011 Uri Gordon, "Israel's "Tent Protests": The Chilling Effect of Nationalism," *Social Movement Studies Journal of Social, Cultural and Political Protest* 11, nos. 3–4 (2012), accessed April 17, 2020, https://tinyurl.com/ych92jpc; "A Short Guide to Israel's Social Protest," *Ha'aretz*, July 11, 2012, accessed April 17, 2020, https://www.haaretz.com/a-short-guide-to-the-social-protest-1.5265752.

July 15, 1971 Christopher Perkins, *United Red Army on Screen: Cinema, Aesthetics and The Politics of Memory* (Houndmills, UK: Palgrave Macmillan, 2015).

July 15, 2009 "S Africa Strike Hits Stadium Work," BBC News, July 8, 2009, accessed April 17, 2017, http://news.bbc.co.uk/1/hi/world/africa/8140433.stm.

July 16, 1977 Steven Johns, "The Great Northampton General Hospital Lie in, 1977," libcom.org, accessed April 17, 2020, https://libcom.org/history/1977-great-northampton-general-hospital-lie.

July 16, 1978 Catrin Nye and Sam Bright, "Altab Ali: The Racist Murder that Mobilised the East End," BBC News, May 4, 2016, accessed April 17, 2020, https://www.bbc.co.uk/news/uk-england-london-36191020; Kenneth Leech, *Brick Lane 1978: The Events and Their Significance*, accessed April 17, 2020, https://libcom.org/files/Brick-Lane-1978.pdf.

July 17, 1936 "Illustrated Timeline of the Spanish Civil War (in-depth)," University of Warwick, accessed April 17, 2020, http://www2.warwick.ac.uk/services/library/mrc/explorefurther/digital/scw/more/timeline; Adam Hochschild, "How Texaco Helped Franco Win the Spanish Civil War," *Mother Jones*, March 29, 2016, accessed April 17, 2020, https://www.motherjones.com/politics/2016/03/texaco-franco-spanish-civil-war-rieber; Anthony Beevor, *The Battle for Spain: The Spanish Civil War 1936-1939* (London: Weidenfeld & Nicolson, 2006).

July 17, 1978 Kenneth Leech, *Brick Lane 1978: The Events and Their Significance*, accessed April 17, 2020, https://libcom.org/files/Brick-Lane-1978.pdf.

July 18, 1917 Colin Everett, "Organised: Labour in Brazil 1900–1937: From Anarchist Origins to Government Control," libcom.org, accessed April 16, 2020, https://tinyurl.com/y8bg3uq2.

July 18, 1969 William "Preacherman" Fesperman, "Young Patriots at the United Front Against Fascism Conference, 1969" (speech), July 18–21, 1969, accessed April 17, 2020, https://libcom.org/history/young-patriots-united-front-against-fascism-conference-1969; James Tracy, "Revolutionary Hillbilly: An Interview with Hy Thurman of the Young Patriots Association" (blog), accessed April 17, 2020, https://tinyurl.com/yczrbuq4.

July 19, 1958 Matthew Heck, "Wichita Students Sit-in for US Civil Rights, 1958," Global Nonviolent Action Database, September 12, 2011, accessed April 17, 2020, https://nvdatabase.swarthmore.edu/content/wichita-students-sit-us-civil-rights-1958.

July 19, 1984 "How 11 Striking Irish Workers Helped to Fight Apartheid," *Irish Times*, December 6, 2013, accessed April 17, 2020, https://tinyurl.com/y78pvum5; "This Day 30 Years Ago the Dunnes Stores Anti-Apartheid Strike Began," thejournal.ie, July 19, 2014, accessed April 17, 2020, https://www.thejournal.ie/30-years-dunnes-stores-strike-1579724-Jul2014.

July 20, 1943 Chris Webb, *Sobibor Death Camp: History, Biographies, Remembrance* (New York: Columbia University Press, 2017), ix; Stanislaw Smajzner, "Extracts from the Tragedy of a Jewish Teenager," Holocaust Education & Archive Research Team, accessed April 17, 2020, http://www.holocaustresearchproject.org/ar/sobibor/smajzner2.html; "Jewish Revolts and Uprisings in the Lublin District," accessed April 17, 2020, http://chelm.freeyellow.com/revolts.html. Some sources claim the breakout occurred on July 27, but this is probably incorrect.

July 20, 1979 "As Clinton Contemplates Clemency for Leonard Peltier, a Debate between the FBI and Defense Attorneys," Democracy Now!, December 11, 2000, accessed April 17, 2020, https://www.democracynow.org/2000/12/11/as_clinton_contemplates_clemency_for_leonard; Resolution on the Case of Leonard Peltier, European Parliament, accessed April 17, 2020, https://web.archive.org/web/20070520182106/http://users.skynet.be/kola/epres2.htm; "Quick Facts: Case of Leonard Peltier," Free Leonard, accessed April 17, 2020, http://www.freeleonard.org/case/index.html; Peter Matthiessen, *In the Spirit of Crazy Horse* (New York: Penguin Books, 1992 [1983]), accessed May 14, 2020, https://leonardpeltiersymposium.files.wordpress.com/2017/01/matthiessen-1992-in-the-spirit-of-crazy-horse-c.pdf.

July 21, 1921 Andrea Ventura, *I Primi Antifascisti* (Sestri Levante, IT: Gammarò Editori, 2010).

July 21, 1945 "The 1945 Laundry Strike," Irish Women Workers Union, accessed April 17, 2020, https://womenworkersunion.ie/history/the-1945-laundry-strike.

July 22, 1920 "Chile: Anarchism, the IWW and the Workers Movement," *Rebel Worker*, accessed April 17, 2020, https://libcom.org/files/Chile.pdf.

July 22, 2005 Hannah Jones, "Tonga Public Servants General Strike, 2005," Global Nonviolent Action Database, April 11, 2020, accessed April 19, 2020, https://nvdatabase.swarthmore.edu/content/tongan-public-servants-strike-higher-wages-2005.

July 23, 1918 libcom, "1918: Rice Riots and Strikes in Japan," libcom.org, August 15, 2007, accessed April 17, 2020, https://libcom.org/library/1918-rice-riots-strikes-japan.

July 23, 1967 Tabitha C. Wang, "The Detroit Riot (1967)," Black Past, July 3, 2008, accessed April 17, 2020, https://tinyurl.com/ybh7fgge; Traqina Quarks Emeka, "Detroit Riot of 1967," Encyclopaedia Britannica, accessed April 17, 2020, https://www.britannica.com/event/Detroit-Riot-of-1967.

July 24, 1777 Barbara Clark Smith, "Food Rioters and the American Revolution," libcom.org, accessed April 17, 2020, http://libcom.org/history/food-rioters-american-revolution-barbara-clark-smith.

July 24, 2009 "Chinese Workers Beat Capitalist to Death," libcom.org, accessed April 17, 2020, https://libcom.org/news/workers-beat-capitalist-death-26072009; Sky Canaves and James T. Areddy, "Murder Bares Worker Anger Over China Industrial Reform," *Wall Street Journal*, July 31, 2009, accessed April 17, 2020, https://www.wsj.com/articles/SB124899768509595465.

July 25, 1867 Karl Marx, *Capital*, vols. 1–3 (Moscow: Progress Publishers, 1965), accessed April 17, 2020, https://libcom.org/library/capital-karl-marx.

July 25, 1972 Jean Heller, "Syphilis Victims in US Study Went Untreated for 40 Years," *New York Times*, July 26, 1972, 1, accessed April 18, 2020, https://tinyurl.com/ybnfbhge.

July 26, 1937 Richard Hart, *Labour Rebellions in the 1930s in the British Caribbean* (London: Socialist History Society, 2002).

July 26, 1950 "The No Gun Ri Massacre, 1950," Zinn Education Project, accessed April 18, 2020, http://libcom.org/history/no-gun-ri-massacre-1950.

July 27, 1816 Adam Wasserman, "The Negro Fort Massacre," libcom.org, accessed April 18, 2020, https://libcom.org/history/negro-fort-massacre.

July 27, 1933 George Lakey and Olivia Ensign, "Cuban General Strike, 1933," Global Nonviolent Action Database, June 15, 2011, accessed April 19, 2020, https://nvdatabase.swarthmore.edu/content/cubans-general-strike-overthrow-president-1933.

July 28, 1915 Robert Fatton Jr., "Killing Haitian Democracy," *Jacobin*, July 2015, accessed April 18, 2020, https://www.jacobinmag.com/2015/07/monroe-doctrine-1915-occupation-duvalier.

July 28, 1932 Mickey Z, "The Bonus Army," Zinn Education Project, accessed April 18, 2020, https://www.zinnedproject.org/materials/bonus-army; "July 28, 1932: Bonus Army Attacked,"

Zinn Education Project, accessed April 18, 2020, https://www.zinnedproject.org/news/tdih/bonus-army-attacked; Andrew Glass, "Bonus Army Expelled," Politico, July 28, 2015, accessed April 18, 2020, https://www.politico.com/story/2015/07/this-day-politics-july-28-1932-120658.

July 29, 1910 "The Slocum Massacre, 1910," Zinn Education Project, accessed April 18, 2020, https://libcom.org/history/slocum-massacre-1910.

July 29, 1962 "1962: Violence Flares at Mosley Rally," BBC, accessed May 28, 2020, http://news.bbc.co.uk/onthisday/hi/dates/stories/july/31/newsid_2776000/2776295.stm; "Mosley Tries Again (1962)" (video), British Pathé, April 13, 2014, accessed May 28, 2020, https://www.youtube.com/watch?v=RRS4NR_BZ1w.

July 30, 1766 Pablo Velasco, "1766: The Real Del Monte Miners' Strike," libcom.org, accessed April 18, 2020, https://libcom.org/history/1766-the-real-del-monte-miners-strike; Allana Akhtar, "The GM Auto Workers Strike Is Entering into Its 4th Week. Here Are 10 of the Most Impactful Strikes in History—for Better or Worse," Business Insider, October 7, 2019, accessed April 18, 2020, https://tinyurl.com/y8g82wxu.

July 30, 1913 Temma Kaplan, "The Socialist Origins of International Women's Day," Feminist Studies 11, no. 1 (1985): 163–71, accessed April 15, 2020, https://libcom.org/files/International%20Women's%20Day.pdf.

July 31, 1922 Giordano Bruno Guerri, Fascisti (Milan: Mondadori Editore, 1995), 89.

July 31, 1945 The Labour Government vs the Dockers 1945–1951, Solidarity Pamphlet 19 (Spring 1965), accessed April 18, 2020, https://libcom.org/library/labour-party-dockers-1945-1951-solidarity; Geoff Ellen, "Labour and Strike-Breaking 1945–1951," International Socialism Journal 2, no. 24 (summer 1984): 45–73, accessed April 18, 2020, https://www.marxists.org/history/etol/newspape/isj2/1984/isj2-024/ellen.html.

August

August 1, 1917 "The Man That Was Hung," International Socialist Review (September 1917), accessed April 18, 2020, https://libcom.org/library/man-was-hung; Rory Carroll, "The Mysterious Lynching of Frank Little: Activist Who Fought Inequality and Lost," Guardian, September 21, 2016, accessed April 18, 2020, https://tinyurl.com/jrjx59s.

August 1, 1938 William J Puette, "The Hilo Massacre, 1938," Center for Labor Education & Research, 1988, accessed April 18, 2020, https://libcom.org/history/hilo-massacre-1938; "Hilo Massacre," University of Hawaii, accessed April 18, 2020, http://www.hawaii.edu/uhwo/clear/Pubs/HiloMassacre.html.

August 2, 1944 Helena Kubica and Piotr Setkiewicz, "The Last Stage of the Functioning of the Zigeunerlager in the Birkenau Camp (May–August, 1944)," Memoria 10 (July 2018), accessed April 18, 2020, https://view.joomag.com/memoria-en-no-10-july-2018/0531301001532506629/p6?short; "16 May: Romani Resistance Day," Romedia Foundation," May 16, 2016, accessed April 18, 2020, https://romediafoundation.wordpress.com/2016/05/16/16-may-romani-resistance-day.

August 2, 1980 Fiona Leney, "The Terror Trial That Won't Grow Cold," Independent, October 10, 1993, accessed April 18, 2020, https://tinyurl.com/yd6qxzej; "Bologna Blast Leaves Dozens Dead," BBC Home, accessed April 18, 2020, http://news.bbc.co.uk/onthisday/hi/dates/stories/august/2/newsid_4532000/4532091.stm.

August 3, 1492 Howard Zinn, "Columbus, the Indians and the 'Discovery' of America," libcom.org, accessed April 18, 2019, https://libcom.org/history/columbus-indians-discovery-america; "Columbus and His Voyages," Cornell University Library, accessed April 18, 2020, https://olinuris.library.cornell.edu/columbia-or-america/columbus.

August 3, 1929 Stromberg v. California, 283 U.S. 359 (1931) No. 584, United States Supreme Court, accessed April 18, 2020, https://caselaw.findlaw.com/us-supreme-court/283/359.html; "Stromberg Arrested for Violating California Red Flag Law," Today in Civil Liberties History, accessed April 18, 2020, http://todayinclh.com/?event=stromberg-arrested-for-violating-california-red-flag-law; The California Red Flag Case (New York: American Civil Liberties Union, 1930), accessed April 18, 2020, http://debs.indstate.edu/a505c3_1930.pdf.

August 4, 2011 (Chile) Jonathan Franklin, "Chile Student Protests Explode into Violence," *Guardian*, August 5, 2011, accessed May 20, 2020, https://www.theguardian.com/world/2011/aug/05/chile-student-protests-violence; "Bases Para un Acuerdo Social por la Educación Chilena," *El Chileno*, accessed May 20, 2020, https://tinyurl.com/y89mj7kb; "Gobierno Regional detalla importante paquete de medidas educacionales," Ministerio de Educación, August 18, 2011, accessed May 20, 2020, https://tinyurl.com/y9r2ocbb.

August 4, 2011 (UK) "Man Killed in Shooting Incident Involving Police Officer," *Telegraph*, August 4, 2011, accessed April 18, 2020, https://tinyurl.com/yayeeh26; "Mark Duggan's Family Have Little Confidence in Police Probe, Court Hears," *Guardian*, December 12, 2011, accessed April 18, 2020, https://www.theguardian.com/uk/2011/dec/12/mark-duggan-family-police-court.

August 5, 1964 Edward J. Marolda, *The Approaching Storm* (Washington, DC: Naval History and Heritage Command Department of the Navy, 2009), 68–80, accessed April 18 2020, https://tinyurl.com/y78uyswm; "Week of August 4," United States of America Vietnam War Commemoration, accessed April 18, 2020, https://www.vietnamwar50th.com/education/week_of_august_4; "Secret War in Laos," Legacies of War, accessed April 18, 2020, http://legaciesofwar.org/about-laos/secret-war-laos.

August 5, 1981 Andrew Glass, "Reagan Fires 11,000 Striking Air Traffic Controllers," Politico, August 5, 1981 accessed April 18, 2020, https://tinyurl.com/y7cvtkty; A.E. Martinez, "Lessons of the Air Traffic Controllers Strike 1981," Ideas and Action, August 25, 2014, accessed April 18, 2020, http://ideasandaction.info/2014/08/lessons-air-traffic-controllers-strike-1981.

August 6, 1945 "1945: US Responses to the Atomic Bombing of Hiroshima and Nagasaki," libcom.org, accessed April 18, 2020, https://libcom.org/history/1945-us-responses-atomic-bombing-hiroshima-nagasaki; Gar Alperovitz, *The Decision to Use the Atomic Bomb* (New York: Vintage, 1996).

August 6, 1970 Jim Hill, "Yippie-Dee-Doo-Dah, Part 1: When the Yippies Invaded Disneyland," Huffpost, April 8, 2011, accessed April 18, 2020, http://www.huffingtonpost.com/jim-hill/yippies-disneyland_b_917731.

August 7, 1842 "The General Strike of 1842," Chartist Ancestors, accessed April 18, 2020, http://www.chartistancestors.co.uk/general-strike-1842.

August 7, 1900 W. Dirk Raat, "Flores Magon, Ricardo," Texas State Historical Association, accessed April 18, 2020, https://tshaonline.org/handbook/online/articles/ffl28; Kevan Aguilar, "Ricardo Flores Magón & the Ongoing Revolution," Oxford Research Encyclopedia of Latin America, accessed April 18, 2020, https://tinyurl.com/yae8vsen.

August 8, 1845 "Inclosure Act 1845," legislation.gov.uk, accessed April 18, 2020, http://www.legislation.gov.uk/ukpga/Vict/8-9/118/introduction; "Enclosing the Land," Parliament.uk, accessed April 18, 2020, https://tinyurl.com/y8zyt4pb.

August 8, 1936 "Spanish Civil War: Chronology," Spartacus Educational, accessed April 18, 2020, https://spartacus-educational.com/SPAchronology.htm; John F. Coverdale, *Italian Intervention in the Spanish Civil War* (Princeton, NJ: Princeton University Press, 1975), 91.

August 9, 1956 M Bahati Kuumba, "'You've Struck a Rock,' Gender and Transformation in the US and South Africa," libcom.org, accessed April 18, 2020, https://tinyurl.com/y7umto6a; Meruschka Govender, "Women's Day: Remembering 9th August 1956," Mzansi Girl, accessed August 7, 2017, unavailable April 18, 2020, http://www.mzansigirl.com/womens-day-remembering-9-august-1956.

August 9, 1970 Robin Bunce and Paul Field, "Mangrove Nine: The Court Challenge against Police Racism in Notting Hill," *Guardian*, November 29, 2010, accessed April 18, 2020, https://www.theguardian.com/law/2010/nov/29/mangrove-nine-40th-anniversary; Anne-Marie Angelo, "The Black Panthers in London, 1967–1972: A Diasporic Struggle Navigates the Black Atlantic," *Radical History Review* 103 (Winter 2009), accessed April 18, 2020, https://tinyurl.com/y9gt88ec.

August 10, 1956 M. Bouraib, "Attentat de la rue de Thèbes du 10 aout 1956: L'abject terrorisme des Ultras," *El Moudjahid*, August 11, 2013, accessed April 18, 2020, http://www.elmoudjahid.com/fr/mobile/detail-article/id/44679; Florence Beaugé, "50 ans après: les survivants du 'nettoyage d'Alger,'" *Le Monde*, January 29, 2007, accessed April 18, 2020, https://tinyurl.com/ybx99pjn; John LeJeune, "Revolutionary Terror and Nation-Building: Frantz Fanon and the Algerian Revolution," *Journal for the Study of Radicalism* 13, no. 2 (Fall 2019): 1–44; Donald Reid, *Germaine Tillion, Lucie Aubrac, and the Politics of Memories of the French Resistance* (Newcastle, UK: Cambridge Scholars Publishing, 2009), 69.

August 10, 2005 "Strikes and Legislation Timelines," Striking Women, accessed April 18, 2020, http://www.leeds.ac.uk/strikingwomen/strikes.

August 11, 1965 Jill A. Eddy, "Watts Riots of 1965," Encyclopaedia Britannica, accessed April 18, 2020, https://www.britannica.com/event/Watts-Riots-of-1965; Learning Network, "Aug. 11, 1965 Riots in the Watts Section of Los Angeles," *New York Times*, August 11, 2011, accessed April 18, 2020, https://tinyurl.com/ycn3v2ts.

August 11, 1984 Elli Narewska, "Jean Stead and the Women of the Miners' Strike," *Guardian*, June 2, 2014, accessed April 18, 2020, https://tinyurl.com/y7ebwlxb; "'Women against Pit Closures' during the 1984–85 British Miners' Strike," libcom.org, accessed April 18, 2020, https://libcom.org/history/women-against-pit-closures-during-1984-85-british-miners-strike.

August 12, 1937 Nick Heath, "August 12, 1937: Killing Day at Tobolsk," libcom.org, accessed April 18, 2020, https://libcom.org/history/august-12th-1937-killing-day-tobolsk; Editors, "Great Purge," Encyclopaedia Britannica, accessed April 18, 2020, https://www.britannica.com/event/Great-Purge.

August 12, 2017 "Violent White Supremacist Rally in Charlottesville Ends in Murder," Unicorn Riot, August 12, 2017, accessed April 18, 2020, https://unicornriot.ninja/2017/violent-white-supremacist-rally-charlottesville-ends-murder; Mitch Smith, "James Fields Sentenced to Life in Prison for Death of Heather Heyer in Charlottesville," *New York Times*, June 28, 2019, accessed April 18, 2020, https://www.nytimes.com/2019/06/28/us/james-fields-sentencing.html.

August 13, 1973 Earl Caldwell, "2 Virgin Islands Jurors Charge Pressure for Slayings Verdict," *New York Times*, August 15, 1973, 15, accessed April 18, 2020, https://timesmachine.nytimes.com/timesmachine/1973/08/15/90466084.html?pageNumber=15; Peter Kerr, "New York-Bound Flight Hijacked to Cuba by Convicted Murderer," *New York Times*, January 1, 1985, 1, accessed April 18, 2020, https://timesmachine.nytimes.com/timesmachine/1985/01/01/186833.html?pageNumber=1; Sean Pennington, "Cuban Diary: Fountain Valley Killer LaBeet Alive and Well in Cuba," St. Croix Source, April 23, 2015, accessed April 18, 2020, https://tinyurl.com/yc357bh9.

August 13, 1977 libcom group, "1977: The Battle of Lewisham," libcom.org, September 10, 2006, accessed April 18, 2020, https://libcom.org/history/1977-the-battle-of-lewisham; Mark Townsend, "How the Battle of Lewisham Helped to Halt the Rise of Britain's Far-Right," *Guardian*, August 13, 2017, accessed April 18, 2020, https://tinyurl.com/y6uv5ejm.

August 14, 1889 "The Great London Dock Strike, 1889," libcom.org, accessed April 18, 2020, https://libcom.org/history/1889-the-great-london-dock-strike; Louise Raw, *Striking a Light: The Bryant and May Matchwomen and their Place in History* (New York: Continuum, 2011).

August 14, 1945 "Danh nhân lịch sử: Nguyễn An Ninh," TaiLieu, accessed April 18, 2020, http://tailieu.vn/doc/danh-nhan-lich-su-nguyen-an-ninh-897574.html.

August 15, 1947 Editors, "Independence Day," Encyclopaedia Britannica, accessed April 18, 2020, https://www.britannica.com/topic/Independence-Day-Indian-holiday; Joseph McQuade, "The Forgotten Violence That Helped India Break Free from Colonial Rule," *Independent*, November 10, 2016, accessed April 18, 2020, https://tinyurl.com/yby5flkn; Sarah Ansari, "How the Partition of India Happened—and Why Its Effects Are Still Felt Today," *Independent*, August 11, 2017, accessed April 18, 2020, https://tinyurl.com/ybqkmnr2.

August 15, 1961 Robert F. Williams, *Negroes with Guns* (Detroit: Wayne State University Press, 1962), accessed April 18, 2020, https://libcom.org/history/negroes-guns-robert-f-williams; Truman Nelson, "People with Strength: The Story of Monroe, North Carolina" (1962), in *Robert and Mabel Williams Resource Guide* (San Francisco: Freedom Archives, 2005), 38, 55–59; "Charges Dropped against Williams," *Star News*, January 17, 1976, 2.

August 16, 1819 "E15: The Peterloo Massacre with Mike Leigh" (podcast), Working Class History, November 7, 2018, accessed July 3, 2020, https://workingclasshistory.com/2018/11/07/e15-the-peterloo-massacre-with-mike-leigh; "History of the Peterloo Massacre, 1819," Peterloo Memorial Campaign, accessed July 3, 2020, https://libcom.org/history/history-peterloo-massacre-1819; Percy Bysshe Shelley, "The Masque of Anarchy" (1819), accessed July 3, 2020, https://libcom.org/library/masque-anarchy-percy-bysshe-shelley.

August 16, 2012 Mouvement Communiste and Kolektivně proti Kapitálu, "South Africa: The Partial Re-emergence of Workers Autonomy," Letter no. 37 (May 2013), accessed April 18, 2020, https://tinyurl.com/yaf9slsh; Sipho Hlongwane, "Marikana Commission: NUM in a Deep Hole Over the Fight That Started It All," Daily Maverick, February 1, 2013, accessed April 18, 2020, https://tinyurl.com/yd6g7pja.

August 17, 1795 Gert Oostindie, "Slave Resistance, Colour Lines, and the Impact of the French and Haitian Revolutions in Curaçao," in Gert Oostindie and Wim Klooster, eds., *Curaçao in the Age of Revolutions, 1795–1800* (Leiden, NL: Brill, 2011), 1–22.

August 17, 1987 "1987: The Great Workers Struggle," libcom.org, August 18, 2008, accessed April 18, 2020, https://libcom.org/history/1987-the-great-workers-struggle; Berch Berberoglu, *The Political Economy of Development: Development Theory and the Prospects for Change in the Third World* (New York: State University of New York Press, 1992), 63.

August 18, 1812 "18th August 1812: Food Riots in Leeds Headed by 'Lady Ludd'—Similar Scenes in Sheffield," Luddite Bicentenary, August 18, 2012, accessed May 28, 2020, https://ludditebicentenary.blogspot.com/2012/08/18th-august-1812-food-riots-in-leeds.html.

August 18, 1823 "Demerara Rebellion 1823," Black Past, June 25, 2017, accessed April 18, 2020, http://www.blackpast.org/gah/demerara-rebellion-1823; Colleen A. Vaconcellos, "Demerara Revolt," Encyclopedia.com, updated April 14, 2020, accessed April 18, 2020, https://tinyurl.com/ya7dx68k.

August 19, 1936 James Badcock, "Spanish Poet Lorca Was 'Killed on Official Orders' After the Outbreak of Spanish Civil War," *Telegraph*, April 23, 2015, accessed April 18, 2020, https://tinyurl.com/k32ft27.

August 19, 1953 "CIA Confirms Role in 1953 Iran Coup," National Security Archive, August 19, 2013, accessed April 18, 2020, https://nsarchive2.gwu.edu/NSAEBB/NSAEBB435; Stephen Kinzer, "The Iranian Coup, 1953," libcom.org, accessed April 18, 2020, https://libcom.org/history/iranian-coup-1953.

August 20, 1948 Olivia Ensign, "Zanzibar Workers General Strike in Zanzibar City, Tanzania, 1948," Global Nonviolent Action Database, March 28, 2010, accessed April 19, 2020, https://tinyurl.com/y7zx2d3l.

August 20, 1976 "E1: The Grunwick Strike, 1976" (podcast), *Working Class History*, February 28, 2018, accessed April 18, 2020, https://workingclasshistory.com/2018/02/28/episode-1-the-grunwick-strike-1976; Bethan Bell and Shabnam Mahmood, "Grunwick Dispute: What Did the 'Strikers in Saris' Achieve?" BBC News, September 10, 2016, accessed April 18, 2020, https://www.bbc.com/news/uk-england-london-37244466.

August 21, 1831 Howard Zinn, *A People's History of the United States: 1492–Present* (New York: Harper & Row, 2009 [1980]), chapter 9, accessed April 18, 2020, https://libcom.org/library/peoples-history-of-united-states-howard-zinn; "Nat Turner's Revolt 1831," Encyclopedia Virginia, updated June 18, 2019, accessed April 18, 2020, https://www.encyclopediavirginia.org/Revolt_Nat_Turner_s_1831.

August 21, 1981 Susan Lochrie, "Greenock Jeans Factory Sit-in's Soundtrack," *Greenock Telegraph*, January 12, 2016, accessed April 18, 2020, https://www.greenocktelegraph.co.uk/news/14197832.greenock-jeans-factory-sit-ins-soundtrack; Andy Clarke, "'And the Next Thing, the Chairs Barricaded the Door': The Lee Jeans Factory Occupation, Trade Unionism and Gender in Scotland in the 1980s," accessed April 18, 2020, https://tinyurl.com/y9swpsv7.

August 22, 1943 Cormac Ó Gráda, "Making Famine History," *Journal of Economic Literature* 45, no. 1 (2007): 5–38, accessed April 18, 2020, https://papers.ssrn.com/sol3/papers.cfm?abstract_id=2764326; Bard Wilkinson, "Churchill's Policies to Blame for Millions of Indian Famine Deaths

Study Says," CNN, March 29, 2019, accessed April 18, 2020, https://www.cnn.com/2019/03/29/asia/churchill-bengal-famine-intl-scli-gbr/index.html; Tom Heyden, "The 10 Greatest Controversies of Winston Churchill's Career," BBC News, January 26, 2015, accessed April 18, 2020, https://www.bbc.com/news/magazine-29701767; Philip Hensher, "*Churchill and Empire*, by Lawrence James—a Review," *Spectator*, July 2013, accessed April 18, 2020, https://www.spectator.co.uk/2013/07/churchill-and-empire-by-lawrence-james-a-review; "In Conversation to Leo Amery, Secretary of State for India," in John Barnes and David Nicholson, eds., *Leo Amery: Diaries* (London: Hutchinson, 1988), 832.

August 22, 1947 Makhan Singh, "Jomo Kenyatta, Post-War Labour Party, Strikes and the Pass System," libcom.org, accessed April 18, 2020, https://tinyurl.com/y8xxlp64.

August 23, 1851 "1851: Sydney Sailors Riot," Radical Tradition, libcom.org, accessed April 18, 2020, https://libcom.org/history/1851-sydney-sailors-riot.

August 23, 1966 "The Wave Hill Walk-Off, 1966–1975," libcom.org, accessed April 18, 2020, https://libcom.org/history/wave-hill-walk-1966-1975; "Wave Hill Walk-Off," National Museum of Australia, accessed April 18, 2020, https://www.nma.gov.au/defining-moments/resources/wave-hill-walk-off.

August 24, 1800 "Gabriel's Rebellion," Virginia Historical Markers, accessed April 18, 2020, http://www.markerhistory.com/tag/gabriels-rebellion.

August 24, 2011 Randy Woods and Matt Craze, "Thousands of Chileans Protest for Education, Labour Reforms," Bloomberg, August 25, 2011, accessed April 18, 2020, https://tinyurl.com/yaoj6wjz.

August 25, 1921 "E7: The West Virginia Mine Wars, 1902–1922," (podcast), *Working Class History*, June 9, 2018, accessed April 18, 2020, https://workingclasshistory.com/2018/06/09/wch-e7-the-west-virginia-mine-wars-1902-1922; "Battle of Blair Mountain 1921 Photo Gallery," libcom.org, accessed April 18, 2020, https://libcom.org/gallery/battle-blair-mountain-1921-photo-gallery; "Battle of Blair Mountain: Topics in Chronicling America," Library of Congress, accessed April 18, 2020, https://www.loc.gov/rr/news/topics/blair.html.

August 25, 1944 "1939–1945: Spanish Resistance in France," libcom.org, accessed April 18, 2020, https://libcom.org/history/1939-1945-spanish-resistance-in-france. This document has the incorrect date. Alberto Fernández, *La España de los maquis* (Mexico City: Ediciones ERA, 1971), accessed April 18, 2020, https://tinyurl.com/ycg68e35; Steven Johns, "The Whitewashing of French Forces in the Liberation of Paris," libcom.org, August 24, 2016, accessed April 18, 2020, https://libcom.org/history/whitewashing-french-forces-liberation-paris-steven-johns.

August 26, 1919 "Fannie Sellins Historical Marker," ExplorePAhistory.com, accessed April 18, 2020, https://explorepahistory.com/hmarker.php?markerId=1-A-244.

August 26, 1930 "Mob Violence," *Advertiser*, August 27, 1930, accessed April 18, 2020, http://trove.nla.gov.au/newspaper/article/30504075.

August 27, 1889 David Rosenberg, "The Rebels Who Brought London to a Standstill," *Jewish Chronicle*, March 19, 2015, accessed April 18, 2020, https://www.thejc.com/culture/books/the-rebels-who-brought-london-to-a-standstill-1.65742; "The Significance of the Great Dock Strike of 1889," London Agora, October 23, 2013, accessed April 18, 2020, http://londonagora.blogspot.com/2013/10/the-significance-of-great-dock-strike.html.

August 27, 1974 "40th Anniversary of Joan Little's Pivotal Murder Acquittal" (video), CBS News, August 14, 2015, accessed April 18, 2020, https://www.cbsnews.com/video/40th-anniversary-of-joan-littles-pivotal-murder-acquittal; Angela Davis, "Joan Little: The Dialectics of Rape," *Ms*, accessed August 27, 2018, unavailable April 18, 2020, http://www.msmagazine.com/spring2002/davis.asp.

August 28, 1830 Marjorie Bloy, "Rural Unrest in the 1830s: The 'Swing' Riots," A Web of English History, accessed April 18, 2020, http://www.historyhome.co.uk/peel/ruralife/swing.htm.

August 28, 1968 Lorraine Perlman and Fredy Perlman, "Chicago 1968," *Black and Red* 2 (October 1968), accessed April 18, 2020, https://libcom.org/history/chicago-1968; Herbert Hill, *Black Labor and the American Legal System: Race, Work, and the Law* (Madison: University of Wisconsin Press, 1985), 331–32.

August 29, 1979 Steven Johns, "The Occupation of the Swedish National Board of Health and Welfare, 1979," libcom.org, accessed April 18, 2020, https://tinyurl.com/y7z6ojrr; "Socialstyrelsen klassar homosexualitet som friskt," Levandehistoria, accessed April 18, 2020, https://tinyurl.com/ydb2mtsn; "- Jag kan inte jobba idag. Jag är homo," QX, March 24, 2009, accessed April 18, 2020, https://www.qx.se/samhalle/9784/jag-kan-inte-jobba-idag-jag-ar-homo.

August 29, 1997 Lily Burana, "What It Was Like to Work at the Lusty Lady, a Unionized Strip Club," *Atlantic*, August 31, 2013, accessed April 18, 2020, https://tinyurl.com/y9ypg79t; Yin Xiao, "San Francisco Strippers Win Right to Form Union 1996–1997," Global Nonviolent Action Database, March 30, 2017, accessed April 18, 2020, https://tinyurl.com/ya6ry7fu.

August 30, 1908 Brian Kelly, "Birmingham District Coal Strike of 1908," libcom.org, accessed April 18, 2020, https://libcom.org/history/birmingham-district-coal-strike-1908.

August 30, 1979 "Jean Seberg: Screen Icon and Black Panther Supporter," libcom.org, July 12, 2007, accessed April 18, 2020, https://libcom.org/library/jean-seberg-screen-icon-black-panther-supporter; Allan M. Jalon, "A Faulty Tip, a Ruined Life and Hindsight," *Los Angeles Times*, April 14, 2002, accessed May 19, 2020, https://www.latimes.com/archives/la-xpm-2002-apr-14-lv-bellows_side14-story.html; Sara Jordan-Heintz, "Jean Seberg Would Have Turned 80 This Week," *Times-Republican*, November 11, 2018, accessed April 18, 2020, https://tinyurl.com/y7bw5ma9.

August 31, 1942 George Kieffer, "General Strike against Military Conscription in German-Occupied Luxembourg, 1942," libcom.org, accessed April 18, 2020, https://libcom.org/library/1942-luxembourg-post-office-strike.

August 31, 1944 "Ποιος σκότωσε τη Μαρία Δημάδη," agrinionews.gr, September 6, 2014, accessed April 18, 2020, https://bit.ly/2KcSCyZ.

September

September 1, 1939 Nikola Budanovic, "Defence of the Polish Post Office in Danzig," warhistoryonline.com, accessed April 18, 2020, https://libcom.org/history/defence-polish-post-office-danzig; "Controversial Museum Planned in Poland at Site of First Nazi Invasion," DW, September 1, 2009, accessed April 18, 2020, https://tinyurl.com/y8kxolxn.

September 1, 2007 Robert Evans, "Military Scientists Tested Mustard Gas on Indians," *Guardian*, September 1, 2007, accessed April 18, 2020, https://www.theguardian.com/uk/2007/sep/01/india.military.

September 2, 1962 "Mosley Gets Rough House (1962)," British Pathé, April 13, 2014, accessed April 18, 2020, https://www.youtube.com/watch?v=Y-Ef3WYWJYc; "III. Behind the Race Laws," Searchlight, accessed April 18, 2020, http://www.searchlight.org.uk/ross/racelaws.html.

September 2, 2005 Michael Kunzelman, "Ex-Cops Go to Prison in Post-Katrina Killing," Associated Press, March 31, 2011, accessed April 18, 2020, https://tinyurl.com/ycukcsqw.

September 3, 1791 Constitution of 1791, September 3, 1791, accessed April 18, 2020, https://tinyurl.com/y9k2rgj3.

September 3, 1934 Jeremy Brecher, "The US National Textile Workers' Strike, 1934," libcom.org, accessed April 18, 2020, https://libcom.org/history/us-national-textile-workers-strike-1934-jeremy-brecher.

September 4, 1919 Alessandro Portelli, *They Say in Harlan County: An Oral History* (Oxford: Oxford University Press, 2012), 180; Federal Writers' Project, *The WPA Guide to West Virginia: The Mountain State* (San Antonio, TX: Trinity University Press, 2013), 91; Melissa Walker, *All We Knew Was to Farm: Rural Women in the Upcountry South, 1919–1941* (Baltimore: Johns Hopkins University Press, 2002), 215.

September 4, 2005 "Ex-Officers Sentenced in Post-Katrina Shootings," *New York Times*, April 5, 2012, accessed April 18, 2020, https://www.nytimes.com/2012/04/05/us/5-ex-officers-sentenced-in-post-katrina-shootings.html.

September 5, 1911 Dave Marson, "Children's Strikes in 1911," libcom.org, accessed April 18, 2020, https://libcom.org/history/childrens-strikes-1911.

September 5, 1917 "1917 Raids on the Socialist Party and the IWW," *International Socialist Review* 17, no. 4 (October 1917): 205–09, accessed April 18, 2020, https://libcom.org/history/1917-raids-socialist-party-iww.

September 6, 1921 "Dail Eireann Halts Cork Harbor," *New York Times*, September 7, 1921, accessed April 18, 2020, https://tinyurl.com/yck9w94a.

September 6, 1966 Nikos Konstandaras, "The Truth Behind the Assassination of the South African PM," *Nation*, August 16, 2019, accessed April 18, 2020, https://www.thenation.com/article/hendrik-verwoerd-assassination-dimitri-tsafendas; "Dimitri Tsafendas," South African History Online, accessed April 18, 2020, https://www.sahistory.org.za/people/dimitri-tsafendas; David Beresford, "Dimitri Tsafendas," October 11, 1999, *Guardian*, accessed April 18, 2020, https://www.theguardian.com/news/1999/oct/11/guardianobituaries.davidberesford; Gerry Loughran, "South Africa Hero Who Changed Course of Apartheid but Got No Reward," *Daily Nation*, September 7, 2016, accessed April 18, 2020, https://tinyurl.com/y7qve927; Danny Morrison, "The Life of Dimitri Tsafendas" (blog), accessed April 18, 2020, http://www.dannymorrison.com/wp-content/dannymorrisonarchive/144.htm; Niren Tolsi, "Tsafendas: Setting the Record Straight," New Frame, September 10, 2018, accessed April 18, 2020, https://www.newframe.com/tsafendas-setting-record-straight.

September 7, 1934 Communist Party of Great Britain, *Drowned in a Sea of Working Class Activity, September* 9th, (London: CPGB, 1934).

September 7, 1977 "The Cycle of Struggle 1973 to 1979 in India," GurgaonWorkersNews 60 (November 2013), accessed April 17, 2020, https://libcom.org/history/cycle-struggle-1973-1979-india.

September 8, 1941 Tore Pryser, "Melkestreiken," in Hans Fredrik Dahl, Guri Hjeltnes, Berit Nøkleby, Nils Johan Ringdal, and Øystein Sørensen, eds., *Norsk krigsleksikon 1940–45* (Oslo: Cappelen, 1995); Per Voksø, *Krigens Dagbok* (Oslo: Det Beste, 1984), 165–66; "Norge i krigen 1939–45," accessed April 18, 2020, https://web.archive.org/web/20110525024739/http://mediabase1.uib.no/krigslex/l/l3.html.

September 8, 1972 Henry P. Leifermann, "A Sort of Mutiny: The Constellation Incident," *New York Times*, February 18, 1973, accessed April 18, 2020, https://www.nytimes.com/1973/02/18/archives/the-constellation-incident-a-sort-of-mutiny.html.

September 9, 1739 Editors, "Stono Rebellion," Encyclopaedia Britannica, accessed April 18, 2020, https://www.britannica.com/event/Stono-rebellion.

September 9, 1945 Martin Hart-Landsberg, *Korea: Division, Reunification, and U.S. Foreign Policy* (New York: Monthly Review Press, 1998).

September 10, 1897 Paul A. Shackel, "How a 1897 Massacre of Pennsylvania Coal Miners Morphed from a Galvanizing Crisis to Forgotten History," *Smithsonian Magazine*, March 13, 2019, accessed April 18, 2020, https://tinyurl.com/ya2uysdc; Kenneth C. Wolensky, "Freedom to Assemble and the Lattimer Massacre of 1897," *Pennsylvania Legacies* 8, no. 1 (May 2008): 24–31.

September 10, 1962 Chana Kai Lee, *For Freedom's Sake: The Life of Fannie Lou Hamer* (Urbana: University of Illinois Press, 2000), 34; "Fannie Lou Hamer: Papers of a Civil Rights Activist, Political Activist and Woman," Archives Unbound, accessed May 19, 2020, https://tinyurl.com/ybp7966w.

September 11, 1973 "Chile Dictatorship Victim Toll Bumped to 40,018," CBC, August 18, 2011, accessed April 18, 2020, https://tinyurl.com/yae76yl5; Jonathan Franklin, "Chilean Army Admits 120 Thrown into Sea," *Guardian*, January 9, 2001, accessed April 8, 2020, https://www.theguardian.com/world/2001/jan/09/chile.pinochet; "Ex-Army Chief Juan Emilio Cheyre Admits Chile Adoption," BBC News, August 20, 2013, accessed April 18, 2020, https://www.bbc.com/news/world-latin-america-23770222; Marianela Jarroud, "Children Stolen by Chilean Dictatorship Finally Come to Light," Inter Press Service, December 31, 2014, accessed April 18, 2020, https://tinyurl.com/ycavgofk; Sarah Malm, "The Stolen Children: 'Hundreds' of Babies Were Taken from Their Mothers to Be Adopted in Sweden through an Agency Later Run by the Man Readying Himself to Become Prime Minister," *Daily Mail*, January 2, 2019, accessed April 18, 2020, https://bit.ly/34OvYXe; Peter Kornbluh, *The Pinochet File: A Declassified Dossier* on *Atrocity and Accountability* (New York: New Press, 2003), 169–170, Comisión Nacional sobre Prisión Política y Tortura, *Informe de la Comisión Nacional sobre Prisión Política y Tortura (Valech I)* (Santiago, CL: Ministerio del Interior, 2005); Editors, "Augusto Pinochet," Encyclopaedia Britannica, accessed April 18, 2020, https://www.britannica.com/biography/Augusto-Pinochet; James Petras and Steve Vieux, "The Chilean "Economic Miracle": An Empirical Critique," *Critical Sociology* 17, no. 2 (July 1990): 57–72; Pointblank, "Strange Defeat: the Chilean Revolution, 1973," libcom.org, accessed April 18, 2020, https://libcom.org/library/strange-defeat-chilean-revolution-1973-pointblank.

September 11, 2017 "We Are Being Oppressed, Taxi Hailing Apps Drivers Say," *Daily Nation*, September 11, 2017, accessed April 18, 2020, https://tinyurl.com/y8k7undr; "Uber Drivers in Kenya on Indefinite Strike," libcom.org, accessed April 18, 2020, https://libcom.org/news/uber-drivers-kenya-indefinite-strike-21092017; Benjamin Muriuki, "Digital Taxi Operators to Begin Strike Today," Citizen Digital, July 15, 2019, accessed April 18, 2020, https://citizentv.co.ke/news/digital-taxi-operators-to-begin-strike-today-263902.

September 12, 1945 Martin Hart-Landsberg, *Korea: Division, Reunification, and U.S. Foreign Policy* (New York: Monthly Review Press, 1998).

September 12, 1969 John Lauritsen, "The First Gay Liberation Front Demonstration," GayToday.com, accessed April 18, 2020, http://gaytoday.com/viewpoint/011904vp.asp.

September 13, 1911 Dave Marson, "Children's Strikes in 1911," libcom.org, accessed April 18, 2020, https://libcom.org/history/childrens-strikes-1911.

September 13, 1971 "1971: The Attica Prison Uprising," libcom.org, September 10, 2006, accessed April 18, 2020, https://libcom.org/history/1971-the-attica-prison-uprising; Larry Getlen, "The True Story of the Attica Prison Riot," *New York Post*, August 20, 2016, accessed April 18, 2020, https://nypost.com/2016/08/20/the-true-story-of-the-attica-prison-riot.

September 14, 1960 Larry Devlin, *Chief of Station Congo: Fighting the Cold War in a Hot Zone* (New York: Public Affairs, 2007); Agence France-Presse, "Apology for Lumumba Killing," *New York Times*, February 6, 2002, accessed April 18, 2020, https://tinyurl.com/y8psk456; "Memorandum for the Record," National Security Archive, February 14, 1972, accessed April 18, 2020, http://www.gwu.edu/~nsarchiv/NSAEBB/NSAEBB222/top06.pdf.

September 14, 1989 Youth Greens, *Anarchism and AIDS Activism* (Minneapolis: Youth Green Clearinghouse, nd), accessed April 18, 2020, https://libcom.org/files/Anarchism_and_AIDS_Activism_Reduced.pdf; "ACTUP Capsule History 1989," ACT UP Historical Archive, accessed April 18, 2020, https://actupny.org/documents/cron-89.html; Paul Finkelman, *Encyclopedia of American Civil Liberties: A-F* (Milton Park, UK: Taylor & Francis, 2006), 26.

September 15, 1845 "Pittsburgh Women in Organized Labor @ Pitt Archives: the Early Years," University of Pittsburgh, accessed April 18, 2020, https://pitt.libguides.com/pittsburghwomen_organizedlabor/early_history; Erik Loomis, "This Day in Labor History: September 15, 1845," Lawyers, Guns & Money, September 15, 2017, accessed April 18, 2020, https://www.lawyersgunsmoneyblog.com/2017/09/day-labor-history-september-15-1845; "Allegheny Cotton Mill Strikes Historical Marker," ExplorePAhistory.com, accessed April 18, 2020, http://explorepahistory.com/hmarker.php?markerId=1-A-BD.

September 15, 1954 Crawford Morgan, "Excerpts of Congressional Testimony," Abraham Lincoln Brigade Archives, accessed April 18, 2020, https://tinyurl.com/y7s2mdcc.

September 16, 1923 Patricia Morley, *The Mountain Is Moving: Japanese Women's Lives* (Vancouver: University of British Columbia Press, 1999), 19; Anarchist Federation, "Noe, Ito, 1895–1923," *Organize!* 59, accessed April 18, 2020, https://libcom.org/history/articles/1895-1923-ito-noe.

September 16, 1973 Adam Augustyn, "Victor Jara," Encyclopaedia Britannica, accessed April 18, 2020, https://www.britannica.com/biography/Victor-Jara; "Victor Jara Killing: Nine Chilean Ex-Soldiers Sentenced," BBC News, July 4, 2018, accessed April 18, 2020, https://www.bbc.com/news/world-latin-america-44709924; "Victor Jara: Military Officers Sentenced in Chile for 1973 Death," *Guardian*, July 3, 2018, accessed April 18, 2020, https://tinyurl.com/y7qwkcjv; J. Patrice McSherry, "¡Compañero Víctor Jara Presente!," *Jacobin*, November 11, 2019, accessed May 19, 2020, https://www.jacobinmag.com/2019/11/victor-jara-chile-protests-songs-salvador-allende.

September 17, 1849 "How Did Harriet Tubman Escape?" Harriet Tubman Historical Society, accessed April 18, 2020, http://www.harriet-tubman.org/escape; "Short Biography," Harriet Tubman Historical Society, accessed April 18, 2020, http://www.harriet-tubman.org/short-biography; Kate Clifford Larson, *Bound for the Promised Land: Harriet Tubman, Portrait of an American Hero* (New York: Ballantine Books, 2004).

September 17, 1922 Cathal Brennan, "The Postal Strike of 1922," libcom.org, accessed April 18, 2020, https://libcom.org/history/postal-strike-1922.

September 18, 1963 "10,000 in Jakarta Attacked and Burned British Embassy," *New York Times*, September 19, 1963, accessed April 18, 2020, https://tinyurl.com/yd5nay48.

September 18, 1974 Victoria Aldunate Morales, "En Memoria de Flora Sanhueza Rebolledo: 'Ni dios ni patron ni marido,'" El Desconcierto, May 7, 2018, accessed April 18, 2020, https://tinyurl.com/y9bfxfvf.

September 19, 1793 Bob Corbett, "The Haitian Revolution, Part II," Webster University, accessed April 18, 2020, http://faculty.webster.edu/corbetre/haiti/history/revolution/revolution2.htm.

September 19, 2007 Prol-Position, "Occupied Bike Factory in Germany, 2007," *Wildcat* 79 (Winter 2007), accessed April 18, 2020, https://libcom.org/history/occupied-bike-factory-germany-2007; "First 'Strike Bikes' Roll Out of Occupied German Factory," DW, October 22, 2007, accessed April 18, 2020, https://www.dw.com/en/first-strike-bikes-roll-out-of-occupied-german-factory/a-2835642.

September 20, 1763 Anne Commire and Deborah Klezmer, *Women in World History: A Biographical Encyclopedia* (Waterford, CT: Yorkin Publications, 2002).

September 20, 1898 Edgar Rodrigues, "A History of the Anarchist Movement in Brazil," Kate Sharpley Library, accessed April 18, 2020, https://www.katesharpleylibrary.net/vq84ck.

September 21, 1945 Jeremy Brecher, "The World War II and Post-War Strike Wave," libcom.org, accessed April 18, 2020, https://libcom.org/history/world-war-ii-post-war-strike-wave.

September 21, 1976 "This Was Not an Accident. This Was a Bomb," *Washington Post*, September 20, 2016, accessed April 18, 2020, http://www.washingtonpost.com/sf/national/2016/09/20/this-was-not-an-accident-this-was-a-bomb.

September 22, 1912 "La Casa del Obrero Mundial," Historia Sindical, updated December 13, 2012, accessed September 3, 2019, unavailable April 18, 2020, http://www.conampros.gob.mx/historiasind_03.html; "Anarcho-Syndicalists in the Mexican Revolution: The Casa del Obrero Mundial," libcom.org, accessed April 18, 2020, https://libcom.org/history/anarcho-syndicalists-mexican-revolution-casa-del-obrero-mundial.

September 22, 1918 Tico Jossifort, "The Revolt at Radomir," *Revolutionary History* 8, no. 2 (2002), accessed April 18, 2020, https://tinyurl.com/ya8h2cwf.

September 23, 1945 Ngo Van Xuyet, "1945: The Saigon Commune," libcom.org, accessed April 18, 2020, https://libcom.org/history/articles/saigon-commune-1945.

September 23, 1969 Robert Lumley, *States of Emergency: Cultures of Revolt in Italy from 1968 to 1978* (London: Verso, 1990), accessed April 18, 2020, https://bit.ly/3bmylTn.

September 24, 1934 Howard A Dewitt, "The Filipino Labor Union: The Salinas Lettuce Strike of 1934," *Amerasia* 5, no. 2 (1978): 1–21.

September 24, 2003 Conal Urquhart, "Israeli Pilots Refuse to Fly Assassination Missions," *Guardian*, September 25, 2003, accessed April 18, 2020, https://www.theguardian.com/world/2003/sep/25/israel.

September 25, 1968 Linda Holden Givens, "Seattle Black Panther Party Protests Gun-Control Bill in Olympia on February 28, 1969," History Link, October 16, 2018, accessed April 18, 2020, https://historylink.org/File/20649.

September 25, 2005 Gregor Gall, *Sex Worker Unionization: Global Developments, Challenges and Possibilities* (London: Palgrave Macmillan, 2016), chapter 7, accessed April 18, 2020, https://libcom.org/history/sex-work-organisation-global-south.

September 26, 1919 Peter Arshinov, *History of the Makhnovist Movement, 1918–1921* (Detroit: Black & Red, 1974), accessed April 19, 2020, https://libcom.org/history/history-makhnovist-movement-1918-1921-peter-arshinov.

September 26, 1955 Antonio Tellez, *Sabate: Guerrilla Extraordinary* (London: Davis-Poynter Publishers, 1974), accessed April 19, 2020, https://libcom.org/history/sabate-guerrilla-extraordinary-antonio-tellez.

September 27, 1915 "Hellraisers Journal: 5,000 Chicago Garment Workers on Strike, 30,000 More Will Soon Be Called Out," Daily Kos, September 28, 2015, accessed April 19, 2020, https://tinyurl.com/y9hxycyo; "1915: Clothing Workers Strike on S Green Street," Homicide in Chicago 1870–1930, accessed April 19, 2020, http://homicide.northwestern.edu/historical/timeline/1915/73.

September 27, 1917 "Industrial Workers of Africa (IWA)," South African History Online, accessed July 16, 2019, unavailable April 19, 2020, https://www.sahistory.org.za/organisations/industrial-workers-africa-iwa.

September 28, 1975 Jenny Bourne, "The 1975 Spaghetti House Siege: Making Rhetoric Real," *Race & Class* 53, no. 2 (October 2011): 113, accessed April 19, 2020, http://libcom.org/history/1975-spaghetti-house-siege-making-rhetoric-real-jenny-bourne; "1975: London's Spaghetti House Siege Ends," BBC Home, accessed April 19, 2020, http://news.bbc.co.uk/onthisday/hi/dates/stories/october/3/newsid_4286000/4286414.stm.

September 28, 1991 Bharat Dogra, "Remembering Shankar Guha Niyoga, The Legendary Labour Leader of Chhattisgarh," Wire, September 28, 2016, accessed April 19, 2020, https://thewire.in/labour/shankar-guha-niyogi; V. Venkatesan, "A Verdict and Some Questions," *Frontline* 22, no. 5 (February–March 2005), accessed May 20, 2020, https://tinyurl.com/ya3j2yaj.

September 29, 1920 "Jose Domingo Gomez Rojas (1896–1920)," Memoria Chilena, accessed April 19, 2020, http://www.memoriachilena.gob.cl/602/w3-article-3476.html.

September 29, 2007 Ed Goddard, "Mahalla Strikers Score Victory," libcom.org, September 29, 2007, accessed April 19, 2020, https://libcom.org/news/mahalla-strikers-score-victory-29092007; Joel Beinin, "The Militancy of Mahalla al-Kubra," Middle East Report Online, September 29, 2007, accessed April 19, 2020, https://merip.org/2007/09/the-militancy-of-mahalla-al-kubra.

September 30, 1918 Christian Koller, "Labour, Labour Movements, Trade Unions and Strikes (Switzerland)," updated October 29, 2015, International Encyclopedia of the First World War, accessed April 19, 2020, https://tinyurl.com/y8qbokng.

September 30, 1919 Nan Elizabeth Woodruff, "The Forgotten History of America's Worst Racial Massacre," *New York Times*, September 30, 2019, accessed April 19, 2020, https://www.nytimes.com/2019/09/30/opinion/elaine-massacre-1919-arkansas.html; "Elaine Massacre of 1919," Encyclopedia of Arkansas, updated May 11, 2019, accessed April 19, 2020, https://encyclopediaofarkansas.net/entries/elaine-massacre-of-1919-1102.

October

October 1, 1935 Richard Hart, *Labour Rebellions in the 1930s in the British Caribbean* (London: Socialist History Society, 2002).

October 1, 1946 "The Koreas," Lumen: Boundless World History, accessed April 19, 2020, https://courses.lumenlearning.com/boundless-worldhistory/chapter/the-koreas.

October 2, 1937 Marlon Bishop and Tatiana Fernandez, "80 Years On, Dominicans and Haitians Revisit Painful Memories of Parsley Massacre," NPR, October 7, 2017, accessed April 19, 2020, https://tinyurl.com/yb93muws.

October 2, 1968 "La noche más triste de Tlatelolco, 2 de Octubre de 1968," Posta, October 2, 2017, accessed April 19, 2020, https://tinyurl.com/y82vswrx; "Mexico's 1968 Massacre: What Really Happened?" NPR, December 1, 2008, accessed April 19, 2020, https://www.npr.org/templates/story/story.php?storyId=97546687; Kate Doyle, "Tlatelolco Massacre: U.S. Documents on Mexico and the Events of 1968," National Security Archive Electronic Briefing Book 99 (October 10, 2003), accessed April 19, 2020, https://nsarchive2.gwu.edu/NSAEBB/NSAEBB99.

October 3, 1935 Editors, "Italo-Ethiopian War," Encyclopaedia Britannica, accessed April 19, 2020, https://www.britannica.com/event/Italo-Ethiopian-War-1935-1936.

October 3, 1952 Caroline Elkins, *Imperial Reckoning: The Untold Story of Britain's Gulag in Kenya* (New York: Henry Holt, 2010).

October 4, 1936 Harriet Sherwood, "'I'd Do It All Over Again': Last Hurrah for the Veterans of Cable Street," *Guardian*, September 25, 2016, accessed April 19, 2020, https://tinyurl.com/jka5kv2; "The Battle of Cable Street: 80 Years On," Hope Not Hate, October 4, 2016, accessed July 29, 2019, http://www.cablestreet.uk.

October 4, 1939 Paul Avrich, *Anarchist Voices: An Oral History of Anarchism in America* (Oakland: AK Press, 2005), 175–88; Attilio Bortolotti and Rossella Di Leo, "Between Canada and the USA: A Tale of Immigrants and Anarchists," *Bollettino Archivio G. Pinelli* 24 (December 2004), accessed April 19, 2020, https://www.katesharpleylibrary.net/8pk1h4; Vivian Gornick, *Emma Goldman: Revolution as a Way of Life* (New Haven, CT: Yale University Press, 2011), 137–38.

October 5, 1789 "Women's March to Versailles 1789," French Revolution II, accessed April 19, 2020, https://tinyurl.com/y9zsmkr4; Jennifer Llewellyn and Steve Thompson, "The October March on Versailles," Alpha History, July 27, 2018, accessed April 19, 2020, https://alphahistory.com/frenchrevolution/october-march-on-versailles.

October 5, 1945 "Strikers during the Conference of Studio Unions Strike against all Hollywood Studios, Los Angeles, October 19, 1945," UCLA, accessed April 19, 2020, https://tinyurl.com/y86hl5bs; "From the Archives: Hollywood's Bloody Friday," *Los Angeles Times*, October 3, 2019, accessed April 19, 2020, https://tinyurl.com/yaf9h8od.

October 6, 1976 Michael Peel, "Students Defy Thai Rulers to Mark Thammasat University Massacre," *Financial Times*, October 4, 2016, accessed April 19, 2020, https://www.ft.com/content/244a9ea8-8a00-11e6-8cb7-e7ada1d123b1; "Thailand 1976 Massacre Anniversary: Lynching Photo Both Dark Mark and Blind Spot for Thais," *Indian Express*, December 11, 2019, accessed April 19, 2020, https://tinyurl.com/y99l2op6.

October 6, 1985 "What Caused the Tottenham Broadwater Farm Riot?" BBC News, March 3, 2014, accessed April 19, 2020, https://www.bbc.com/news/uk-england-london-26362633.

October 7, 1944 Marcus Bennett, "Life in the Century's Midnight," *Jacobin*, accessed April 19, 2020, https://tinyurl.com/y9d5q8t6; "Sonderkommando Revolt—Auschwitz-Birkenau: 7 October 1944," Holocaust Education and Archive Research Team, accessed April 19, 2020, http://www.holocaustresearchproject.org/revolt/sonderevolt.html; Auschwitz Museum tweet, October 7, 2019, accessed April 19, 2020, https://twitter.com/AuschwitzMuseum/status/1181096658156826624.

October 7, 1985 "The Victoria Nurses' Strike, 1985," libcom.org, accessed April 19, 2020, https://libcom.org/history/articles/victoria-nurses-strike-1985; Liz Ross, "Dedication Doesn't Pay the Rent—The 1986 Victorian Nurses Strike," Australian Society for the Study of Labour History: Canberra, updated 2012, accessed April 19, 2020, https://tinyurl.com/y7xe5ke4.

October 8, 1967 Patricia G. Steinhoff, "Memories of New Left Protest, 2013," *Contemporary Japan* 25, no. 2 (August 2013): 127–65, accessed April 19, 2020, https://www.degruyter.com/downloadpdf/j/cj.2013.25.issue-2/cj-2013-0007/cj-2013-0007.pdf; Patricia G. Steinhoff, "Student Protest in the 1960s," *Social Science Japan* 15 (March 1999).

October 8, 1970 *The Angry Brigade 1967–1984: Documents and Chronology* (London: Elephant Editions, 1985 [1978]), accessed April 19, 2020, https://libcom.org/history/angry-brigade-documents-chronology.

October 9, 1912 Brendan Maslauskas Dunn, "In November We Remember: The Centennial of the 1912 Little Falls Textile Strike," *Industrial Worker* 109, no. 9 (November 2012), accessed April 19, 2020, https://tinyurl.com/y9pmnfnb; "The Red Sweater Girls of 1912," *Little Falls Evening Times*, June 20, 1911, accessed April 19, 2020, https://upstateearth.blogspot.com/2013/01/the-red-sweater-girls-of-1912.html.

October 9, 1945 Richard Cleminson, "Spanish Anti-Fascist 'Prisoners of War' in Lancashire, 1944–46," *International Journal of Iberian Studies* 22, no. 3 (December 2009), accessed April 19, 2020, https://libcom.org/history/spanish-anti-fascist-prisoners-war-lancashire-1944-46; "Spanish Nationals (Detention)," Hansard 414 cc47-8W, October 9, 1945, accessed April 19, 2020, http://hansard.millbanksystems.com/written_answers/1945/oct/09/spanish-nationals-detention.

October 10, 1947 Aurora Muñoz, "French West African Rail Workers Strike for Benefits, 1947–1948," Global Nonviolent Action Database, November 12, 2009, accessed April 19, 2020, https://tinyurl.com/y8cpmfrj.

October 10, 1971 Richard Boyle, *GI Revolts: The Breakdown of the US Army in Vietnam* (San Francisco: United Front Press, 1973), accessed April 19, 2020, https://libcom.org/history/gi-revolts-breakdown-us-army-vietnam; S. Brian Wilson, *Don't Thank Me for My Service* (Atlanta, GA: Clarity Press, 2018 [1980]), 328.

October 11, 1972 Mark Jones, "Hostage Stand-Off at the DC Jail, October 11, 1972," Boundary Stones, October 15, 2018, accessed April 19, 2020, https://blogs.weta.org/boundarystones/2018/10/15/hostage-standoff-dc-jail-october-11-1972; Michael Buchanan, "October 11, 1972, Inmates Riot Over Conditions at Washington DC Jail—Today in Crime History," DeThomasis & Buchanan, October 11, 2011, accessed October 11, 2018, unavailable April 19, 2020, http://reasonabledoubt.org/criminallawblog/entry/october-11-1972-inmates-riot-over-conditions-at-washington-dc-jail-today-in-crime-history; "Rebellion against System: DC Jail 1972," Washington Area Spark, accessed April 19, 2020, https://www.flickr.com/photos/washington_area_spark/sets/72157627531793620.

October 11, 1972 David Wilma, "Chicano Activists Occupy Abandoned School in Seattle, Which Will Become El Centro, on October 11, 1972," History Link, August 2, 2000, accessed April 19, 2020, http://www.historylink.org/File/2588; "El Centro de la Raza: News Coverage," Seattle Civil Rights & Labor History Project, accessed April 19, 2020, https://depts.washington.edu/civilr/mecha_news_centro.htm; Madeline Ostrander and Valerie Schloredt, "1972–74: Native Activists Fight for Their Rights to Fish," *Seattle Met*, November 21, 2017, accessed April 19, 2020, https://tinyurl.com/y8u322b8.

October 12, 1925 J.A. Zumoff, "The 1925 Tenants' Strike in Panama: West Indians, the Left, and the Labor Movement," *The Americas* 74, no. 4 (October 2017): 513–54, accessed April 19, 2020, https://bit.ly/2Ke0Jeu; "Panama Tenants Revolt," Juan Manuel Pérez, Encyclopedia.com, updated March 15, 2020, accessed April 19, 2020, https://tinyurl.com/y9ltryva.

October 12, 1972 Earl Caldwell, "Kitty Hawk Back at Home Port; Sailors Describe Racial Conflict," *New York Times*, November 29, 1972, accessed April 19, 2020, https://tinyurl.com/yadxjdmj; "Some Very Unhappy Ships," *New York Times*, November 12, 1972; Mark D. Faram, "Race Riot at Sea—1972 Kitty Hawk Incident Fueled Fleet-Wide Unrest," *Navy Times*, February 28, 2017, accessed April 19, 2020, https://tinyurl.com/yarzwphv.

October 13, 1157 BCE Joshua J. Mark, "The First Labor Strike in History," Ancient History Encyclopedia, July 4, 2017, accessed April 19, 2020, https://www.ancient.eu/article/1089; William F. Edgerton, "The Strikes in Ramses III's Twenty-Ninth Year," *Journal of Near Eastern Studies* 10, no. 3 (1951), 137–45; The Little Egyptologist tumblr, November 14, 2019, accessed February 19, 2020, https://tinyurl.com/y9zozbjt.

October 13, 1970 Linda Charlton, "FBI Seizes Angela Davis in Motel Here," *New York Times*, October 14, 1970, accessed April 19, 2020, http://movies2.nytimes.com/books/98/03/08/home/davis-fbi.html; Sean Peterson, "Angela Davis and the Marin County Courthouse Incident," Black Power in American History, accessed April 19, 2020, https://tinyurl.com/ybur3svu.

October 14, 1973 "1973: Thai Army Shoots Protesters," BBC Home, accessed April 19, 2020, http://news.bbc.co.uk/onthisday/hi/dates/stories/october/14/newsid_2534000/2534347.stm; Giles Ji Ungpakorn, "The 14 October 1973 Thai Uprising," Uglytruth-Thailand, October 14, 2014, accessed April 19, 2020, https://uglytruththailand.wordpress.com/2014/10/14/the-14th-october-1973-uprising.

October 14, 1977 "Anita Bryant's Pie to the Face" (video), NBC Universal Archives, June 9, 2014 [October 14, 1977], accessed April 19, 2020, https://www.youtube.com/watch?v=5tHGmSh7f-0; Cliff Jahr, "Anita Bryant's Startling Reversal," *Ladies Home Journal*, December 1980, 60–68; Tyler Ward, "Florida Gay Rights Activists Boycott Orange Juice, 1977–80," Global Nonviolent Action Database, accessed April 19, 2020, https://tinyurl.com/y7uovltz.

October 15, 1964 Ian Cobain, "Britain's Secret Wars," *Guardian*, September 8, 2016, accessed April 19, 2020, https://www.theguardian.com/uk-news/2016/sep/08/britains-secret-wars-oman;

"Politics in America," *Congressional Quarterly* (1969), 53; "Oman—Mortality rate," Index Mundi, accessed May 15, 2020, https://www.indexmundi.com/facts/oman/mortality-rate.

October 15, 1966 Garrett Albert Duncan, "Black Panther Party," Encyclopaedia Britannica, updated April 2, 2020, accessed April 19, 2020, https://www.britannica.com/topic/Black-Panther-Party; Richard Kreitner, "October 15, 1966: The Black Panther Party Is Founded," *Nation*, October 15, 2015, accessed April 19, 2020, https://www.thenation.com/article/october-15-1966-the-black-panther-party-is-founded; "Oct 15, 1966: Black Panther Party Founded," Zinn Education Project, accessed April 19, 2020, https://www.zinnedproject.org/news/tdih/black-panther-founded; Salamishah Tillet, "The Panthers' Revolutionary Feminism," *New York Times*, October 2, 2015, accessed April 19, 2020, https://tinyurl.com/ybm52ock.

October 16, 1859 Howard Zinn, *A People's History of the United States: 1492—Present* (New York: Harper & Row, 2009 [1980]), chapter 9, accessed, April 18, 2020, https://libcom.org/library/peoples-history-of-united-states-howard-zinn; "John Brown's Harpers Ferry Raid," American Battlefields Trust, accessed April 19, 2020, https://www.battlefields.org/learn/topics/john-browns-harpers-ferry-raid; Eugene L Meyer, "Five Black Men Raided Harpers Ferry with John Brown. They've Been Forgotten," *Washington Post*, October 13, 2019, accessed April 19, 2020, https://tinyurl.com/y9xqkthr.

October 16, 1968 Tommie Smith, *Silent Gesture* (Philadelphia: Temple University Press, 2007); Andrew Webster, "Finally, the Real Story about Peter Norman and the Black Power Salute," *Sydney Morning Herald*, October 20, 2018, accessed April 19, 2020, https://tinyurl.com/yafyfxf8; James Montague, "The Third Man: The Forgotten Black Power Hero," CNN, April 25, 2012, accessed April 19, 2020, https://tinyurl.com/y7uwfmca. Some sources date the event October 17 due to the time zone. In Mexico City, the date was October 16.

October 17, 1950 Carl R. Weinberg, "Salt of the Earth: Labor, Film, and the Cold War," *OAH Magazine of History* 24, no. 4 (October 2010): 41–45; Ronald Young, "Salt of the Earth Strike," Encyclopedia.com, updated April 17, 2020, accessed April 19, 2020, https://tinyurl.com/y9djct59.

October 17, 1961 Tahar Hani, "The Paris Massacre That Time Forgot, 51 Years On," France 24, October 17, 2012, accessed April 19, 2020, https://tinyurl.com/ybkpwlh2; "Le 17 octobre 1961, la réalité d'un massacre face à un mensonge d'Etat," *Le Monde*, October 16, 2001, accessed April 19, 2020, https://tinyurl.com/yd3srddv.

October 18, 1931 Eve Rosenhaft, "Beating the Fascists? The German Communists and Political Violence 1929–1933," libcom.org, accessed April 19, 2018, https://tinyurl.com/y9phomq5.

October 18, 1948 A. H. Raskin, "Talk Fails to End Beer Drivers' Row," *New York Times*, October 19, 1948, 17.

October 19, 1920 "Chronology: The Pre-War Korean Anarchist Movement, Part 1," *Libero International* 1 (January 1975), accessed April 15, 2020, https://libcom.org/library/chronology-pre-war-korean-anarchist-movement.

October 19, 1920 Edward Crouse, "Upheld by Force: Sylvia Pankhurst's Edition of 1920" (under-graduate thesis, Columbia University, April 4 2018), 4, accessed April 19, 2020, https://history.columbia.edu/wp-content/uploads/sites/20/2016/06/Crouse-Edward-Thesis.pdf.

October 20, 1877 David Fieldhouse, "For Richer, for Poorer?" in P.J. Marshall, ed., *The Cambridge Illustrated History of the British Empire* (Cambridge: Cambridge University Press, 1996), 108–46; *Imperial Gazetteer of India*, vol. 3 (Oxford: Clarendon Press, 1907), 488, accessed April 19, 2020, https://archive.org/details/in.ernet.dli.2015.207356/page/n3/mode/2up; David Hall-Matthews, "Historical Roots of Famine Relief Paradigms: Ideas on Dependency and Free Trade in India in the 1870s," *Disasters* 20, no. 3 (1996): 216–30; David Hall-Matthews, "Inaccurate Conceptions: Disputed Measures of Nutritional Needs and Famine Deaths in Colonial India," *Modern Asian Studies* 42, no. 1 (2008): 1–24; Mike Davis, *Late Victorian Holocausts* (London: Verso, 2001), 400; Adam Jones, *Genocide: A Comprehensive Introduction* (London: Routledge, 2016), chapter 2.

October 20, 1952 David Anderson, "Smallholder Agriculture in Colonial Kenya: The Official Mind and the Swynnerton Plan," *African Affairs* 87, no. 348 (July 1988); Caroline Elkins, *Imperial Reckoning: The Untold Story of Britain's Gulag in Kenya* (New York: Henry Holt, 2010); "The

Mau Mau Uprising, 1952–1956," South African History Online, accessed April 19, 2020, https://www.sahistory.org.za/article/mau-mau-uprising.

October 21, 1935 Richard Hart, *Labour Rebellions in the 1930s in the British Caribbean* (London: Socialist History Society, 2002).

October 21, 1970 Sonni Efron, "Japan OKs Birth Control Pill After Decades of Delay," *Los Angeles Times*, June 3, 1999, accessed April 19, 2020, http://articles.latimes.com/1999/jun/03/news/mn-43662; Masimi Itō, "Women of Japan Unite: Examining the Contemporary State of Feminism," *Japan Times*, October 3, 2015, accessed April 19, 2020, https://tinyurl.com/y8bbmukq; Oguma Eiji, "Japan's 1968: A Collective Reaction to Rapid Economic Growth in an Age of Turmoil," *The Asia-Pacific Journal* 13, no. 12/1 (March 2015), accessed April 19, 2020, http://apjjf.org/2015/13/11/Oguma-Eiji/4300.html.

October 22, 1905 José Antonio Gutiérrez Danton, "1872–1995: Anarchism in Chile," libcom.org, accessed April 16, 2020, https://libcom.org/history/articles/anarchism-in-chile.

October 22, 1972 Julia Smith, "An 'Entirely Different' Kind of Union: The Service, Office, and Retail Workers' Union of Canada (SORWUC), 1972–1986," *Labour/Le Travail* 73 (2014), accessed April 19, 2020, https://bit.ly/2YtKJNN.

October 23, 1901 Leónidas "Noni" Ceruti, "Maldita esa maldita costumbre de matar," La Izquierda Diario, October 20, 2017, accessed April 19, 2020, http://www.laizquierdadiario.com/Maldita-esa-maldita-costumbre-de-matar.

October 23, 1956 Peter Fryer, *Hungarian Tragedy* (London: New Park Publications, 1986 [1957]), accessed April 19, 2020, https://libcom.org/library/hungarian-tragedy-peter-fryer; Andy Anderson, *Hungary '56* (Oakland: AK Press, 2002 [1964]), accessed April 19, 2020, https://libcom.org/library/hungary-56-andy-anderson; "1956: Hungarians Rise Up against Soviet Rule," BBC Home, accessed April 19, 2020, http://news.bbc.co.uk/onthisday/hi/dates/stories/october/23/newsid_3140000/3140400.stm.

October 24, 1975 "Iceland: Women Strike," *New York Times*, October 25, 1975, accessed April 19, 2020, https://www.nytimes.com/1975/10/25/archives/iceland-women-strike.html; Kirstie Brewer, "The Day Iceland's Women Went on Strike," BBC News, October 23, 2015, accessed April 19, 2020, https://www.bbc.com/news/magazine-34602822.

October 24, 2007 Gregor Gall, *Sex Worker Unionization: Global Developments, Challenges and Possibilities* (London: Palgrave Macmillan, 2016), chapter 7, accessed April 18, 2020, https://libcom.org/history/sex-work-organisation-global-south.

October 25, 1983 "Hayes Cottage Hospital Occupation, 1983," Hayes People's History, November 27, 2006, accessed April 19, 2020, https://ourhistory-hayes.blogspot.com/search?q=Hayes+Cottage+hospital+occupation.

October 25, 1983 "Invasion of Grenada," *New York Times*, October 26, 1983, accessed April 19, 2020, https://tinyurl.com/ycxkhb5v; Ronald H. Cole, *Operation Urgent Fury: Grenada* (Washington, DC: Joint History Office, Office of the Chairman of the Joint Chiefs of Staff, 1997), accessed April 19, 2020, https://tinyurl.com/y7ve2f5m; "1983: US Troops Invade Grenada," BBC Home, accessed April 19, 2020, http://news.bbc.co.uk/onthisday/hi/dates/stories/october/25/newsid_3207000/3207509.stm.

October 26, 1977 Dilip Bobb, "Swadeshi Cotton Mills in Kanpur Explodes in an Unprecedented Paroxysm of Violence," *India Today*, October 30, 2014, accessed April 19, 2020, https://tinyurl.com/y7zsctjf; "India: Leaflet on 1977 Swadeshi Mill Police Firing in Kanpur," South Asia Citizens Web, October 10, 2007, accessed April 19, 2020, http://www.sacw.net/article2320.html; "The Cycle of Struggle 1973 to 1979 in India," GurgaonWorkersNews 60 (November 2013), accessed April 17, 2020, https://libcom.org/history/cycle-struggle-1973-1979-india.

October 26, 1983 Tony Ellis, "The Northwood and Pinner Community Hospital—a Potted History," *Northwood Residents' Association Newsletter* 151 (October 2011): 13, accessed April 19, 2020, https://www.northwoodresidents.co.uk//images/stories/DocsLink/Newsletters/oct11.pdf; "The Northwood and Pinner Hospital Occupation, 1983," libcom.org, accessed April 19, 2020, https://libcom.org/history/northwood-pinner-hospital-occupation-1983.

October 27, 1962 Nicola Davis, "Soviet Submarine Officer Who Averted Nuclear War Honoured with Prize," *Guardian*, October 27, 2017, accessed April 19, 2020, https://tinyurl.com/yd6b8qa5; Robert Krulwich, "You (and Almost Everyone You Know) Owe Your Life to This Man," *National Geographic*, March 24, 2016, accessed April 19, 2020, https://tinyurl.com/y8kngdc4.

October 27, 1970 Public Law 91-513-Oct. 27, 1970, goveinfo.gov, accessed April 19, 2020, https://www.govinfo.gov/content/pkg/STATUTE-84/pdf/STATUTE-84-Pg1236.pdf; Tom LoBianco, "Report: Aide Says Nixon's War on Drugs Targeted Blacks, Hippies," CNN, March 24, 2016, accessed April 19, 2020, https://tinyurl.com/ybp22w2d.

October 28, 1916 "Conscription Referendums, 1916 and 1917," National Archives of Australia, 2017, accessed November 19, 2018, unavailable April 19, 2020, http://www.naa.gov.au/collection/fact-sheets/fs161.aspx; "E19: The IWW in Australia" (podcast), *Working Class History*, January 28, 2019, accessed April 19, 2020, https://workingclasshistory.com/2019/01/28/e19-the-iww-in-australia.

October 28, 2016 Nadir Bouhmouch, "The Rif and the Moroccan State's Economic Pressure Cooker," *Counterpunch*, July 14, 2017, accessed April 19, 2020, https://tinyurl.com/y8ycwv39; "La mort d'un vendeur de poissons dans une opération de police choque le Maroc," *Le Monde*, October 30, 2016, accessed April 19, 2020, https://tinyurl.com/ycaqob67.

October 29, 1918 Gabriel Kuhn, *All Power to the Councils! A Documentary History of the German Revolution of 1918–1919* (Oakland: PM Press, 2012), 3.

October 29, 1940 "Abdol Hossein Sardari (1895–1981)," Holocaust Encyclopedia, accessed April 19, 2020, https://www.ushmm.org/wlc/en/article.php?ModuleId=10007452.

October 30, 1919 "Working Home Blind Threaten to Strike; Inmates of Pennsylvania Institution Demand More Pay for Making Brooms," *New York Times*, October 31, 1919, 3, accessed April 19, 2020, https://nyti.ms/2VY4dsp.

October 30, 1944 Annette B. Fromm, "Hispanic Culture in Exile: Sephardic Life in the Ottoman Balkans," in Zion Zohar, ed., *Sephardic and Mizrahi Jewry: From the Golden Age of Spain to Modern Times* (New York: New York University Press, 2005), 162; Evangelos Kofos, "The Impact of the Macedonian Question on Civil Conflict in Greece, 1943–1949," in John O. Iatrides and Linda Wrigley, eds., *Greece at the Crossroads: The Civil War and Its Legacy* (University Park: Pennsylvania State University Press, 1995), 288.

October 31, 1978 "Key Moments in Iran 1979 Islamic Revolution," Associated Press, February 11, 2019, accessed April 19, 2020, https://www.apnews.com/3c3e6ec7476240978080842a0329bcee; Misagh Parsa, *Democracy in Iran: Why It Failed and How It Might Succeed* (Cambridge, MA: Harvard University Press, 2016), 76.

October 31, 1986 Liz Ross, "Dedication Doesn't Pay the Rent—The 1986 Victorian Nurses Strike," Australian Society for the Study of Labour History: Canberra, updated 2012, accessed April 19, 2020, https://tinyurl.com/y7xe5ke4.

November

November 1, 1954 "Algerian War of Independence from France Begins," *Guardian*, November 2, 2015, accessed April 19, 2020, https://tinyurl.com/ycwb6xy2; "The Algerian War of Independence Begins," South African History Online, accessed April 19, 2020, https://www.sahistory.org.za/dated-event/algerian-war-independence-begins.

November 1, 1972 Bennie Bunsee, "Women in Struggle: The Mansfield Hosiery Strike," *Spare Rib* 21 (1974), accessed April 19, 2020, https://libcom.org/library/women-struggle-mansfield-hosiery-strike; Peter Braham, Ali Rattansi, and Richard Skellington, eds., *Racism and Antiracism: Inequalities, Opportunities and Policies* (Thousand Oaks, CA: SAGE Publications, 1992); "Mansfield Hosiery Mills Ltd," National Archives, accessed April 19, 2020, http://discovery.nationalarchives.gov.uk/details/r/5726a3db-0e77-4eec-aba0-6abe3008d85f.

November 2, 1912 "Site of Grabow Riot/Beauregard Regional Airport," Clio, accessed April 17, 2020, https://www.theclio.com/web/entry?id=48463; "1912 Grabow Riot Centennial Observation," July 7, 2012, Friends of DeRidder Army Air Base, accessed April 17, 2020, https://tinyurl.com/y7wgrfcj;" W.T. Block, "'Leather Britches' Smith and the Grabow Riot," Calcasieu

Parish, accessed April 17, 2020, http://theusgenweb.org/la/calcasieu/block/leatherbritches. html.

November 2, 1970 "Jane Fonda Accused of Smuggling," *New York Times*, November 4, 1970, accessed April 19, 2020, https://www.nytimes.com/1970/11/04/archives/jane-fonda-accused-of-smuggling.html; Jane Fonda, "Mug Shot," JaneFonda.com, March 26, 2009, accessed April 19, 2020, https://www.janefonda.com/mug-shot; "Jane Fonda 11/70," Smoking Gun, January 1, 2001, accessed April 19, 2020, http://www.thesmokinggun.com/mugshots/celebrity/hollywood/jane-fonda-1170-0; Mackenzie Wagoner, "Jane Fonda's 1970 Mugshot Started a Beauty Revolution 47 Years Ago Today," *Vogue*, November 3, 2017, accessed April 19, 2020, https://www.vogue.com/article/jane-fonda-hair-mugshot-1970-klute-anniversary-vietnam-war; Nikola Budanovic, "Jane Fonda Said about the Infamous Hanoi Jane Photo: 'I Made a Huge Mistake,'" War History Online, September 6, 2016, accessed April 19, 2020, https://tinyurl.com/y99rcwzl.

November 3, 1970 "Hollister Office Dynamited," *El Macriado* 4, no. 10 (November 1970): 14, accessed April 19, 2020, https://tinyurl.com/yag25phl.

November 3, 1979 Rebecca Boger, Cat McDowell, and David Gwynn, "The Greensboro Massacre," UNC Greensboro, accessed April 19, 2020, http://libcdm1.uncg.edu/cdm/essay1979/collection/CivilRights.

November 4, 1910 François Bonal, "Revolution in the Vineyards," Grand Marques & Maisons de Champagne, accessed April 19, 2020, https://tinyurl.com/y7c9e9wd; "La Révolte des vignerons en 1911 à Cumières," Cumieres, accessed April 19, 2020, https://www.cumieresenchampagne.com/historique/revolte-de-1911; Don and Petie Kladstrup, *Champagne* (New York: HarperCollins, 2006) 129–51; "We Buy Fake Champagne and the Vineyards Revolt," *New York Times*, February 12, 1911, 51, accessed April 19, 2020, https://timesmachine.nytimes.com/timesmachine/1911/02/12/issue.html.

November 4, 1913 Rosemary Taylor, *In Letters of Gold: The Story of Sylvia Pankhurst and the East London Federation of the Suffragettes in Bow* (London: Stepney Books, 1993), 22; "Sylvia Pankhurst and the East London Suffragettes," Inspiring City, November 25, 2015, accessed May 29, 2020, https://tinyurl.com/yb4f7x6l.

November 5, 1843 Jae Jones, "Carlota: Enslaved African Woman Leader of the 1843 Slave Rebellion Who Used a 'Machete' as Weapon," Black Then, November 14, 2018, accessed April 19, 2020, https://tinyurl.com/ycyfygqp; Myra Ann Houser, "Avenging Carlota in Africa: Angola and the Memory of Cuban Slavery," Ouachita Baptist University, January 2, 2015, 4–6, accessed April 19, 2020, https://scholarlycommons.obu.edu/cgi/viewcontent.cgi?article=1041&context=articles.

November 5, 1916 Margaret Riddle, "Everett Massacre (1916)," History Link, December 18, 2011, accessed April 19 2020, http://www.historylink.org/File/9981; Walt Crowley, "Five IWW Members and Two Deputies Die in Gunbattle Dubbed the Everett Massacre on November 5, 1916," History Link, March 1, 2003, accessed April 19, 2020, https://www.historylink.org/File/5326.

November 6, 1913 "Gandhi and the Passive Resistance Campaign 1907–1914," South African History Online, accessed April 19, 2020, http://www.sahistory.org.za/article/gandhi-and-passive-resistance-campaign-1907-1914.

November 6, 1986 "The Iran-Contra Affairs," Understanding the Iran-Contra Affair, accessed April 19, 2020, https://bit.ly/2WgM6Ng; Daniel Pipes, "Breaking the Iran/Contra Story," Daniel Pipes Middle East Forum, Spring 1987, accessed April 19, 2020, http://www.danielpipes.org/13852/breaking-the-iran-contra-story; "News Summary: Friday, November 1986," *New York Times*, November 7, 1986, accessed April 19, 2020, https://www.nytimes.com/1986/11/07/world/news-summary-friday-november-7-1986.html; "Iran-Contra Affair," Encyclopaedia Britannica, accessed April 19, 2020, https://www.britannica.com/event/Iran-Contra-Affair; Noam Chomsky, "The Contra War in Nicaragua," libcom.org, accessed April 19, 2020, https://libcom.org/history/1970-1987-the-contra-war-in-nicaragua.

November 7, 1917 The Learning Network, "Nov. 7, 1917: Russian Government Overthrown in Bolshevik Revolution," *New York Times*, November 7, 2011, accessed April 19, 2020, https://nyti.

ms/2KTs5Hi; "Timeline of the Russian Revolution," British Library, accessed April 19, 2020, https://www.bl.uk/russian-revolution/articles/timeline-of-the-russian-revolution.

November 7, 1968 Aileen Eisenberg, "Pakistani Students, Workers and Peasants Bring Down a Dictator, 1968–1969," Global Nonviolent Action Database, February 22, 2013, accessed April 19, 2020, https://bit.ly/2zNvMvH.

November 8, 1965 Dr. Paul Monaghan, "Britain's Shame: The Ethnic Cleansing of the Chagos Islands," Politics First, April 23, 2016, accessed May 28, 2020, https://tinyurl.com/y9q3t49g.

November 8, 2004 William Lawrence, "New Caledonia Strike to Reinstate Fired Workers, 2005," Global Nonviolent Action Database, March 28, 2011, accessed April 19, 2020, https://bit.ly/3bY4hhb; "Strike Action Hits Output at New Caledonia's SLN Nickel Plant," RNZ, November 9, 2005, accessed April 19, 2020, https://bit.ly/2VTeUMA.

November 9, 1918 "Long Live the Republic—November 9, 1919," DW, November 16, 2009, accessed April 19, 2020, https://www.dw.com/en/long-live-the-republic-november-9-1918/a-4746952; Gilles Dauvé and Denis Authier, *The Communist Left in Germany 1918–1921*, chapter 12, accessed April 15, 2020, https://libcom.org/library/communist-left-germany-1918-1921; Ralf Hoffrogge, *Working-Class Politics in the German Revolution: Richard Müller, the Revolutionary Shop Stewards and the Origins of the Council Movement* (Leiden, NL: Brill, 2014), 61–79.

November 9, 1988 William Pedreira, "Massacre de Volta Redonda completa 26 anos," CUT Brasil, November 7, 2014, accessed April 19, 2020, https://www.cut.org.br/noticias/memoria-de-luta-e-resistencia-1cbc; "29 anos do Massacre de Volta Redonda," Sindicato dosPortuários do Rio de Janeiro, November 9, 2017, accessed April 19, 2020, http://portuariosrio.org.br/29-anos-do-massacre-de-volta-redonda.

November 10, 1970 Alfonso A. Narvaez, "Young Lords Seize Lincoln Hospital Building," *New York Times*, July 15, 1970, accessed April 19, 2020, https://nyti.ms/3bVHRxh; "Palente! A Brief History of the Young Lords," libcom.org, accessed April 19, 2020, https://libcom.org/library/palante-brief-history-young-lords.

November 10, 1995 Editors, "Ken Saro Wiwa," Encyclopaedia Britannica, accessed April 19, 2020, https://www.britannica.com/biography/Ken-Saro-Wiwa; Jon Entine, "Seeds of NGO Activism: Shell Capitulates in Saro-Wiwa Case," NGO Watch, June 18, 2009, accessed April 19, 2020, https://bit.ly/2z4UEPq; Frank Aigbogun, "It Took Five Tries to Hang Saro Wiwa," *Independent*, November 13, 1995, accessed April 19, 2020, https://bit.ly/2Wmcp4J; Salil Tripathi, "Praise the Lord and Buy Insurance," *Index on Censorship* 34, no. 4 (November 2005): 188–192.

November 11, 1918 Christian Koller, "Labour, Labour Movements, Trade Unions and Strikes (Switzerland)," International Encyclopedia of the First World War, October 30, 2015, accessed April 19, 2020, https://libcom.org/history/world-war-i-struggles-switzerland.

November 11, 1948 A.H. Raskin, "Beer Flows Again as Strike Is Ended," *New York Times*, November 12, 1948, 1, 4.

November 12, 1977 "Why Reclaim the Night?" Reclaim the Night, accessed April 16, 2020, http://www.reclaimthenight.co.uk/why.html; Laura Mackenzie, "Leeds Women Marched through Streets to 'Reclaim the Night,'" *Guardian*, December 6, 2010, accessed April 19, 2020, https://www.theguardian.com/leeds/2010/dec/06/leeds-reclaim-the-night-women-march.

November 12, 1984 Philip Berrigan and Elizabeth McAlister, *The Time's Discipline: The Beatitudes and Nuclear Resistance* (Eugene, OR: Wipf & Stock Publishers, 2010 [1989]), 256; "Letters from Prison," *Peace*, December 1985, 5, accessed April 19, 2020, http://peacemagazine.org/archive/v01n9p05.htm.

November 13, 1909 Anny Cullum, "Theresa Garnett vrs. Winston Churchill," Bristol Radical History Group, accessed April 19, 2020, http://www.brh.org.uk/site/articles/theresa-garnette-vrs-winston-churchill; Lucienne Boyce, *The Bristol Suffragettes* (Bristol, UK: SilverWood, 2013), 35.

November 13, 1974 Jennifer Latson, "The Nuclear-Safety Activist Whose Mysterious Death Inspired a Movie," *Time*, November 13, 2014, accessed April 19, 2020, http://time.com/3574931/karen-silkwood; Richard L Rashke, *The Killing of Karen Silkwood: The Story Behind the Kerr-McGee Plutonium Case* (Ithaca, NY: Cornell University Press, 2000).

November 14, 1917 "'Night of Terror': The Suffragists Who Were Beaten and Tortured for Seeking the Vote," *Washington Post*, November 10, 2017, accessed April 19, 2020, https://wapo.st/2KQydQr; "Nov. 15, 1917: Suffragists Beaten and Tortured in the 'Night of Terror,'" Zinn Education Project, accessed April 19, 2020, https://www.zinnedproject.org/news/tdih/suffragists-beaten-and-tortured.

November 14, 1973 "November 17, 1973, Uprising of the Polytechnic," *Greek City Times*, November 17, 2018, accessed April 19, 2020, https://greekcitytimes.com/2018/11/17/november-17-1973-uprising-of-the-polytechnic/?amp; "Οι 24 νεκροί του Πολυτεχνείου: Τα σημεία που έχασαν την ζωή τους σε χάρτη," News 24 7, accessed April 19, 2020, https://www.news247.gr/ereyna-aytoi-einai-oi-24-nekroi-toy-polytechneioy.7533202.html; "1973: Army Deposes Hated Greek President," BBC Home, accessed April 19, 2020, http://news.bbc.co.uk/onthisday/hi/dates/stories/november/25/newsid_2546000/2546297.stm.

November 15, 1922 Proletarios Revolucionarios, "[Ecuador] November 15: Class War, Memory War!" Třídní Válka # Class War # Guerre de Classe, November 2014, accessed April 19, 2020, https://www.autistici.org/tridnivalka/ecuador-november-15-class-war-memory-war; Ronn F. Pineo, "Guayaquil General Strike 1922," Encyclopedia.com, updated March 9, 2020, accessed April 19, 2020, https://bit.ly/3d54VcX.

November 15, 2011 Nick Palazzolo, "Disabled Bolivians March to La Paz, 2011–2012," Global Nonviolent Action Database, April 10, 2013, accessed April 19, 2020, https://bit.ly/2xvQr6U.

November 16, 1984 "South Africa: Now and Then," libcom.org, accessed April 19, 2020, libcom.org/library/south-africa-now-then.

November 16, 1989 "Nov. 16, 1989: Jesuit Scholars/Priests and Staff Massacred in El Salvador," Zinn Education Project, accessed April 19, 2020, https://www.zinnedproject.org/news/tdih/scholars-priests-killed; "6 Priests Killed in a Campus Raid in San Salvador," *New York Times*, November 17, 1989, accessed April 19, 2020, https://nyti.ms/3aWnI8E.

November 17, 1915 Anarchist Federation, "1915: The Glasgow Rent Strike," libcom.org, accessed April 19, 2020, https://libcom.org/history/1915-the-glasgow-rent-strike; Brenda Grant, "A Woman's Fight: The Glasgow Rent Strike 1915" (honours thesis, University of the Highlands and Islands, 2018), accessed April 19, 2020, https://bit.ly/35mnTJo; "Mary Barbour," Their Names Will Be Remembered for Evermore, accessed April 19, 2020, https://www.firstworldwarglasgow.co.uk/index.aspx?articleid=11384.

November 17, 1983 "EZLN: 35 Anniversary of Its Foundation in a Chiapas Rainforest," telesurtv.net, November 17, 2018, accessed April 19, 2020, https://bit.ly/2WgVv7r; "A Commune in Chiapas? Mexico and the Zapatista Rebellion, 1994–2000," *Aufheben* 9 (Autumn 2000), accessed April 19, 2018, https://libcom.org/library/commune-chiapas-zapatista-mexico; "Zapatistas on Gay Rights: 'Let Those Who Persecute Be Ashamed!'" *Green Left* 368, July 21, 1999, accessed April 19, 2020, https://www.greenleft.org.au/content/zapatistas-gay-rights-let-those-who-persecute-be-ashamed.

November 18, 1965 "Feminism Friday: The Origins of the Word 'Sexism'" (blog), Finally, a Feminism 101 Blog, October 19, 2007, accessed April 19, 2020, https://bit.ly/2KOtbEb; F. Shapiro, "Historical Notes on the Vocabulary of the Women's Movement," *American Speech* 60, no. 1 (Spring 1985): 3–16.

November 18, 1967 Shelby L. Stanton, *The Rise and Fall of an American Army: U.S. Ground Forces in Vietnam 1965–1973* (New York: Ballantine Books, 2003), 215–16.

November 19, 1915 "1915: The Murder of Joe Hill," libcom.org, accessed April 20, 2020, https://libcom.org/history/1915-the-murder-of-joe-hill; William Adler, *The Man Who Never Died: The Life, Times and Legacy of Joe Hill, American Labour Icon* (London: Bloomsbury Publishing, 2011).

November 19, 1984 "PEMEX LPG Terminal, Mexico City, Mexico. November 19, 1984," Health and Safety Executive, accessed April 20, 2020, http://www.hse.gov.uk/comah/sragtech/casepemex84.htm.

November 20, 1913 Olga Alicia Aragón Castillo, "Merecen tres revolucionarias ser rescatadas del olvido," *La Jornada*, November 22, 2009, 27, accessed April 20, 2020, https://www.jornada.com.

mx/2009/11/22/estados/027n2est; Anarchist Federation, "Ortega, Margarita, ?–1914," *Organise!* 51, accessed April 20, 2020, https://libcom.org/history/articles/-1914-margarita-ortega.

November 20, 1969 "Nov. 20, 1969: Alcatraz Occupation," Zinn Education Project, accessed April 20, 2020, https://www.zinnedproject.org/news/tdih/alcatraz-occupation.

November 21, 1920 John Dorney, "Today in Irish History, Bloody Sunday, 21 November 1920," The Irish Story, November 21, 2011, accessed April 20, 2020, https://bit.ly/3bVxTMl.

November 21, 1922 Alan MacSimóin, "Magon, Ricardo Flores, 1873–1922," libcom.org, accessed April 20, 2020, https://libcom.org/history/magon-ricardo-flores-1873-1922; Andrew Grant Wood, "Death of a Political Prisoner: Revisiting the Case of Ricardo Flores Magón," University of Tulsa, 2005, accessed April 20, 2020, https://projects.ncsu.edu/project/acontracorriente/fall_05/Wood.pdf; David Poole, ed., *Land and Liberty: Anarchist Influences in the Mexican Revolution* (Montréal: Black Rose, 1977), 5.

November 22, 1919 "Nov. 22, 1919: Bogalusa Labor Massacre," Zinn Education Project, accessed April 20, 2020, https://www.zinnedproject.org/news/tdih/bogalusa-labor-massacre; Josie Alexandra Burks, "Bloody Bogalusa and the Fight for a Bi-Racial Lumber Union: A Study in the Burkean Rebirth Cycle" (master's thesis, University of Alabama, 2016), accessed April 20, 2020, https://ir.ua.edu/bitstream/handle/123456789/2580/file_1.pdf.

November 22, 1968 Oguma Eiji, "Japan's 1968: A Collective Reaction to Rapid Economic Growth in an Age of Turmoil," *Social Science Japan* 13, no. 12 (March 2015), accessed April 20, 2020, https://apjjf.org/2015/13/11/Oguma-Eiji/4300.html.

November 23, 1887 Stephen Kliebert, "The Thibodaux Massacre, 1887," libcom.org, accessed April 19, 2020, https://libcom.org/library/us-thibodaux-massacre-1887; Calvin Schermerhorn, "The Thibodaux Massacre Left 60 African Americans Dead and Spelled the End of Unionized Farm Labor in the South for Decades," *Smithsonian Magazine*, November 21, 2017, accessed April 19, 2020, https://bit.ly/2zR4LaT.

November 23, 1969 Chicago FBI DOJ memo: NW 55176 DocId: 32989646, United States Department of Justice, December 4, 1969, 191, accessed April 20, 2020, https://www.archives.gov/files/research/jfk/releases/docid-32989646.pdf#page=191; Wolfgang Saxon, "Luis Kutner, Lawyer Who Fought for Human Rights, Is Dead at 84," *New York Times*, March 4, 1993, accessed April 20, 2020, https://nyti.ms/3faHYHo.

November 24, 1995 Sam Lowry, "The French Pensions Strike, 1995," libcom.org, April 12, 2007, accessed April 19, 2020, https://libcom.org/history/french-pensions-strikes-1995; Dong Shin You, "French Public Sectors Strike against the Juppe Plan 1995," Global Nonviolent Action Database, accessed April 20, 2020, https://bit.ly/2KTfXGc; Martin Schludi, *The Reform of Bismarckian Pension Systems* (Amsterdam: Amsterdam University Press, 2005), 200–4; Glenn Hubbard and Tim Kane, *Balance: The Economics of Great Powers From Ancient Rome to Modern America* (New York: Simon & Schuster, 2013), 204.

November 24, 2010 G. Keeley, "General Strike Brings Portugal to Standstill as Bailout Fears Grow," *Times*, November 25, 2010, accessed April 20, 2020, https://bit.ly/2VTATTG; "Portugal Readies Austerity Measures," *New York Times*, March 8, 2010, accessed May 18, 2020, https://www.nytimes.com/2010/03/09/business/global/09escudo.html.

November 25, 1941 Alexander Mejstrik, "Urban Youth, National-Socialist Education and Specialised Fun: The Making of the Vienna Schlurfs 1941–44," in Axel Schildt and Detlef Siegfried, eds., *European Cities, Youth and the Public Sphere in the Twentieth Century* (London: Routledge, 2016); Anarchist Federation, "The Schlurfs—Youth against Nazism," Winter 2008, libcom.org, accessed April 20, 2020, https://libcom.org/history/schlurfs-%E2%80%93-youth-against-nazism; "E4: Anti-Nazi Youth Movements in World War II" (podcast), *Working Class History*, April 4, 2018, accessed April 20, 2020, https://bit.ly/2yklzq7.

November 25, 1960 Larry Rohter, "Santo Domingo Journal—The Three Sisters Avenged—A Dominican Drama," *New York Times*, February 15, 1997, accessed April 20, 2020, https://www.nytimes.com/1997/02/15/world/the-three-sisters-avenged-a-dominican-drama.html; Luigi Morris, "The Mirabal Sisters and the International Day for the Elimination of Violence against Women," *Left Voice*, November 25, 2017, accessed April 19, 2020, https://bit.ly/2YqXt.

November 26, 1926 Central Department of Research and Survey, National Council of the Churches of Christ in the United States of America, "End of the British Mine Strike," *Information Service* 6, no 3 (January 1927): 3; "The 1926 General Strike and the Defeat of the Miners," Spartacus Educational, accessed April 20, 2020, https://spartacus-educational.com/ExamIR23.htm.

November 26, 1938 "Association Football Match," ticket, Aid for Spain Committee—Pontypridd, 1938; Richard Burton Archives tweet, June 15, 2018, accessed April 20, 2020, https://twitter.com/SwanUniArchives/status/1007552303099011073.

November 27, 1835 Frank Ryan, "Pratt and Smith—The Last UK Men Hanged for Sodomy," Peter Tatchell Foundation, accessed April 20, 2020, https://www.petertatchellfoundation.org/pratt-smith-last-uk-men-hanged-for-sodomy; "The Execution of James Pratt and John Smith," British Library, accessed April 19, 2020, https://www.bl.uk/collection-items/the-execution-of-james-pratt-and-john-smith.

November 27, 1868 "Colonel George Custer Massacres Cheyenne on Washita River," History.com, November 16, 2009, accessed April 20, 2020, https://www.history.com/this-day-in-history/custer-massacres-cheyenne-on-washita-river; "Washita Battlefield," National Park Service, accessed April 20, 2020, https://www.nps.gov/waba/learn/historyculture/index.htm.

November 28, 1971 Dave Hann, *Physical Resistance: A Hundred Years of Anti-Fascism* (UK: Zero, 2013); "A History of the 62 Group," libcom.org, accessed May 20, 2020, https://libcom.org/history/history-62-group.

November 28, 1985 "1988 Shell Confidential Report: 'The Greenhouse Effect,'" ClimateFiles, accessed April 20, 2020, http://www.climatefiles.com/shell/1988-shell-report-greenhouse; Benjamin Franta, "Shell and Exxon's Secret 1980s Climate Change Warnings," *Guardian*, September 19, 2018, accessed April 19, 2020, https://bit.ly/2yiUnIs.

November 29, 1830 Stuart Booth, "Captain Swing Was Here!" libcom.org, March 19, 2017, accessed April 20, 2020, https://libcom.org/history/captain-swing-was-here.

November 29, 1864 Helen Hunt Jackson, "Helen Hunt Jackson's Account of Sand Creek" (1881), accessed April 20, 2020, https://bit.ly/2YpvZPT; Helen Hunt Jackson, *A Century of Dishonor: A Sketch of the United States Government's Dealings with Some of the Indian Tribes* (New York: Indian Head Books, 1994 [1889]), 344; Dee Brown, *Bury My Heart at Wounded Knee: An Indian History of the American West* (New York: Holt, Rinehart & Winston, 1970), 91.

November 30, 1961 Jacinto Valdés-Dapena Vivanco, Operation Mongoose: Prelude of a Direct Invasion on Cuba (Barcelona: Ruth, 2016); Nora Gamez Torres, "The CIA Offered Big Bucks to Kill Cuban Communists. For Fidel Himself? Just Two Cents," *Miami Herald*, October 27, 2017, accessed May 20, 2020, https://www.miamiherald.com/news/nation-world/world/americas/cuba/article181288881.html; Jane Franklin, *Cuba and the U.S. Empire: A Chronological History* (New York: NYU Press, 2016), 45.

November 30, 1966 "Barbados Independence Celebrations," Go Barbados, accessed April 20, 2020, https://barbados.org/indepen.htm; CR Sutton, "Continuing the Fight for Economic Justice: The Barbados Sugar Workers' 1958 Wildcat Strike," in C.R. Sutton, ed., *Revisiting Caribbean Labour: Essays in Honour of O. Nigel Bolland* (Kingston, JM: Ian Randle Publishers, 2005).

December

December 1, 1919 Keith Look, "T & T's First General Strike," *Hold the Fort* 6, no. 2 (June 1988), accessed April 20, 2020, http://www.workersunion.org.tt/our-history/historical-documents-1/1919-general-strike.

December 1, 1955 Editors, "Rosa Parks," Encyclopaedia Britannica, accessed April 20, 2020, https://www.britannica.com/biography/Rosa-Parks; Bahati Kuumba, "'You've Struck a Rock,' Gender and Transformation in the US and South Africa," *Gender & Society* 16, no. 4 (August 2002), accessed April 19, 2020, 504–23, https://libcom.org/files/You've%20Struck%20a%20Rock.pdf; Dara Lind, "This 50-Year-Old Article Shows How the Myth of Rosa Parks Was

Made," Vox, December 1, 2016, accessed April 19, 2020, https://www.vox.com/2015/12/2/9834798/rosa-parks-tired-civil-rights.

December 2, 1980 Larry Rohter, "4 Salvadorans Say They Killed US Nuns on Order of Military," *New York Times*, April 3, 1998, accessed April 20, 2020, https://nyti.ms/3dbMKlJ.

December 2, 1984 Luke David, "Night of the Gas: Bhopal India," *New Internationalist* (December 2002), accessed April 20, 2020, https://libcom.org/library/night-gas-bhopal-india; Alan Taylor, "Bhopal: The World's Worst Industrial Disaster, 30 Years Later," *Atlantic*, December 2, 2014, accessed April 20, 2020, https://bit.ly/35orF4Z.

December 3, 1944 Ed Vulliamy and Helena Smith, "Athens 1944: Britain's Dirty Secret," *Guardian*, November 30, 2014, accessed April 20, 2020, https://bit.ly/3aXp4jw; Stephen Pritchard, "The Readers' Editor on . . . Athens, 1944," *Observer*, March 28, 2015, accessed April 20, 2020, https://www.theguardian.com/media/2015/mar/28/readers-editor-on-athens-44-british-army.

December 3, 1946 Stan Weir, "The Oakland General Strike," libcom.org, accessed April 19, 2020, https://libcom.org/library/oakland-general-strike-stan-weir; Philip J. Wolman, "The Oakland General Strike of 1946," *Southern California Quarterly* 57, no. 2 (1975): 147–78, accessed April 19, 2020, https://www.jstor.org/stable/41170592.

December 4, 1956 "Andy Anderson, *Hungary 56*, (London: Solidarity, 1964), chapter 21, accessed April 19, 2020, https://libcom.org/library/Hungary5621; "Hungarian Women Defy Russian Tanks to March on Budapest," accessed April 20, 2020, https://www.theguardian.com/world/2015/dec/05/hungary-russia-invasion-1956-budapest.

December 4, 1969 FBI Chicago Illinois Memo #60604, US Department of Justice, December 8, 1969, in SSC Request 8/20/75 Part II Item 3, 200–2, accessed April 20, 2020, https://www.archives.gov/files/research/jfk/releases/docid-32989646.pdf; "The FBI Sets Goals for COINTELPRO," HERB: Social History for Every Classroom, accessed April 20, 2020, https://herb.ashp.cuny.edu/items/show/814; Jakobi Williams, *From the Bullet to the Ballot: The Illinois Chapter of the Black Panther Party and Racial Coalition Politics in Chicago* (Chapel Hill: University of North Carolina Press, 2013).

December 5, 1955 Daniel Maguire, "More Than a Seat on the Bus," We Are History, December 1, 2015, accessed April 20, 2020, http://werehistory.org/rosa-parks; "Montgomery Bus Boycott," Martin Luther King, Jr. Research and Education Institute, accessed April 20, 2020, https://kinginstitute.stanford.edu/encyclopedia/montgomery-bus-boycott.

December 5, 2008 Jessica Siegel, "Chicago Workers Sit-in, Gain Benefits after Factory Shutdown, 2008 (Republic Windows and Doors)," Global Nonviolent Action Database, February 21, 2013, accessed April 20, 2020, https://bit.ly/2VZ9wb7.

December 6, 1918 Steven Johns, "The British West Indies Regiment Mutiny, 1918," libcom.org, August 7, 2013, accessed April 20, 2020, https://libcom.org/history/british-west-indies-regiment-mutiny-1918; Richard W.P. Smith, "The British West Indies Regiment Mutiny at Taranto and Multicultural Memories of the First World War," in *Voices of the Homes Fronts*, National Archives, United Kingdom, updated December 13, 2018, accessed April 20, 2020, http://research.gold.ac.uk/25273.

December 6, 1989 "The Montreal Massacre," CBC Digital Archives, December 6, 1989, accessed April 20, 2020, https://bit.ly/2WjiIWv.

December 7, 1959 William Lawrence, "Fijian Oil Industry Workers Strike for Higher Wages and Benefits, 1959," Global Nonviolent Action Database, November 24, 2010, accessed April 20, 2020, https://bit.ly/2SrWJf8.

December 7, 2006 "Egyptian Textile Workers Confront the New Economic Order," Middle East Research and Information Project, accessed April 20, 2020, https://merip.org/2007/03/egyptian-textile-workers-confront-the-new-economic-order.

December 8, 1949 "Marseille Dockers Refuse to Load Arms Headed to Saudi Arabia," libcom.org, June 18, 2019, accessed April 20, 2020, https://libcom.org/news/marseille-dockers-refuse-load-arms-headed-saudi-arabia-18062019.

December 8, 2008 A.G. Schwarz, T. Sagris, and Void Network, *We Are an Image from the Future: The Greek Revolt of December 2008* (Oakland: AK Press, 2010), chapter 3, accessed April 20, 2020, https://bit.ly/2VWoT3G.

December 9, 1959 Ian Cobain, Owen Bowcott, and Richard Norton-Taylor, "Britain Destroyed Records of Colonial Crimes," *Guardian*, April 18, 2012, accessed April 20, 2020, https://www.theguardian.com/uk/2012/apr/18/britain-destroyed-records-colonial-crimes.

December 9, 1987 Edward Said, "Intifada and Independence," in Zachary Lockman and Joel Beinin, eds., *Intifada: The Palestinian Uprising Against Israeli Occupation* (Cambridge, MA: South End Press, 1989) 5; "Behind the 21st Century Intifada," *Aufheben* 10 (2002), accessed April 20, 2020, https://libcom.org/library/21st-century-intifada-israel-palestine-aufheben.

December 10, 1924 Carl Nash, "Gay and Lesbian Rights Movements," Encyclopedia of Chicago, accessed April 20, 2020, http://www.encyclopedia.chicagohistory.org/pages/508.html; "Henry Gerber House National Historic Landmark," National Park Service, accessed April 20, 2020, https://www.nps.gov/articles/henry-gerber-house-national-historic-landmark.htm.

December 10, 1984 "Bronski Bash Nets £5,000 for Miners," *Capital Gay*, December 14, 1984, 1, accessed April 20, 2020, https://twitter.com/LGSMpride/status/1014042459012255744/photo/1; Colin Clews, "1984. Lesbians and Gays Support the Miners. Part One," Gay in the 80s, accessed April 20, 2020, https://www.gayinthe80s.com/2012/09/1984-lesbians-and-gays-support-the-miners-part-one/3.

December 11, 1981 Tim Golden, "Salvador Skeletons Confirm Reports of Massacre in 1981," *New York Times*, October 22, 1992, accessed April 20, 2020, https://nyti.ms/2SsSRdx.

December 11, 1983 "Your Greenham Chronology," YourGreenham.co.uk, accessed April 20, 2020, https://bit.ly/2yiLONN.

December 12, 1948 Mark Townsend, "Revealed: How Britain Tried to Legitimise Batang Kali Massacre," *Guardian*, May 6, 2012, accessed April 20, 2020, https://www.theguardian.com/world/2012/may/06/britain-batang-kali-massacre-malaysia; "Settle Massacre Case, Britain Told," Condemning Batang Kali Massacre, accessed April 20, 2020, https://batangkalimassacre.wordpress.com.

December 12, 1969 "1969-?: The Strategy of Tension in Italy," libcom.org, September 17, 2006, accessed April 20, 2020, https://libcom.org/history/articles/strategy-of-tension-italy; Philip Willan, "Three Jailed for 1969 Milan Bomb," *Guardian*, July 2, 2001, accessed April 20, 2020, https://www.theguardian.com/world/2001/jul/02/philipwillan.

December 13, 1905 Nick Heath, "1890–1924: Anarchism in Hungary," libcom.org, September 13, 2006, accessed April 20, 2020, https://libcom.org/history/articles/hungary-anarchism-1890-1924.

December 13, 1971 Max Rennebohm, "Ovambo Migrant Workers General Strike for Rights, Namibia: 1971–72," Global Nonviolent Action Database, October 18, 2009, accessed April 20, 2020, https://bit.ly/3f8nvCJ.

December 14, 1914 "Entre el dolor y la ira. La venganza de Antonio Ramón Ramón," accessed April 20, 2020, https://bit.ly/3bWYY1t.

December 14, 1951 "Bagel Famine Threatens in City; Labor Dispute Puts Hole in Supply," *New York Times*, December 17, 1951, 1; "Lox Strike Expert Acts to End the Bagel Famine," *New York Times*, December 18, 1951, 27; "Return of the Bagel Near as Drivers Settle Dispute," *New York Times*, February 7, 1952, 17.

December 15, 1890 Robert M. Utley, *The Last Days of The Sioux Nation* (New Haven, CT: Yale University Press, 2004), 158–60; "Sitting Bull Killed by Indian Police," History.com, accessed April 20, 2020, https://www.history.com/this-day-in-history/sitting-bull-killed-by-indian-police.

December 15, 1912 Steven Hirsch, "Anarcho-Syndicalism in Peru, 1905–1930," accessed April 20, 2020, https://libcom.org/library/anarcho-syndicalism-peru-1905-1930-steven-hirsch; Ángel Cappalletti, *Anarchism in Latin America*, Gabriel Palmer-Fernández, trans., (Oakland: AK Press, 1990), 131; Steven Hirsch, "Peruvian Anarcho-Syndicalism: Adapting Transnational Influences and Forging Counterhegemonic Practices, 1905–1930," in Steven Hirsch and Lucien Van Der Walt, eds., *Anarchism and Syndicalism in the Colonial and Postcolonial World, 1870–1940* (Leiden, NL: Brill, 2010).

December 16, 1871 Jayacintha Danaswamy, "Michel, Louise, 1830–1905," Workers Solidarity Movement, accessed April 20, 2020, https://libcom.org/history/michel-louise-1830-1905; "Louise Michel Biography," International Institute of Social History, accessed April 20, 2020, http://www.iisg.nl/collections/louisemichel/biography.php.

December 16, 1910 Pauls Bankovskis, "Peter the Painter (Janis Zhaklis) and the Siege of Sidney Street," Bulletin of the Kate Sharpley Library 50–51, (July 2007), accessed April 20, 2020, https://www.katesharpleylibrary.net/rjdgpg; Pietro Di Paola, *The Knights Errant of Anarchy: London and the Italian Anarchist Diaspora (1880–1917)* (Liverpool: Liverpool University Press, 2013), 115–16.

December 17, 1933 Slava Mogutin, "Gay in the Gulag," *Index on Censorship* 24, no. 1 (1995), accessed April 20, 2020, http://slavamogutin.com/gay-in-the-gulag; Resource Information Center, "Russia: Information on the Treatment of Homosexuals in Russia, Including Imprisonment and Involuntary Medical Treatment, and the Situation of HIV-Positive Citizens of Russia," United States Bureau of Citizenship and Immigration Services, accessed April 20, 2020, https://www.refworld.org/docid/3df0ba597.html; Professor Igor Kon, "Soviet Homophobia," gay.ru, 1998, accessed April 20, 2020, http://www.xgay.ru/english/history/kon/soviet.htm; Dan Healey, *Homosexual Desire in Revolutionary Russia: The Regulation of Sexual and Gender Dissent* (Chicago: University Of Chicago Press, 2001).

December 17, 1970 "1970–71: Uprising in Poland," libcom.org, October 31, 2008, accessed April 20, 2020, https://libcom.org/history/1970-71-uprising-poland; "1970 Gdynia Massacre of 42 Workers Remembered," Radio Poland, December 17, 2012, accessed April 20, 2020, http://archiwum.thenews.pl/1/9/Artykul/121690.

December 18, 2010 "Tunisia: People Power Overthrows Dictator Ben Ali," Workers Solidarity Movement, January 14, 2011, accessed April 20, 2020, http://www.wsm.ie/c/tunisia-people-power-overthrows-dictator-ben-ali; Kamal Eldin Osman Salih, "The Roots and Causes of the 2011 Arab Uprisings," *Arab Studies Quarterly* 35, no. 2 (2013): 184–206, accessed April 20, 2020, https://pdfs.semanticscholar.org/79bb/74a0476dda6d03e2879ba6e5370662a30c82.pdf.

December 18, 2012 "Sierra Leone Koidu Mine: Foreigners 'Holed Up' After Clashes," BBC News, December 19, 2012, accessed April 20, 2020, https://www.bbc.co.uk/news/world-africa-20781940.

December 19, 1996 "1993–1996: The Dublin Fight against Water Charges," Workers Solidarity Movement, accessed April 20, 2020, https://libcom.org/history/articles/dublin-water-charge-campaign-1996; Maol Muire Tynan, "Cabinet Set to Abolish Water Charges," *Irish Times*, December 19, 1996, accessed April 20, 2020, https://www.irishtimes.com/news/cabinet-set-to-abolish-water-charges-1.117314.

December 19, 2001 "Picket and Pot Banger Together—Class Recomposition in Argentina?" *Aufheben* 11, accessed April 20, 2020, https://libcom.org/library/argentina-aufheben-11; Jonathan Gilbert, "Debt Crisis: the Cost of Default—Rioting, Sieges and Death," *Telegraph*, June 14, 2012, accessed April 20, 2020, https://bit.ly/2VXTj5V.

December 20, 1960 Maurice Brinton, "Belgian General Strike Diary, 1960," libcom.org, accessed April 20, 2020, https://libcom.org/history/belgian-general-strike-diary-1960-maurice-brinton.

December 20, 1970 Jon Mitchell, "Military Policeman's 'Hobby' Documented 1970," *Japan Times*, December 17, 2011, accessed April 20, 2020, https://bit.ly/3da3NVA.

December 21, 1848 Magnus Magnusson, *Fakers, Forgers & Phoneys* (Edinburgh, SL: Mainstream Publishing, 2006), 231; Marion Smith Holmes, "The Great Escape from Slavery of Ellen and William Craft," *Smithsonian Magazine*, June 16, 2020, accessed April 20, 2020, https://bit.ly/3d9YPbf.

December 21, 1907 José Antonio Gutiérrez Danton, "1872–1995: Anarchism in Chile," libcom.org, accessed April 16, 2020, https://libcom.org/history/articles/anarchism-in-chile; "Chile: The Siege of Santa Maria de Iquique—A People's Cantata," Smithsonian Folkways, accessed April 20, 2020, https://s.si.edu/2ybwlPJ.

December 22, 1988 Olivia Ensign, "Brazilian Rubber Tappers Campaign against Deforestation of the Brazilian Rainforest Region, 1977–1988,"Global Nonviolent Action Database, February 28, 2010, accessed April 20, 2020, 2020, https://bit.ly/2StmHid; A Revkin, *The Burning Season: The*

Murder of Chico Mendes and the Fight for the Amazon Rainforest (Washington, DC: Island Press, 2004).

December 22, 1997 "A Commune in Chiapas? Mexico and the Zapatista Rebellion, 1994–2000," *Aufheben* 9 (Autumn 2000), accessed April 19, 2018, https://libcom.org/library/commune-chiapas-zapatista-mexico; Martin O Neill, "The 'Low-Intensity War' against Autonomy in Mexico (Part Three)," libcom.org, accessed April 20, 2020, https://bit.ly/2VXR0iY; Andrew Kennis, "Ten Years Later, It's Time to Recognize the U.S. Government's Responsibility for Acteal," Narco News Bulletin, December 30, 2007, accessed April 20, 2020, https://www.narconews.com/Issue48/article2948.html; Marc Lacey, "10 Years Later, Chiapas Massacre Still Haunts Mexico," *New York Times*, December 23, 2007, accessed April 20, 2020, https://www.nytimes.com/2007/12/23/world/americas/23acteal.html.

December 23, 1928 Diane van den Broek, "The 1929 Timber Workers Strike: The Role of Community and Gender," School of Industrial Relations and Organisational Behaviour, 1995, accessed April 20, 2020, http://wwwdocs.fce.unsw.edu.au/orgmanagement/WorkingPapers/WP104.pdf.

December 23, 2013 Steven Johns, "Revenge of a Citibank Worker,"libcom.org, accessed April 20, 2020, https://libcom.org/news/revenge-citibank-worker-01082016; "Former Citibank Employee Sentenced to 21 Months in Federal Prison for Causing Intentional Damage to a Protected Computer," Department of Justice US Attorney's Office North District of Texas, July 25, 2016, accessed April 20, 2020, https://bit.ly/3aZ78oR.

December 24, 1913 "The Christmas Eve Calumet Massacre, 1913," libcom.org, December 22, 2014, accessed April 20, 2020, https://libcom.org/history/christmas-eve-calumet-massacre-1913; Brandon Weber, "When 59 Children Died on Christmas Eve 1913, the World Cried with the Town of Calumet, Michigan," Upworthy, December 18, 2019, accessed April 20, 2020, https://bit.ly/3bYsJiC; Conditions in the Copper Mines of Michigan: Hearings before a Subcommittee of the Committee on Mines and Mining, House of Representatives, Sixty-Third Congress, Second Session, Pursuant to H. Res. 387, a Resolution Authorizing and Directing the Committee on Mines and Mining to Make an Investigation of Conditions in the Copper Mines of Michigan, United States Congress House Committee on Mines and Mining (Washington, DC: Government Printing Office, 1914), accessed April 20, 2020, https://catalog.hathitrust.org/Record/011597245.

December 24, 1983 "Every Official Christmas Number 1 Ever," Official Charts, accessed April 20, 2020, http://www.officialcharts.com/chart-news/every-official-christmas-number-1-ever-__3618; Anthony Hayward, "Brian Hibbard Obituary," *Guardian*, June 19, 2012, accessed May 27, 2020, https://www.theguardian.com/music/2012/jun/19/brian-hibbard; "The Flying Pickets' Taste of Fame," Wales Online, April 12, 2009, accessed May 20, 2020, https://www.walesonline.co.uk/news/wales-news/flying-pickets-taste-fame-2111239.

December 25, 1522, 1831, and 1837 Andrew Lawler, "Muslims Were Banned from the Americas as Early as the 16th Century," *Smithsonian Magazine*, February 7, 2017, accessed April 20, 2020, https://bit.ly/2StIaYu; "Spanish Rule: 1492–1697," History of Haiti 1492–1805, accessed April 20, 2020, https://library.brown.edu/haitihistory/1sr.html; Samuel Momodu, "The Baptist War (1831–1832)," Black Past, July 22, 2017, accessed April 20, 2020, https://www.blackpast.org/global-african-history/baptist-war-1831-1832; "1831 the Jamaica Slave Rebellion," libcom.org, accessed April 20, 2020, https://libcom.org/history/1831-jamaica-slave-rebellion; "Case Study 4: Jamaica (1831)—the Rebellion," Abolition Project, accessed April 20, 2020, http://abolition.e2bn.org/resistance_54.html; William Katz, "Dec. 25, 1837: Seminole Anticolonial Struggle," accessed April 20, 2020, https://www.zinnedproject.org/news/tdih/seminole-anti-colonial-struggle; William Katz, "Battle of Lake Okeechobee (1837)," Black Past, February 3, 2014, accessed April 20, 2020, https://www.blackpast.org/african-american-history/battle-lake-okeechobee-1837; Raymond K. Bluhm, "Battle of Lake Okeechobee," Encyclopaedia Britannica, accessed April 20, 2020, https://www.britannica.com/event/Battle-of-Lake-Okeechobee.

December 25, 1914 Steven Johns, "The Christmas Truce, 1914," libcom.org, December 22, 2014, accessed April 20, 2020, https://libcom.org/history/christmas-truce-1914-steven-johns; Mike Dash, "World War I: 100 Years Later: The Story of the WWI Christmas Truce," *Smithsonian*

Magazine, December 23, 2011, accessed April 20, 2020, https://www.smithsonianmag.com/history/the-story-of-the-wwi-christmas-truce-11972213.

December 26, 1862 Dee Brown, *Bury My Heart at Wounded Knee: An Indian History of the American West* (New York: Holt, Rinehart & Winston, 1970), 59–61.

December 26, 1904 "Baku Strikes," Great Soviet Encyclopedia (1979), accessed April 20, 2020, https://encyclopedia2.thefreedictionary.com/Baku+Strikes; Henry Reichman, *Railwaymen and Revolution: Russia, 1905* (Berkeley: University of California Press, 1987), 134; Rosa Luxemburg, *The Complete Works of Rosa Luxemburg: Political Writings 1—On Revolution, 1897–1905*, vol. 3 (London: Verso, 2019), 41. December 13 in the Old Style calendar.

December 27, 1797 William Clowes, *The Royal Navy: A History from the Earliest Times to 1900*, vol. 4 (London: S. Low Marston, Co., 1897), 549, accessed April 20, 2020, https://archive.org/details/royalnavyhistory04clow/page/n8/mode/2up.

December 27, 1923 Philippe Pelletier, "Anarcho-Syndicalism in Japan: 1911 to 1934," Editions CNT-RP/Nautilus, 2001, accessed April 20, 2020, http://libcom.org/history/anarcho-syndicalism-japan-1911-1934-philippe-pelletier; Richard H. Mitchell, "Japan's Peace Preservation Law of 1925: Its Origins and Significance," *Monumenta Nipponica* 28, no. 3 (Autumn 1973): 317–45.

December 28, 1907 "A Teenager Leads the Great Rent Strike of 1907," Ephemeral New York, June 21, 2014, accessed April 20, 2020, https://bit.ly/2Yq1U2H; David B Green, "This Day in Jewish History: 1907: Teenage Girl Leads Rent Strike in N.Y.," *Ha'aretz*, December 26, 2014, accessed April 20, 2020, https://www.haaretz.com/jewish/1907-teenage-girl-leads-rent-strike-in-n-y-1.5352480.

December 28, 1973 Michael Hiltzik, "The Day When Three NASA Astronauts Staged a Strike in Space," *Los Angeles Times*, December 28, 2015, accessed April 20, 2020, https://lat.ms/2VVxXpx; Erik Loomis "This Day in Labor History: December 28, 1973," accessed April 20, 2020, http://www.lawyersgunsmoneyblog.com/2015/12/this-day-in-labor-history-december-28-1972.

December 29, 1890 Dee Brown, *Bury My Heart at Wounded Knee: An Indian History of the American West* (New York Holt, Rinehart & Winston, 1970), 439–48; Myles Hudson, "Wounded Knee Massacre," Encyclopaedia Britannica, accessed April 20, 2020, https://www.britannica.com/topic/Wounded-Knee-Massacre.

December 29, 1968 Patricia G. Steinhoff, "Student Protest in the 1960s," *Social Science Japan* 15 (March 1999).

December 30, 1930 Marc Becker, "Una Revolución Comunista Indígena: Rural Protest Movements in Cayambe, Ecuador," *Rethinking Marxism* 10, no. 4 (1998): 34–51; Marc Becker, "Comunas and Indigenous Protest in Cayambe, Ecuador," *Americas* 55, no. 4 (April 1999): 531–59, accessed April 20, 2020, https://bit.ly/2xKXlVU.

December 30, 1936 Jeremy Brecher, "The Flint Sit-down Strike, 1936–1937," libcom.org, accessed April 20, 2020, https://libcom.org/history/flint-sit-down-strike-1936-1937-jeremy-brecher; "Sit-down Strike Begins in Flint," History.com, updated December 27, 2019, accessed April 20, 2020, https://www.history.com/this-day-in-history/sit-down-strike-begins-in-flint; "Subject Focus: Remembering the Flint Sit-down," Walter P. Reuther Library, December 17, 2010, accessed April 20, 2020, https://reuther.wayne.edu/node/7092; Martha Grevatt, "Strategic Roles of Black Workers, Women in Flint Sit-down Strike," *Workers World*, March 10, 2007, accessed July 3, 2020, https://www.workers.org/2007/us/flint-0315.

December 31, 1912 "Waiters Attack the Hotel Astor," *New York Times*, January 1, 1913, 1; "Waiters in a Riot around Hotel Astor," *New York Times*, January 9, 1913, 1; "Plan Strike for Thursday," *New York Times*, January 13, 1913, 3; "Leader Ettor's Speech," *New York Times*, January 14, 1913, 16.

December 31, 1969 "3 Bombs Are Found at Wisconsin Plant," *New York Times*, January 7, 1970, accessed April 20, 2020, https://nyti.ms/35qTcTB; Margalit Fox, "Dwight Armstrong, Who Bombed a College Building in 1970, Dies at 58,"*New York Times*, June 27, 2010, accessed April 20, 2020, https://www.nytimes.com/2010/06/27/us/27armstrong.html; Michael Fellner, "The Untold Story: After 15 Years, Karl & Dwight Armstrong Reveal the Drama Behind the Anti-Vietnam War Bombings in Madison," accessed July 9, 2019, unavailable April 20, 2020, https://news.google.com/newspapers?id=M2MaAAAAIBAJ&sjid=bSoEAAAAIBAJ&pg=4997%2C1353813.

Index

Page numbers in *italic* refer to illustrations. "Passim" (literally "scattered") indicates intermittent discussion of a topic over a cluster of pages.

ABOUT PM PRESS

PM Press is an independent, radical publisher of books and media to educate, entertain, and inspire. Founded in 2007 by a small group of people with decades of publishing, media, and organizing experience, PM Press amplifies the voices of radical authors, artists, and activists. Our aim is to deliver bold political ideas and vital stories to all walks of life and arm the dreamers to demand the impossible. We have sold millions of copies of our books, most often one at a time, face to face. We're old enough to know what we're doing and young enough to know what's at stake. Join us to create a better world.

PM Press
PO Box 23912
Oakland, CA 94623
www.pmpress.org

PM Press in Europe
europe@pmpress.org
www.pmpress.org.uk

FRIENDS OF PM PRESS

These are indisputably momentous times—the financial system is melting down globally and the Empire is stumbling. Now more than ever there is a vital need for radical ideas.

In the years since its founding—and on a mere shoestring—PM Press has risen to the formidable challenge of publishing and distributing knowledge and entertainment for the struggles ahead. With over 450 releases to date, we have published an impressive and stimulating array of literature, art, music, politics, and culture. Using every available medium, we've succeeded in connecting those hungry for ideas and information to those putting them into practice.

Friends of PM allows you to directly help impact, amplify, and revitalize the discourse and actions of radical writers, filmmakers, and artists. It provides us with a stable foundation from which we can build upon our early successes and provides a much-needed subsidy for the materials that can't necessarily pay their own way. You can help make that happen—and receive every new title automatically delivered to your door once a month—by joining as a Friend of PM Press. And, we'll throw in a free T-shirt when you sign up.

Here are your options:

- **$30 a month** Get all books and pamphlets plus 50% discount on all webstore purchases

- **$40 a month** Get all PM Press releases (including CDs and DVDs) plus 50% discount on all webstore purchases

- **$100 a month** Superstar—Everything plus PM merchandise, free downloads, and 50% discount on all webstore purchases

For those who can't afford $30 or more a month, we have **Sustainer Rates** at $15, $10, and $5. Sustainers get a free PM Press T-shirt and a 50% discount on all purchases from our website.

Your Visa or Mastercard will be billed once a month, until you tell us to stop. Or until our efforts succeed in bringing the revolution around. Or the financial meltdown of Capital makes plastic redundant. Whichever comes first.

Strike! 50th Anniversary Edition

Jeremy Brecher with a Preface by Sara
Nelson and a Foreword by Kim Kelly

ISBN: 978-1-62963-800-3
$28.95   640 pages

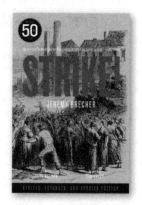

Jeremy Brecher's *Strike!* narrates the dramatic story
of repeated, massive, and sometimes violent revolts
by ordinary working people in America. Involving
nationwide general strikes, the seizure of vast industrial
establishments, nonviolent direct action on a massive
scale, and armed battles with artillery and tanks, this exciting hidden history is told
from the point of view of the rank-and-file workers who lived it. Encompassing the
repeated repression of workers' rebellions by company-sponsored violence, local
police, state militias, and the US Army and National Guard, it reveals a dimension
of American history rarely found in the usual high school or college history course.

Since its original publication in 1972, no book has done as much as *Strike!* to bring
US labor history to a wide audience. Now this fiftieth anniversary edition brings
the story up to date with chapters covering the "mini-revolts of the 21st century,"
including Occupy Wall Street and the Fight for Fifteen. The new edition contains
over a hundred pages of new materials and concludes by examining a wide range
of current struggles, ranging from #BlackLivesMatter, to the great wave of teachers
strikes "for the soul of public education," to the global "Student Strike for Climate,"
that may be harbingers of mass strikes to come.

"*Jeremy Brecher's* Strike! *is a classic of American historical writing. This new edition,
bringing his account up to the present, comes amid rampant inequality and growing
popular resistance. No book could be more timely for those seeking the roots of our
current condition.*"
—Eric Foner, Pulitzer Prize winner and DeWitt Clinton Professor of History at
Columbia University

"*Magnificent—a vivid, muscular labor history, just updated and rereleased by PM
Press, which should be at the side of anyone who wants to understand the deep
structure of force and counterforce in America.*"
—JoAnn Wypijewski, author of *Killing Trayvons: An Anthology of American Violence*

"*An exciting history of American labor. Brings to life the flashpoints of labor history.
Scholarly, genuinely stirring.*"
—*New York Times*

"*Splendid . . . clearly the best single-volume summary yet published of American
general strikes.*"
—*Washington Post*

Asia's Unknown Uprisings
Volume 1
South Korean Social Movements in the 20th Century

George Katsiaficas

ISBN: 978-1-60486-457-1
$28.95   480 pages

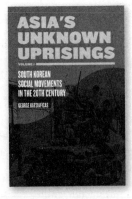

Using social movements as a prism to illuminate the oft-hidden history of 20th century Korea, this book provides detailed analysis of major uprisings that have patterned that country's politics and society. From the 1894 Tonghak Uprising through the March 1, 1919, independence movement and anti-Japanese resistance, a direct line is traced to the popular opposition to US division of Korea after World War Two. The overthrow of Syngman Rhee in 1960, resistance to Park Chung-hee, the 1980 Gwangju Uprising, as well as student, labor, and feminist movements are all recounted with attention to their economic and political contexts. South Korean opposition to neoliberalism is portrayed in detail, as is an analysis of neoliberalism's rise and effects. With a central focus on the Gwangju Uprising (that ultimately proved decisive in South Korea's democratization), the author uses Korean experiences as a baseboard to extrapolate into the possibilities of global social movements in the 21st century.

Asia's Unknown Uprisings
Volume 2
People Power in the Philippines, Burma, Tibet, China, Taiwan, Bangladesh, Nepal, Thailand, and Indonesia, 1947–2009

George Katsiaficas

ISBN: 978-1-60486-488-5
$28.95   448 pages

Ten years in the making, this book provides a unique perspective on uprisings in nine places in East Asia in the 1980s and 1990s. While the 2011 Arab Spring is well known, the wave of uprisings that swept East Asia in the 1980s became hardly visible. This book begins with an overview of late 20th-century history—the context within which Asian uprisings arose. Through a critique of Samuel Huntington's notion of a "Third Wave" of democratization, the author relates Asian uprisings to predecessors in 1968 and shows their subsequent influence on the wave of uprisings that swept Eastern Europe at the end of the 1980s. By empirically reconstructing the specific history of each Asian uprising, significant insight into major constituencies of change and the trajectories of these societies becomes visible.

A History of Pan-African Revolt

C.L.R. James with an Introduction by Robin D.G. Kelley

ISBN: 978-1-60486-095-5
$16.95   160 pages

Originally published in England in 1938 (the same year as his magnum opus *The Black Jacobins*) and expanded in 1969, this work remains the classic account of global black resistance. Robin D.G. Kelley's substantial introduction contextualizes the work in the history and ferment of the times, and explores its ongoing relevance today.

"*A History of Pan-African Revolt* is one of those rare books that continues to strike a chord of urgency, even half a century after it was first published. Time and time again, its lessons have proven to be valuable and relevant for understanding liberation movements in Africa and the diaspora. Each generation who has had the opportunity to read this small book finds new insights, new lessons, new visions for their own age .... No piece of literature can substitute for a crystal ball, and only religious fundamentalists believe that a book can provide comprehensive answers to all questions. But if nothing else, *A History of Pan-African Revolt* leaves us with two incontrovertible facts. First, as long as black people are denied freedom, humanity and a decent standard of living, they will continue to revolt. Second, unless these revolts involve the ordinary masses and take place on their own terms, they have no hope of succeeding." —Robin D.G. Kelley, from the Introduction

"I wish my readers to understand the history of Pan-African Revolt. They fought, they suffered—they are still fighting. Once we understand that, we can tackle our problems with the necessary mental equilibrium." —C.L.R. James

"*Kudos for reissuing C.L.R. James's pioneering work on black resistance. Many brilliant embryonic ideas articulated in* A History of Pan-African Revolt *twenty years later became the way to study black social movements. Robin Kelley's introduction superbly situates James and his thought in the world of Pan-African and Marxist intellectuals.*" —Sundiata Cha-Jua, Penn State University

"*A mine of ideas advancing far ahead of its time.*" —Walter Rodney

"*When one looks back over the last twenty years to those men who were most far-sighted, who first began to tease out the muddle of ideology in our times, who were at the same time Marxists with a hard theoretical basis, and close students of society, humanists with a tremendous response to and understanding of human culture, Comrade James is one of the first one thinks of.*" —E.P. Thompson

The CNT in the Spanish Revolution Vols. 1-3

José Peirats
with an introduction by Chris Ealham

Vol. 1 **ISBN: 978-1-60486-207-2**
$28.00   432 pages

Vol. 2 **ISBN: 978-1-60486-208-9**
$22.95   312 pages

Vol. 3 **ISBN: 978-1-60486-209-6**
$22.95   296 pages

The CNT in the Spanish Revolution is the history of one of the most original and audacious, and arguably also the most far-reaching, of all the twentieth-century revolutions. It is the history of the giddy years of political change and hope in 1930s Spain, when the so-called 'Generation of '36', Peirats' own generation, rose up against the oppressive structures of Spanish society. It is also a history of a revolution that failed, crushed in the jaws of its enemies on both the reformist left and the reactionary right. José Peirats' account is effectively the official CNT history of the war, passionate, partisan but, above all, intelligent. Its huge sweeping canvas covers all areas of the anarchist experience—the spontaneous militias, the revolutionary collectives, the moral dilemmas occasioned by the clash of revolutionary ideals and the stark reality of the war effort against Franco and his German Nazi and Italian Fascist allies.

This new edition is carefully indexed in a way that converts the work into a usable tool for historians and makes it much easier for the general reader to dip in with greater purpose and pleasure.

"José Peirats' **The CNT in the Spanish Revolution** *is a landmark in the historiography of the Spanish Civil War. . . . Originally published in Toulouse in the early 1950s, it was a rarity anxiously searched for by historians and others who gleefully pillaged its wealth of documentation. Even its republication in Paris in 1971 by the exiled Spanish publishing house, Ruedo Ibérico, though welcome, still left the book in the territory of specialists. For that reason alone, the present project to publish the entire work in English is to be applauded."*
—Professor Paul Preston, London School of Economics

The Big Red Songbook:
250+ IWW Songs!

Edited by Archie Green, David Roediger,
Franklin Rosemont, and Salvatore Salerno
with a Foreword by Tom Morello and an
Afterword by Utah Phillips

ISBN: 978-1-62963-129-5
$29.95   560 pages

In 1905, representatives from dozens of radical labor
groups came together in Chicago to form One Big Union—the Industrial Workers
of the World (IWW), known as the Wobblies. The union was a big presence in
the labor movement, leading strikes, walkouts, and rallies across the nation. And
everywhere its members went, they sang.

Their songs were sung in mining camps and textile mills, hobo jungles and flop
houses, and anywhere workers might be recruited to the Wobblies' cause. The
songs were published in a pocketsize tome called the *Little Red Songbook*, which
was so successful that it's been published continuously since 1909. In *The Big Red
Songbook*, the editors have gathered songs from over three dozen editions, plus
additional songs, rare artwork, personal recollections, discographies, and more into
one big all-embracing book.

IWW poets/composers strove to nurture revolutionary consciousness. Each
piece, whether topical, hortatory, elegiac, or comic served to educate, agitate,
and emancipate workers. A handful of Wobbly numbers have become classics,
still sung by labor groups and folk singers. They include Joe Hill's sardonic "The
Preacher and the Slave" (sometimes known by its famous phrase "Pie in the Sky")
and Ralph Chaplin's "Solidarity Forever." Songs lost or found, sacred or irreverent,
touted or neglected, serious or zany, singable or not, are here. The Wobblies and
their friends have been singing for a century. May this comprehensive gathering
simultaneously celebrate past battles and chart future goals.

In addition to the 250+ songs, writings are included from Archie Green, Franklin
Rosemont, David Roediger, Salvatore Salerno, Judy Branfman, Richard Brazier,
James Connell, Carlos Cortez, Bill Friedland, Virginia Martin, Harry McClintock,
Fred Thompson, Adam Machado, and many more.

*"This engaging anthology features the lyrics to 250 or so Wobbly songs, rich with
references to job sharks, shovel stiffs, capitalist tools, and plutocratic parasites. Wobbly
wordsmiths such as the fabled Joe Hill, T-Bone Slim, Haywire Mac, and Richard Brazier
set their fighting words to popular tunes of the day, gospel hymns, old ballads and
patriotic anthems."*
—San Francisco Chronicle

500 Years of Indigenous Resistance

Gord Hill

ISBN: 978-1-60486-106-8
$12.00   96 pages

The history of the colonization of the Americas by Europeans is often portrayed as a mutually beneficial process, in which "civilization" was brought to the Natives, who in return shared their land and cultures. A more critical history might present it as a genocide in which Indigenous peoples were helpless victims, overwhelmed and awed by European military power. In reality, neither of these views is correct.

500 Years of Indigenous Resistance is more than a history of European colonization of the Americas. In this slim volume, Gord Hill chronicles the resistance by Indigenous peoples, which limited and shaped the forms and extent of colonialism. This history encompasses North and South America, the development of nation-states, and the resurgence of Indigenous resistance in the post-WW2 era.

Gord Hill is a member of the Kwakwaka'wakw nation on the Northwest Coast. Writer, artist, and militant, he has been involved in Indigenous resistance, anti-colonial and anti-capitalist movements for many years, often using the pseudonym Zig Zag.

Portugal: The Impossible Revolution?

Phil Mailer, with an afterword
by Maurice Brinton

ISBN: 978-1-60486-336-9
$24.95   288 pages

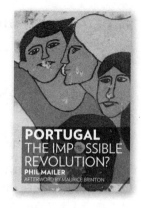

After the military coup in Portugal on April 25, 1974,
the overthrow of almost fifty years of Fascist rule, and
the end of three colonial wars, there followed eighteen
months of intense, democratic social transformation
which challenged every aspect of Portuguese society. What started as a military
coup turned into a profound attempt at social change from the bottom up and
became headlines on a daily basis in the world media. This was due to the intensity
of the struggle as well as the fact that in 1974–75 the moribund, right-wing
Francoist regime was still in power in neighboring Spain and there was huge
uncertainty as to how these struggles might affect Spain and Europe at large.

This is the story of what happened in Portugal between April 25, 1974, and
November 25, 1975, as seen and felt by a deeply committed participant. It
depicts the hopes, the tremendous enthusiasm, the boundless energy, the total
commitment, the released power, even the revolutionary innocence of thousands
of ordinary people taking a hand in the remolding of their lives. And it does so
against the background of an economic and social reality which placed limits on
what could be done.

"An evocative, bitterly partisan diary of the Portuguese revolution, written from a
radical-utopian perspective. The enemy is any type of organization or presumption of
leadership. The book affords a good view of the mood of the time, of the multiplicity of
leftist factions, and of the social problems that bedeviled the revolution."
—Fritz Stern, Foreign Affairs

"Mailer portrays history with the enthusiasm of a cheerleader, the 'home team' in
this case being libertarian communism. Official documents, position papers and
the pronouncements of the protagonists of this drama are mostly relegated to the
appendices. The text itself recounts the activities of a host of worker, tenant, soldier
and student committees as well as the author's personal experiences."
—Ian Wallace, Library Journal

"A thorough delight as it moves from first person accounts of street demonstrations
through intricate analyses of political movements. Mailer has handled masterfully the
enormous cast of politicians, officers of the military peasant and workers councils, and
a myriad of splinter parties, movements and caucuses."
—Choice